THE RECORD OF A

FALLEN VAMPIRE

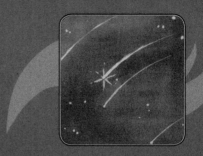

The winter sky is beautiful. A few years ago I stood in the cold to watch the Leonid meteor shower, and it was absolutely stunning. I will never forget the way the meteors sparkled as they rained down.

—Yuri Kimura

Artist Yuri Kimura debuted two short stories in Japan's *Gangan Powered* after winning the Enix Manga Award. Shortly thereafter, she began *The Record of a Fallen Vampire*, which was serialized in Japan's *Monthly Shonen Gangan* through March 2007.

Author Kyo Shirodaira is from Nara prefecture. In addition to *The Record of a Fallen Vampire*, Shirodaira has scripted the manga *Spiral: The Bonds of Reasoning*. Shirodaira's novel *Meitantei ni Hana wo* was nominated for the 8th Annual Ayukawa Tetsuya Award in 1997.

THE RECORD OF A

FALLEN VAMPIRE

STORY BY: KYO SHIRODAIRA ART BY: YURI KIMURA

8

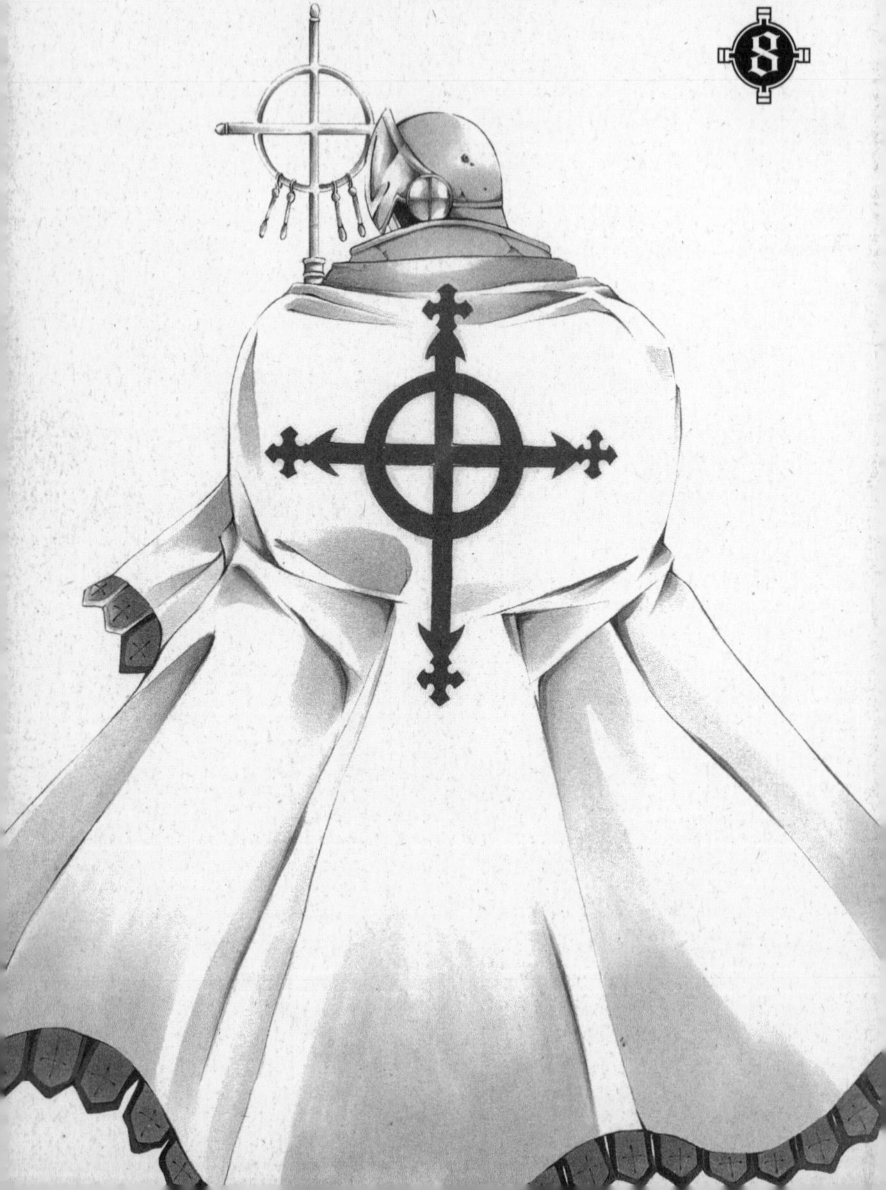

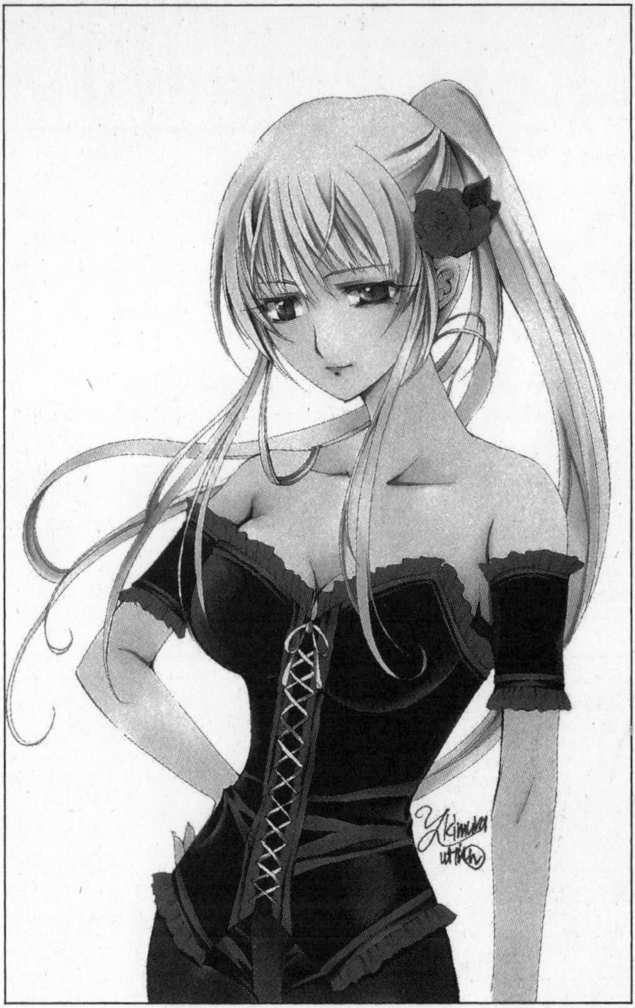

CONTENTS

Chapter 34: Tale of a Beautiful Soul

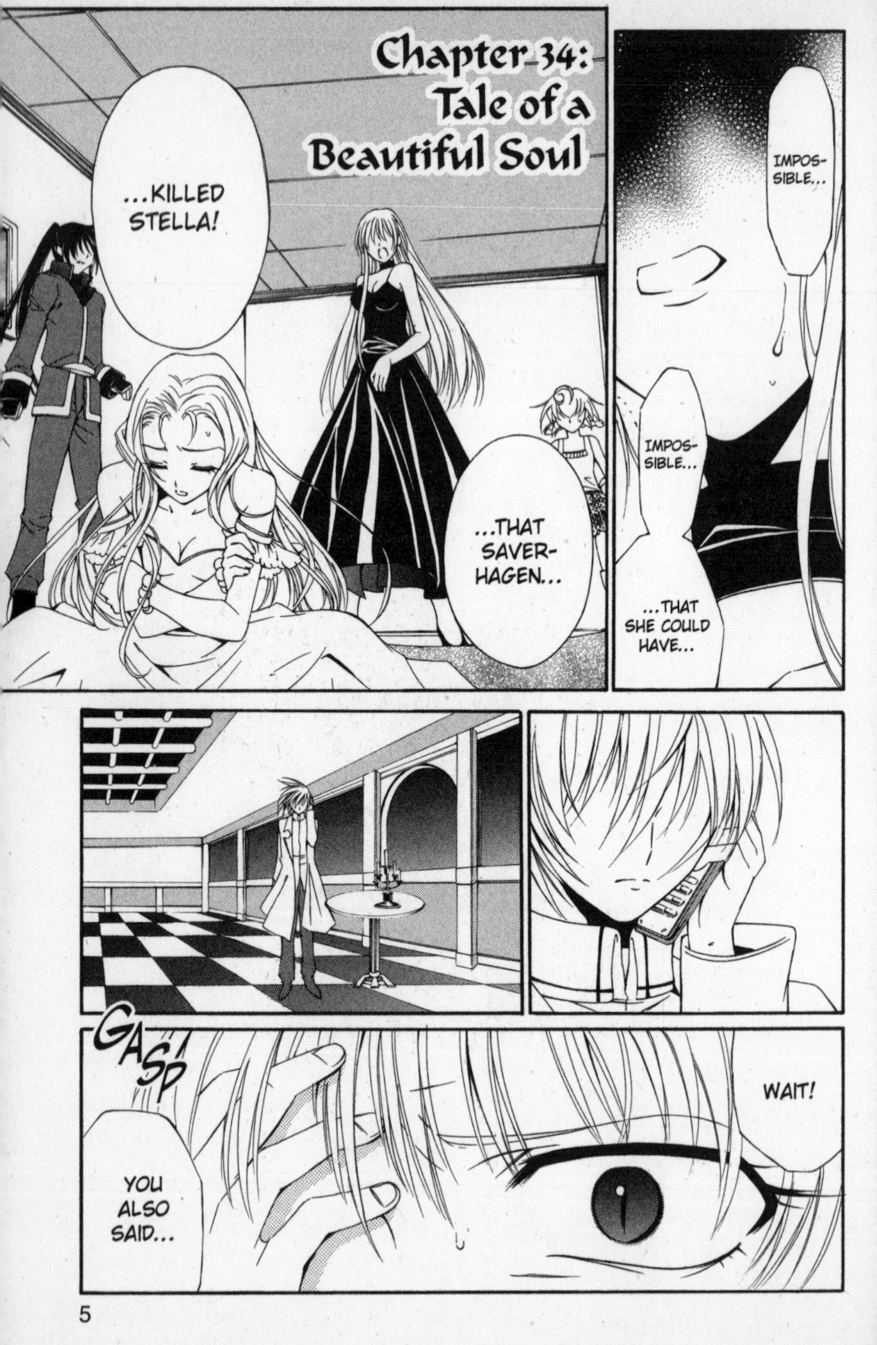
IMPOSSIBLE...
IMPOSSIBLE...
...THAT SHE COULD HAVE...
...THAT SAVERHAGEN...
...KILLED STELLA!
WAIT!
GASP!
YOU ALSO SAID...

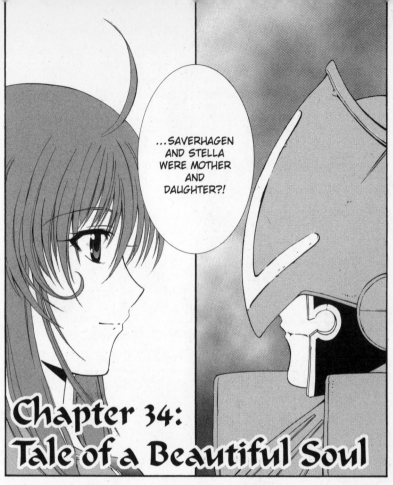

...SAVERHAGEN AND STELLA WERE MOTHER AND DAUGHTER?!

Chapter 34: Tale of a Beautiful Soul

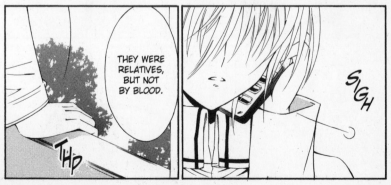

THEY WERE RELATIVES, BUT NOT BY BLOOD.

THP

SIGH

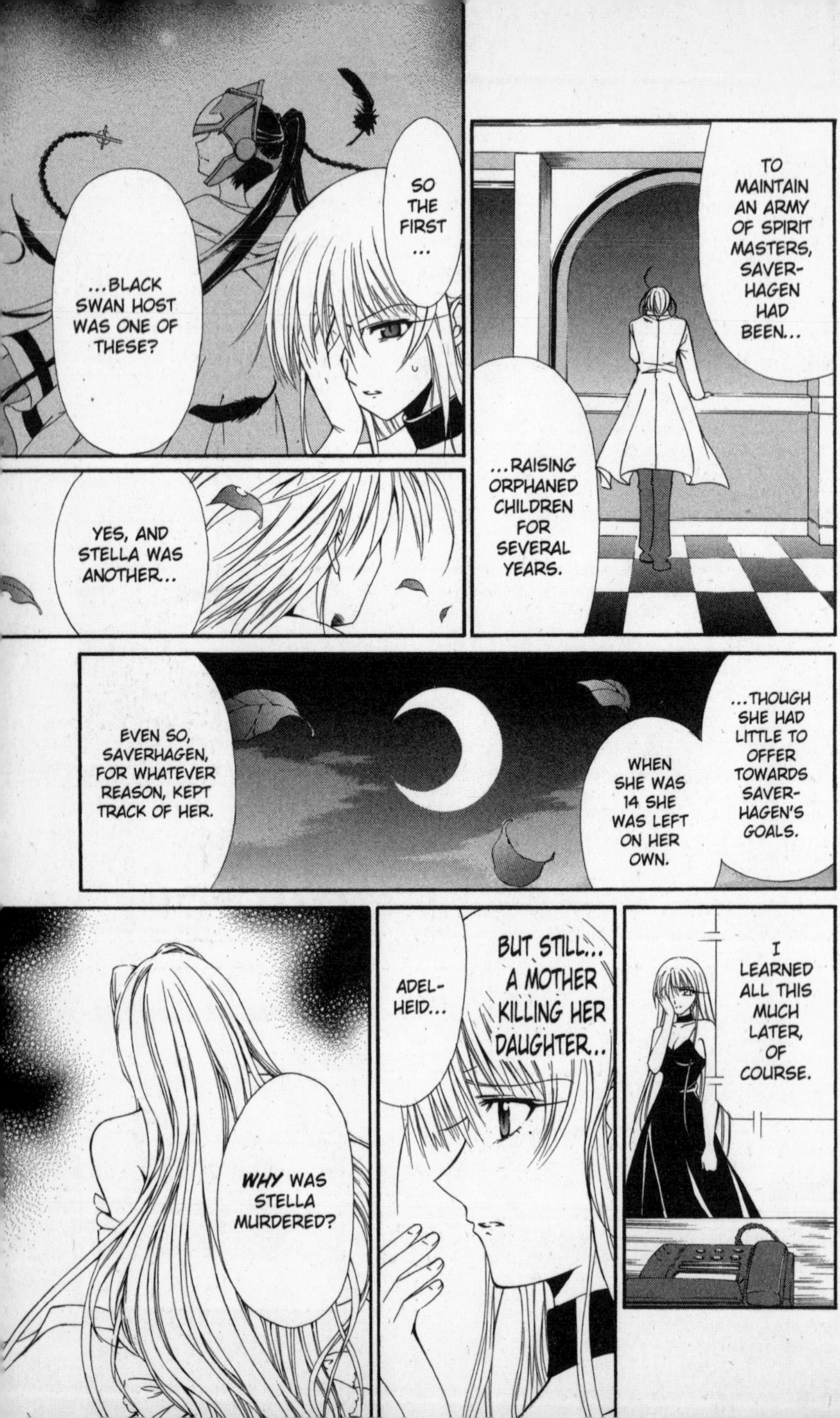
TO MAINTAIN AN ARMY OF SPIRIT MASTERS, SAVERHAGEN HAD BEEN...
...RAISING ORPHANED CHILDREN FOR SEVERAL YEARS.
SO THE FIRST...
...BLACK SWAN HOST WAS ONE OF THESE?
YES, AND STELLA WAS ANOTHER...
...THOUGH SHE HAD LITTLE TO OFFER TOWARDS SAVERHAGEN'S GOALS.
WHEN SHE WAS 14 SHE WAS LEFT ON HER OWN.
EVEN SO, SAVERHAGEN, FOR WHATEVER REASON, KEPT TRACK OF HER.
I LEARNED ALL THIS MUCH LATER, OF COURSE.
BUT STILL... A MOTHER KILLING HER DAUGHTER...
ADELHEID...
WHY WAS STELLA MURDERED?

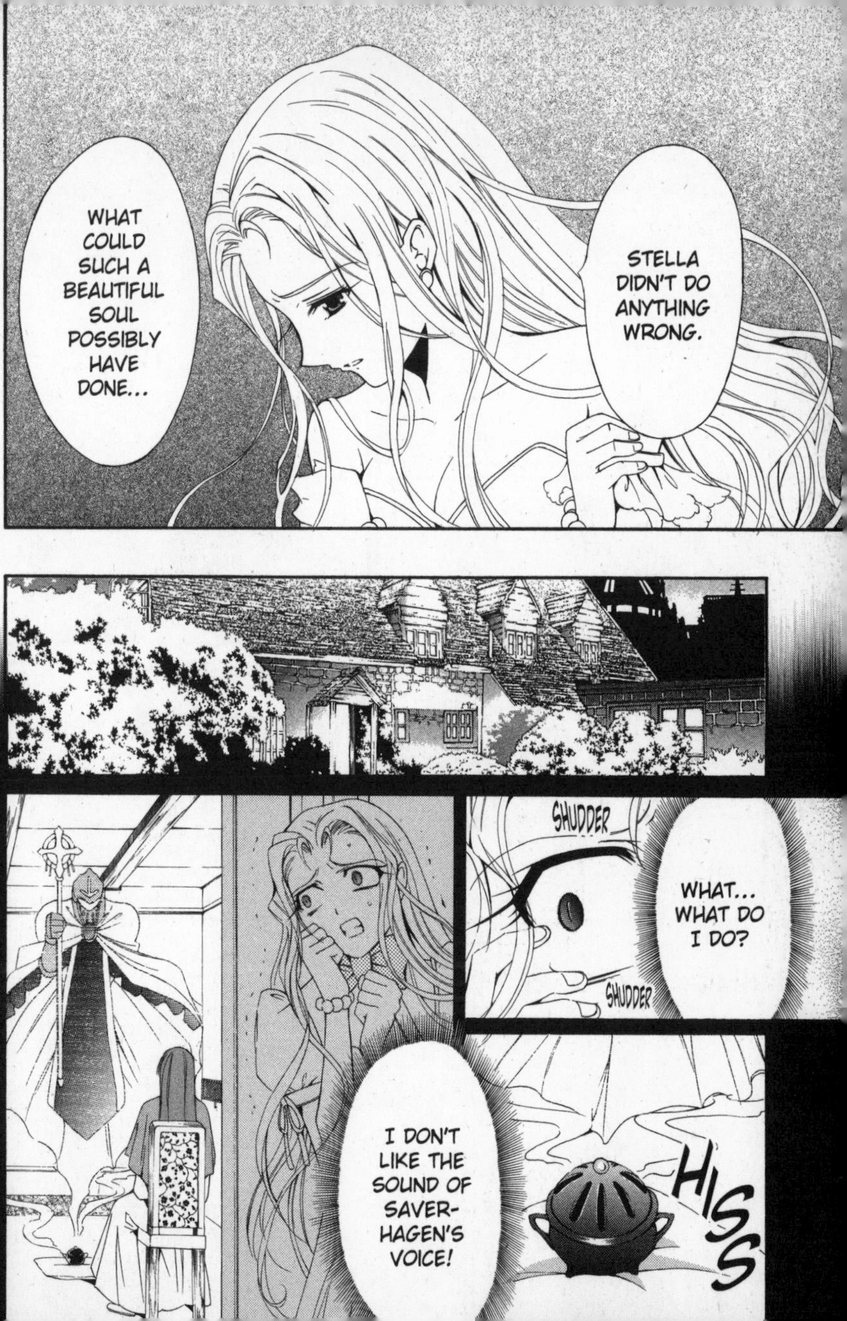
STELLA DIDN'T DO ANYTHING WRONG.
WHAT COULD SUCH A BEAUTIFUL SOUL POSSIBLY HAVE DONE...
SHUDDER
WHAT... WHAT DO I DO?
SHUDDER
HISS
I DON'T LIKE THE SOUND OF SAVER-HAGEN'S VOICE!

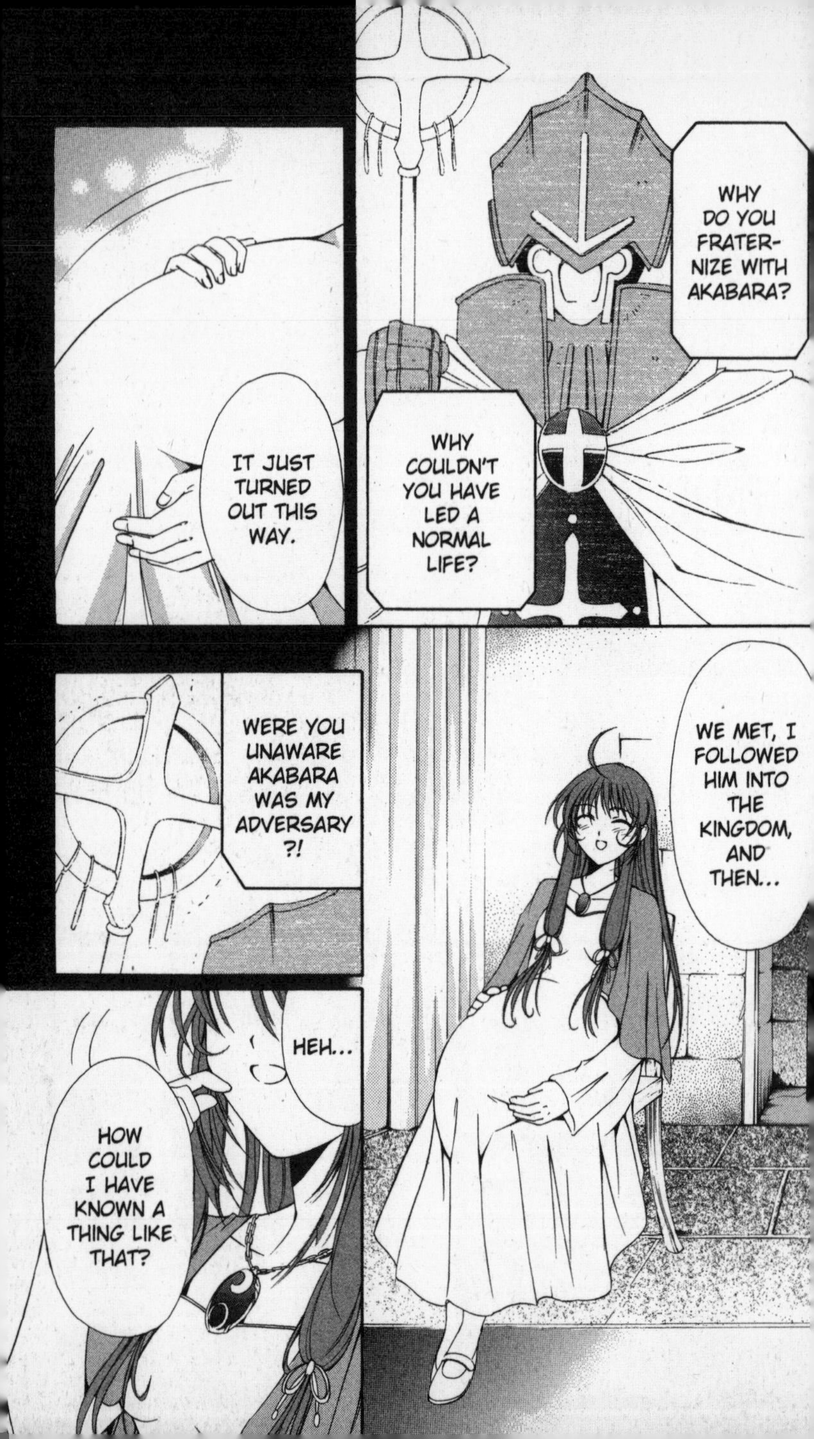
WHY DO YOU FRATER-NIZE WITH AKABARA?
WHY COULDN'T YOU HAVE LED A NORMAL LIFE?
IT JUST TURNED OUT THIS WAY.
WE MET, I FOLLOWED HIM INTO THE KINGDOM, AND THEN...
WERE YOU UNAWARE AKABARA WAS MY ADVERSARY?!
HEH...
HOW COULD I HAVE KNOWN A THING LIKE THAT?

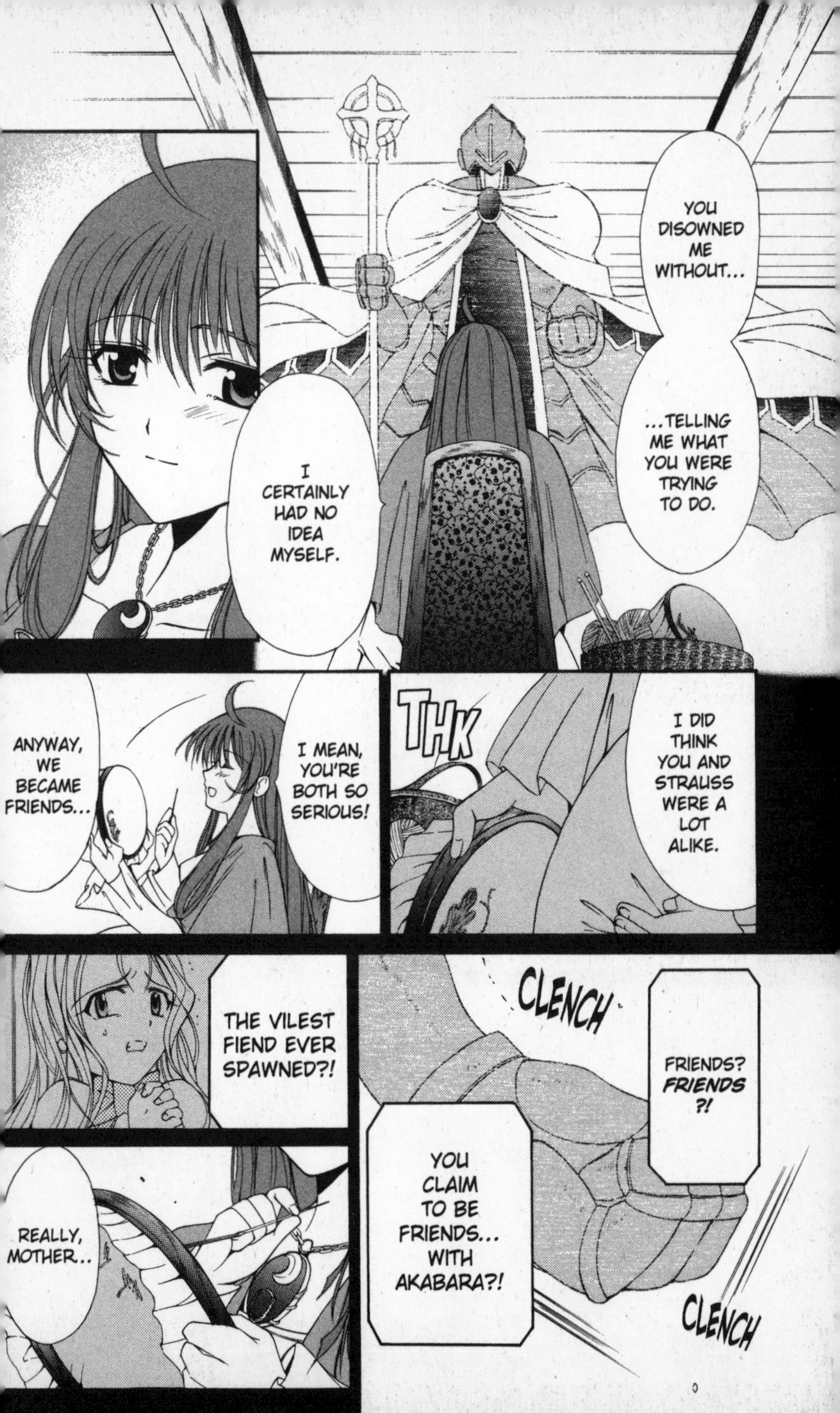
YOU DISOWNED ME WITHOUT...
...TELLING ME WHAT YOU WERE TRYING TO DO.
I CERTAINLY HAD NO IDEA MYSELF.
THK
I DID THINK YOU AND STRAUSS WERE A LOT ALIKE.
I MEAN, YOU'RE BOTH SO SERIOUS!
ANYWAY, WE BECAME FRIENDS...
CLENCH
FRIENDS? FRIENDS?!
YOU CLAIM TO BE FRIENDS... WITH AKABARA?!
CLENCH
THE VILEST FIEND EVER SPAWNED?!
REALLY, MOTHER...

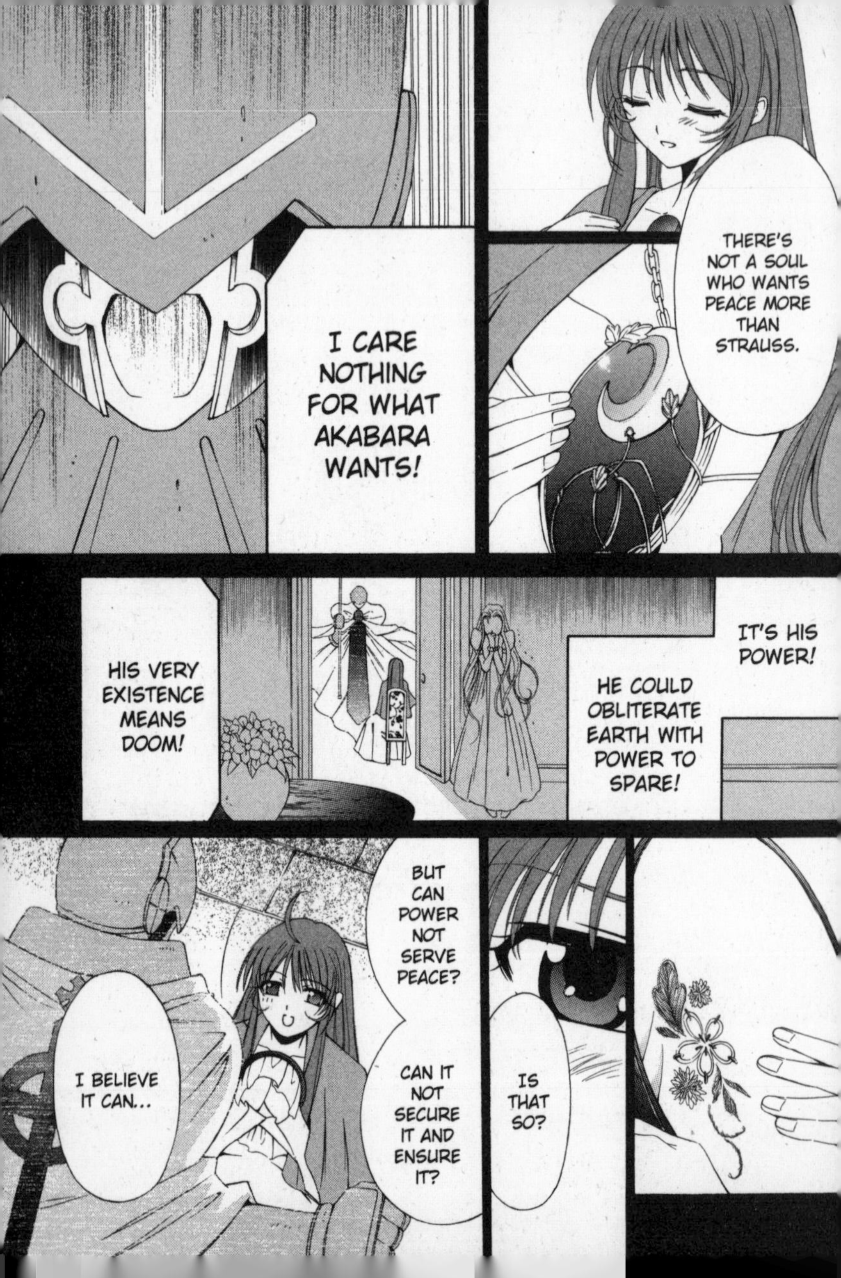
THERE'S NOT A SOUL WHO WANTS PEACE MORE THAN STRAUSS.
I CARE NOTHING FOR WHAT AKABARA WANTS!
IT'S HIS POWER!
HE COULD OBLITERATE EARTH WITH POWER TO SPARE!
HIS VERY EXISTENCE MEANS DOOM!
IS THAT SO?
BUT CAN POWER NOT SERVE PEACE?
CAN IT NOT SECURE IT AND ENSURE IT?
I BELIEVE IT CAN...

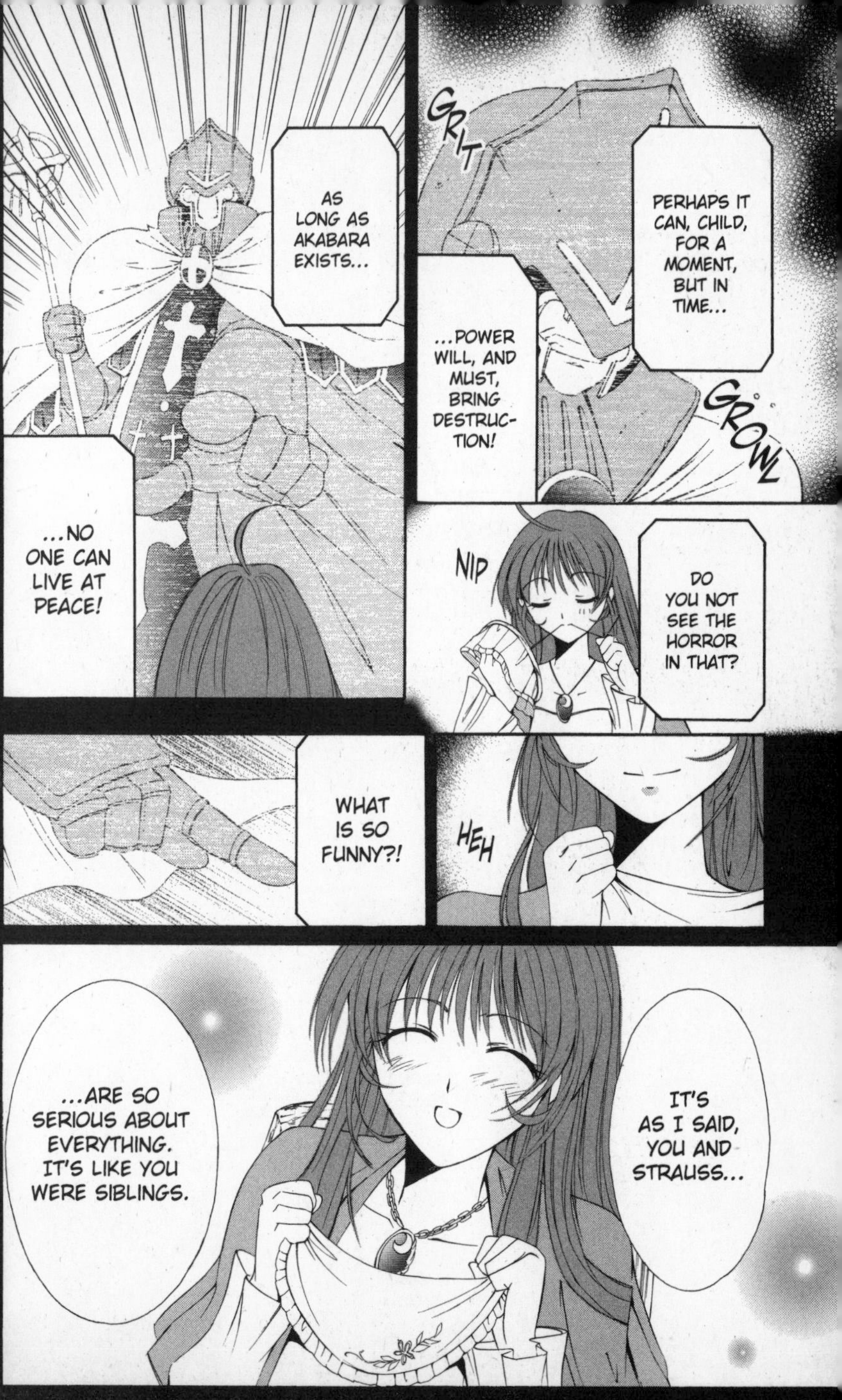
GRIT
PERHAPS IT CAN, CHILD, FOR A MOMENT, BUT IN TIME...
...POWER WILL, AND MUST, BRING DESTRUCTION!
GROWL
DO YOU NOT SEE THE HORROR IN THAT?
NIP
AS LONG AS AKABARA EXISTS...
...NO ONE CAN LIVE AT PEACE!
HEH
WHAT IS SO FUNNY?!
IT'S AS I SAID, YOU AND STRAUSS...
...ARE SO SERIOUS ABOUT EVERYTHING. IT'S LIKE YOU WERE SIBLINGS.

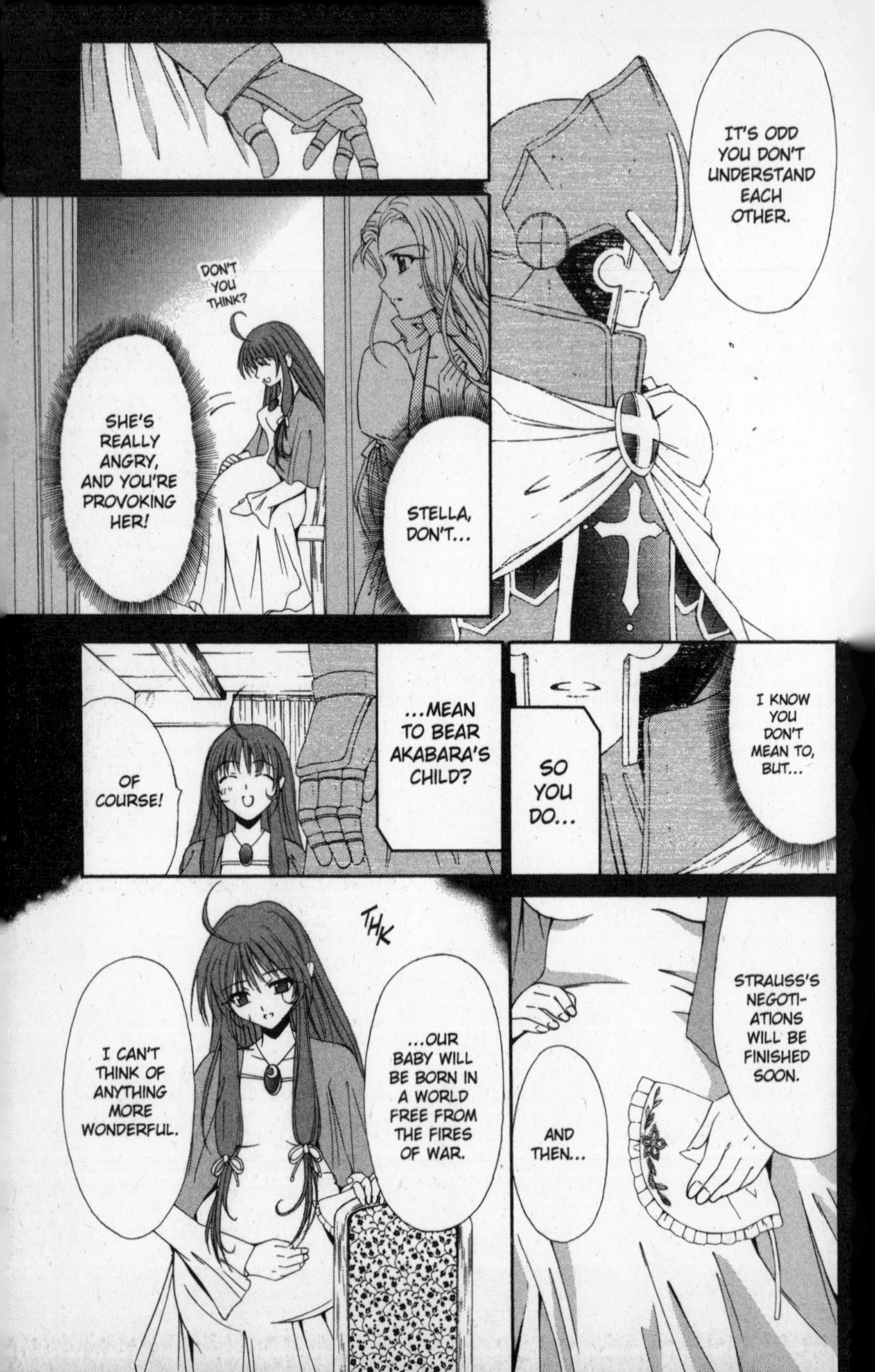
IT'S ODD YOU DON'T UNDERSTAND EACH OTHER.
DON'T YOU THINK?
STELLA, DON'T...
SHE'S REALLY ANGRY, AND YOU'RE PROVOKING HER!
I KNOW YOU DON'T MEAN TO, BUT...
SO YOU DO...
...MEAN TO BEAR AKABARA'S CHILD?
OF COURSE!
STRAUSS'S NEGOTI-ATIONS WILL BE FINISHED SOON.
AND THEN...
THK
...OUR BABY WILL BE BORN IN A WORLD FREE FROM THE FIRES OF WAR.
I CAN'T THINK OF ANYTHING MORE WONDERFUL.

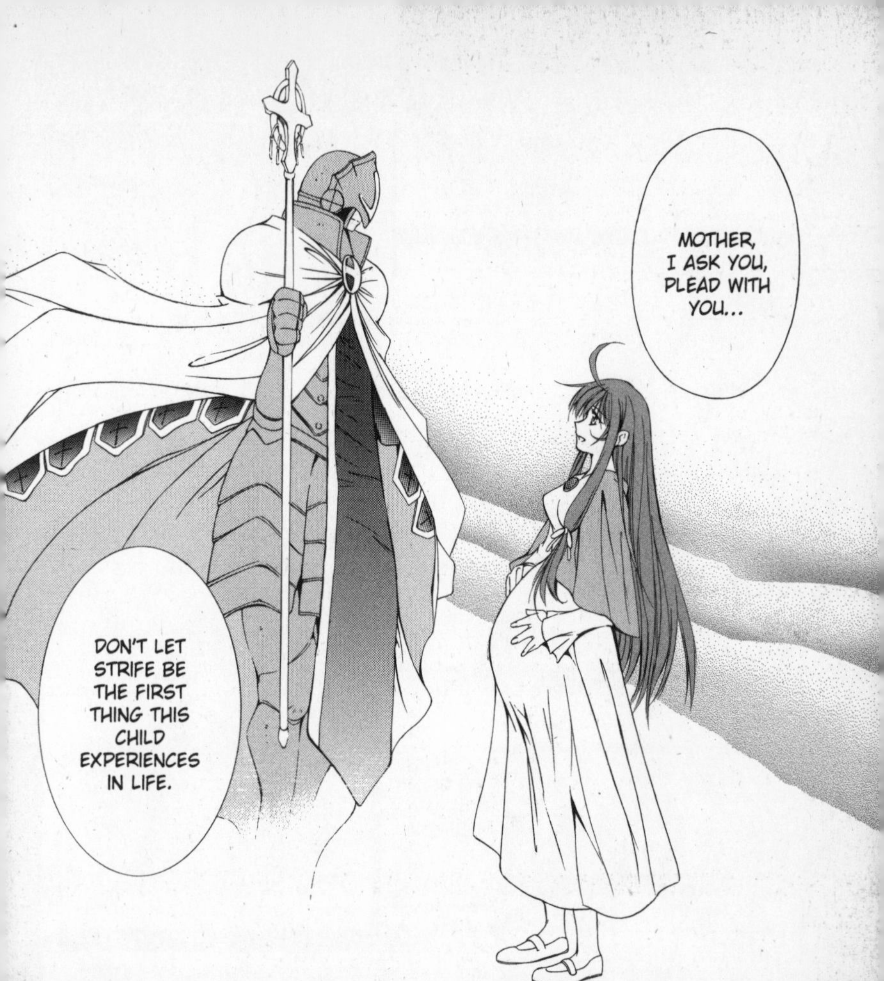
MOTHER, I ASK YOU, PLEAD WITH YOU...
DON'T LET STRIFE BE THE FIRST THING THIS CHILD EXPERIENCES IN LIFE.
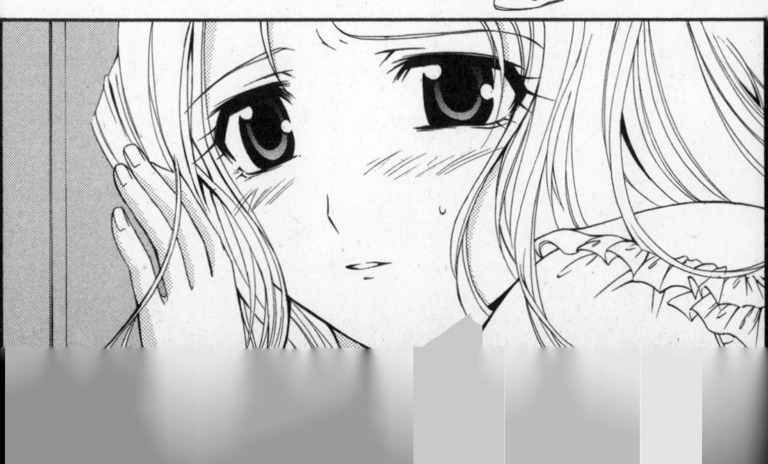

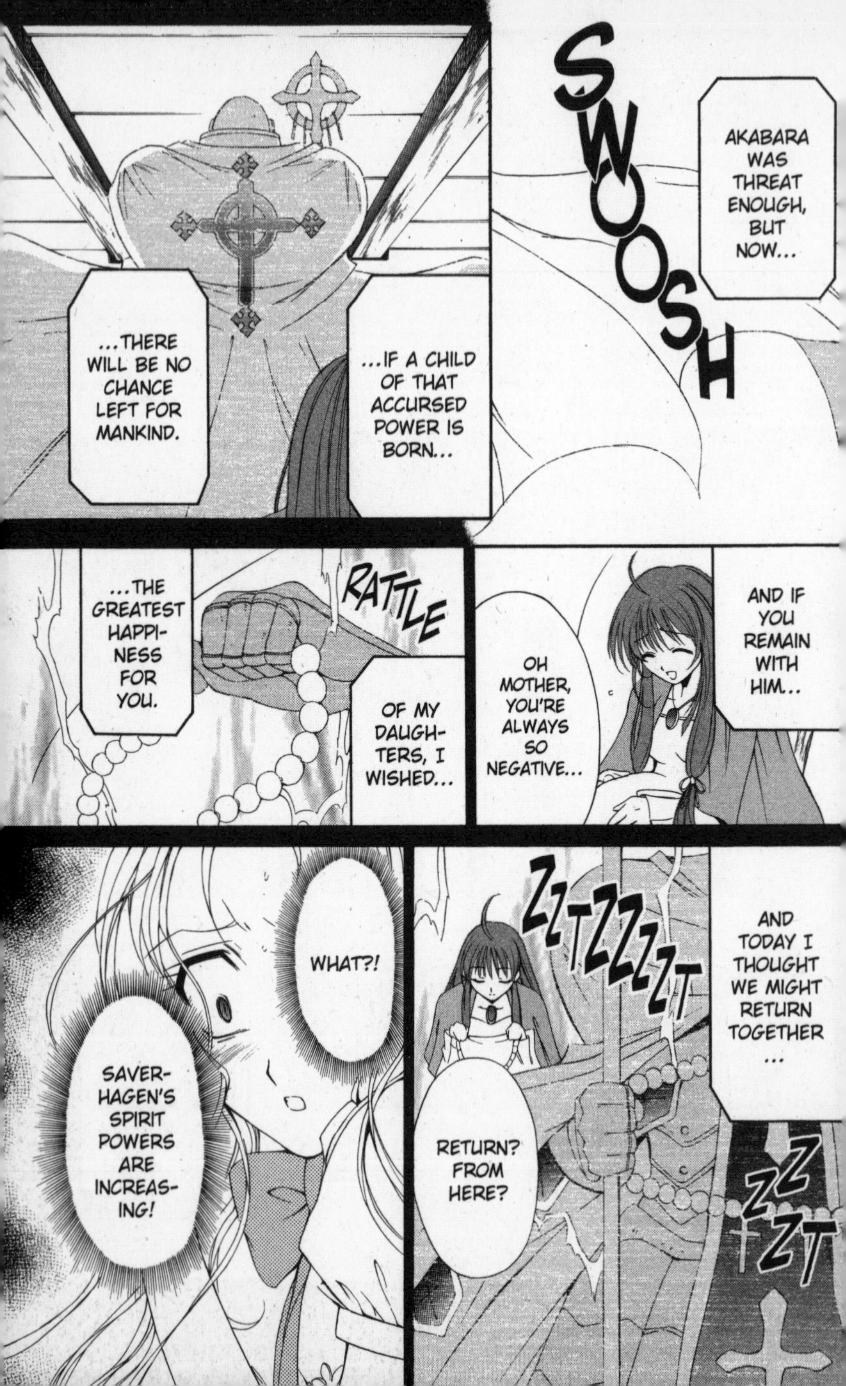

SWOOSH
AKABARA WAS THREAT ENOUGH, BUT NOW...
...IF A CHILD OF THAT ACCURSED POWER IS BORN...
...THERE WILL BE NO CHANCE LEFT FOR MANKIND.
AND IF YOU REMAIN WITH HIM...
OH MOTHER, YOU'RE ALWAYS SO NEGATIVE...
OF MY DAUGHTERS, I WISHED...
RATTLE
...THE GREATEST HAPPINESS FOR YOU.
AND TODAY I THOUGHT WE MIGHT RETURN TOGETHER...
ZZTZZZZZT
RETURN? FROM HERE?
ZZZZT
WHAT?!
SAVERHAGEN'S SPIRIT POWERS ARE INCREASING!

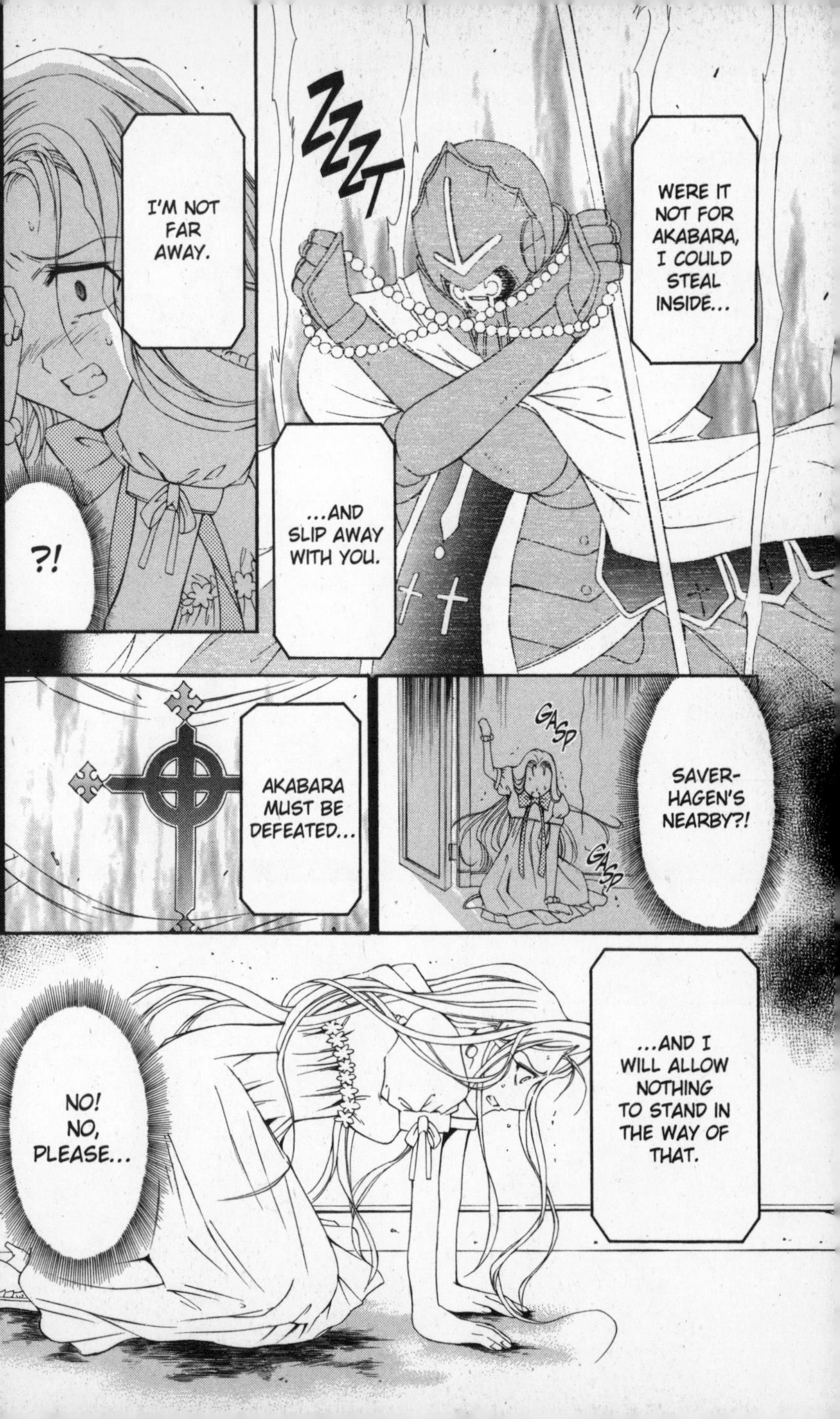
WERE IT NOT FOR AKABARA, I COULD STEAL INSIDE...
ZZZT
...AND SLIP AWAY WITH YOU.
I'M NOT FAR AWAY.
?!
SAVER-HAGEN'S NEARBY?!
GASP
GASP
AKABARA MUST BE DEFEATED...
...AND I WILL ALLOW NOTHING TO STAND IN THE WAY OF THAT.
NO! NO, PLEASE...

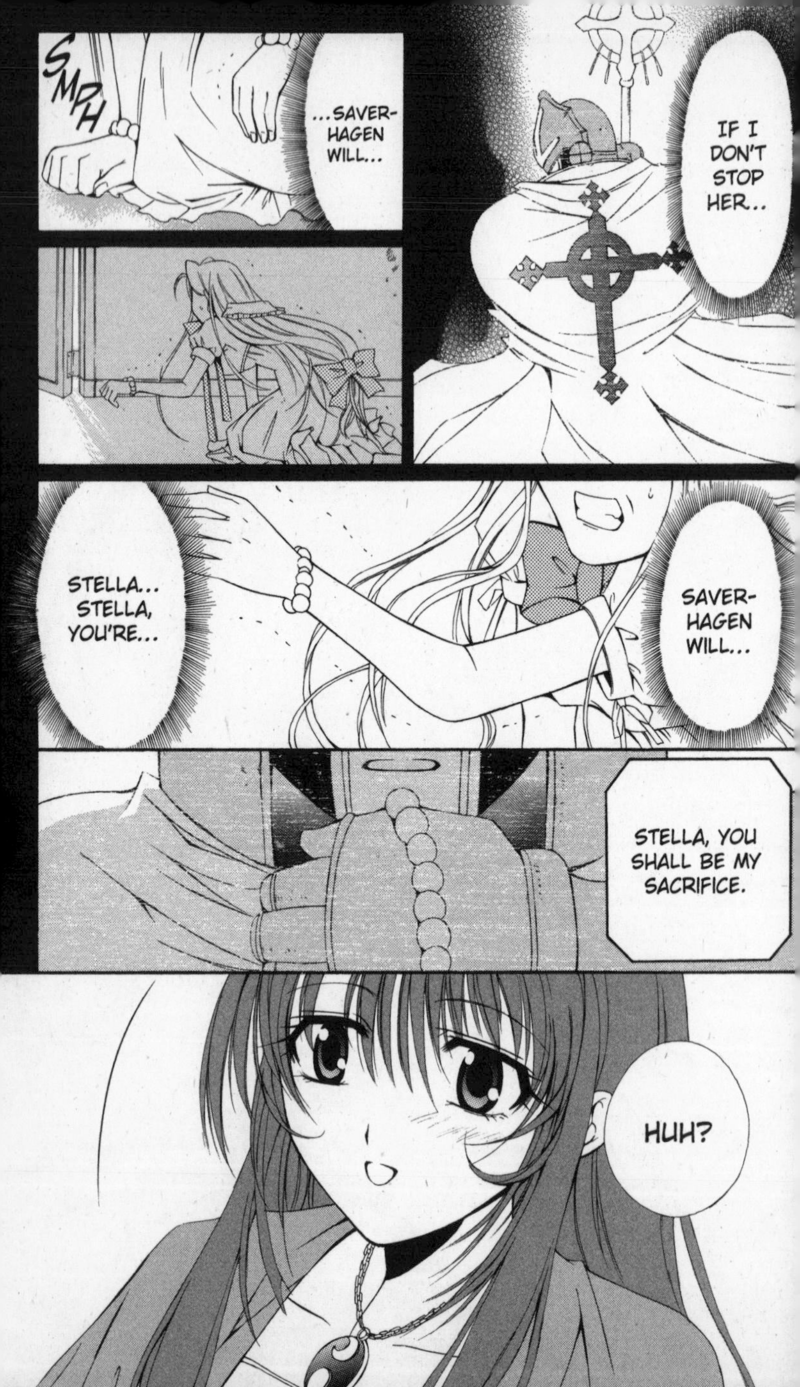
IF I DON'T STOP HER...
...SAVER-HAGEN WILL...
SMDH
SAVER-HAGEN WILL...
STELLA... STELLA, YOU'RE...
STELLA, YOU SHALL BE MY SACRIFICE.
HUH?

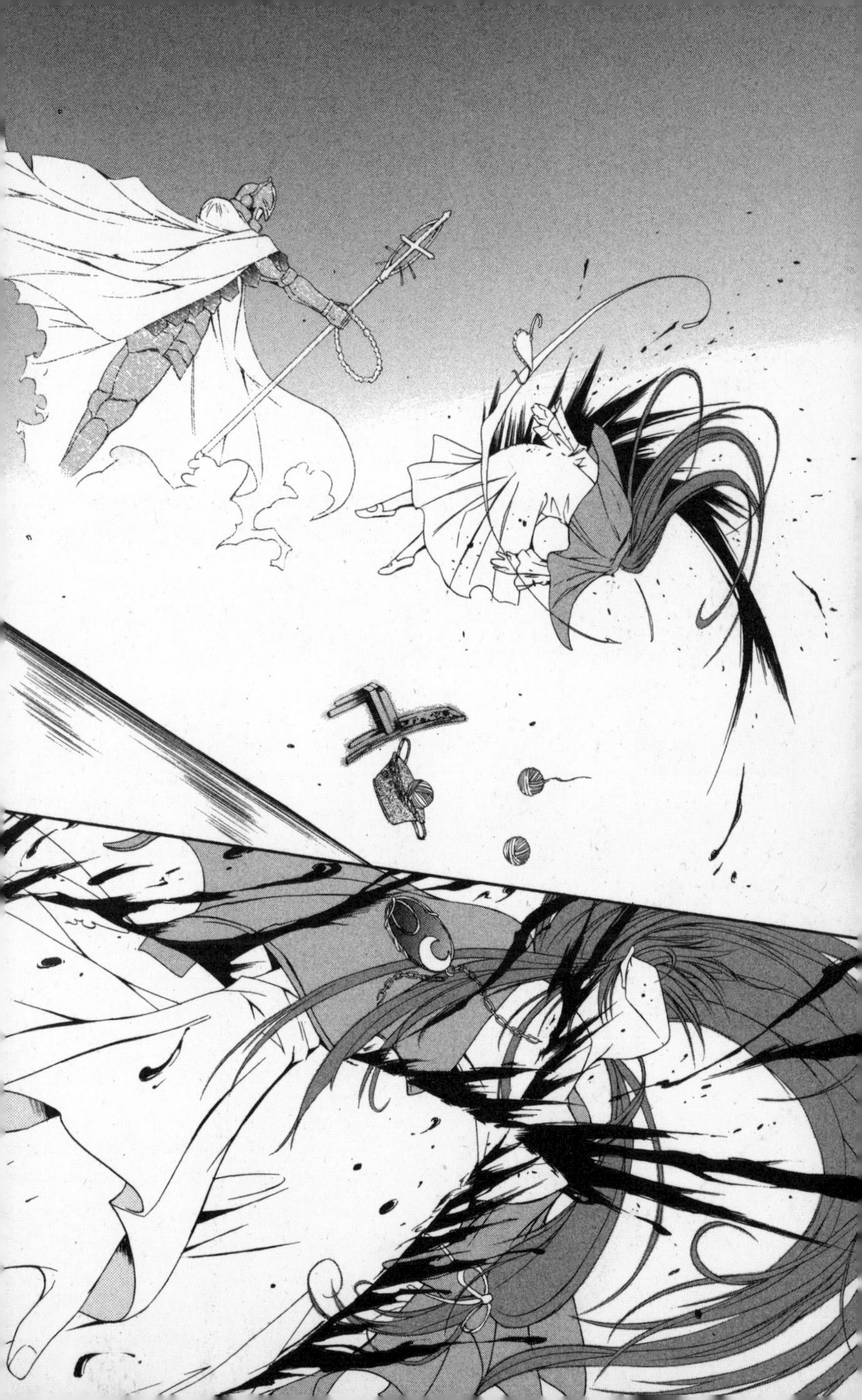

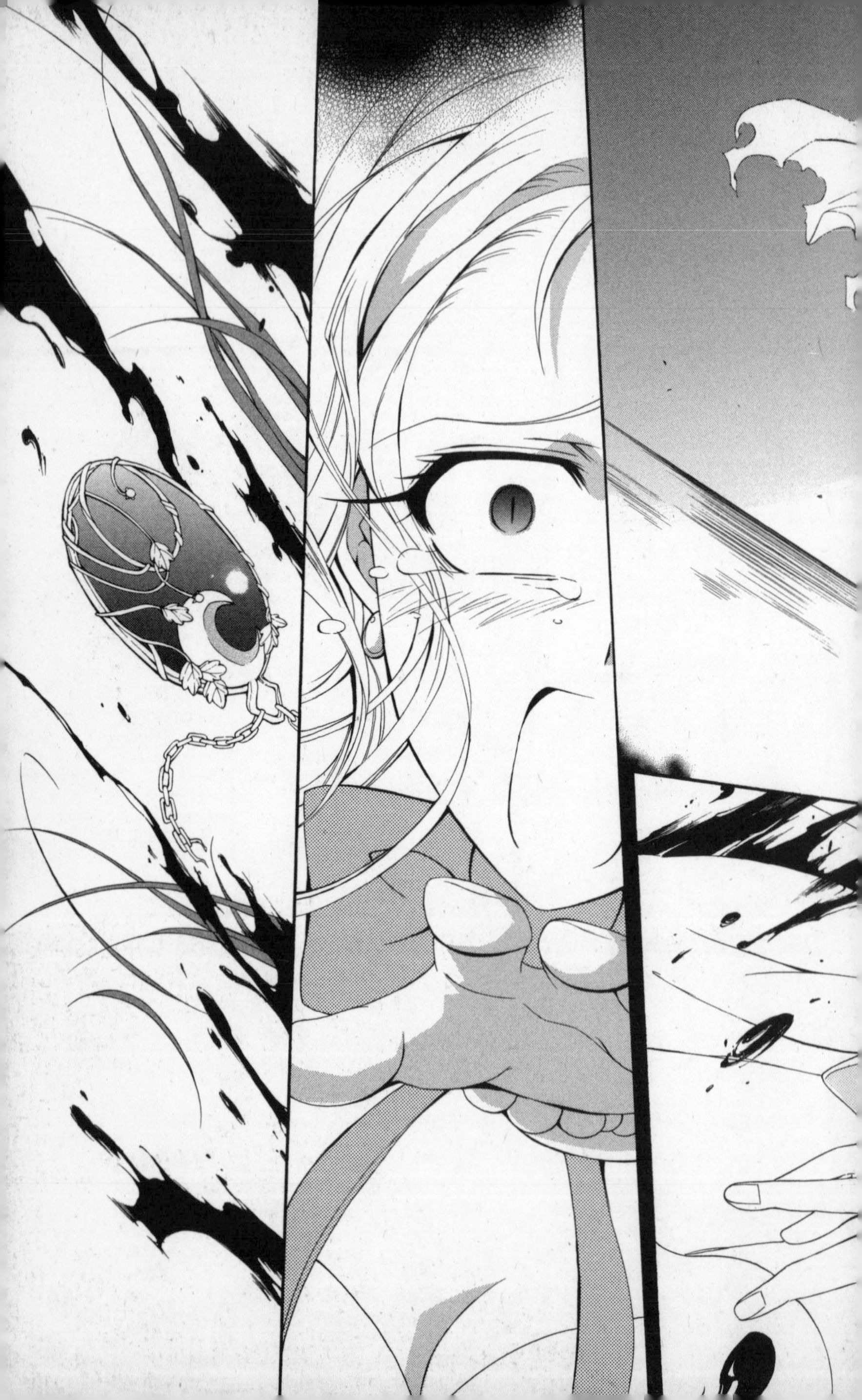

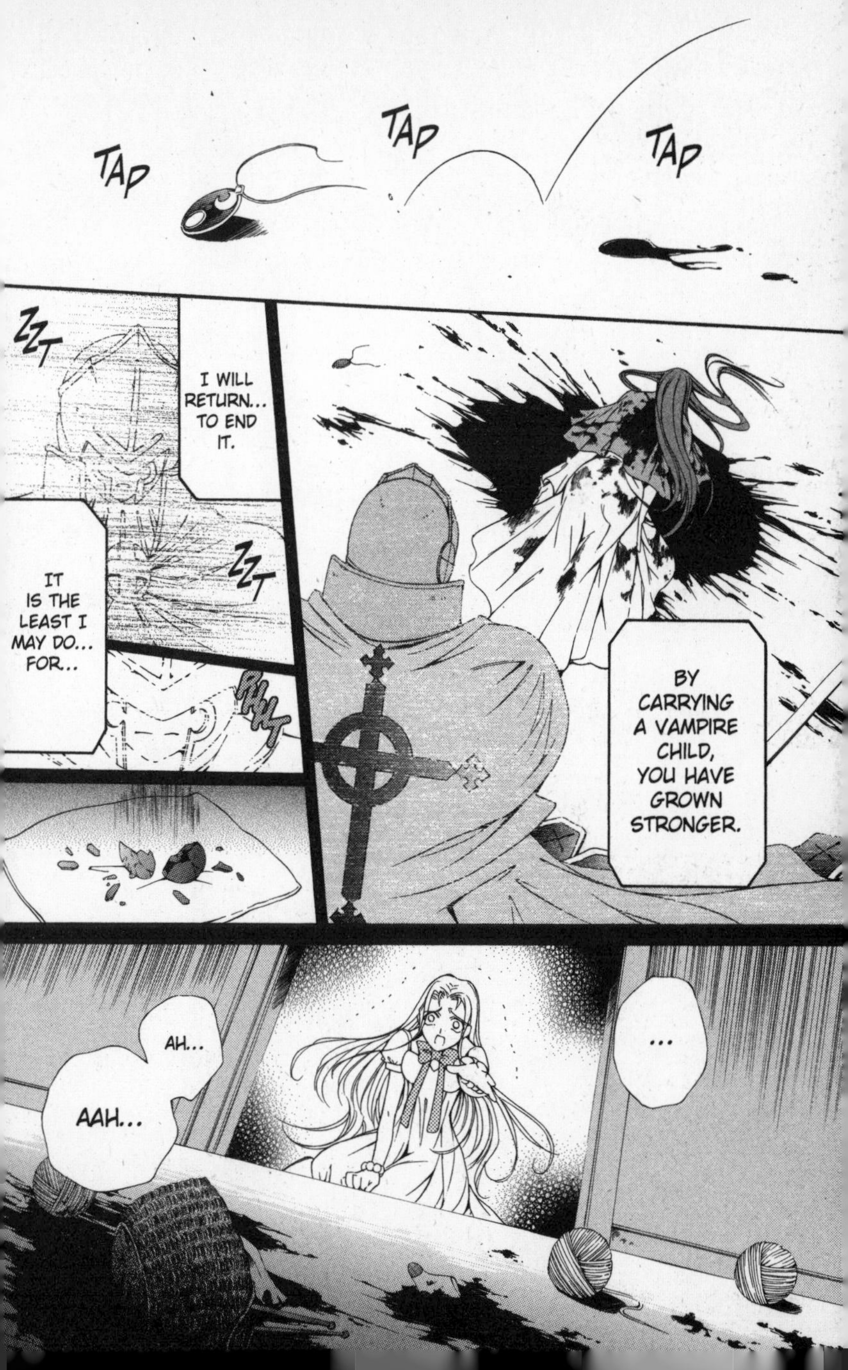
TAP
TAP
TAP
BY CARRYING A VAMPIRE CHILD, YOU HAVE GROWN STRONGER.
I WILL RETURN... TO END IT.
ZZT
ZZT
IT IS THE LEAST I MAY DO... FOR...
...
AH...
AAH...

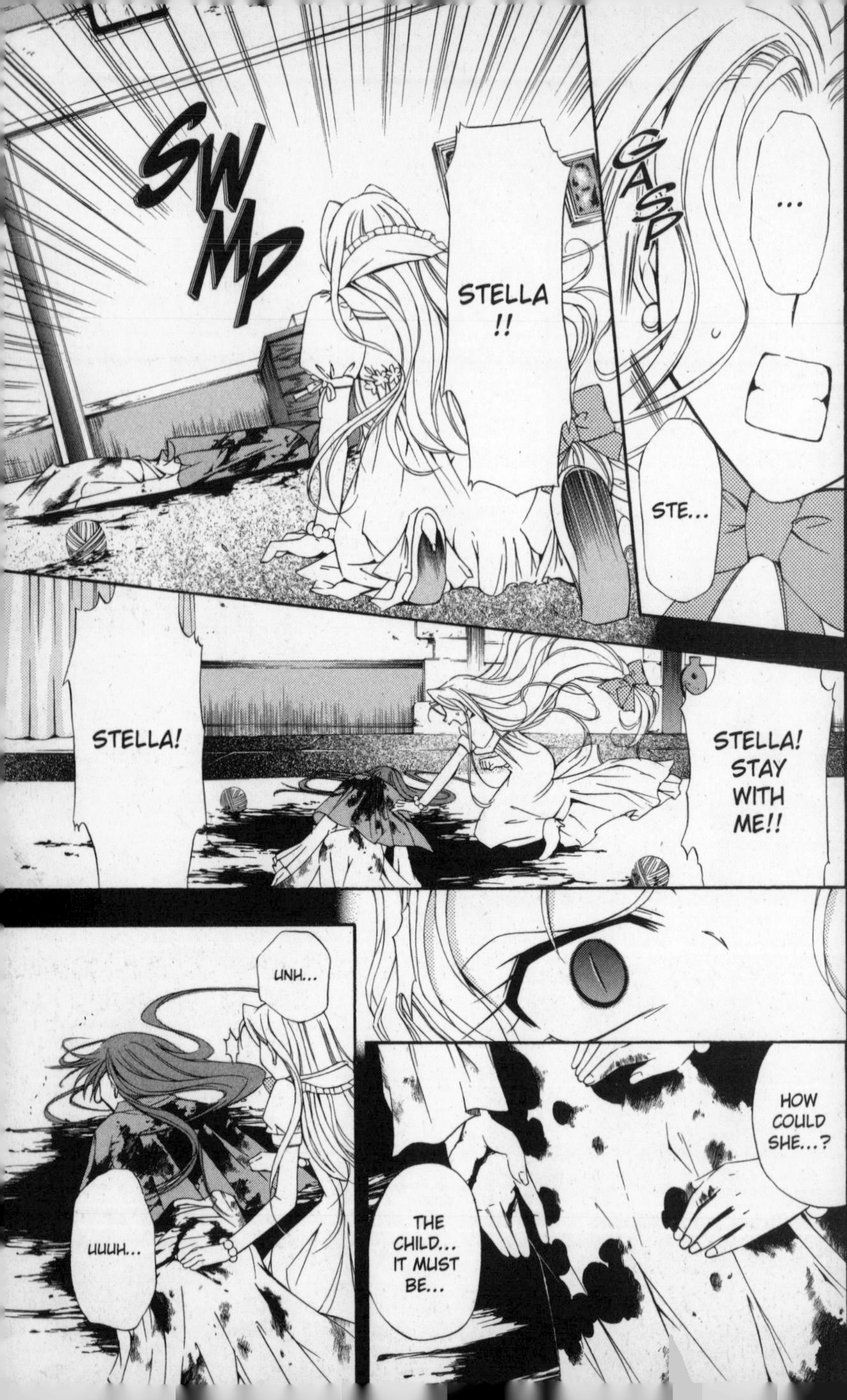
GASP
...
STE...
STELLA !!
SWMP
STELLA! STAY WITH ME!!
STELLA!
HOW COULD SHE...?
THE CHILD... IT MUST BE...
UNH...
UUUH...

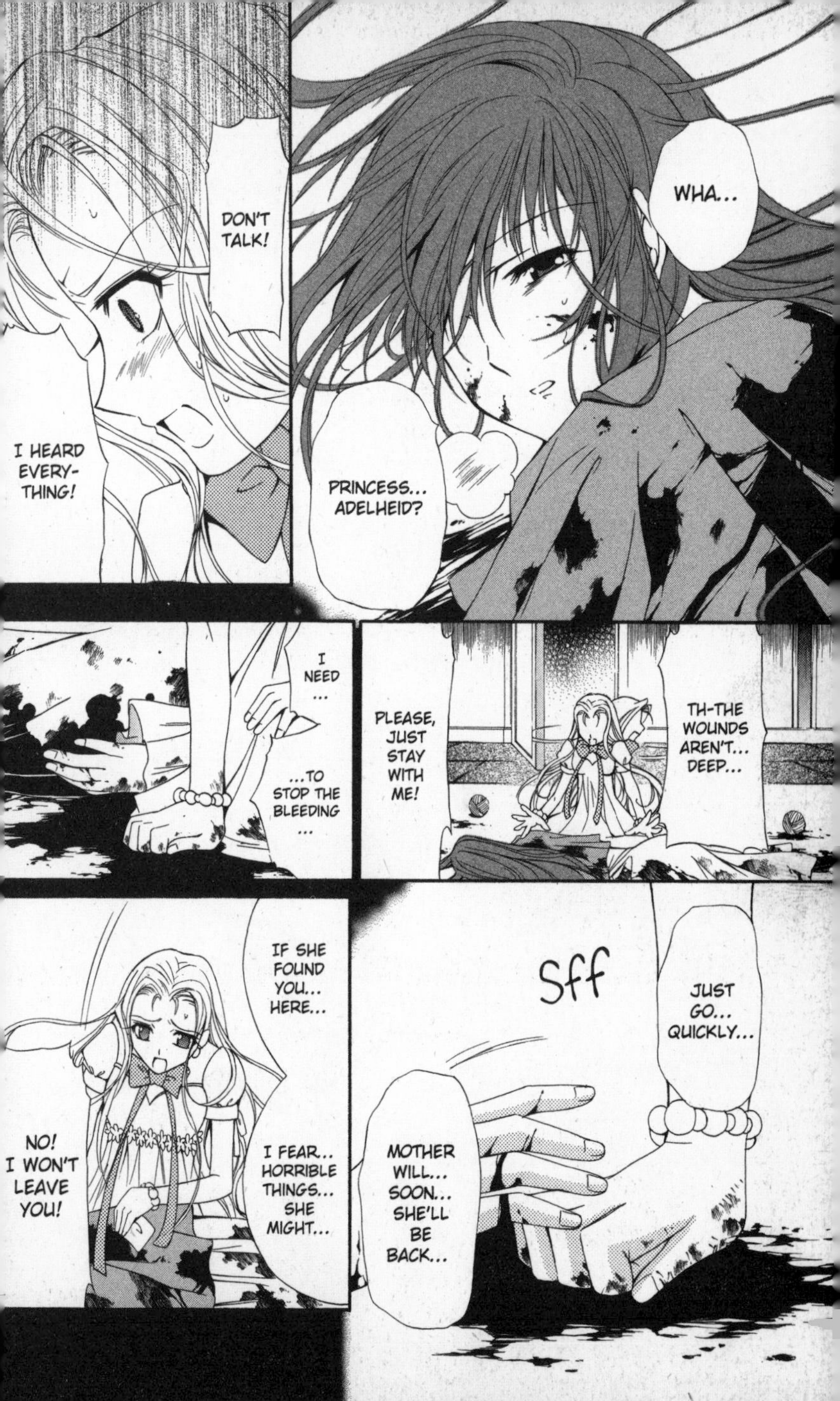
WHA...
PRINCESS... ADELHEID?
DON'T TALK!
I HEARD EVERY-THING!
TH-THE WOUNDS AREN'T... DEEP...
PLEASE, JUST STAY WITH ME!
I NEED ...
...TO STOP THE BLEEDING ...
Sff
JUST GO... QUICKLY...
MOTHER WILL... SOON... SHE'LL BE BACK...
IF SHE FOUND YOU... HERE...
I FEAR.. HORRIBLE THINGS... SHE MIGHT...
NO! I WON'T LEAVE YOU!

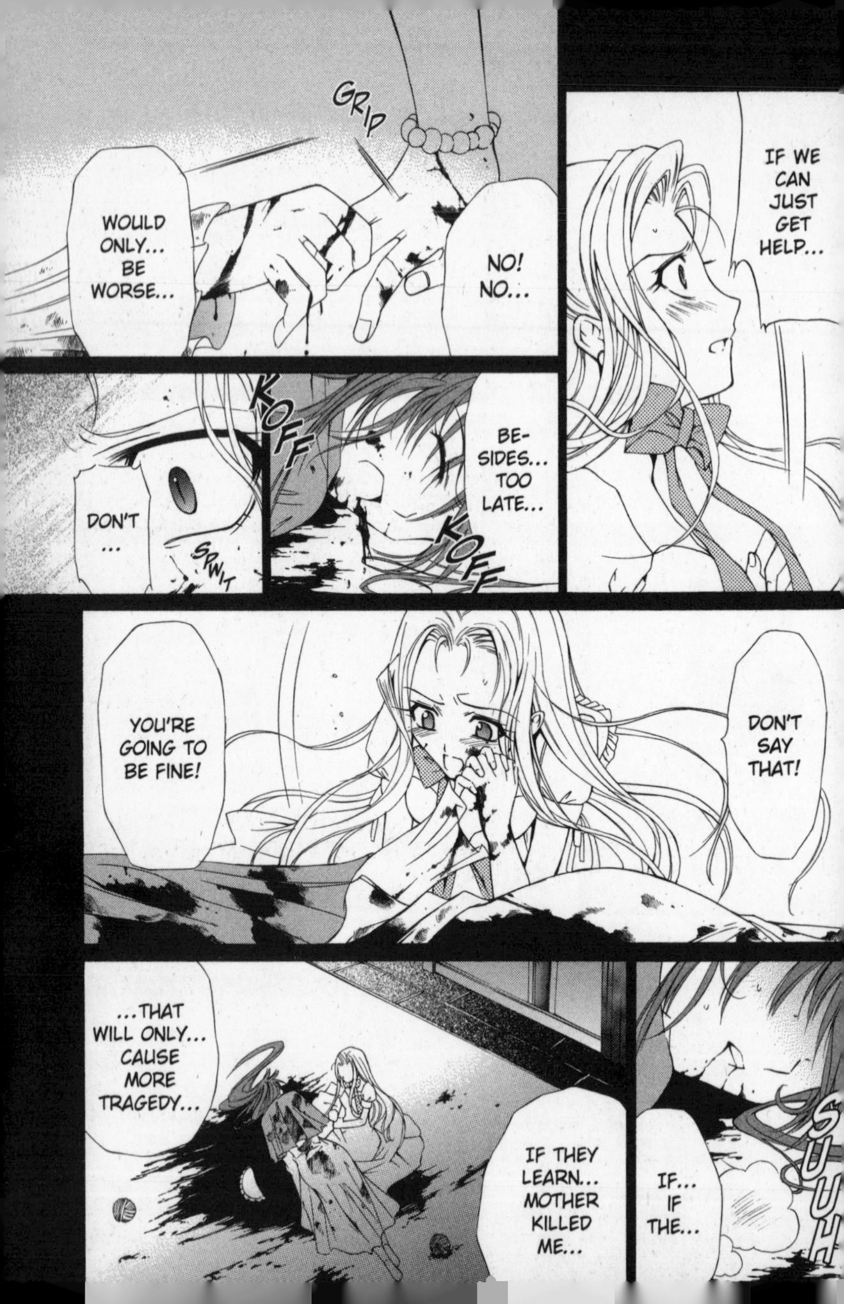
IF WE CAN JUST GET HELP...
GRIP
NO! NO...
WOULD ONLY... BE WORSE...
KOFF
BE-SIDES... TOO LATE...
KOFF
DON'T ...
SPWIT
DON'T SAY THAT!
YOU'RE GOING TO BE FINE!
SUUHH
IF... IF THE...
IF THEY LEARN... MOTHER KILLED ME...
...THAT WILL ONLY... CAUSE MORE TRAGEDY...

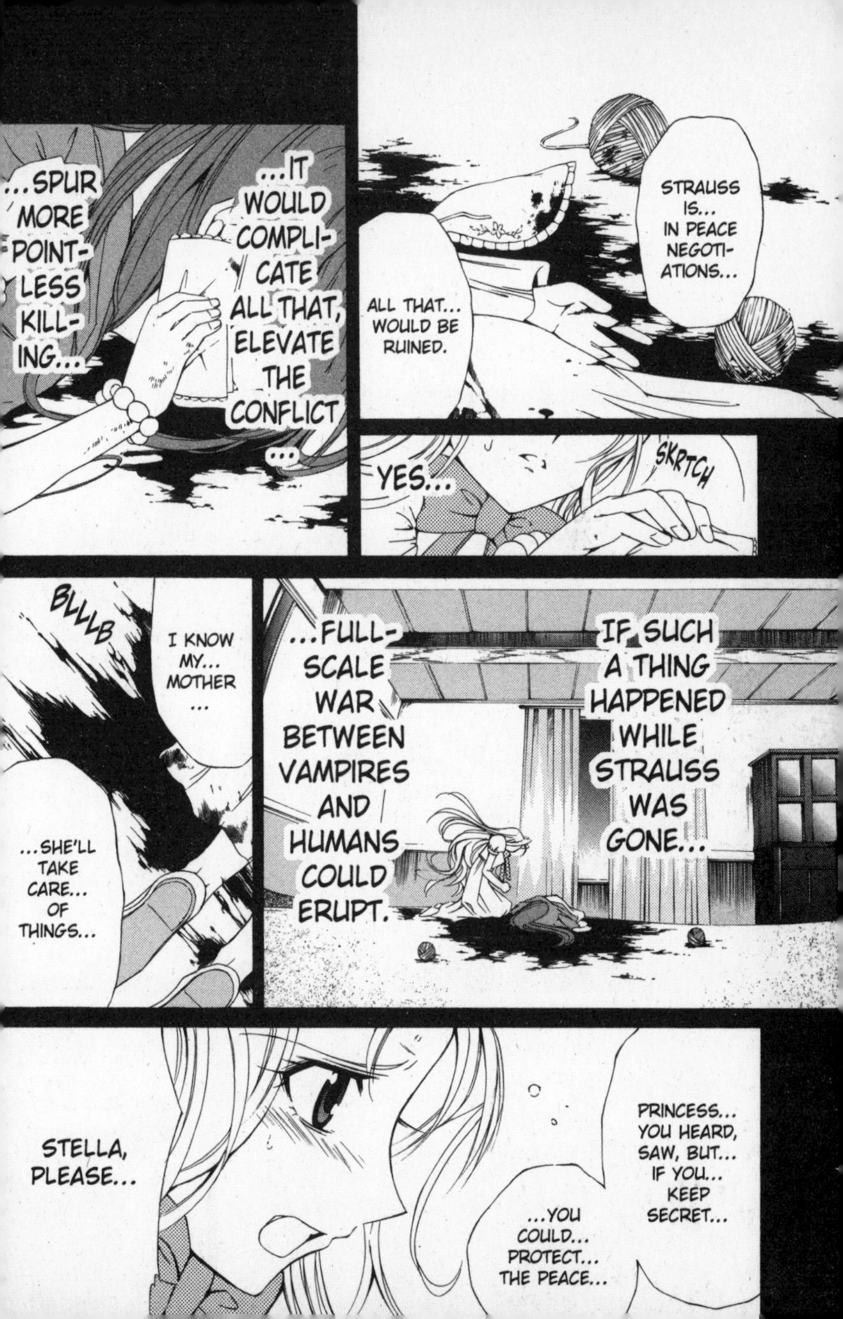
STRAUSS IS... IN PEACE NEGOTI-ATIONS...
ALL THAT... WOULD BE RUINED.
SKRTCH
YES...
...IT WOULD COMPLI-CATE ALL THAT, ELEVATE THE CONFLICT...
...SPUR MORE POINT-LESS KILL-ING...
IF SUCH A THING HAPPENED WHILE STRAUSS WAS GONE...
...FULL-SCALE WAR BETWEEN VAMPIRES AND HUMANS COULD ERUPT.
I KNOW MY... MOTHER...
BLLLB
...SHE'LL TAKE CARE... OF THINGS...
PRINCESS... YOU HEARD, SAW, BUT... IF YOU... KEEP SECRET...
...YOU COULD... PROTECT... THE PEACE...
STELLA, PLEASE...

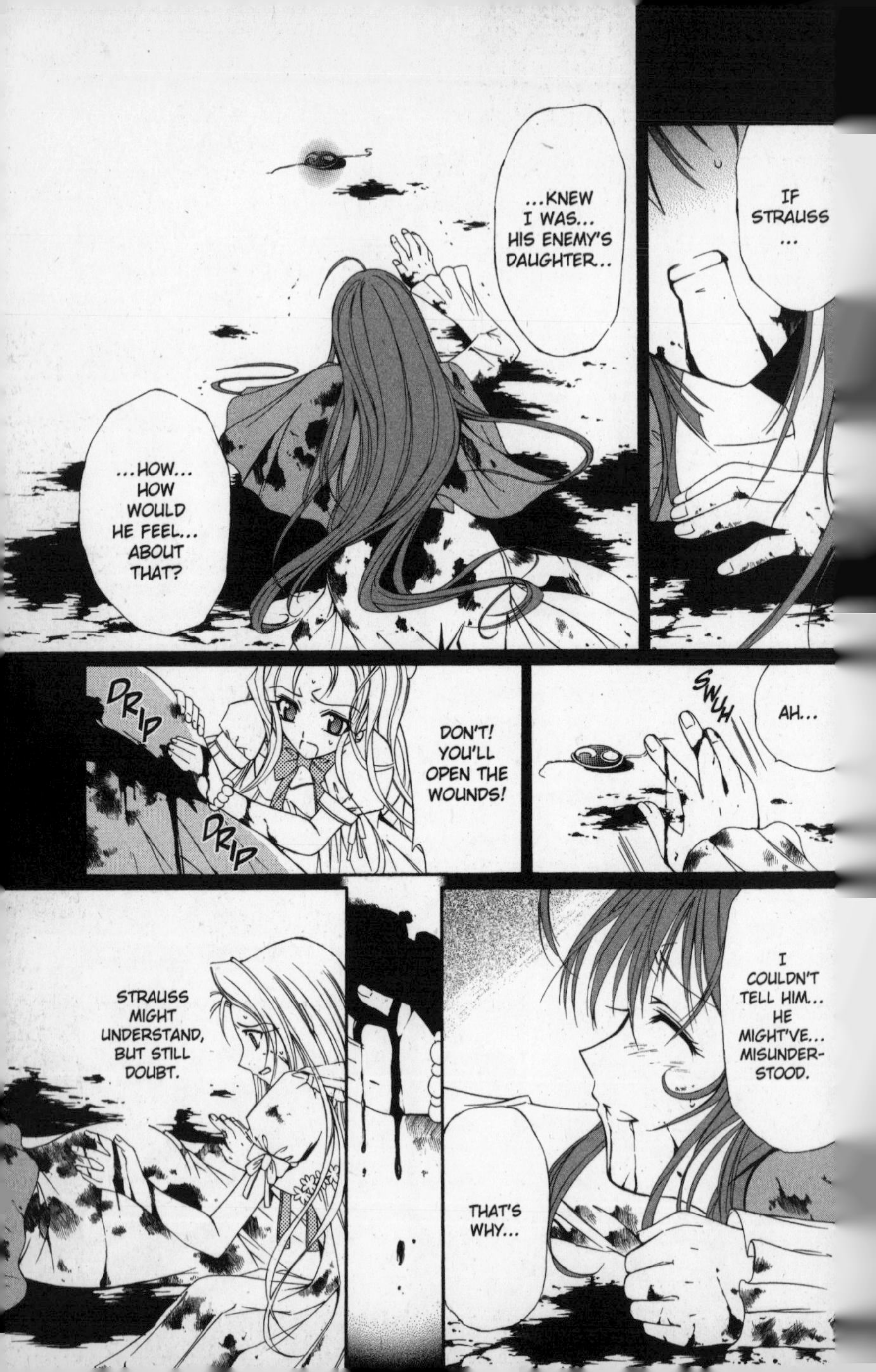
IF STRAUSS ...
...KNEW I WAS... HIS ENEMY'S DAUGHTER...
...HOW... HOW WOULD HE FEEL... ABOUT THAT?
SWUH
AH...
DON'T! YOU'LL OPEN THE WOUNDS!
DRIP
DRIP
I COULDN'T TELL HIM.. HE MIGHT'VE... MISUNDER-STOOD.
THAT'S WHY...
STRAUSS MIGHT UNDERSTAND, BUT STILL DOUBT.

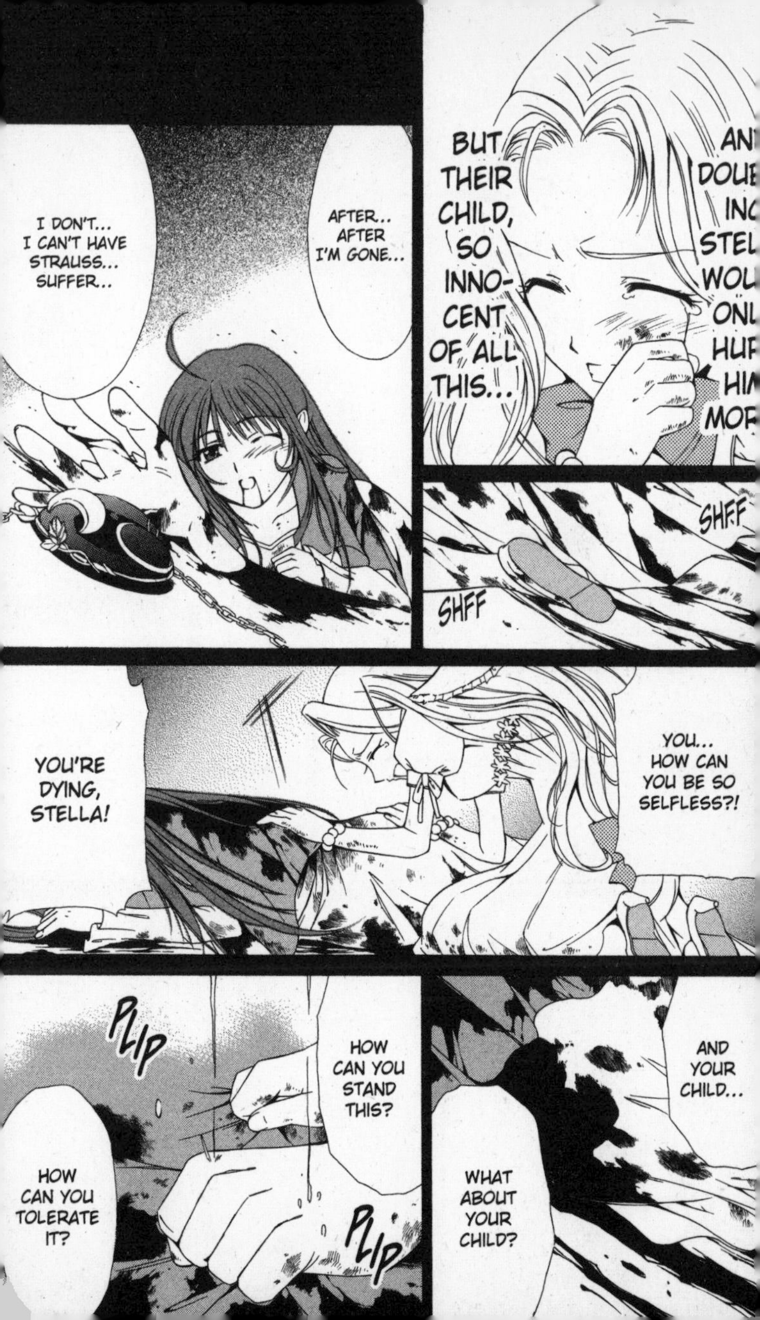
BUT THEIR CHILD, SO INNOCENT OF ALL THIS...
SHFF
SHFF
AFTER... AFTER I'M GONE...
I DON'T... I CAN'T HAVE STRAUSS... SUFFER...
YOU... HOW CAN YOU BE SO SELFLESS?!
YOU'RE DYING, STELLA!
AND YOUR CHILD...
WHAT ABOUT YOUR CHILD?
PLIP
HOW CAN YOU STAND THIS?
HOW CAN YOU TOLERATE IT?
PLIP

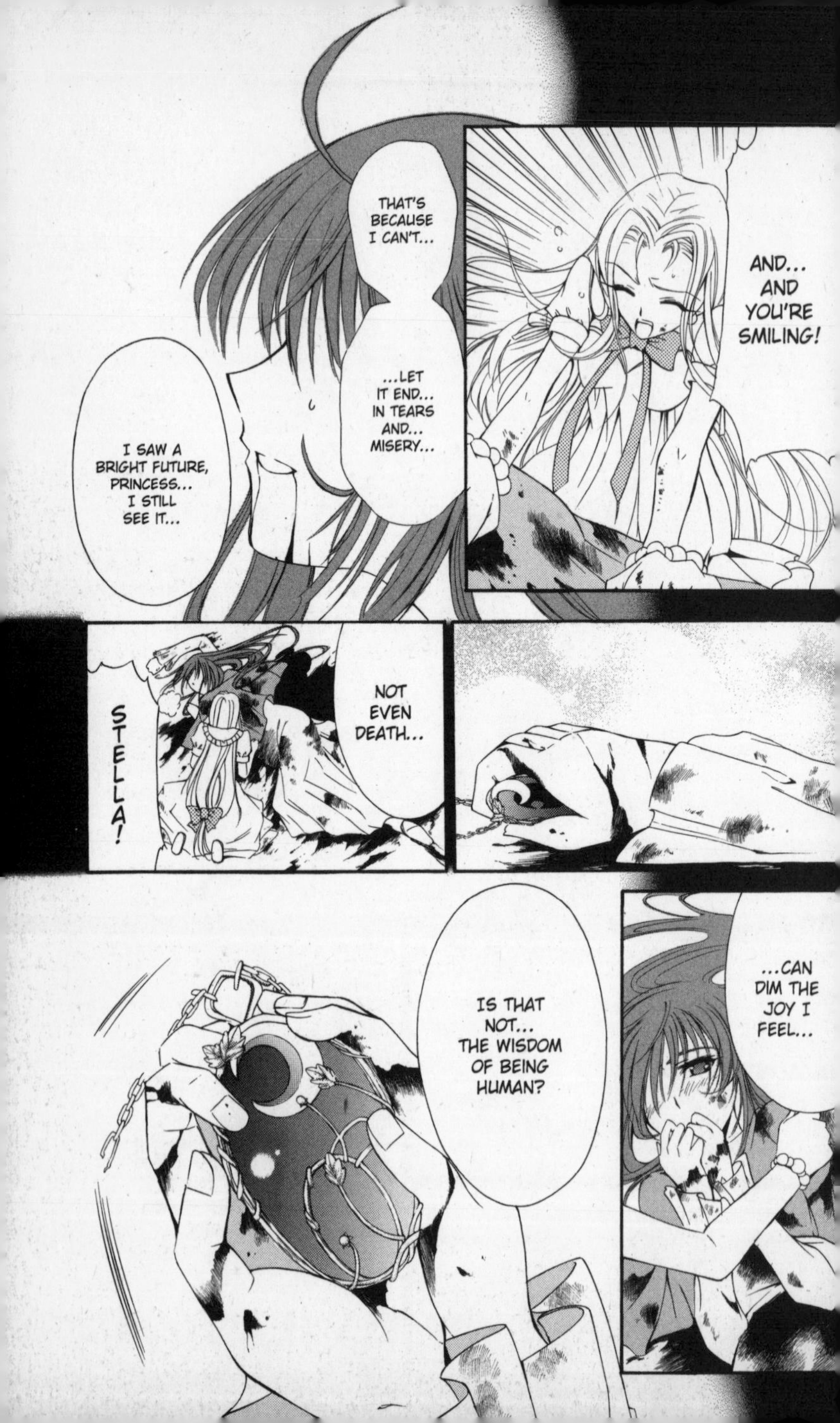
AND... AND YOU'RE SMILING!
THAT'S BECAUSE I CAN'T...
...LET IT END... IN TEARS AND... MISERY...
I SAW A BRIGHT FUTURE, PRINCESS... I STILL SEE IT...
NOT EVEN DEATH...
STELLA!
...CAN DIM THE JOY I FEEL...
IS THAT NOT... THE WISDOM OF BEING HUMAN?

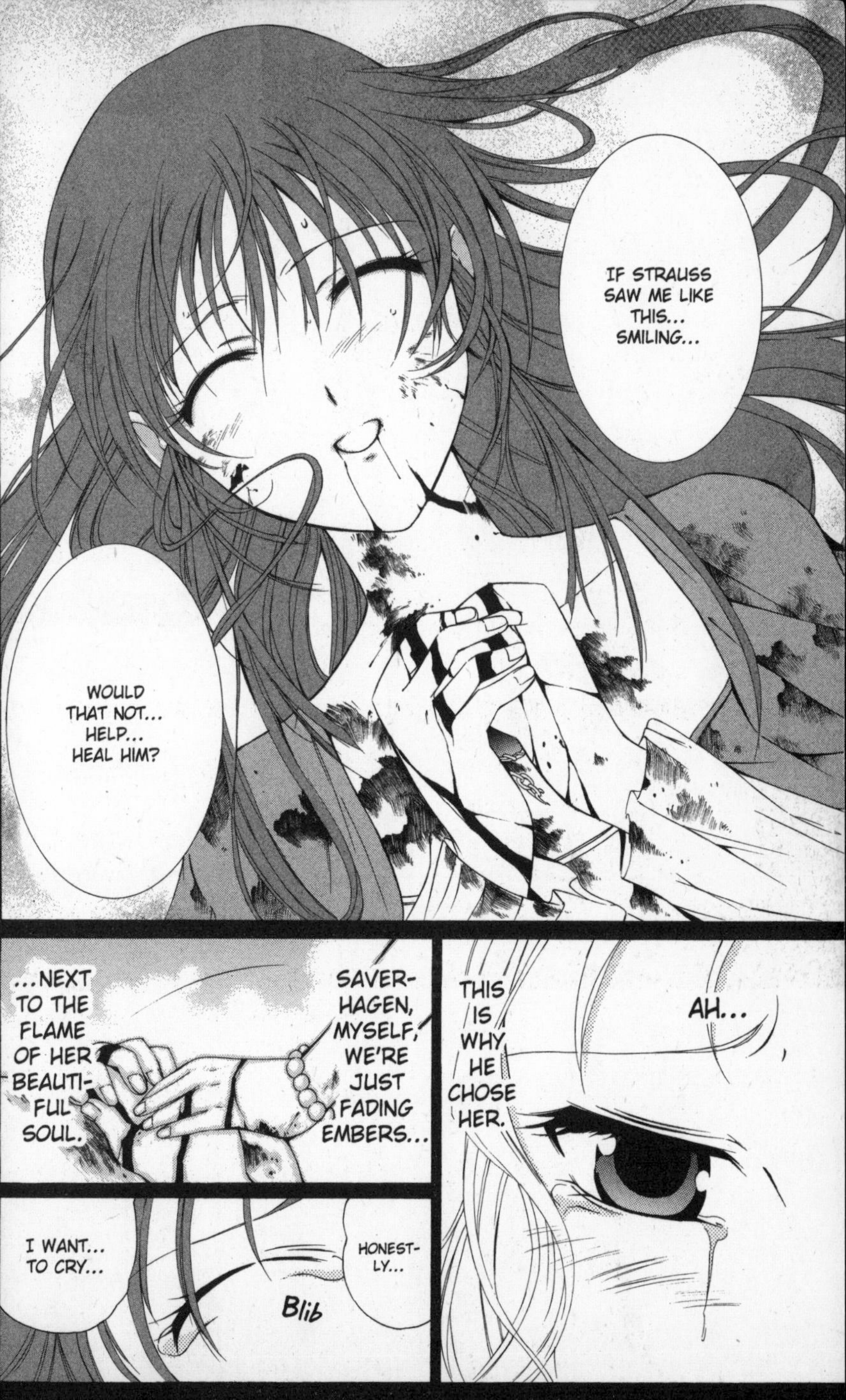
IF STRAUSS SAW ME LIKE THIS... SMILING...
WOULD THAT NOT... HELP... HEAL HIM?
AH...
THIS IS WHY HE CHOSE HER.
SAVERHAGEN, MYSELF, WE'RE JUST FADING EMBERS...
...NEXT TO THE FLAME OF HER BEAUTIFUL SOUL.
HONESTLY...
Blib
I WANT... TO CRY...

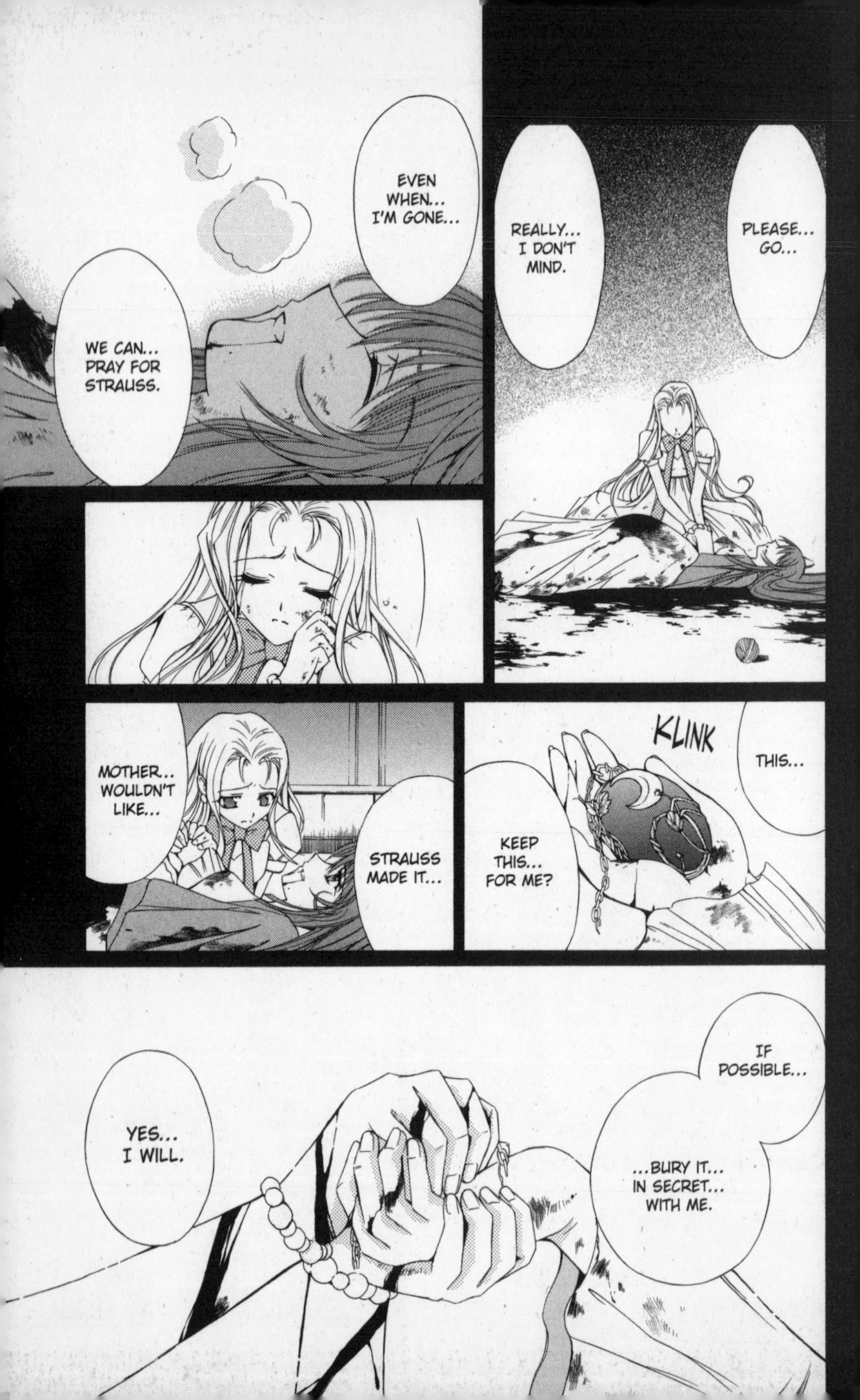
PLEASE... GO...
REALLY... I DON'T MIND.
EVEN WHEN... I'M GONE...
WE CAN... PRAY FOR STRAUSS.
KLINK
THIS...
KEEP THIS... FOR ME?
STRAUSS MADE IT...
MOTHER... WOULDN'T LIKE...
IF POSSIBLE...
...BURY IT... IN SECRET... WITH ME.
YES... I WILL.

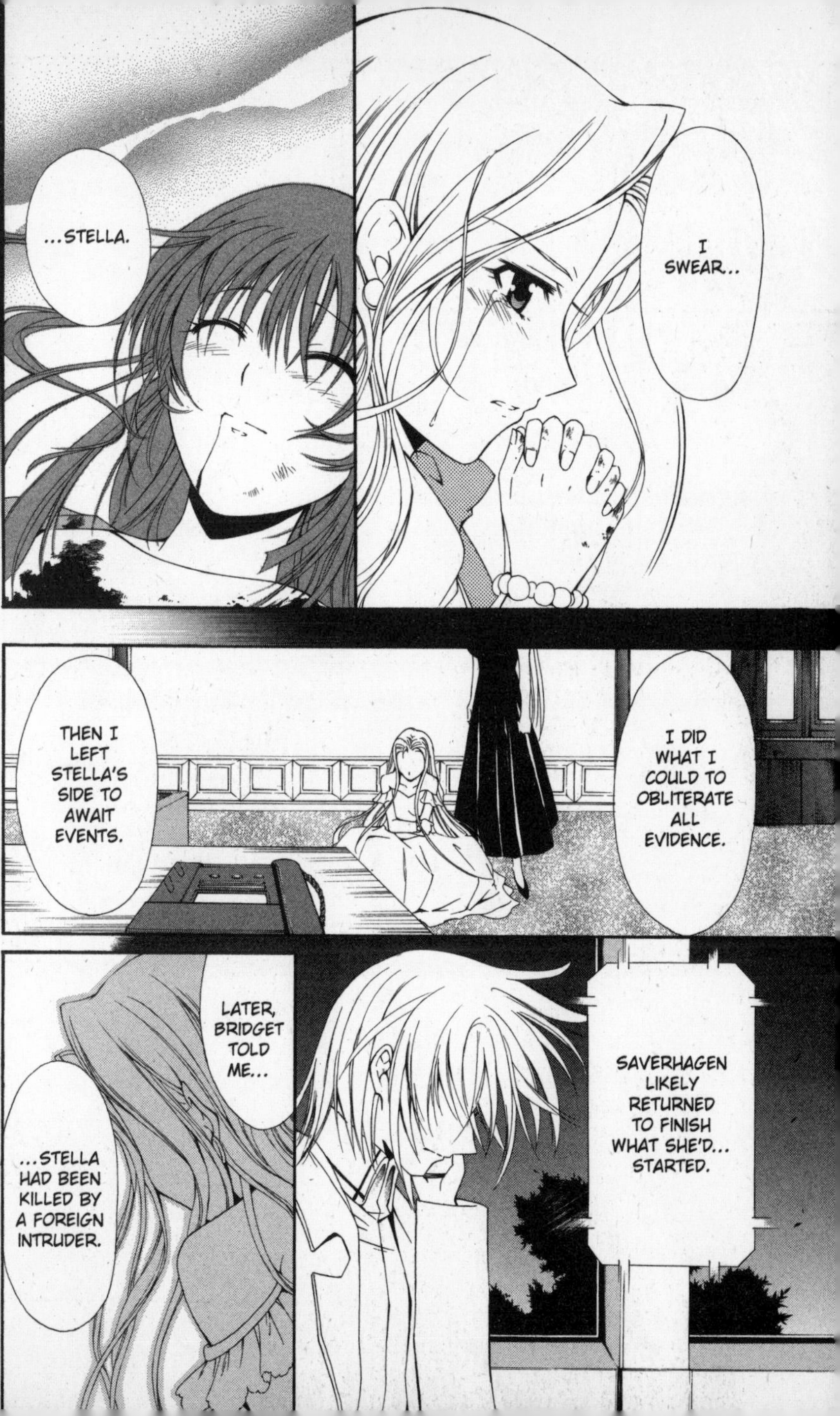
I SWEAR...
...STELLA.
I DID WHAT I COULD TO OBLITERATE ALL EVIDENCE.
THEN I LEFT STELLA'S SIDE TO AWAIT EVENTS.
SAVERHAGEN LIKELY RETURNED TO FINISH WHAT SHE'D... STARTED.
LATER, BRIDGET TOLD ME...
...STELLA HAD BEEN KILLED BY A FOREIGN INTRUDER.

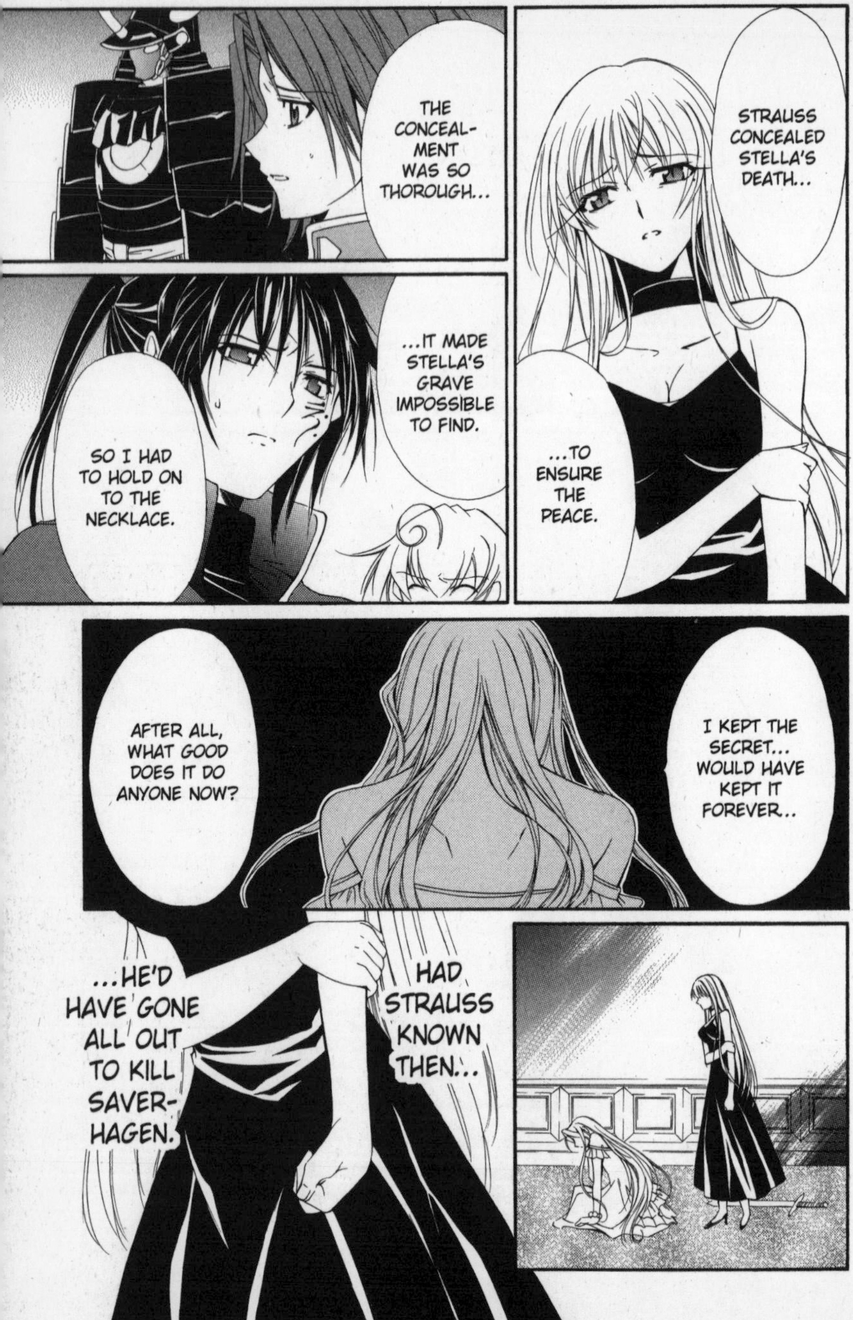
STRAUSS CONCEALED STELLA'S DEATH...
...TO ENSURE THE PEACE.
THE CONCEAL-MENT WAS SO THOROUGH...
...IT MADE STELLA'S GRAVE IMPOSSIBLE TO FIND.
SO I HAD TO HOLD ON TO THE NECKLACE.
I KEPT THE SECRET... WOULD HAVE KEPT IT FOREVER..
AFTER ALL, WHAT GOOD DOES IT DO ANYONE NOW?
HAD STRAUSS KNOWN THEN...
...HE'D HAVE GONE ALL OUT TO KILL SAVER-HAGEN.

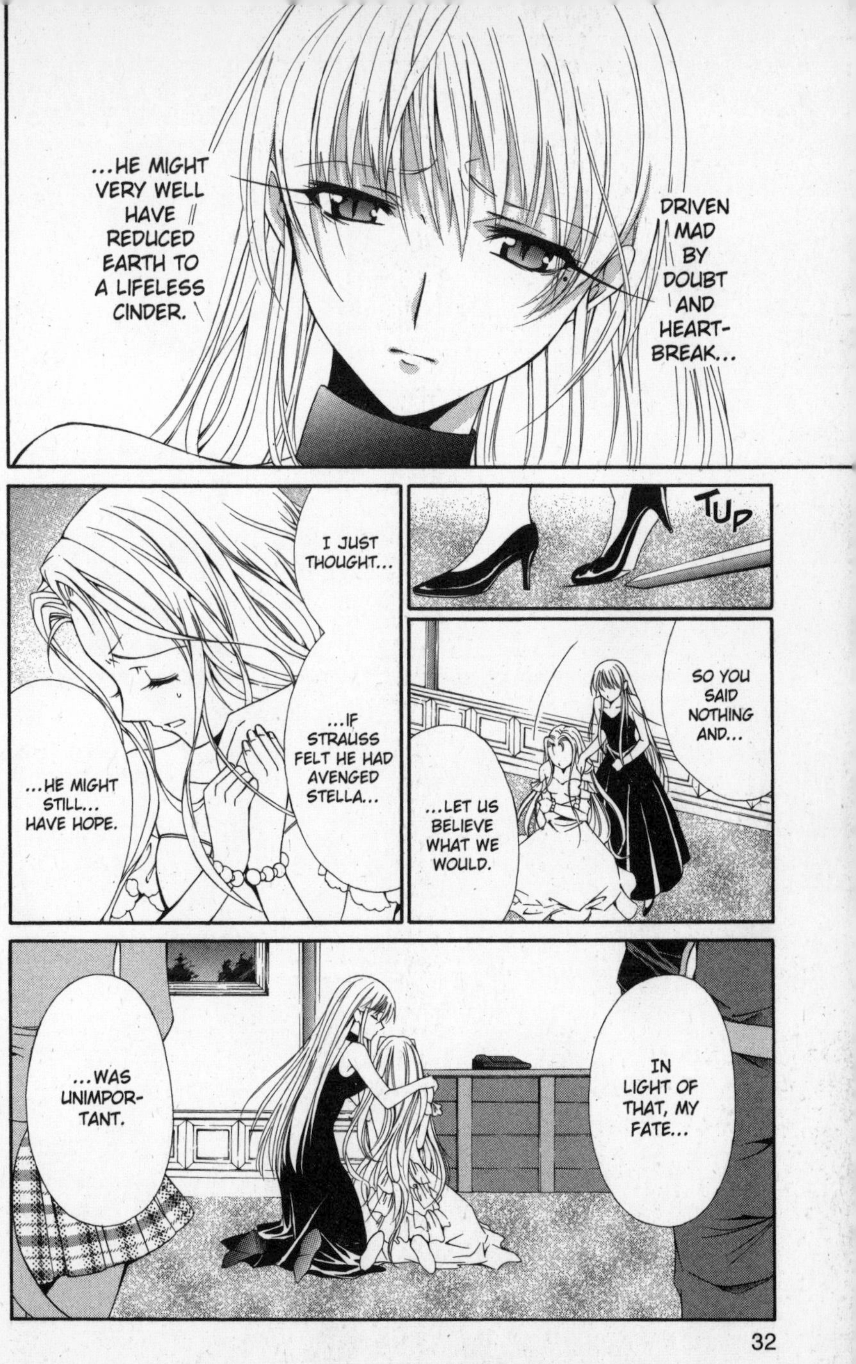
DRIVEN MAD BY DOUBT AND HEART-BREAK...
...HE MIGHT VERY WELL HAVE REDUCED EARTH TO A LIFELESS CINDER.
TUP
SO YOU SAID NOTHING AND...
...LET US BELIEVE WHAT WE WOULD.
I JUST THOUGHT...
...IF STRAUSS FELT HE HAD AVENGED STELLA...
...HE MIGHT STILL... HAVE HOPE.
IN LIGHT OF THAT, MY FATE...
...WAS UNIMPORTANT.

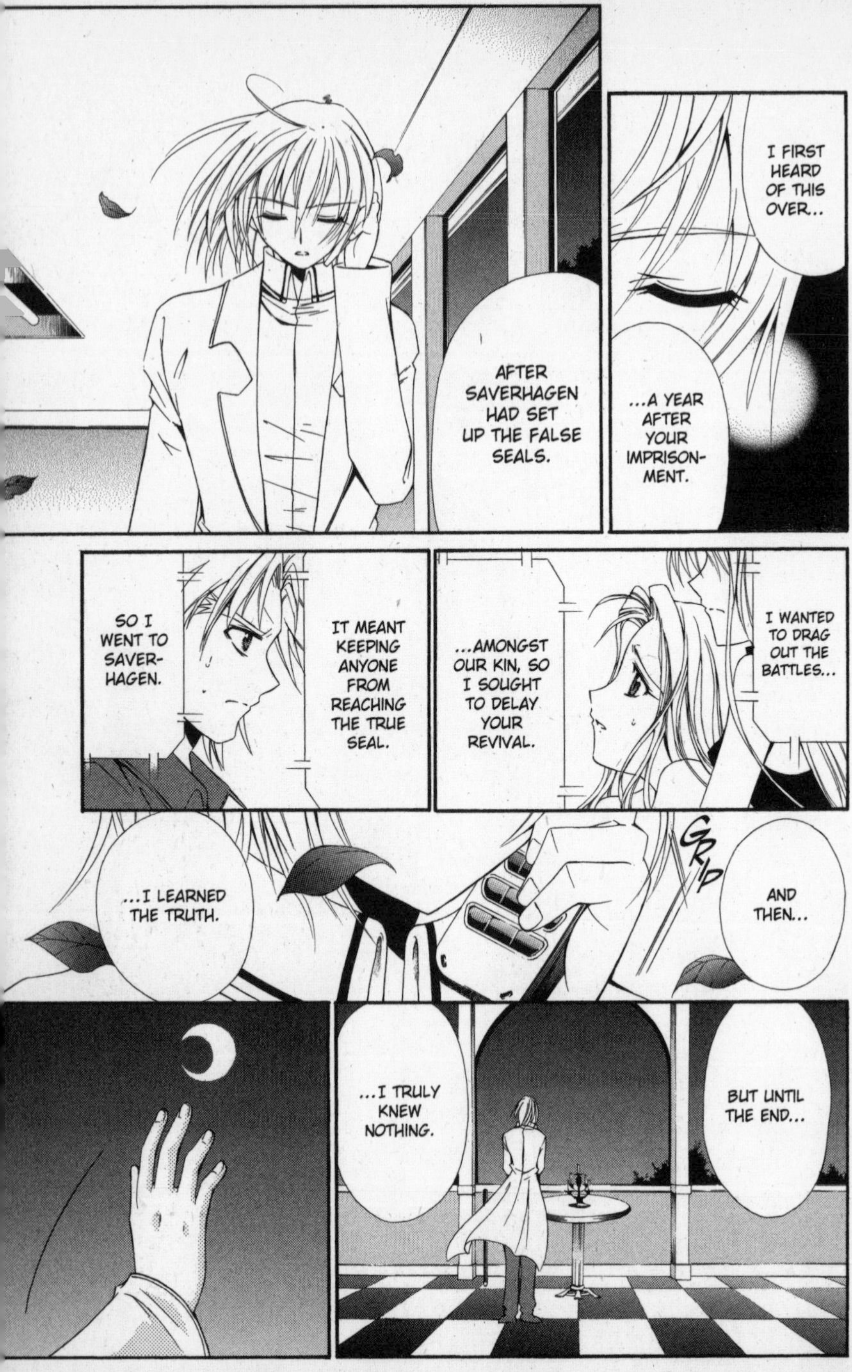
I FIRST HEARD OF THIS OVER...
...A YEAR AFTER YOUR IMPRISONMENT.
AFTER SAVERHAGEN HAD SET UP THE FALSE SEALS.
I WANTED TO DRAG OUT THE BATTLES...
...AMONGST OUR KIN, SO I SOUGHT TO DELAY YOUR REVIVAL.
IT MEANT KEEPING ANYONE FROM REACHING THE TRUE SEAL.
SO I WENT TO SAVERHAGEN.
GRIP
AND THEN...
...I LEARNED THE TRUTH.
BUT UNTIL THE END...
...I TRULY KNEW NOTHING.

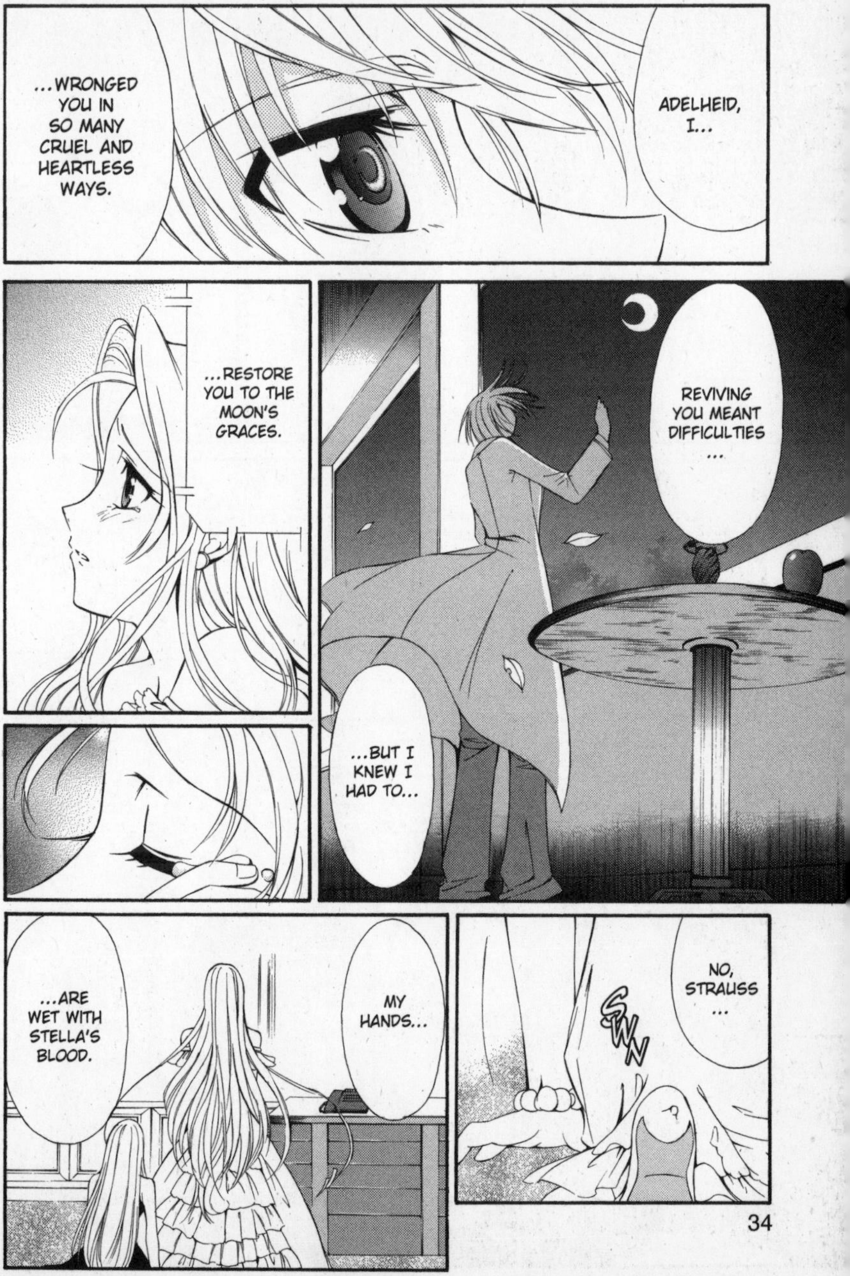
ADELHEID, I...
...WRONGED YOU IN SO MANY CRUEL AND HEARTLESS WAYS.
REVIVING YOU MEANT DIFFICULTIES ...
...BUT I KNEW I HAD TO...
...RESTORE YOU TO THE MOON'S GRACES.
NO, STRAUSS ...
SWN
MY HANDS...
...ARE WET WITH STELLA'S BLOOD.

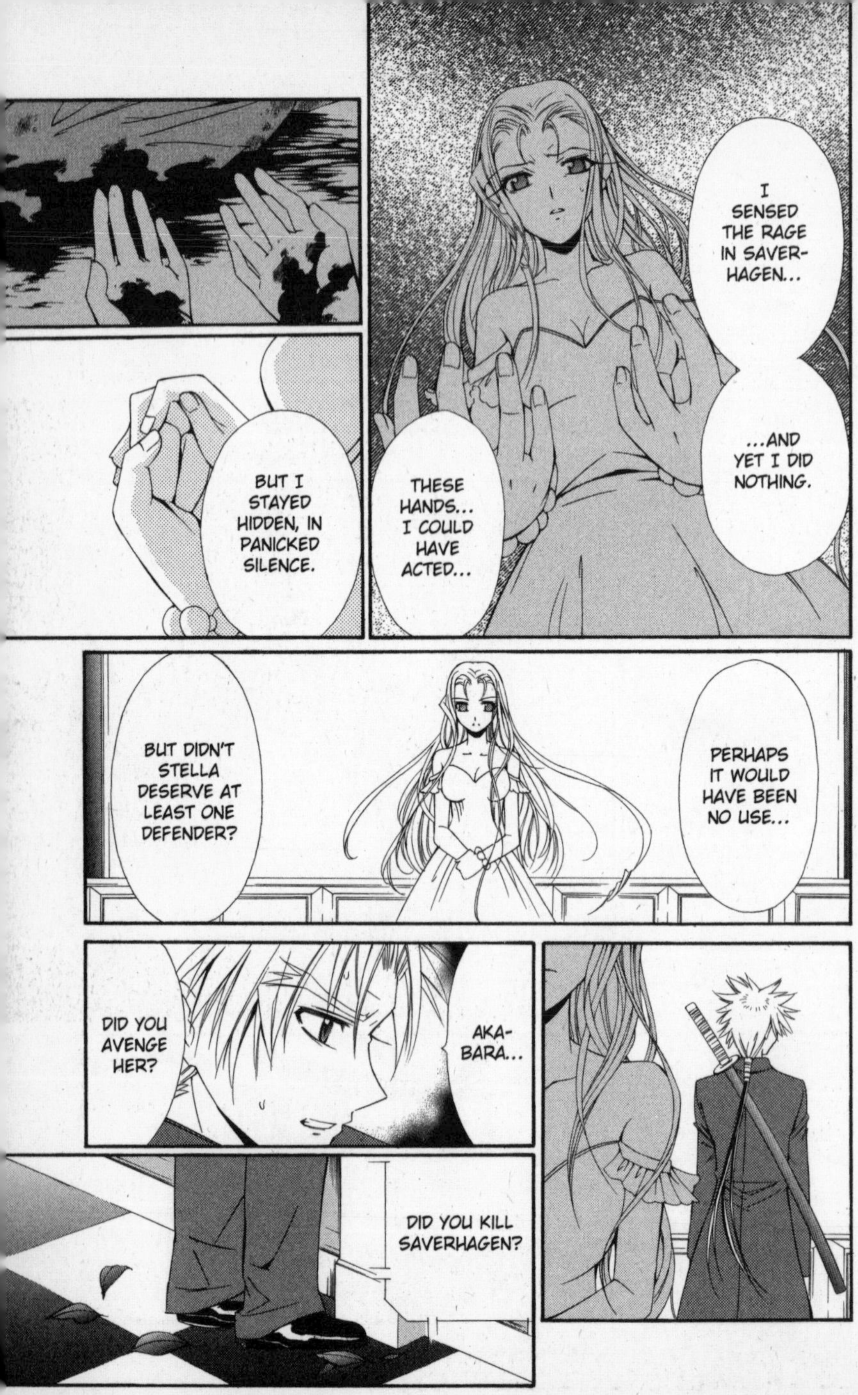
I SENSED THE RAGE IN SAVER-HAGEN...
...AND YET I DID NOTHING.
THESE HANDS... I COULD HAVE ACTED...
BUT I STAYED HIDDEN, IN PANICKED SILENCE.
PERHAPS IT WOULD HAVE BEEN NO USE...
BUT DIDN'T STELLA DESERVE AT LEAST ONE DEFENDER?
AKA-BARA...
DID YOU AVENGE HER?
DID YOU KILL SAVERHAGEN?

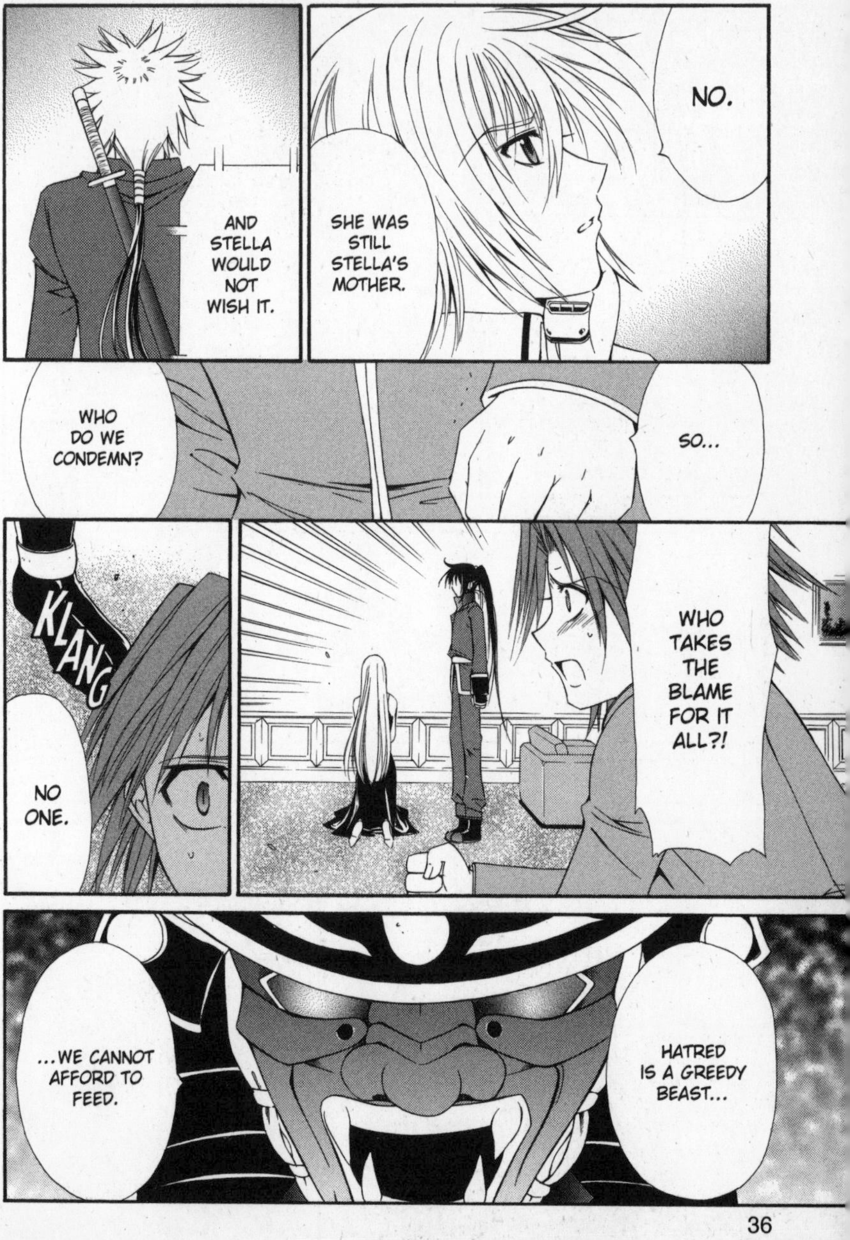
NO.
SHE WAS STILL STELLA'S MOTHER.
AND STELLA WOULD NOT WISH IT.
SO...
WHO DO WE CONDEMN?
WHO TAKES THE BLAME FOR IT ALL?!
KLANG
NO ONE.
HATRED IS A GREEDY BEAST...
...WE CANNOT AFFORD TO FEED.

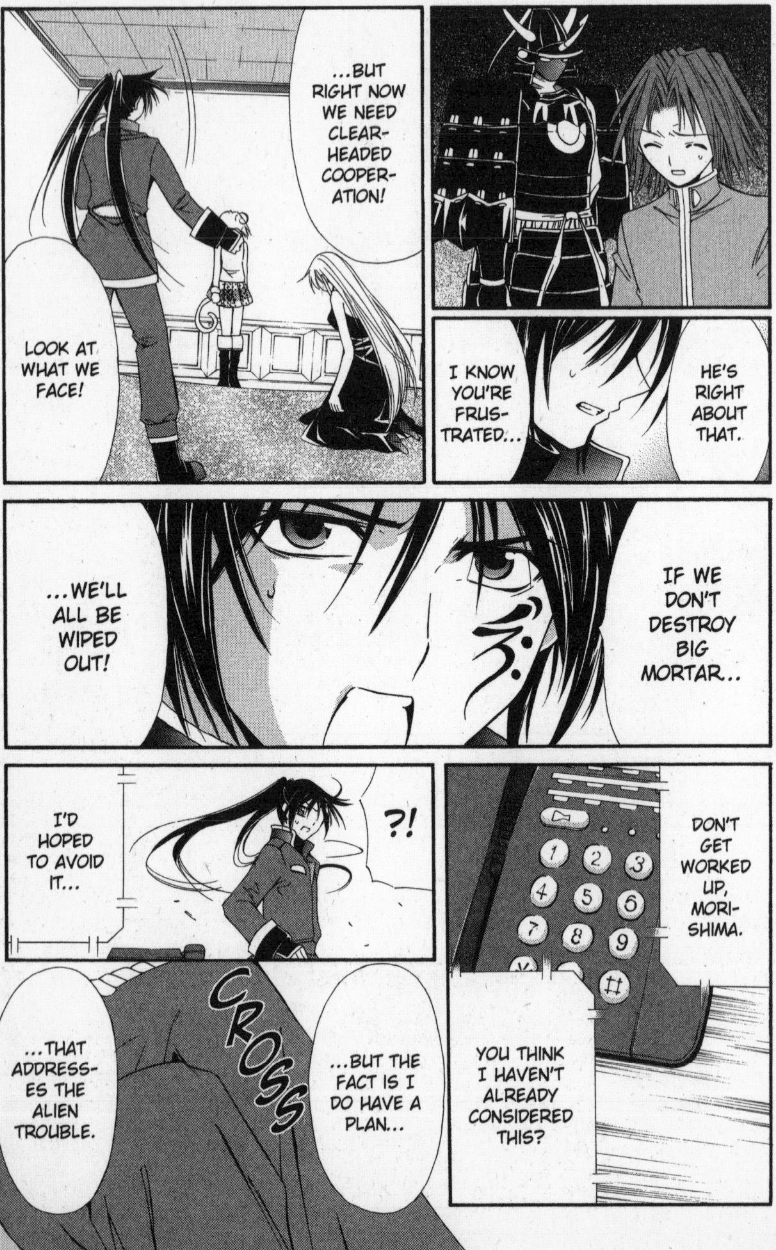
HE'S RIGHT ABOUT THAT.
I KNOW YOU'RE FRUS-TRATED...
...BUT RIGHT NOW WE NEED CLEAR-HEADED COOPER-ATION!
LOOK AT WHAT WE FACE!
IF WE DON'T DESTROY BIG MORTAR...
...WE'LL ALL BE WIPED OUT!
DON'T GET WORKED UP, MORI-SHIMA.
?!
I'D HOPED TO AVOID IT...
YOU THINK I HAVEN'T ALREADY CONSIDERED THIS?
CROSS
...BUT THE FACT IS I DO HAVE A PLAN...
...THAT ADDRESS-ES THE ALIEN TROUBLE.

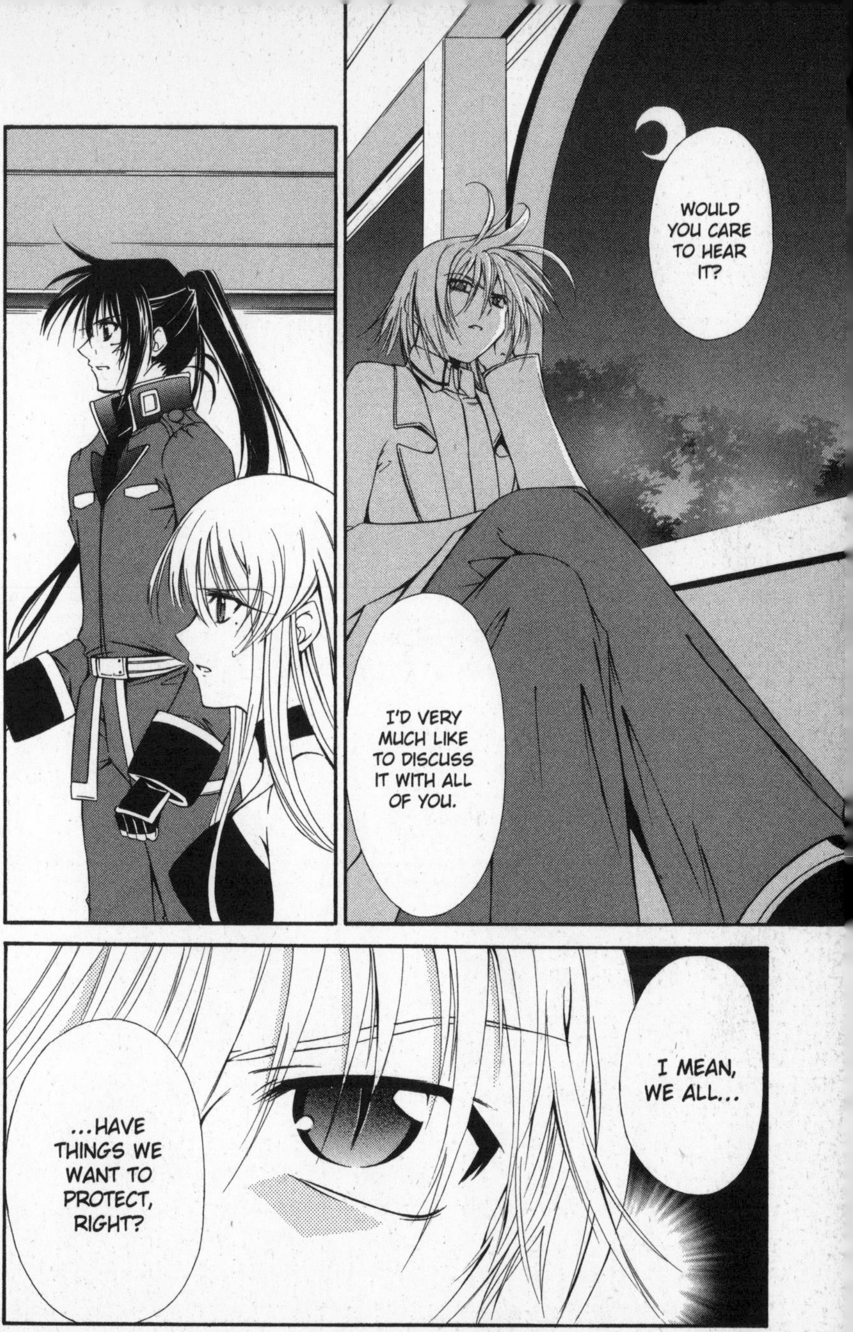
WOULD YOU CARE TO HEAR IT?
I'D VERY MUCH LIKE TO DISCUSS IT WITH ALL OF YOU.
I MEAN, WE ALL...
...HAVE THINGS WE WANT TO PROTECT, RIGHT?

THE RECORD OF A

FALLEN VAMPIRE

THE RECORD OF A

FALLEN VAMPIRE

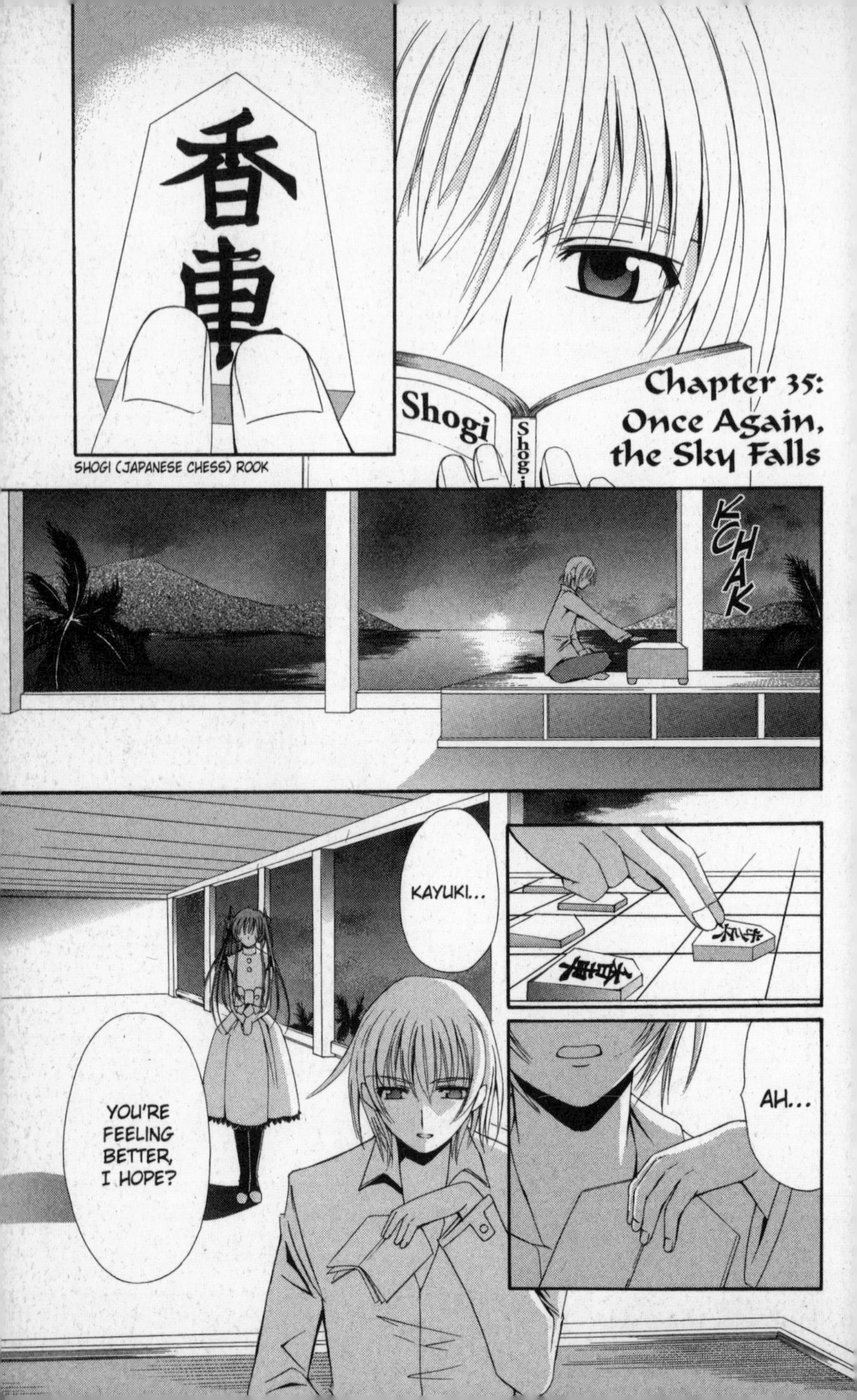
Shogi
Chapter 35: Once Again, the Sky Falls
SHOGI (JAPANESE CHESS) ROOK
KCHAK
AH...
KAYUKI...
YOU'RE FEELING BETTER, I HOPE?

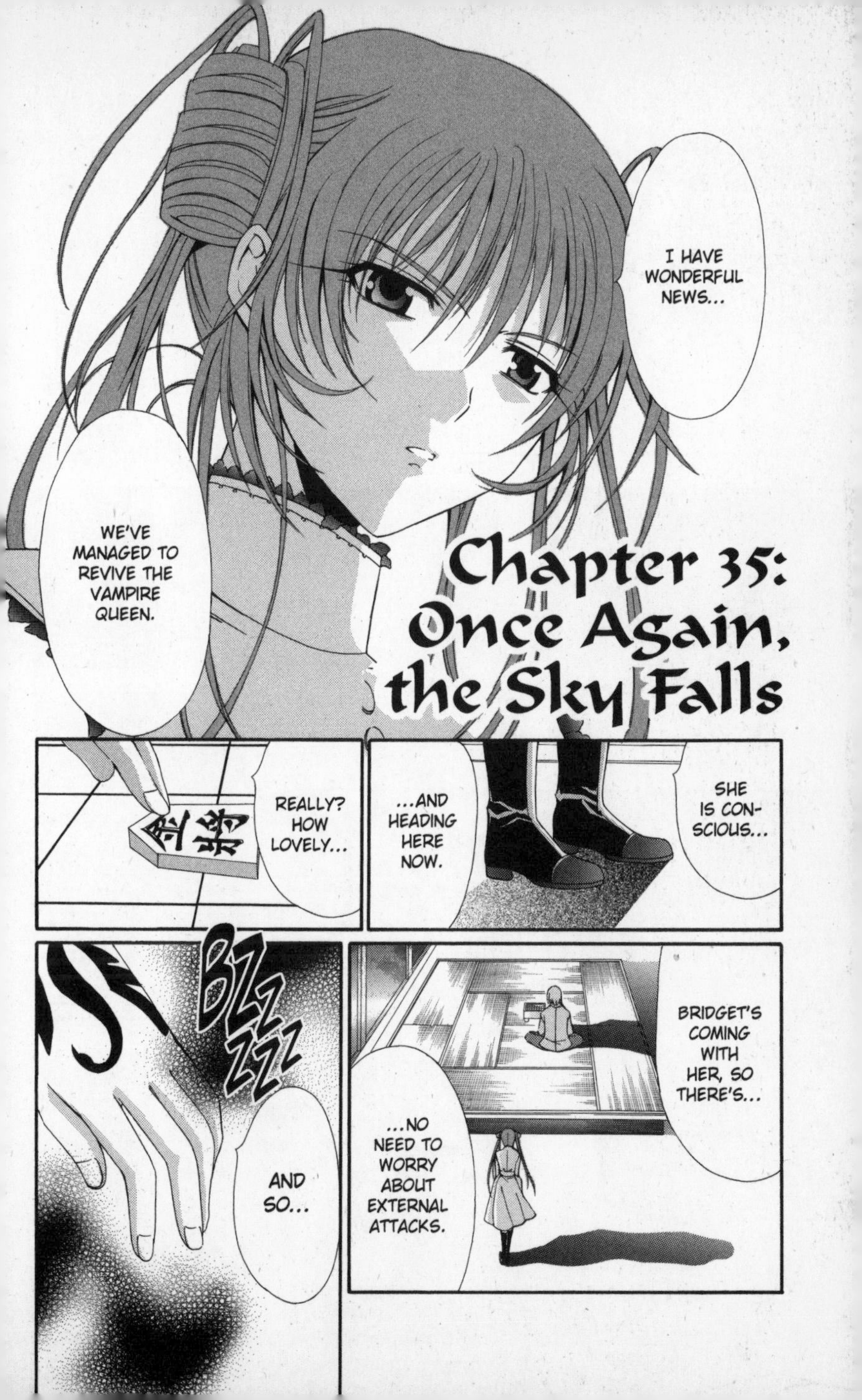
I HAVE WONDERFUL NEWS...
WE'VE MANAGED TO REVIVE THE VAMPIRE QUEEN.
Chapter 35: Once Again, the Sky Falls
SHE IS CONSCIOUS...
...AND HEADING HERE NOW.
REALLY? HOW LOVELY...
BRIDGET'S COMING WITH HER, SO THERE'S...
...NO NEED TO WORRY ABOUT EXTERNAL ATTACKS.
BZZZZZ
AND SO...

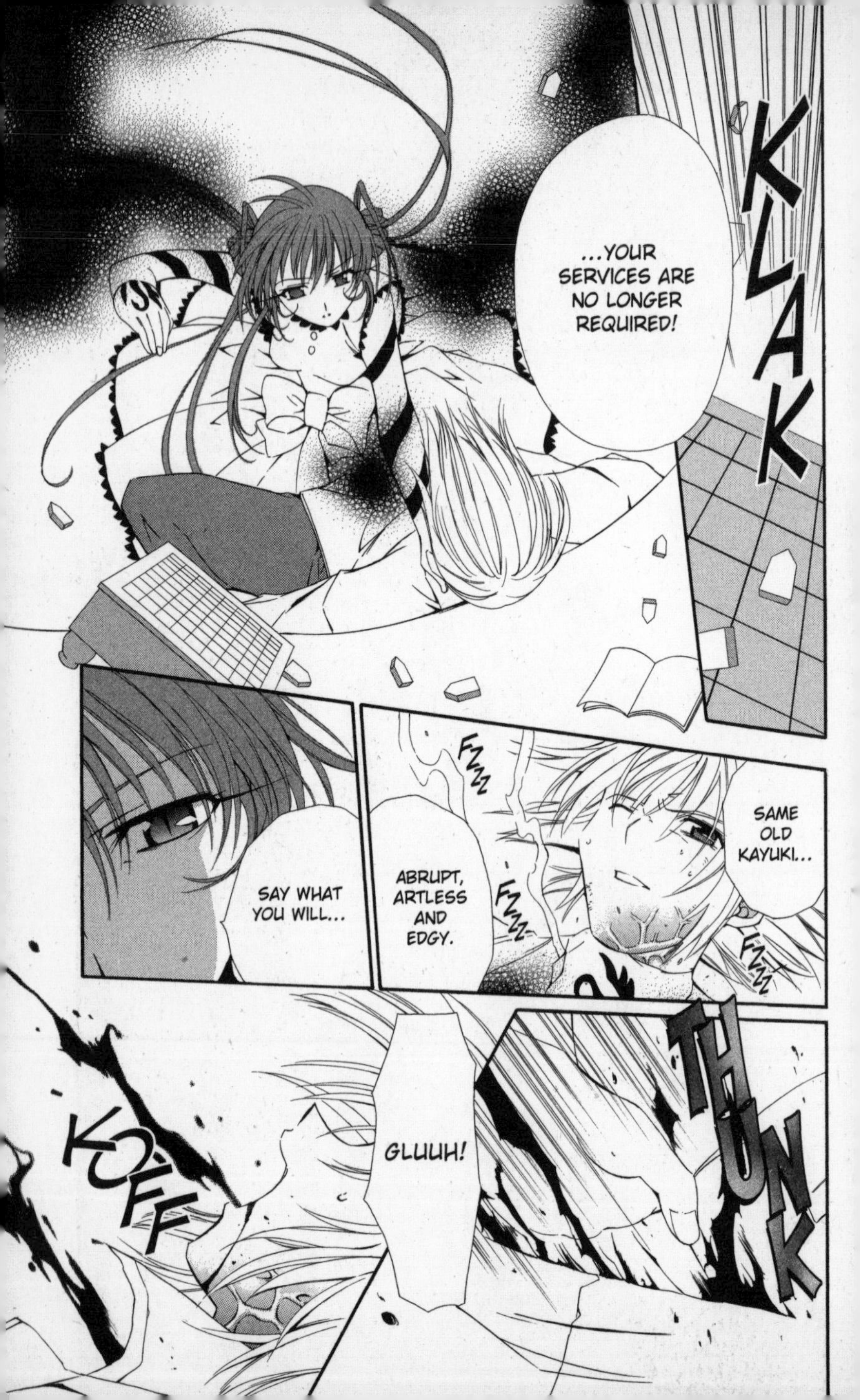
KLAK
...YOUR SERVICES ARE NO LONGER REQUIRED!
SAME OLD KAYUKI...
FZZZ
ABRUPT, ARTLESS AND EDGY.
FZZZ
FZZZ
SAY WHAT YOU WILL...
THUNK
GLUUH!
KOFF

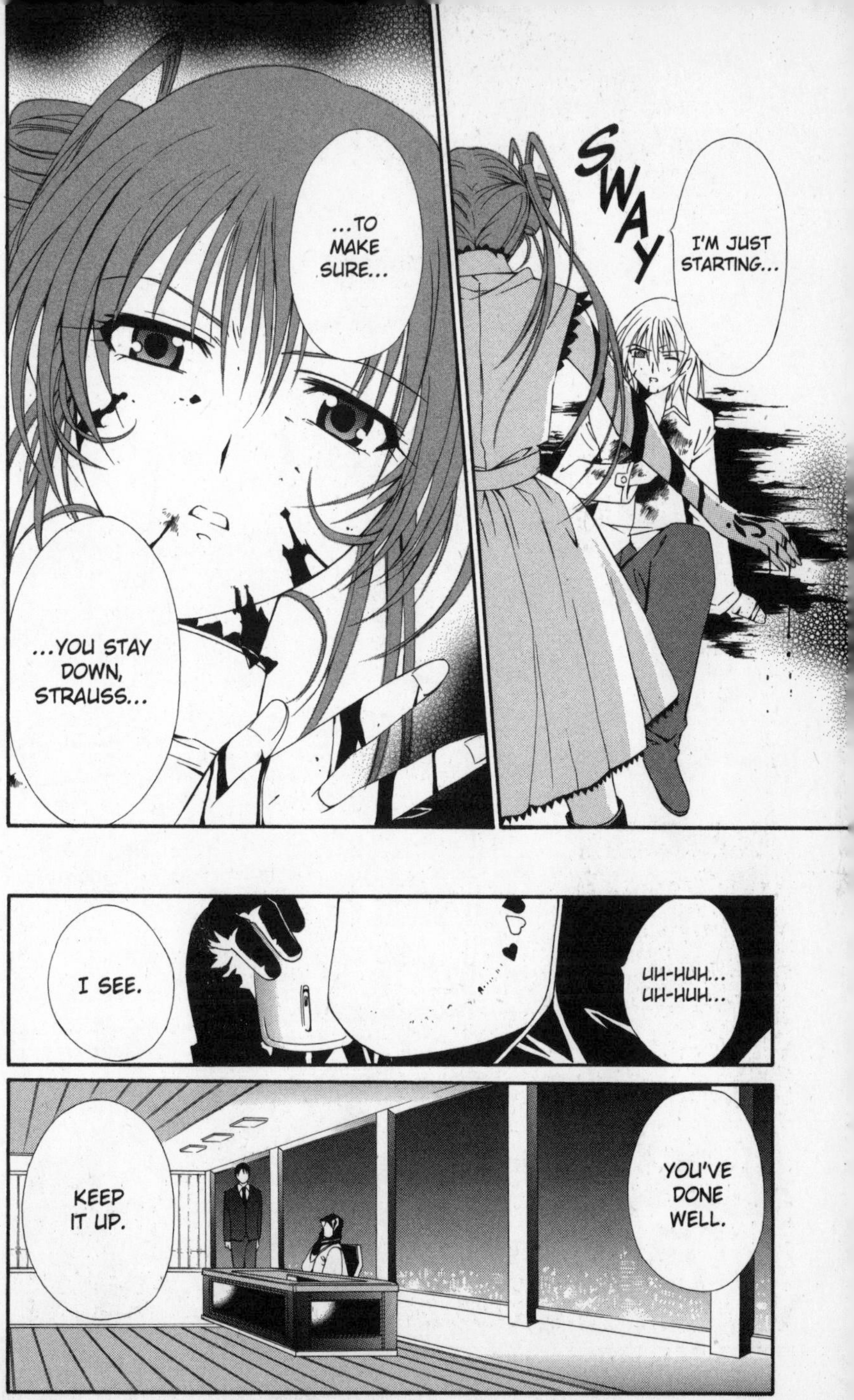
SWAY
I'M JUST STARTING...
...TO MAKE SURE...
...YOU STAY DOWN, STRAUSS...
UH-HUH... UH-HUH...
I SEE.
YOU'VE DONE WELL.
KEEP IT UP.

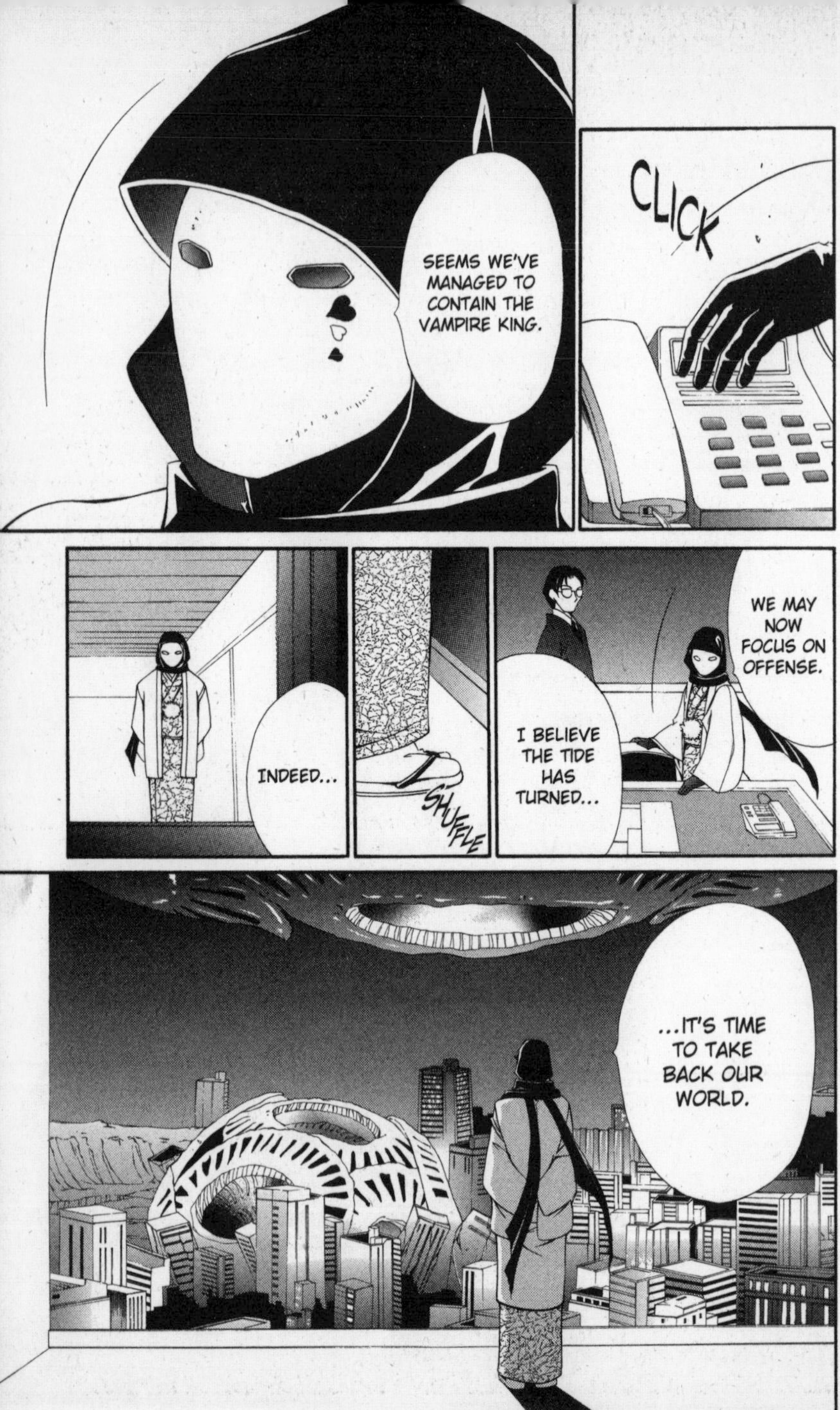
CLICK
SEEMS WE'VE MANAGED TO CONTAIN THE VAMPIRE KING.
WE MAY NOW FOCUS ON OFFENSE.
I BELIEVE THE TIDE HAS TURNED...
SHUFFLE
INDEED...
...IT'S TIME TO TAKE BACK OUR WORLD.

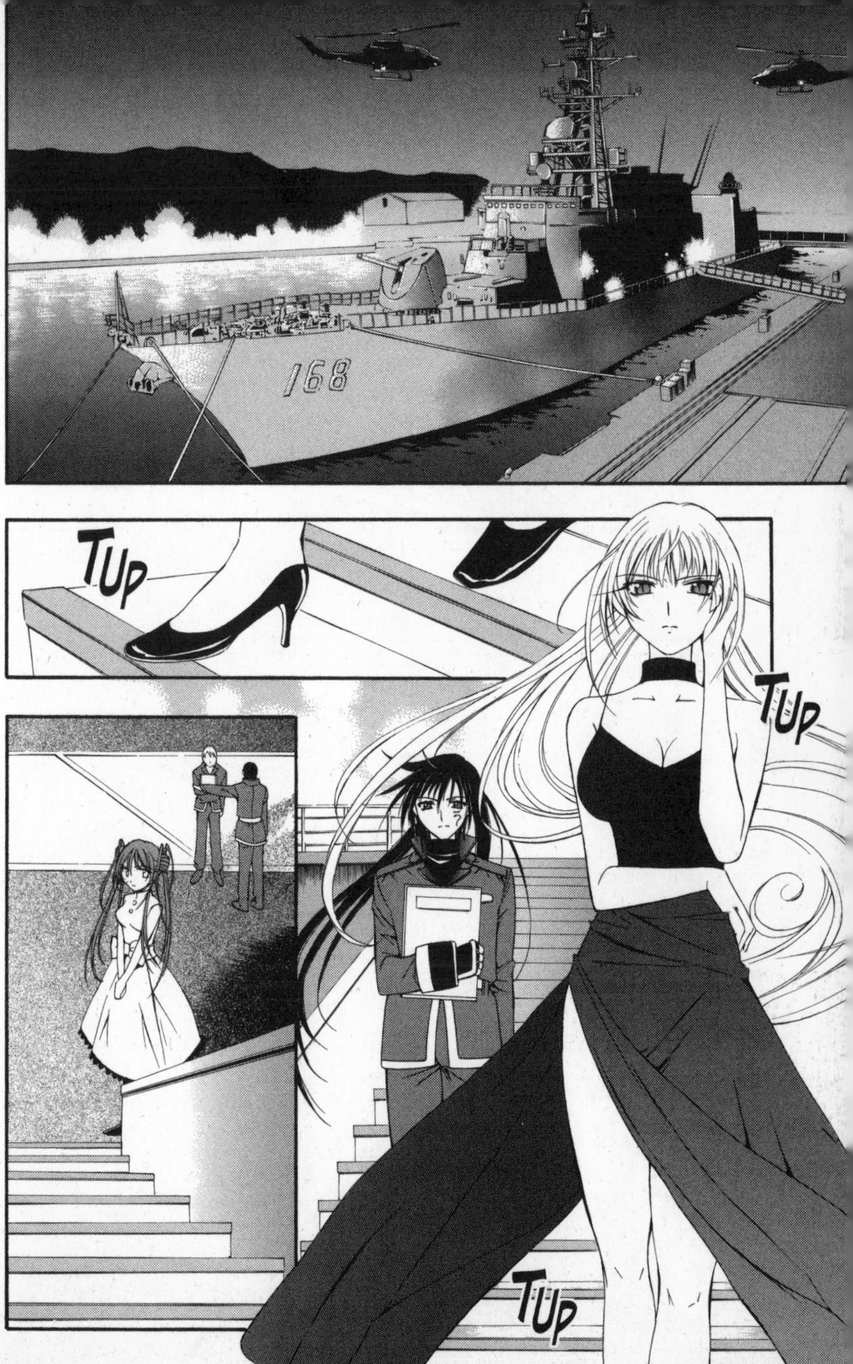
TUP
TUP
TUP

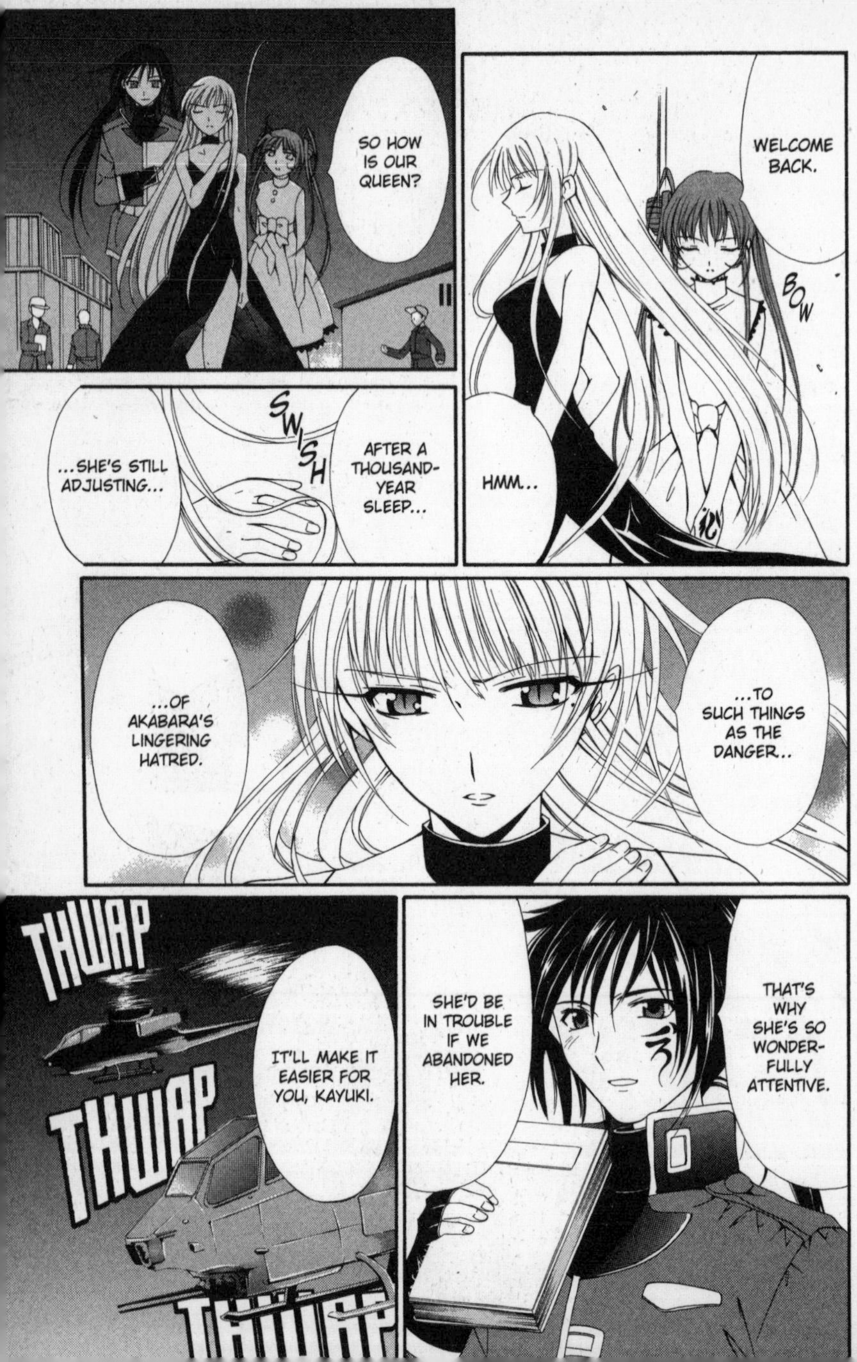
WELCOME BACK.
BOW
HMM...
SO HOW IS OUR QUEEN?
AFTER A THOUSAND-YEAR SLEEP...
SWISH
...SHE'S STILL ADJUSTING...
...TO SUCH THINGS AS THE DANGER..
...OF AKABARA'S LINGERING HATRED.
THAT'S WHY SHE'S SO WONDERFULLY ATTENTIVE.
SHE'D BE IN TROUBLE IF WE ABANDONED HER.
IT'LL MAKE IT EASIER FOR YOU, KAYUKI.
THWAP
THWAP
THWAP

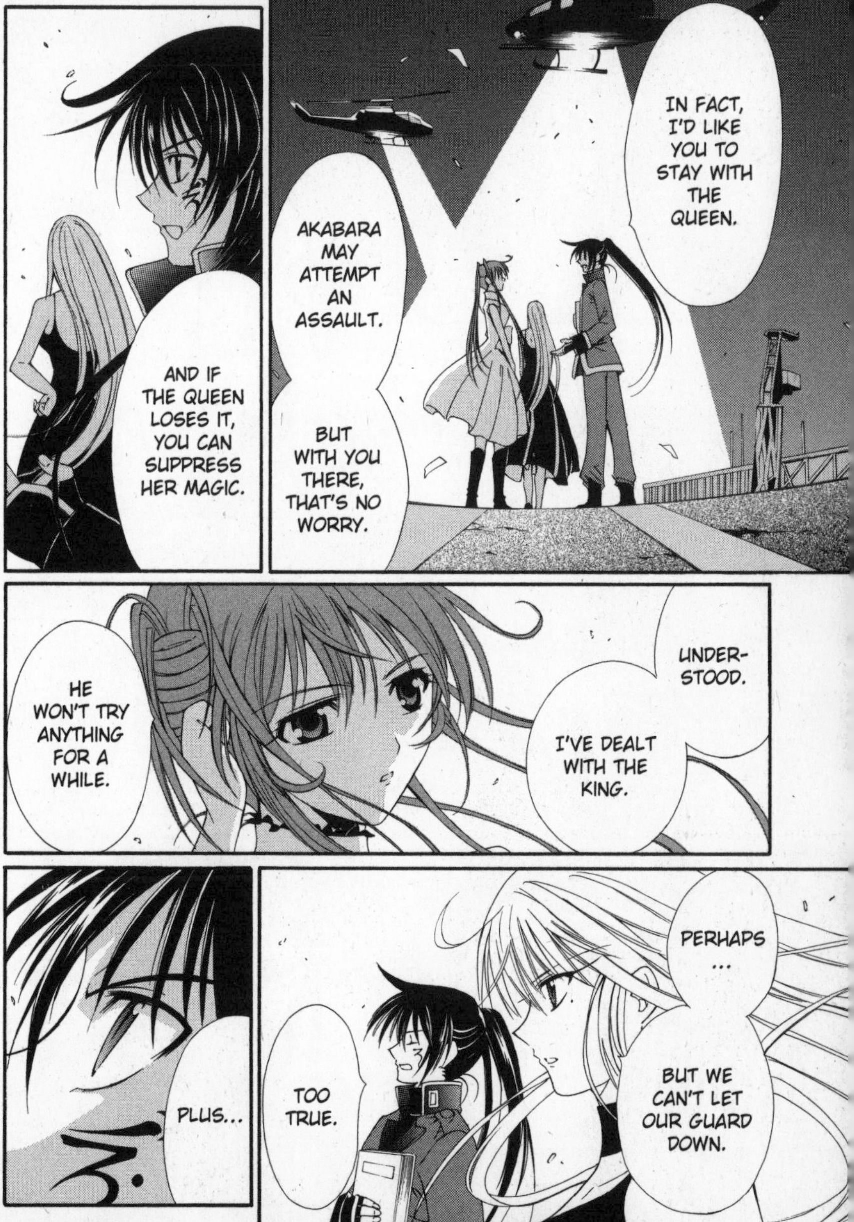
IN FACT, I'D LIKE YOU TO STAY WITH THE QUEEN.
AKABARA MAY ATTEMPT AN ASSAULT.
BUT WITH YOU THERE, THAT'S NO WORRY.
AND IF THE QUEEN LOSES IT, YOU CAN SUPPRESS HER MAGIC.
UNDER-STOOD.
I'VE DEALT WITH THE KING.
HE WON'T TRY ANYTHING FOR A WHILE.
PERHAPS...
BUT WE CAN'T LET OUR GUARD DOWN.
TOO TRUE.
PLUS...

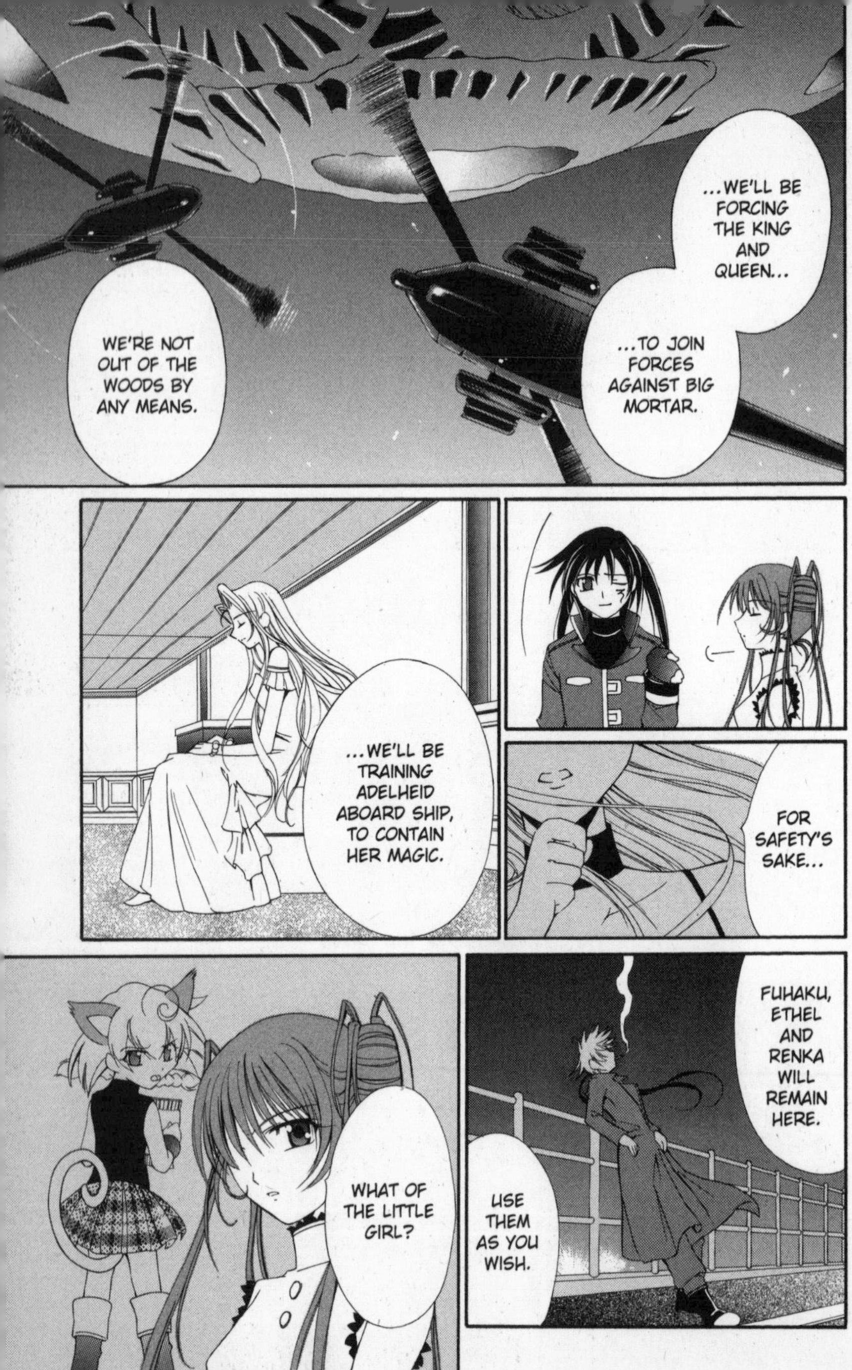
...WE'LL BE FORCING THE KING AND QUEEN...
...TO JOIN FORCES AGAINST BIG MORTAR.
WE'RE NOT OUT OF THE WOODS BY ANY MEANS.
FOR SAFETY'S SAKE...
...WE'LL BE TRAINING ADELHEID ABOARD SHIP, TO CONTAIN HER MAGIC.
FUHAKU, ETHEL AND RENKA WILL REMAIN HERE.
USE THEM AS YOU WISH.
WHAT OF THE LITTLE GIRL?

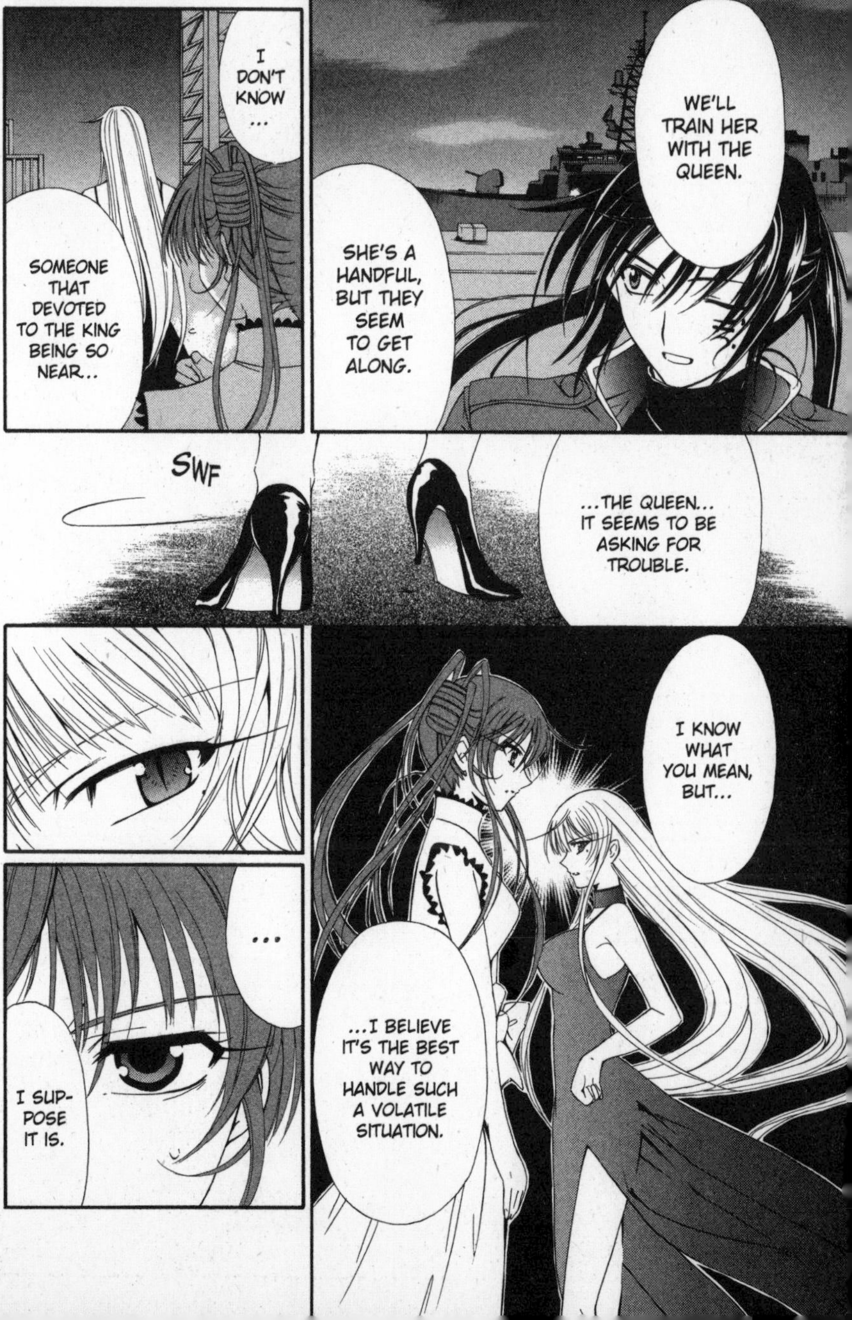
WE'LL TRAIN HER WITH THE QUEEN.
SHE'S A HANDFUL, BUT THEY SEEM TO GET ALONG.
I DON'T KNOW ...
SOMEONE THAT DEVOTED TO THE KING BEING SO NEAR...
...THE QUEEN... IT SEEMS TO BE ASKING FOR TROUBLE.
SWF
I KNOW WHAT YOU MEAN, BUT...
...I BELIEVE IT'S THE BEST WAY TO HANDLE SUCH A VOLATILE SITUATION.
...
I SUP-POSE IT IS.

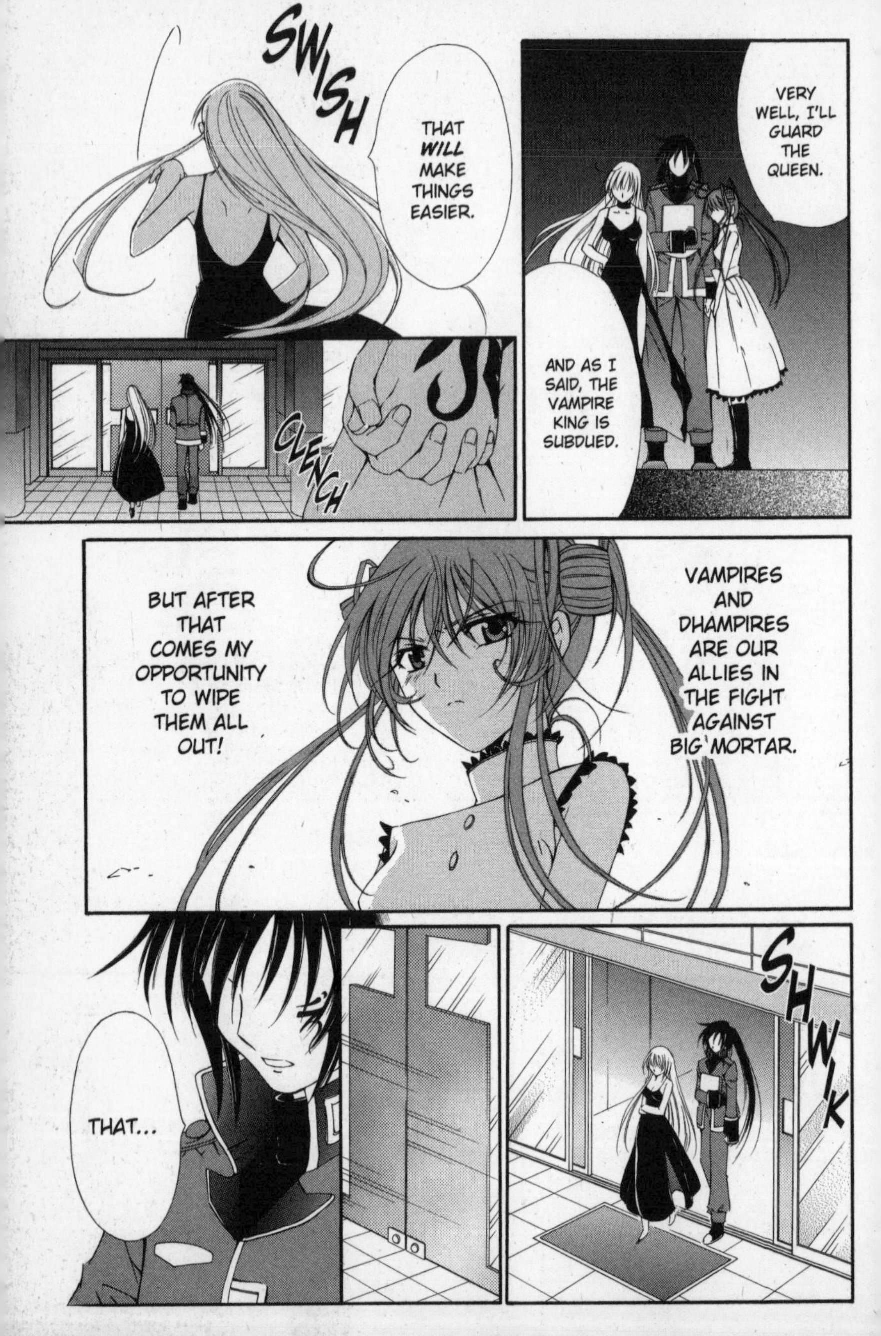
VERY WELL, I'LL GUARD THE QUEEN.
AND AS I SAID, THE VAMPIRE KING IS SUBDUED.
THAT *WILL* MAKE THINGS EASIER.
SWISH
CLENCH
VAMPIRES AND DHAMPIRES ARE OUR ALLIES IN THE FIGHT AGAINST BIG MORTAR.
BUT AFTER THAT COMES MY OPPORTUNITY TO WIPE THEM ALL OUT!
SHWIK
THAT...

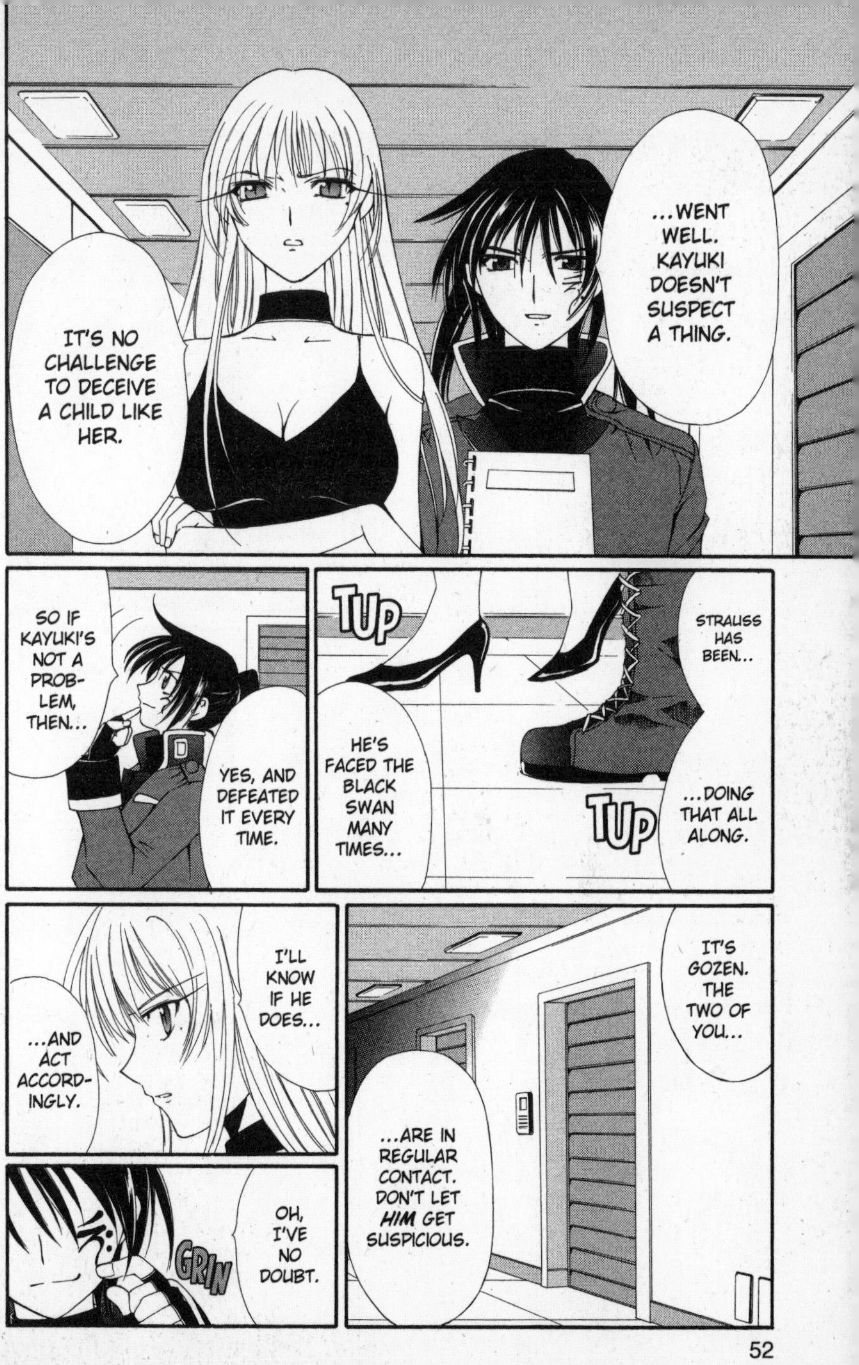
...WENT WELL. KAYUKI DOESN'T SUSPECT A THING.
IT'S NO CHALLENGE TO DECEIVE A CHILD LIKE HER.
STRAUSS HAS BEEN...
TUP
...DOING THAT ALL ALONG.
HE'S FACED THE BLACK SWAN MANY TIMES...
TUP
YES, AND DEFEATED IT EVERY TIME.
SO IF KAYUKI'S NOT A PROB-LEM, THEN...
IT'S GOZEN. THE TWO OF YOU...
...ARE IN REGULAR CONTACT. DON'T LET *HIM* GET SUSPICIOUS.
I'LL KNOW IF HE DOES...
...AND ACT ACCORD-INGLY.
OH, I'VE NO DOUBT.
GRIN

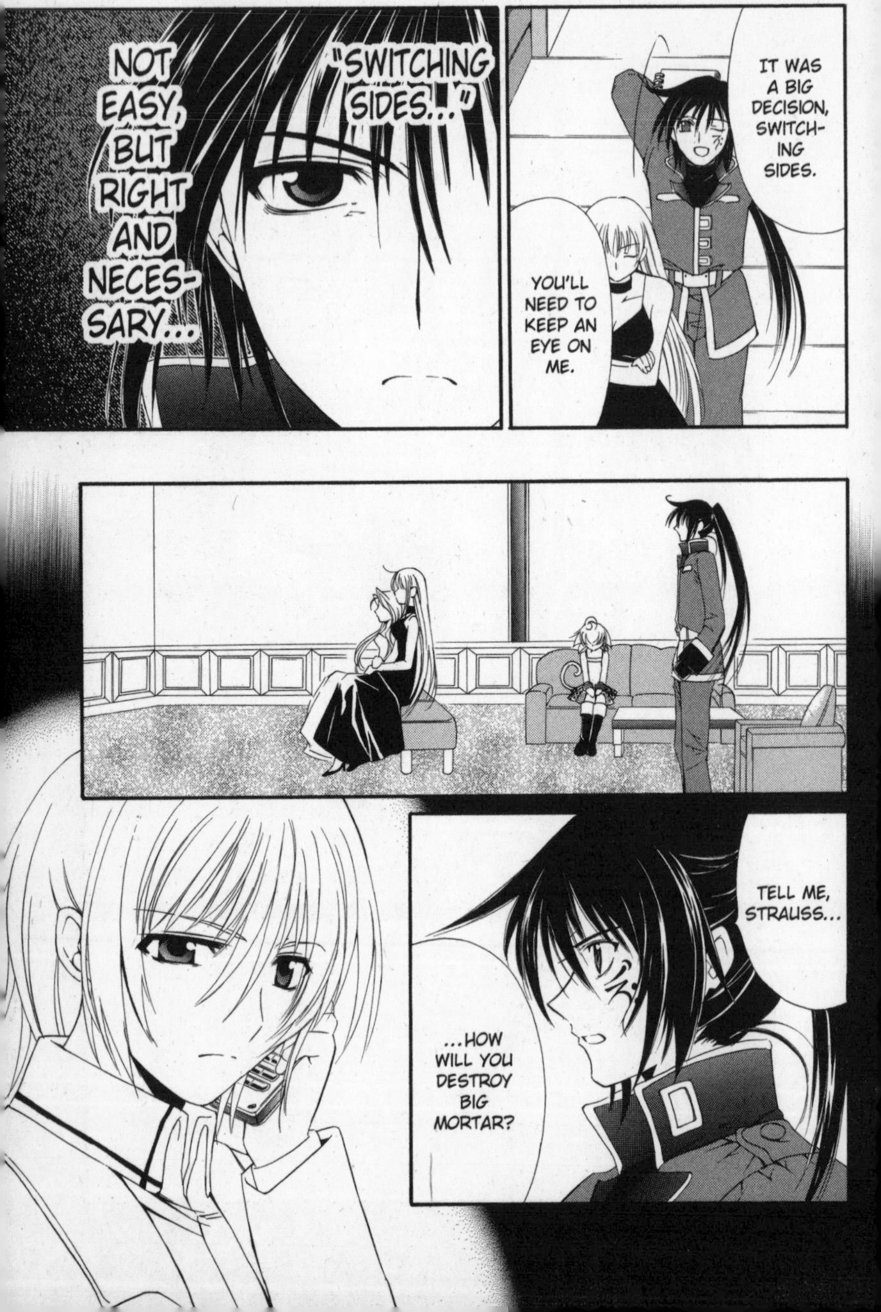
IT WAS A BIG DECISION, SWITCH-ING SIDES.
YOU'LL NEED TO KEEP AN EYE ON ME.
"SWITCHING SIDES..."
NOT EASY, BUT RIGHT AND NECES-SARY...
TELL ME, STRAUSS...
...HOW WILL YOU DESTROY BIG MORTAR?

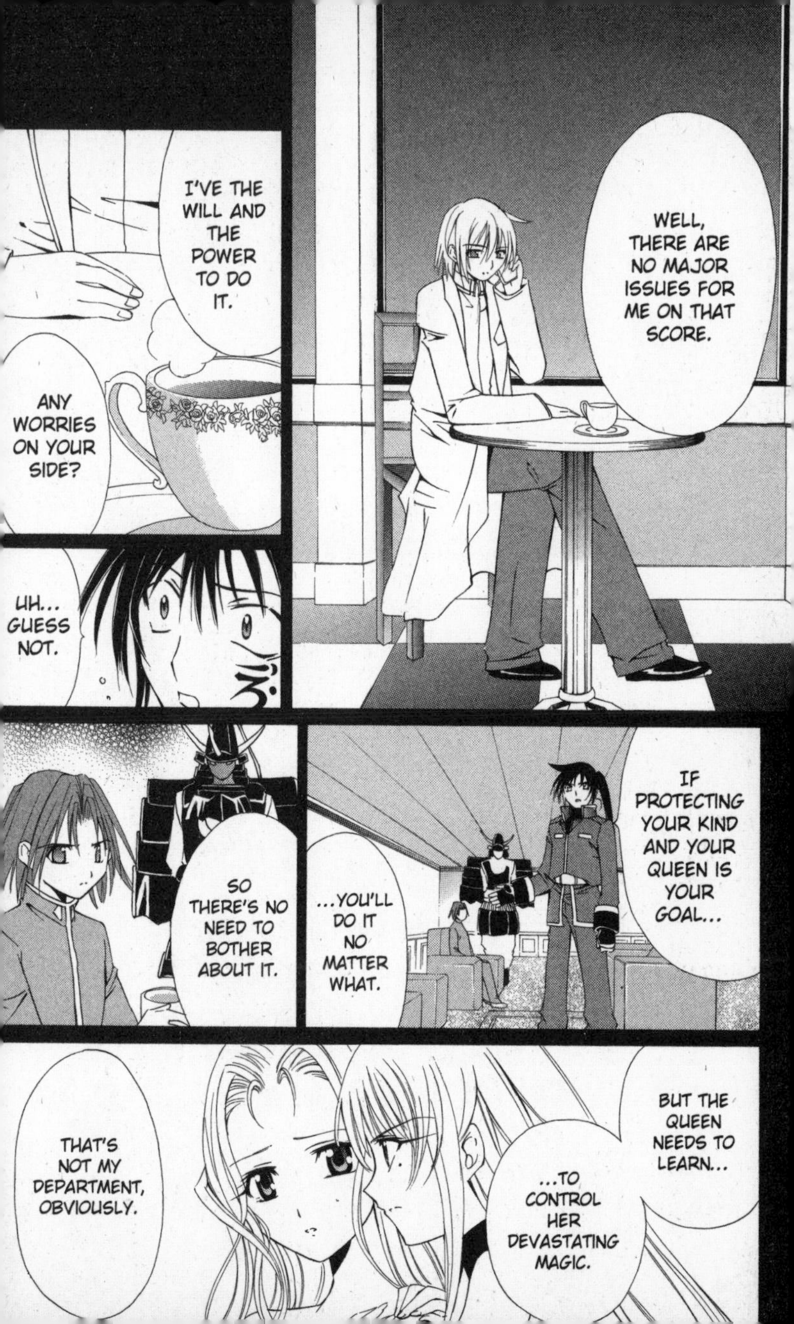
WELL, THERE ARE NO MAJOR ISSUES FOR ME ON THAT SCORE.
I'VE THE WILL AND THE POWER TO DO IT.
ANY WORRIES ON YOUR SIDE?
UH... GUESS NOT.
IF PROTECTING YOUR KIND AND YOUR QUEEN IS YOUR GOAL...
...YOU'LL DO IT NO MATTER WHAT.
SO THERE'S NO NEED TO BOTHER ABOUT IT.
BUT THE QUEEN NEEDS TO LEARN...
...TO CONTROL HER DEVASTATING MAGIC.
THAT'S NOT MY DEPARTMENT, OBVIOUSLY.

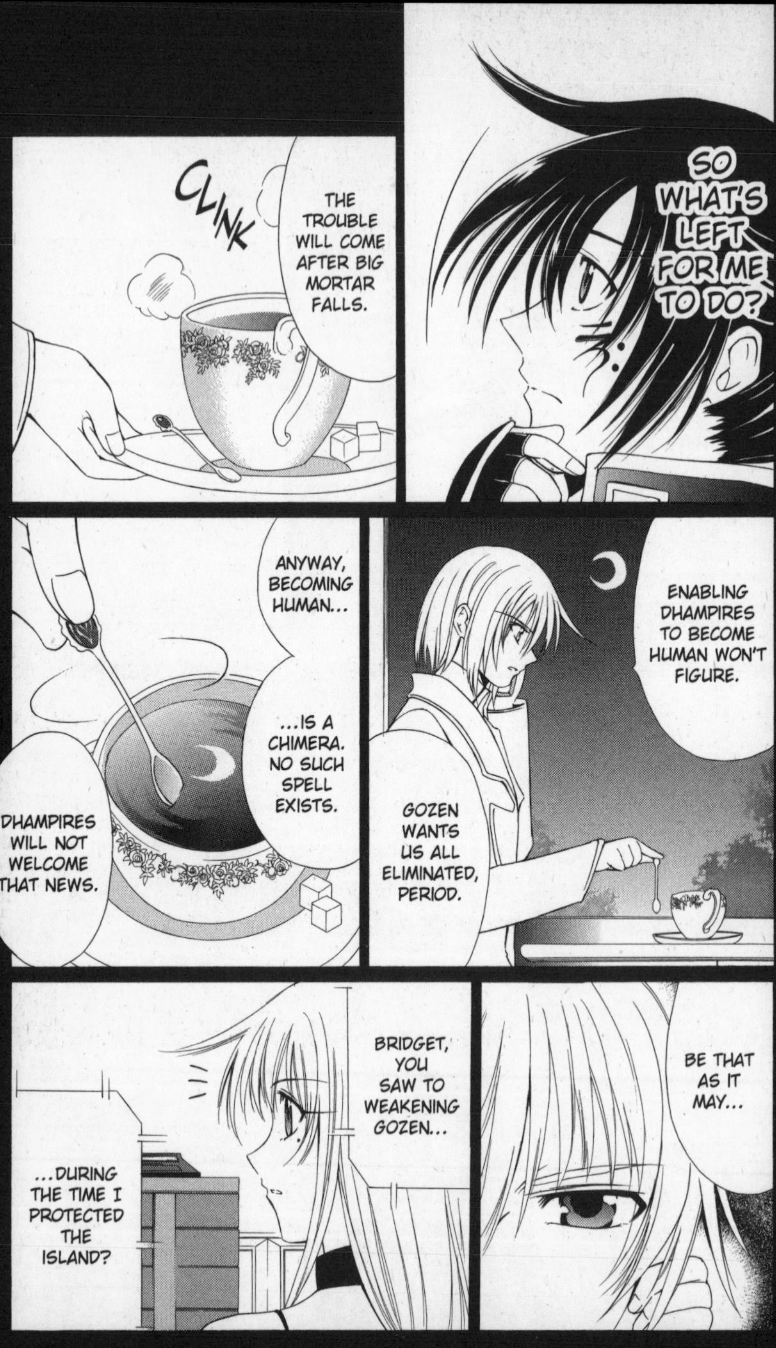
SO WHAT'S LEFT FOR ME TO DO?
CLINK
THE TROUBLE WILL COME AFTER BIG MORTAR FALLS.
ENABLING DHAMPIRES TO BECOME HUMAN WON'T FIGURE.
GOZEN WANTS US ALL ELIMINATED, PERIOD.
ANYWAY, BECOMING HUMAN...
...IS A CHIMERA. NO SUCH SPELL EXISTS.
DHAMPIRES WILL NOT WELCOME THAT NEWS.
BE THAT AS IT MAY...
BRIDGET, YOU SAW TO WEAKENING GOZEN...
...DURING THE TIME I PROTECTED THE ISLAND?

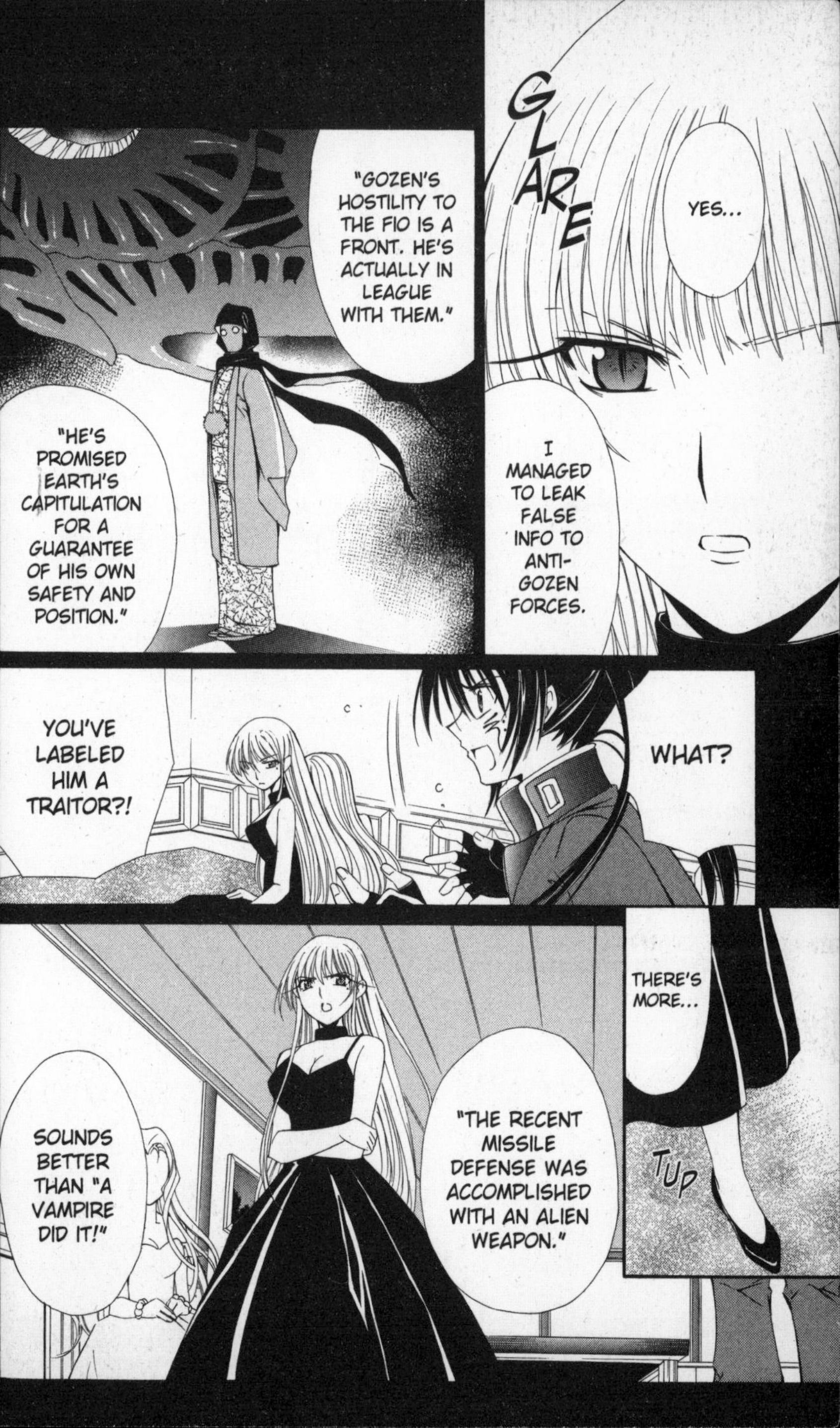
GLARE
YES...
I MANAGED TO LEAK FALSE INFO TO ANTI-GOZEN FORCES.
"GOZEN'S HOSTILITY TO THE FIO IS A FRONT. HE'S ACTUALLY IN LEAGUE WITH THEM."
"HE'S PROMISED EARTH'S CAPITULATION FOR A GUARANTEE OF HIS OWN SAFETY AND POSITION."
WHAT?
YOU'VE LABELED HIM A TRAITOR?!
THERE'S MORE...
TUP
"THE RECENT MISSILE DEFENSE WAS ACCOMPLISHED WITH AN ALIEN WEAPON."
SOUNDS BETTER THAN "A VAMPIRE DID IT!"

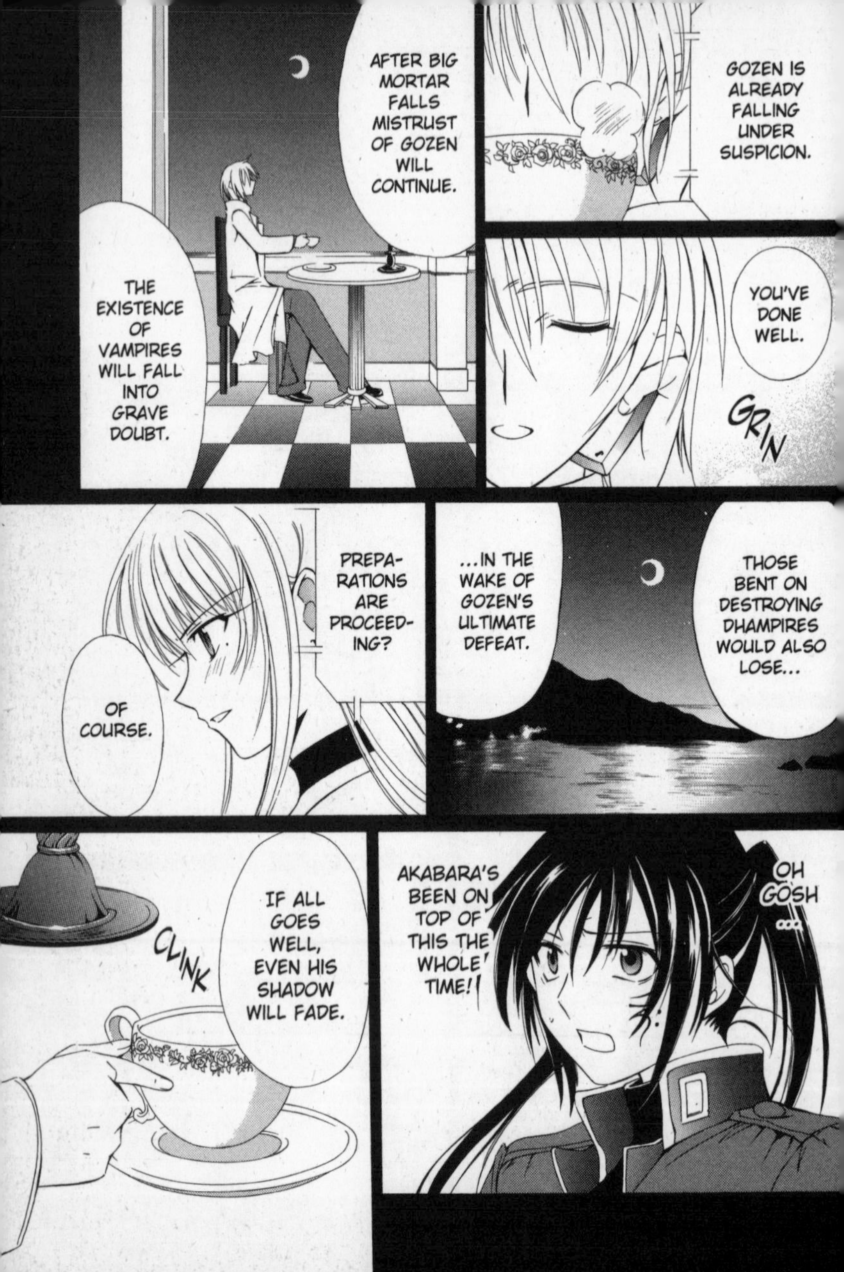
GOZEN IS ALREADY FALLING UNDER SUSPICION.
YOU'VE DONE WELL.
GRIN
AFTER BIG MORTAR FALLS MISTRUST OF GOZEN WILL CONTINUE.
THE EXISTENCE OF VAMPIRES WILL FALL INTO GRAVE DOUBT.
THOSE BENT ON DESTROYING DHAMPIRES WOULD ALSO LOSE...
...IN THE WAKE OF GOZEN'S ULTIMATE DEFEAT.
PREPARATIONS ARE PROCEEDING?
OF COURSE.
AKABARA'S BEEN ON TOP OF THIS THE WHOLE TIME!!
OH GOSH...
IF ALL GOES WELL, EVEN HIS SHADOW WILL FADE.
CLINK

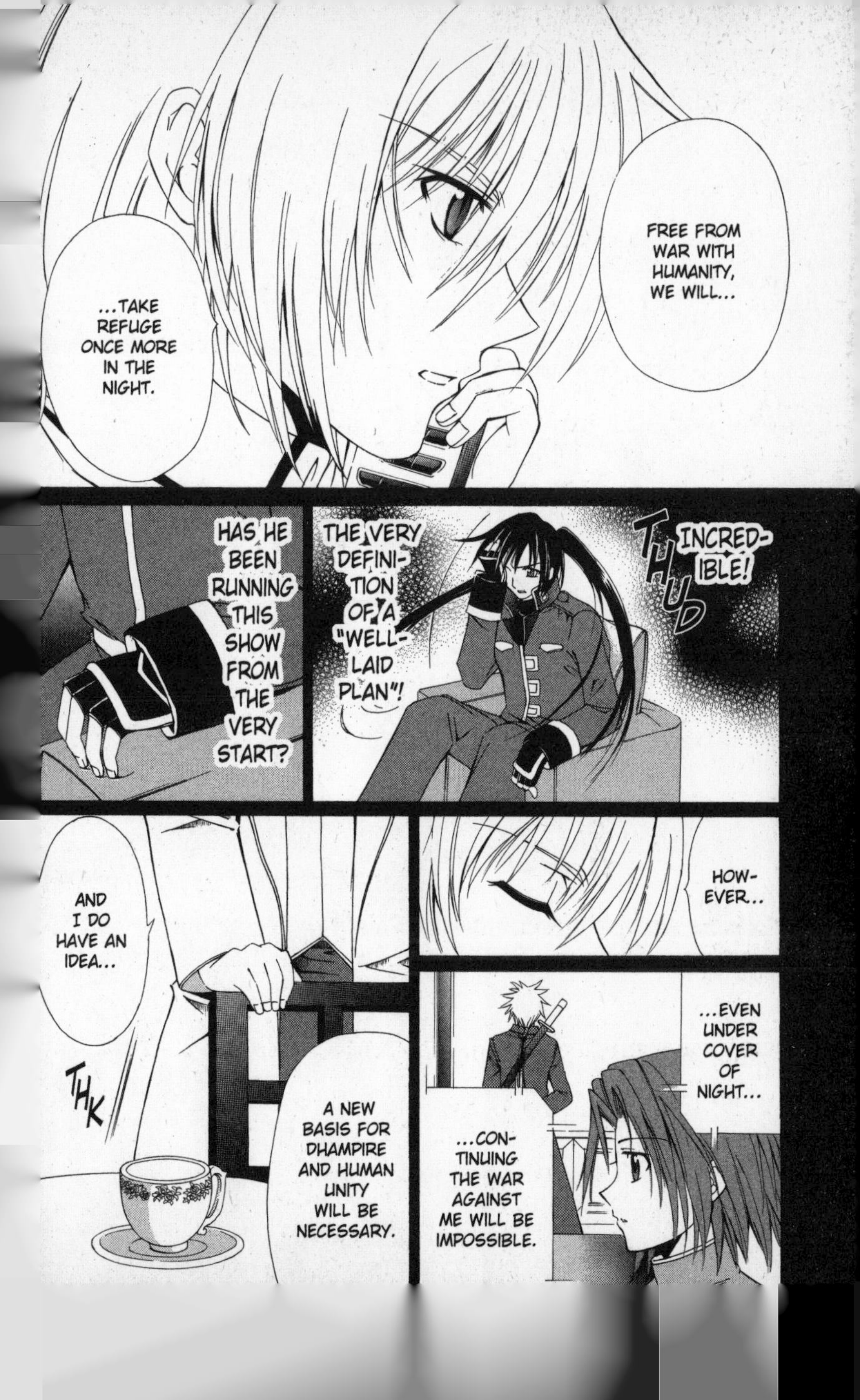
FREE FROM WAR WITH HUMANITY, WE WILL...
...TAKE REFUGE ONCE MORE IN THE NIGHT.
THUD
INCRED-IBLE!
THE VERY DEFINI-TION OF A "WELL-LAID PLAN"!
HAS HE BEEN RUNNING THIS SHOW FROM THE VERY START?
HOW-EVER...
...EVEN UNDER COVER OF NIGHT...
...CON-TINUING THE WAR AGAINST ME WILL BE IMPOSSIBLE.
AND I DO HAVE AN IDEA...
THK
A NEW BASIS FOR DHAMPIRE AND HUMAN UNITY WILL BE NECESSARY.

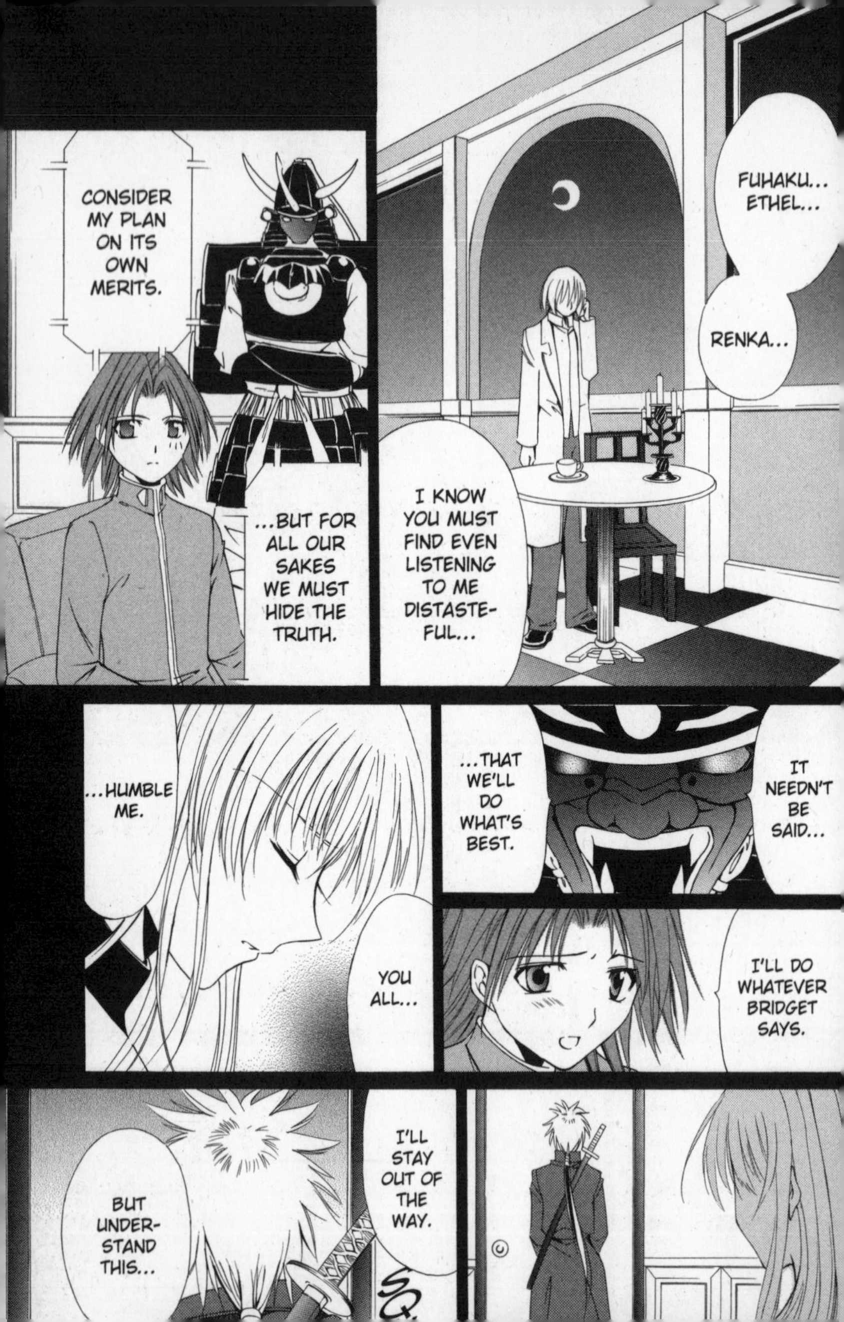
FUHAKU... ETHEL...
RENKA...
I KNOW YOU MUST FIND EVEN LISTENING TO ME DISTASTEFUL...
CONSIDER MY PLAN ON ITS OWN MERITS.
...BUT FOR ALL OUR SAKES WE MUST HIDE THE TRUTH.
IT NEEDN'T BE SAID...
...THAT WE'LL DO WHAT'S BEST.
I'LL DO WHATEVER BRIDGET SAYS.
YOU ALL...
...HUMBLE ME.
I'LL STAY OUT OF THE WAY.
BUT UNDERSTAND THIS...

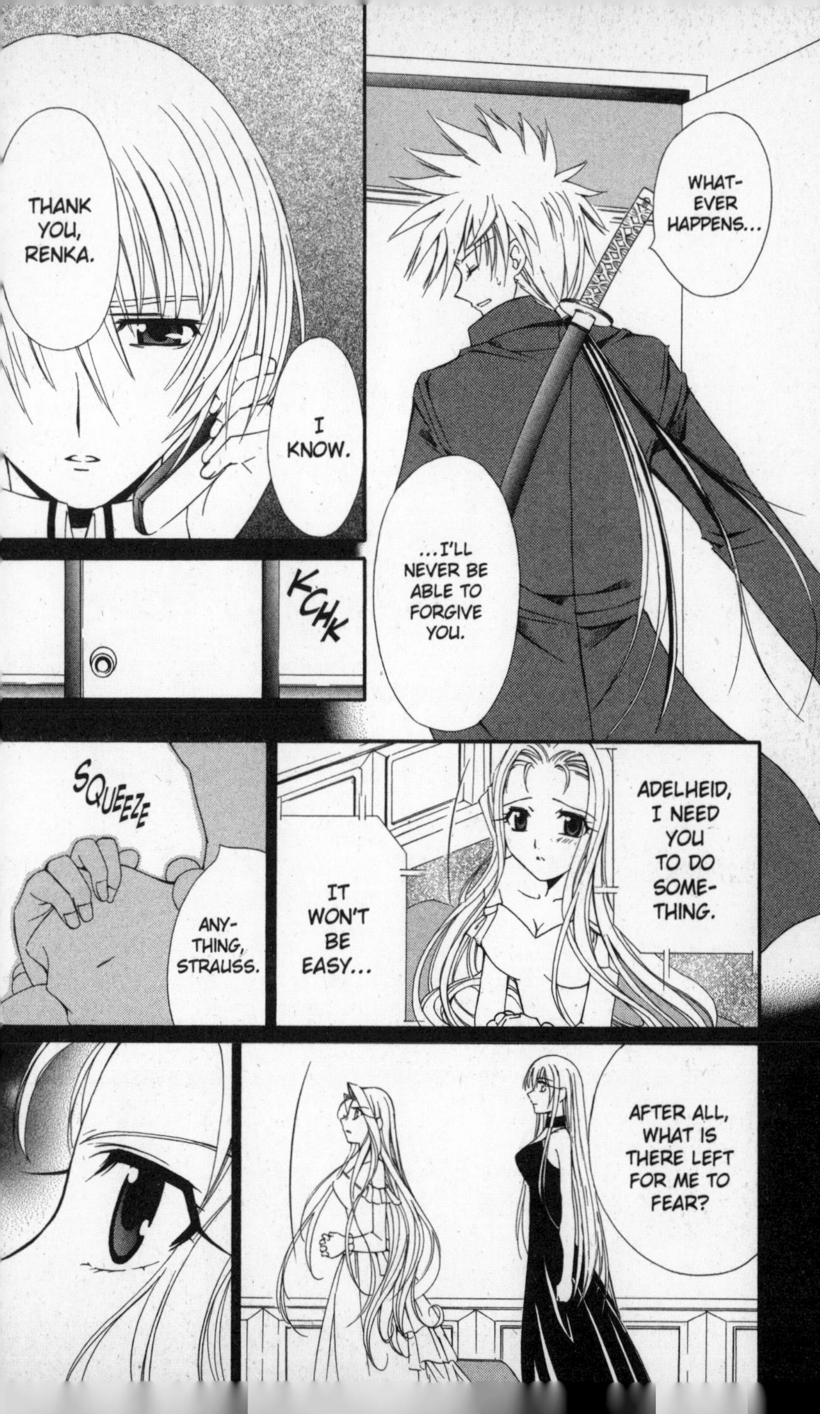
WHAT-EVER HAPPENS...
...I'LL NEVER BE ABLE TO FORGIVE YOU.
I KNOW.
THANK YOU, RENKA.
KCHK
ADELHEID, I NEED YOU TO DO SOME-THING.
IT WON'T BE EASY...
SQUEEZE
ANY-THING, STRAUSS.
AFTER ALL, WHAT IS THERE LEFT FOR ME TO FEAR?

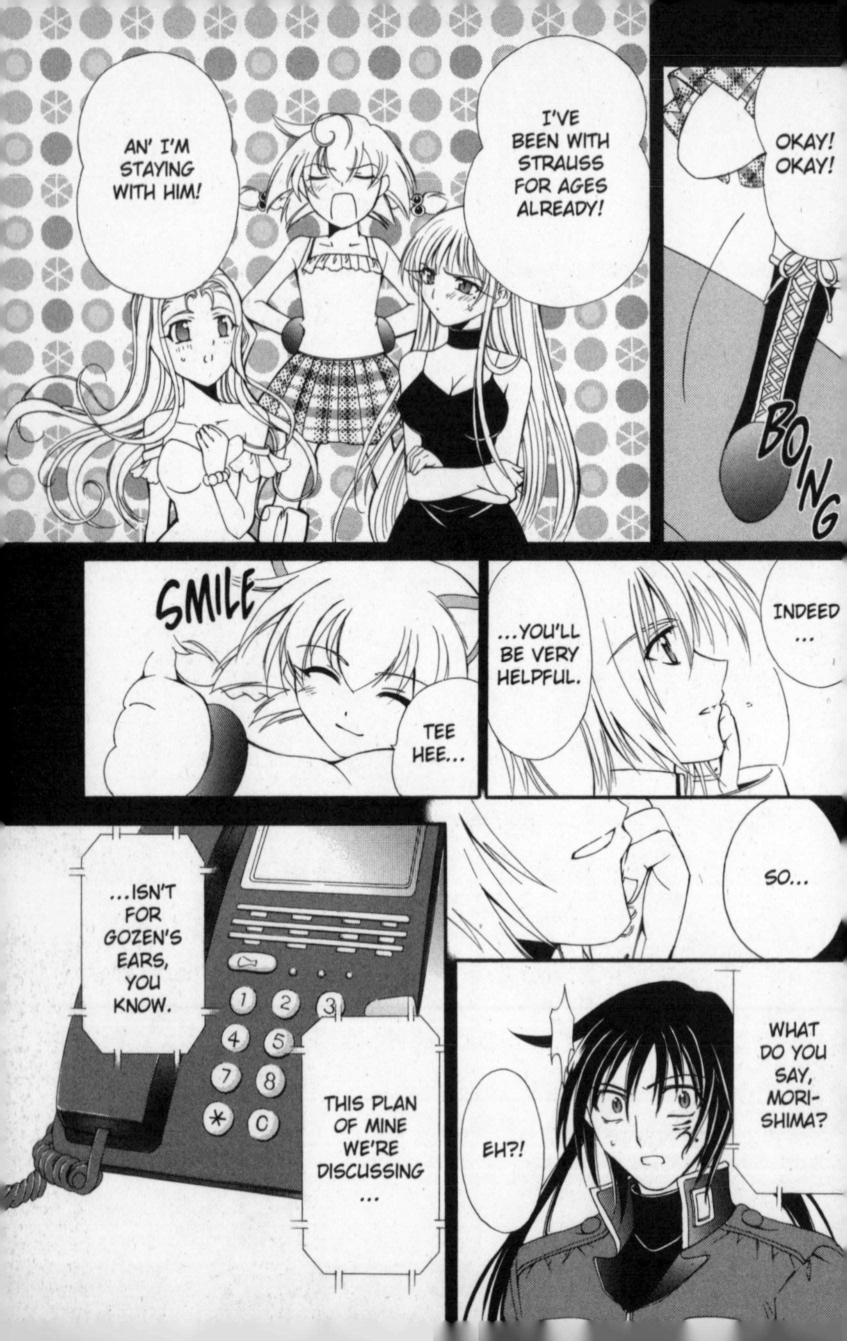
OKAY! OKAY!
BOING
I'VE BEEN WITH STRAUSS FOR AGES ALREADY!
AN' I'M STAYING WITH HIM!
INDEED...
...YOU'LL BE VERY HELPFUL.
SMILE
TEE HEE...
SO...
WHAT DO YOU SAY, MORI-SHIMA?
EH?!
THIS PLAN OF MINE WE'RE DISCUSSING...
...ISN'T FOR GOZEN'S EARS, YOU KNOW.

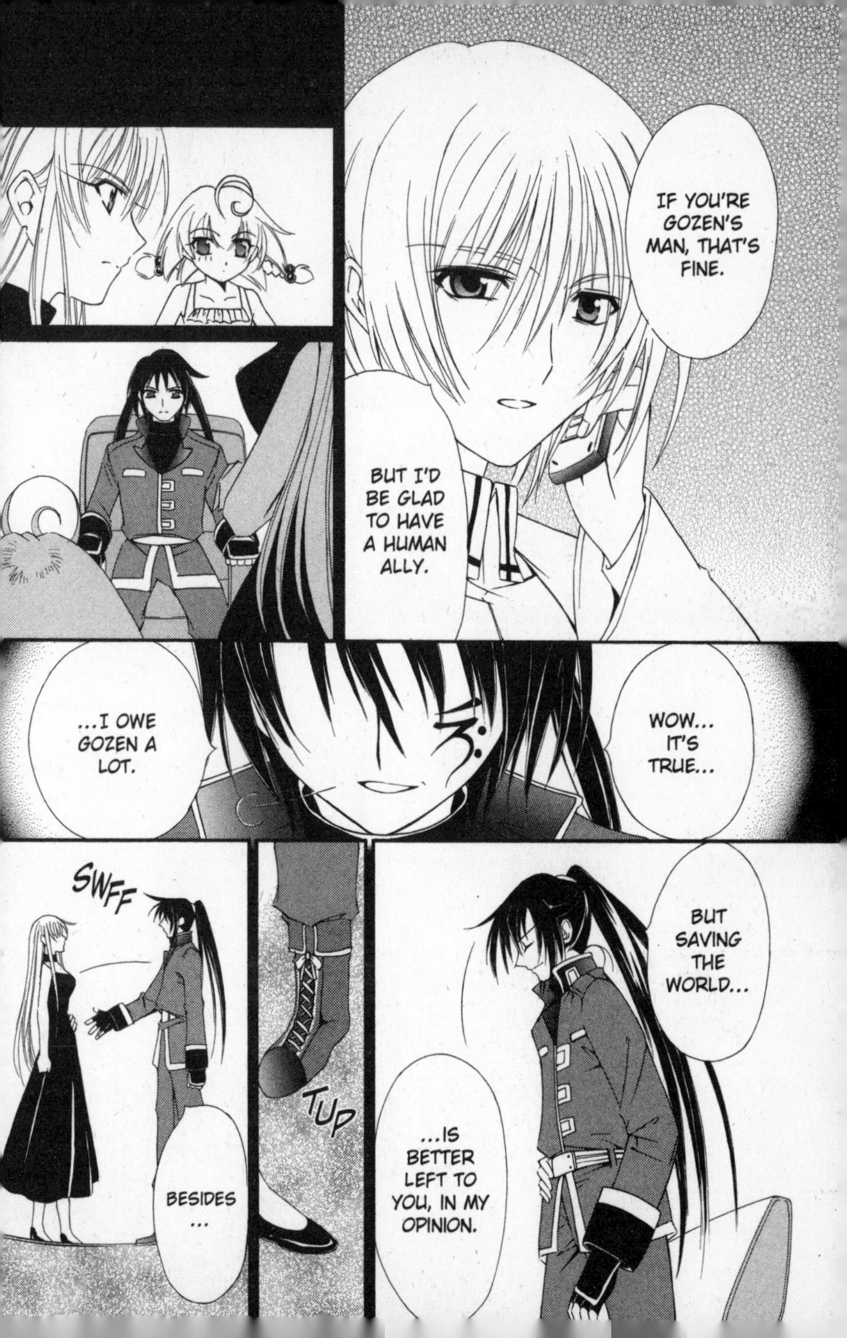
IF YOU'RE GOZEN'S MAN, THAT'S FINE.
BUT I'D BE GLAD TO HAVE A HUMAN ALLY.
WOW... IT'S TRUE...
...I OWE GOZEN A LOT.
BUT SAVING THE WORLD...
...IS BETTER LEFT TO YOU, IN MY OPINION.
TUP
SWFF
BESIDES...

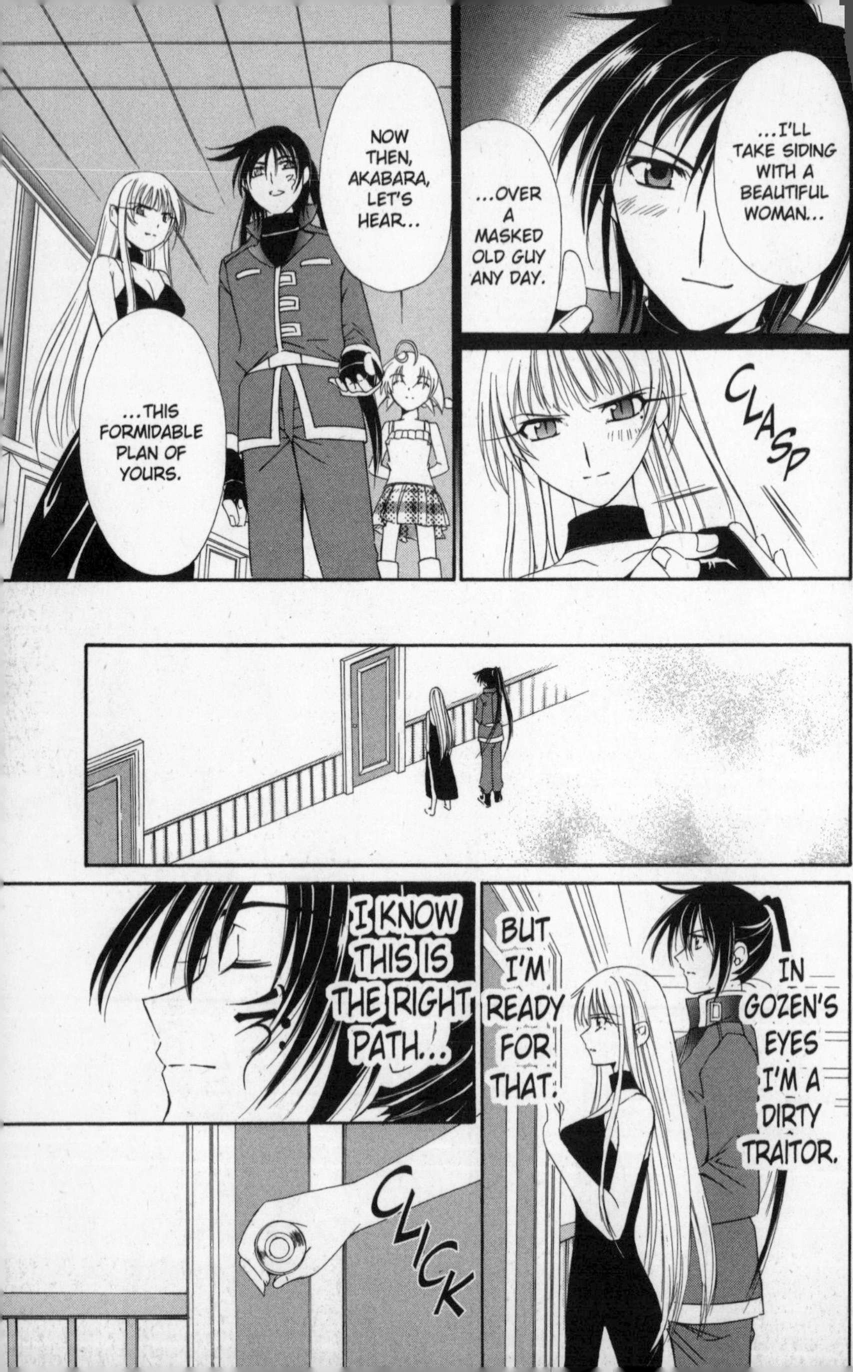
...I'LL TAKE SIDING WITH A BEAUTIFUL WOMAN...
...OVER A MASKED OLD GUY ANY DAY.
CLASP
NOW THEN, AKABARA, LET'S HEAR...
...THIS FORMIDABLE PLAN OF YOURS.
IN GOZEN'S EYES I'M A DIRTY TRAITOR.
BUT I'M READY FOR THAT.
I KNOW THIS IS THE RIGHT PATH...
CLICK

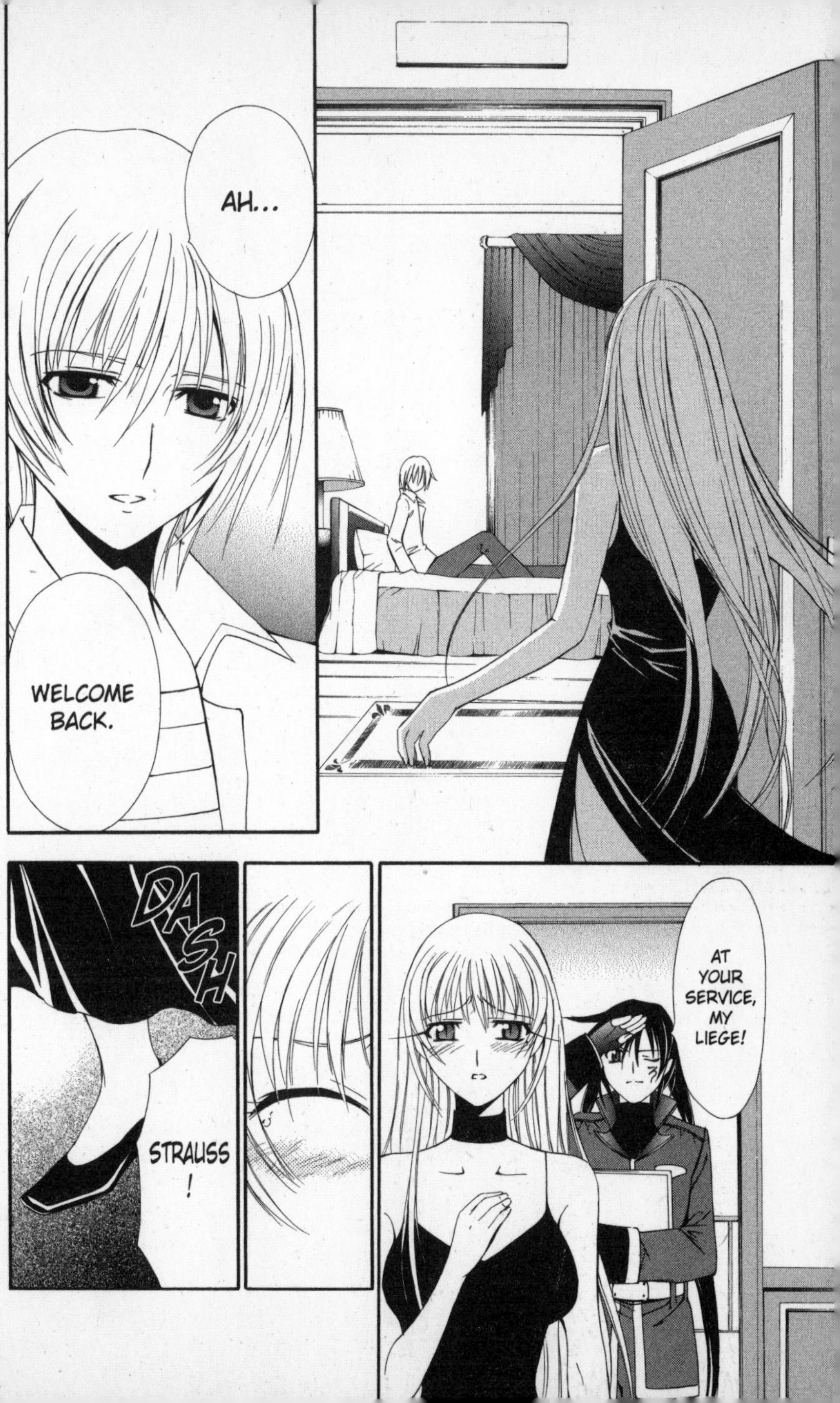
AH...
WELCOME BACK.
AT YOUR SERVICE, MY LIEGE!
DASH
STRAUSS!

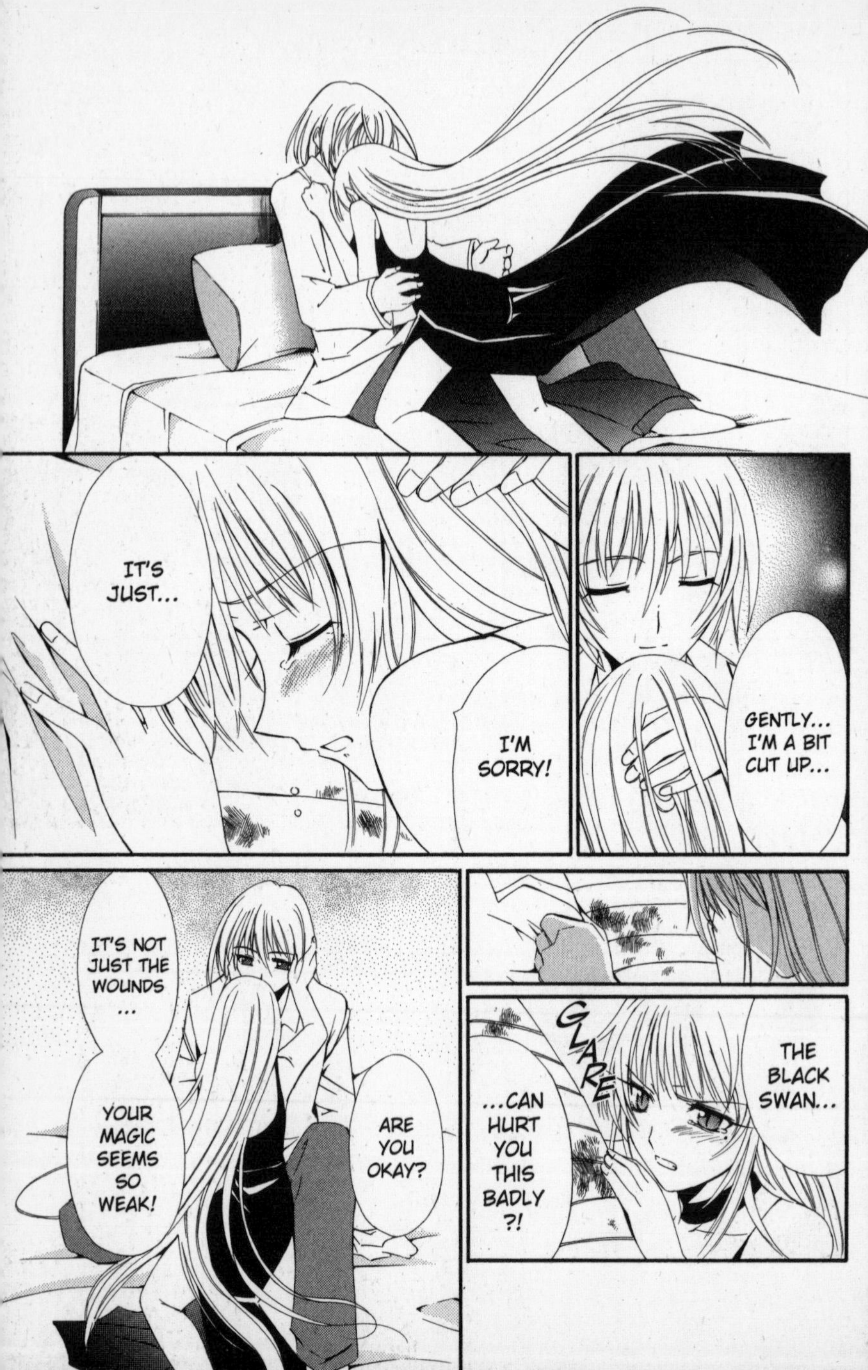
GENTLY... I'M A BIT CUT UP...
I'M SORRY!
IT'S JUST...
THE BLACK SWAN...
GLARE
...CAN HURT YOU THIS BADLY ?!
ARE YOU OKAY?
IT'S NOT JUST THE WOUNDS ...
YOUR MAGIC SEEMS SO WEAK!

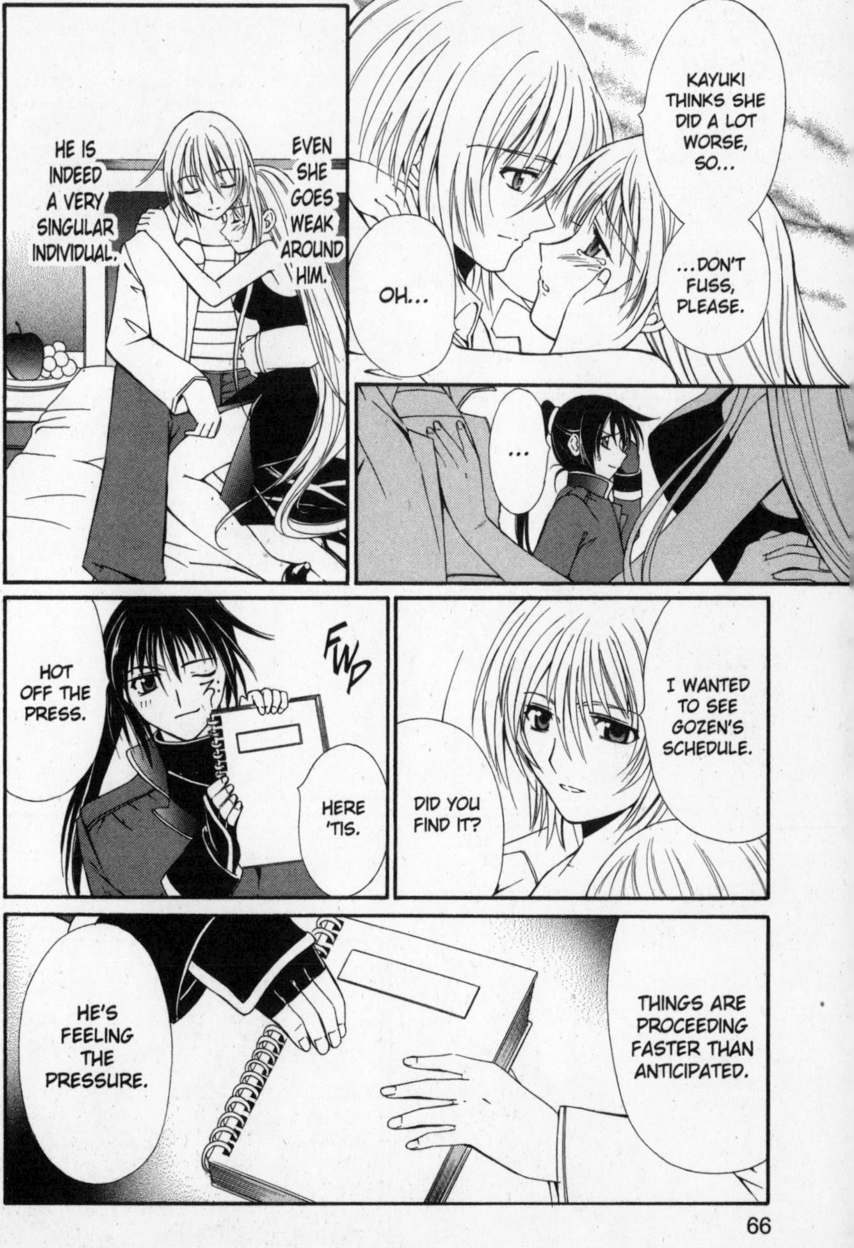
KAYUKI THINKS SHE DID A LOT WORSE, SO...
...DON'T FUSS, PLEASE.
OH...
...
EVEN SHE GOES WEAK AROUND HIM.
HE IS INDEED A VERY SINGULAR INDIVIDUAL.
I WANTED TO SEE GOZEN'S SCHEDULE.
DID YOU FIND IT?
FWP
HOT OFF THE PRESS.
HERE 'TIS.
THINGS ARE PROCEEDING FASTER THAN ANTICIPATED.
HE'S FEELING THE PRESSURE.

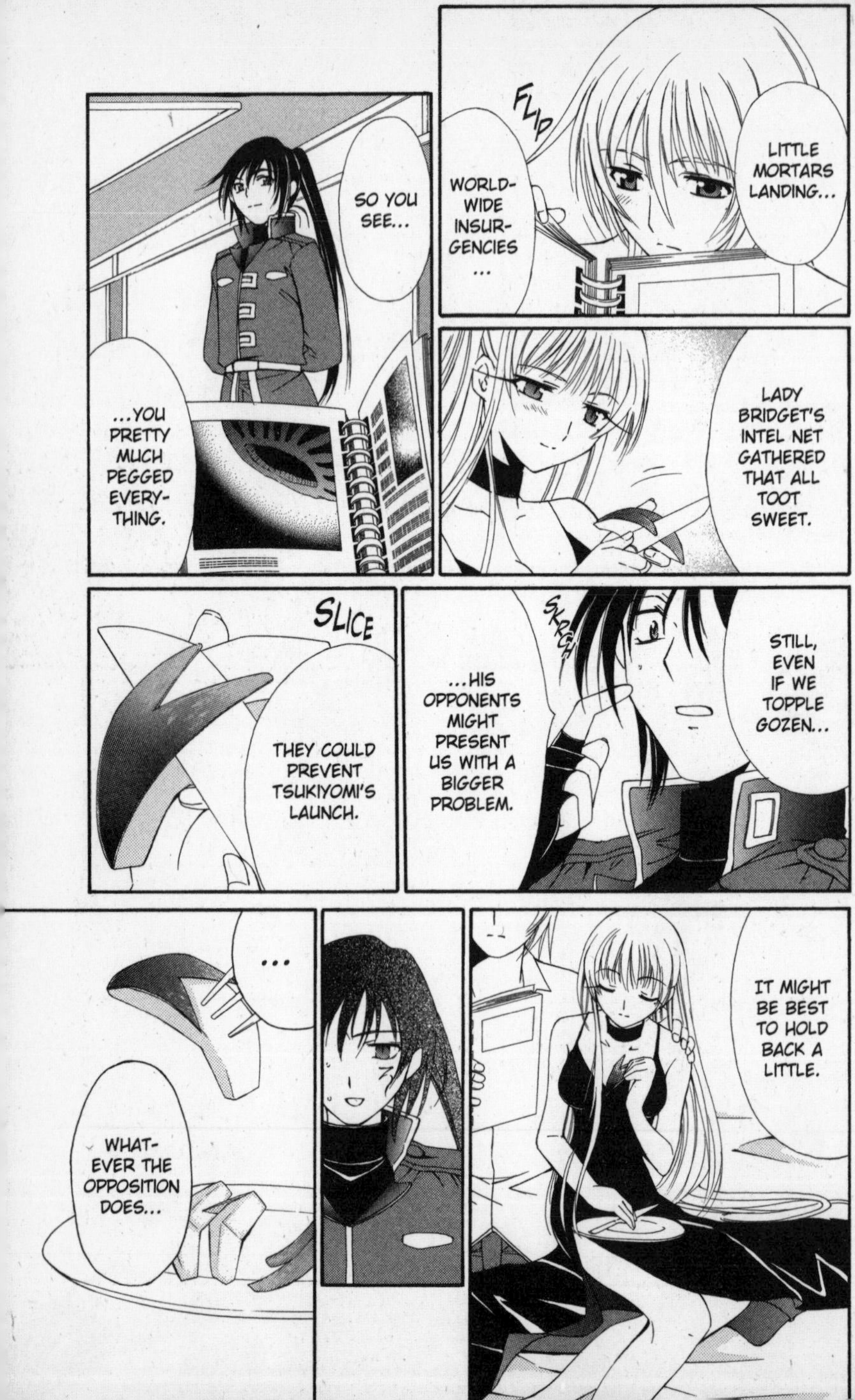
LITTLE MORTARS LANDING...
FLIP
WORLD-WIDE INSURGENCIES ...
LADY BRIDGET'S INTEL NET GATHERED THAT ALL TOOT SWEET.
SO YOU SEE...
...YOU PRETTY MUCH PEGGED EVERYTHING.
STILL, EVEN IF WE TOPPLE GOZEN...
SKRCH
...HIS OPPONENTS MIGHT PRESENT US WITH A BIGGER PROBLEM.
SLICE
THEY COULD PREVENT TSUKIYOMI'S LAUNCH.
IT MIGHT BE BEST TO HOLD BACK A LITTLE.
...
WHATEVER THE OPPOSITION DOES...

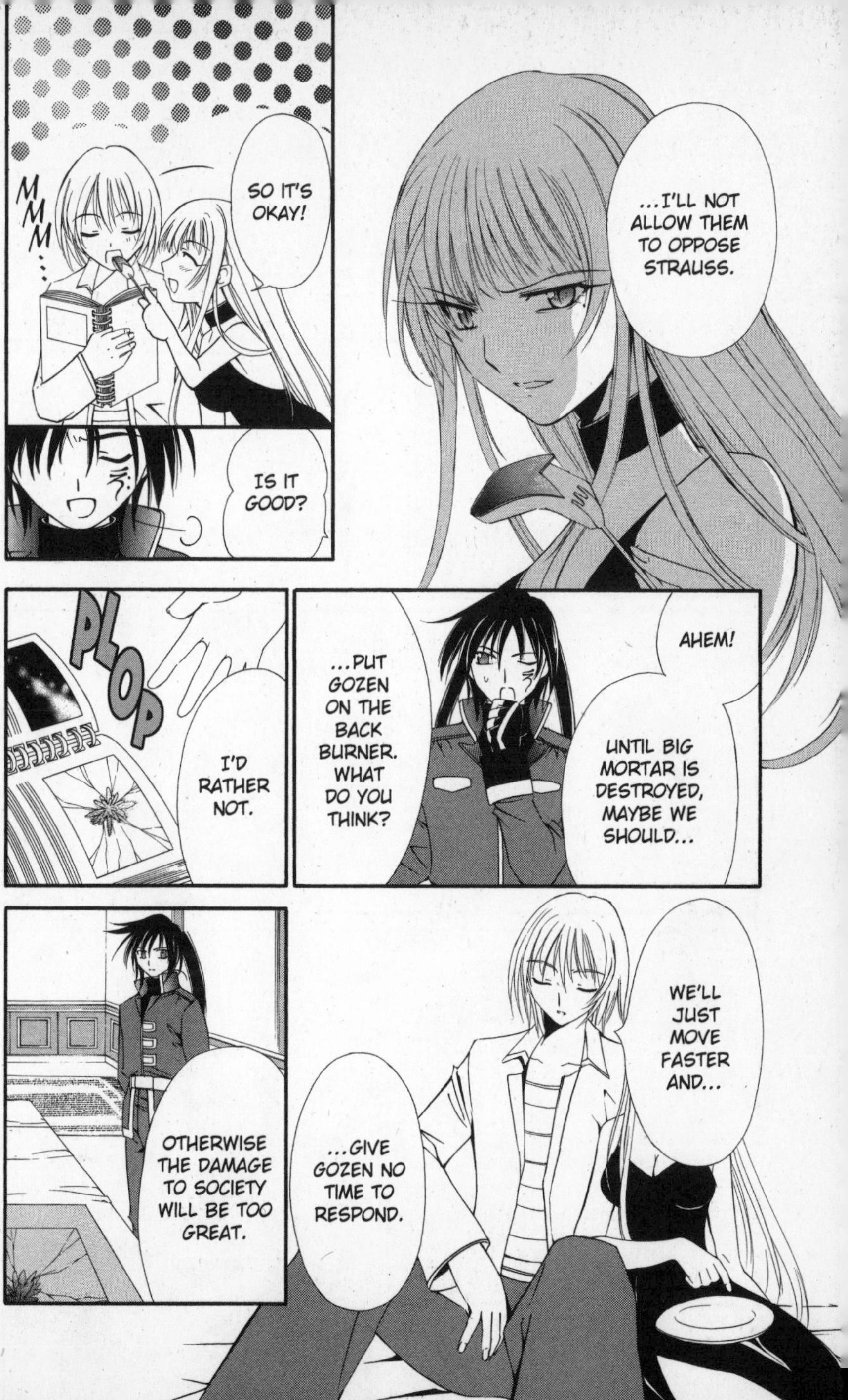
...I'LL NOT ALLOW THEM TO OPPOSE STRAUSS.
SO IT'S OKAY!
MMM...
IS IT GOOD?
AHEM!
UNTIL BIG MORTAR IS DESTROYED, MAYBE WE SHOULD...
...PUT GOZEN ON THE BACK BURNER. WHAT DO YOU THINK?
PLOP
I'D RATHER NOT.
WE'LL JUST MOVE FASTER AND...
...GIVE GOZEN NO TIME TO RESPOND.
OTHERWISE THE DAMAGE TO SOCIETY WILL BE TOO GREAT.

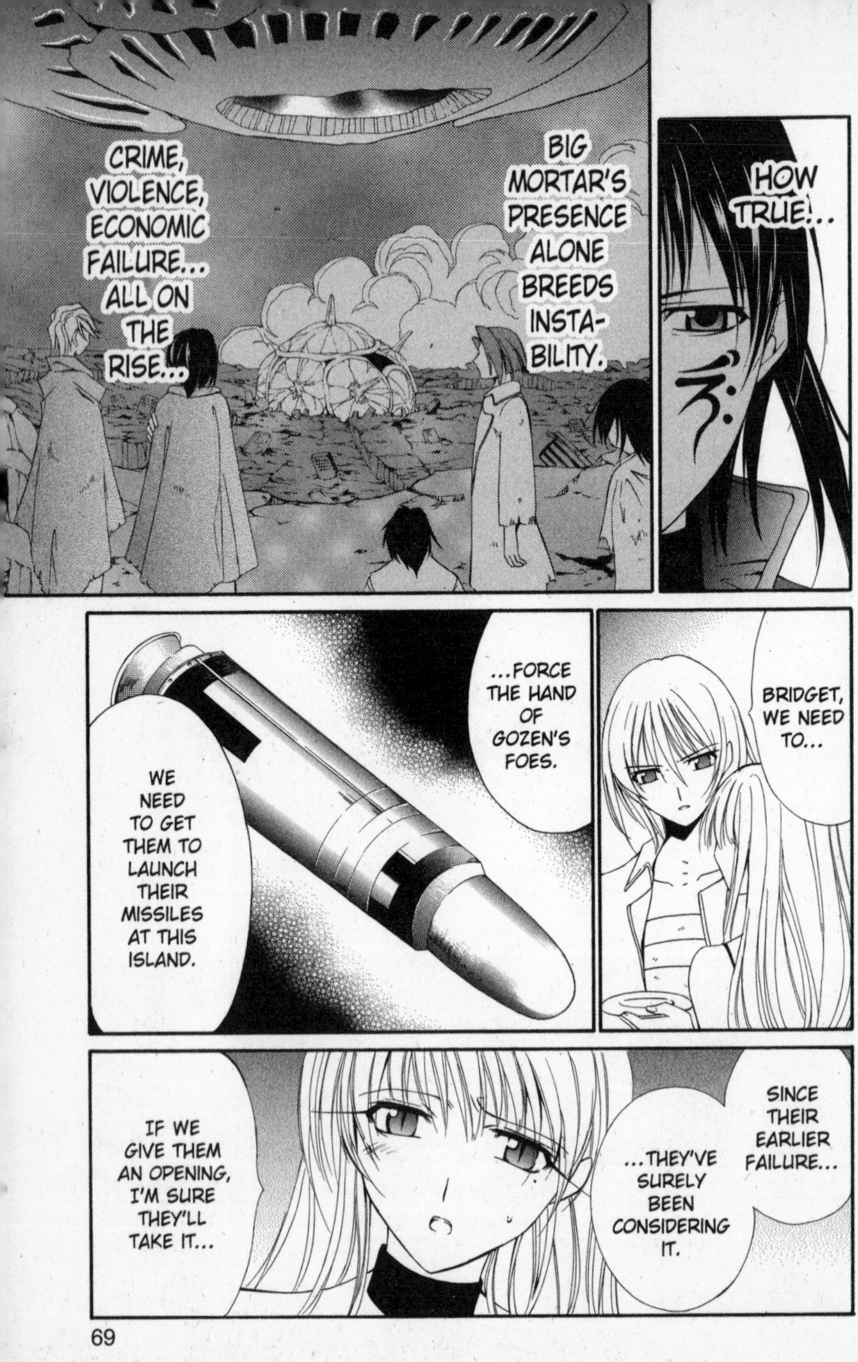
BIG MORTAR'S PRESENCE ALONE BREEDS INSTA-BILITY.
CRIME, VIOLENCE, ECONOMIC FAILURE... ALL ON THE RISE...
HOW TRUE...
BRIDGET, WE NEED TO...
...FORCE THE HAND OF GOZEN'S FOES.
WE NEED TO GET THEM TO LAUNCH THEIR MISSILES AT THIS ISLAND.
SINCE THEIR EARLIER FAILURE...
...THEY'VE SURELY BEEN CONSIDERING IT.
IF WE GIVE THEM AN OPENING, I'M SURE THEY'LL TAKE IT...

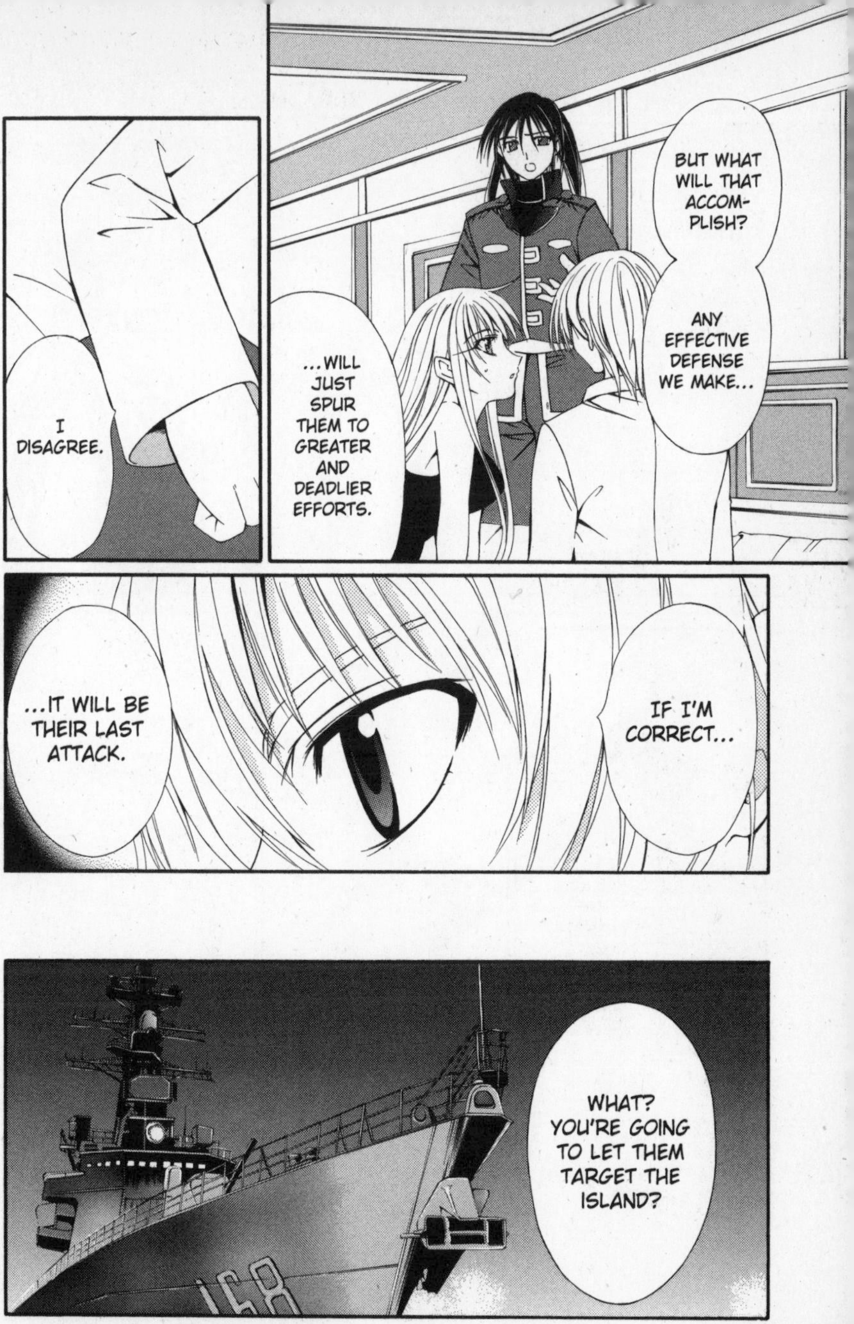
BUT WHAT WILL THAT ACCOM-PLISH?
ANY EFFECTIVE DEFENSE WE MAKE...
...WILL JUST SPUR THEM TO GREATER AND DEADLIER EFFORTS.
I DISAGREE.
IF I'M CORRECT...
...IT WILL BE THEIR LAST ATTACK.
WHAT? YOU'RE GOING TO LET THEM TARGET THE ISLAND?

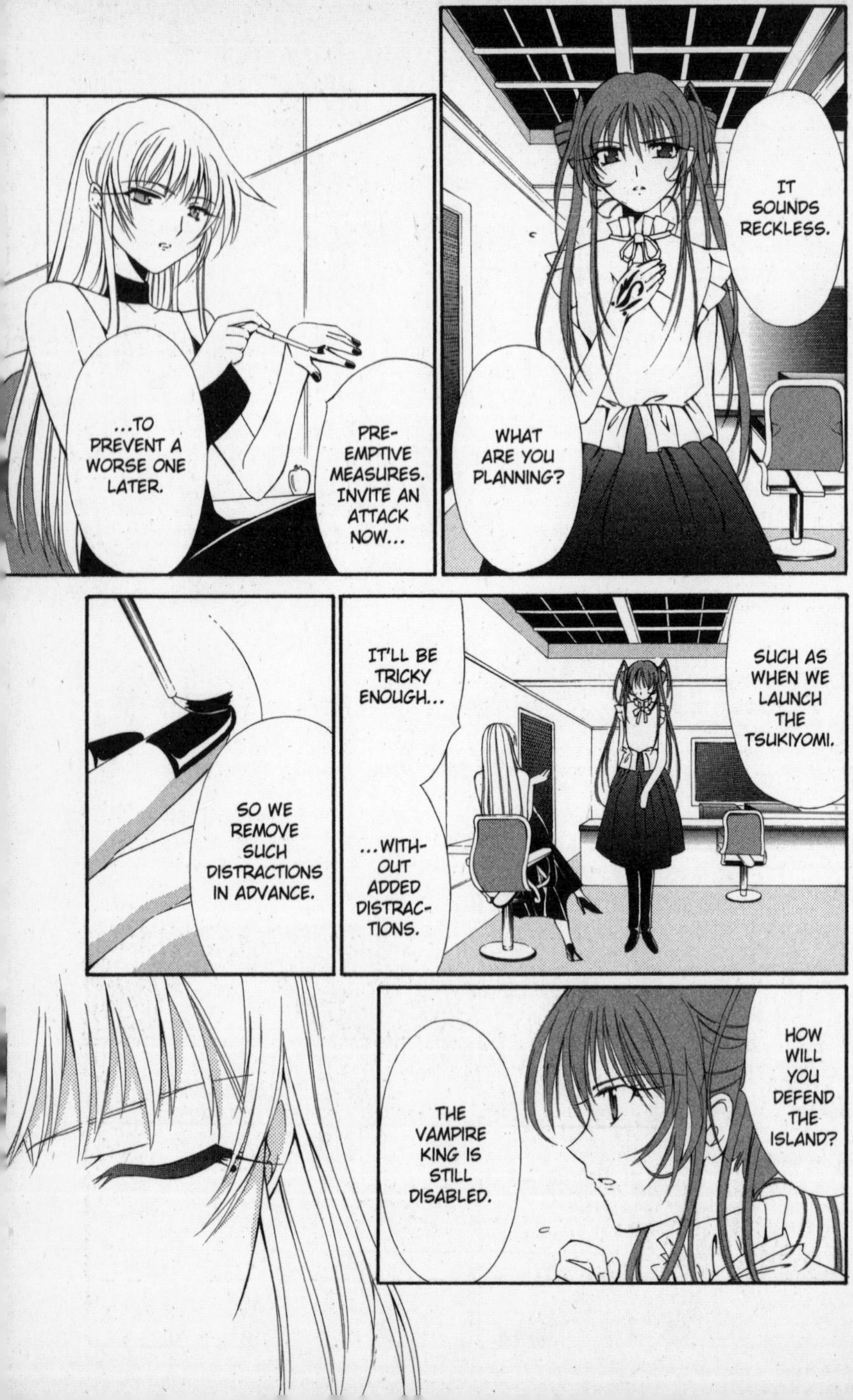
IT SOUNDS RECKLESS.
WHAT ARE YOU PLANNING?
PRE-EMPTIVE MEASURES. INVITE AN ATTACK NOW...
...TO PREVENT A WORSE ONE LATER.
SUCH AS WHEN WE LAUNCH THE TSUKIYOMI.
IT'LL BE TRICKY ENOUGH...
...WITH-OUT ADDED DISTRAC-TIONS.
SO WE REMOVE SUCH DISTRACTIONS IN ADVANCE.
HOW WILL YOU DEFEND THE ISLAND?
THE VAMPIRE KING IS STILL DISABLED.

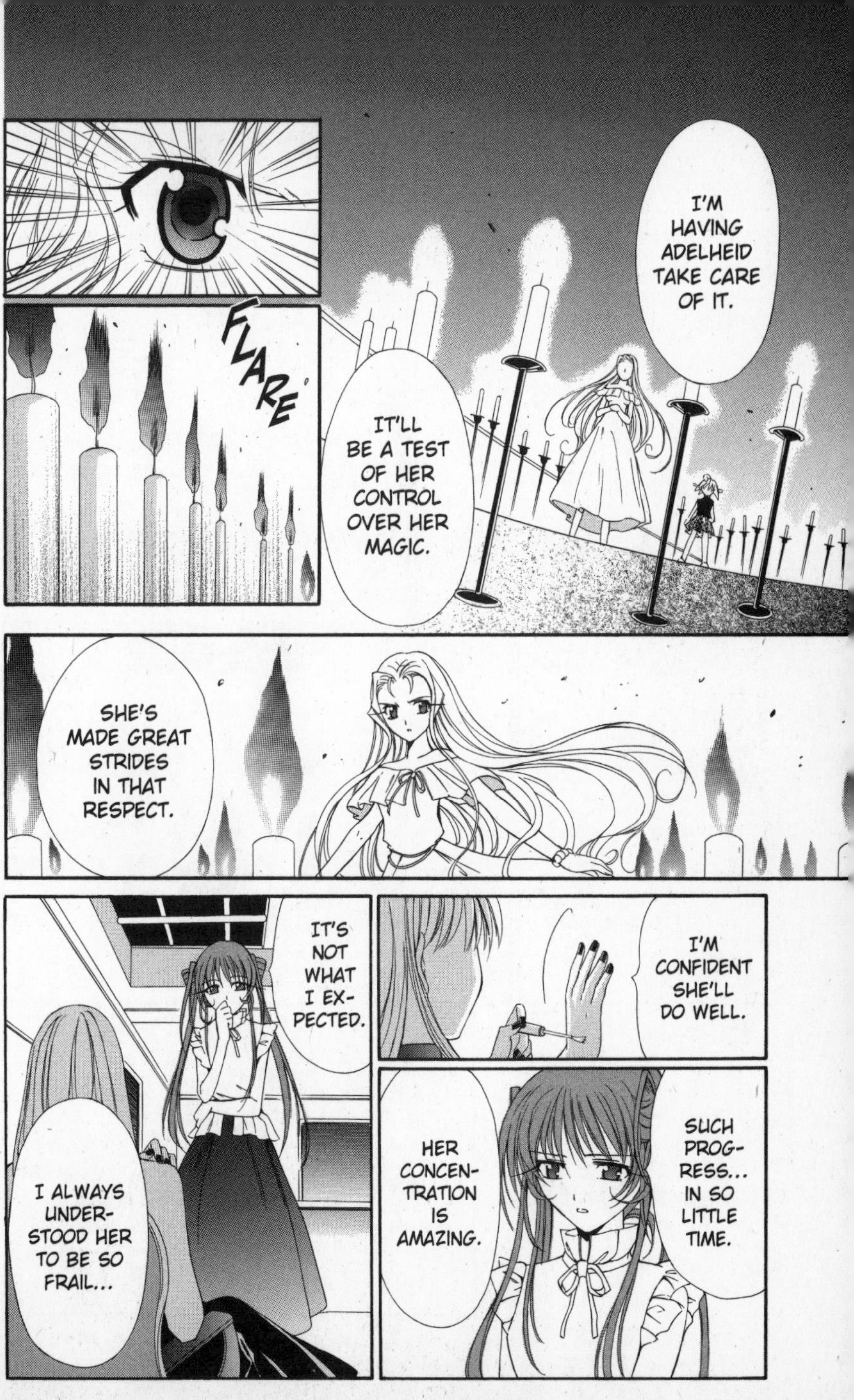
I'M HAVING ADELHEID TAKE CARE OF IT.
IT'LL BE A TEST OF HER CONTROL OVER HER MAGIC.
FLARE
SHE'S MADE GREAT STRIDES IN THAT RESPECT.
I'M CONFIDENT SHE'LL DO WELL.
SUCH PROG-RESS... IN SO LITTLE TIME.
HER CONCEN-TRATION IS AMAZING.
IT'S NOT WHAT I EX-PECTED.
I ALWAYS UNDER-STOOD HER TO BE SO FRAIL...

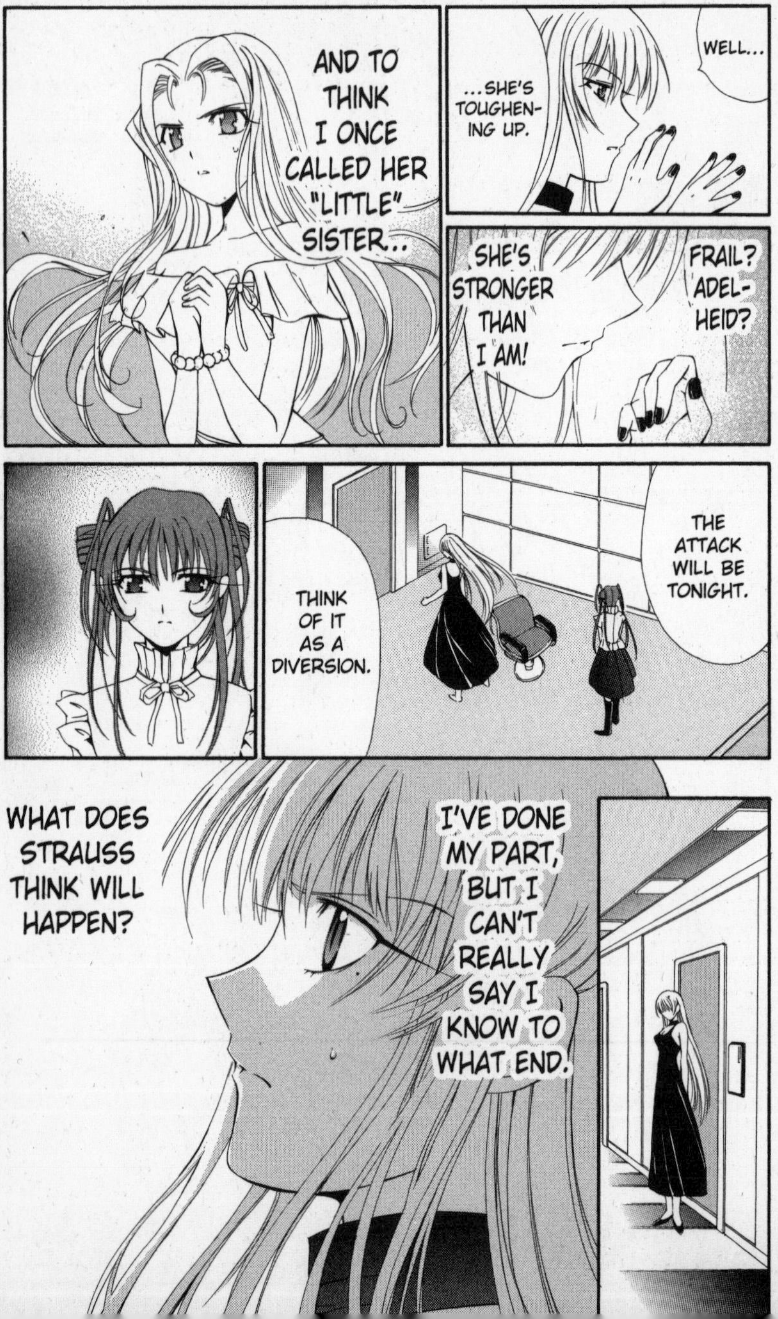
WELL...
...SHE'S TOUGHENING UP.
FRAIL? ADELHEID?
SHE'S STRONGER THAN I AM!
AND TO THINK I ONCE CALLED HER "LITTLE" SISTER...
THE ATTACK WILL BE TONIGHT.
THINK OF IT AS A DIVERSION.
I'VE DONE MY PART, BUT I CAN'T REALLY SAY I KNOW TO WHAT END.
WHAT DOES STRAUSS THINK WILL HAPPEN?

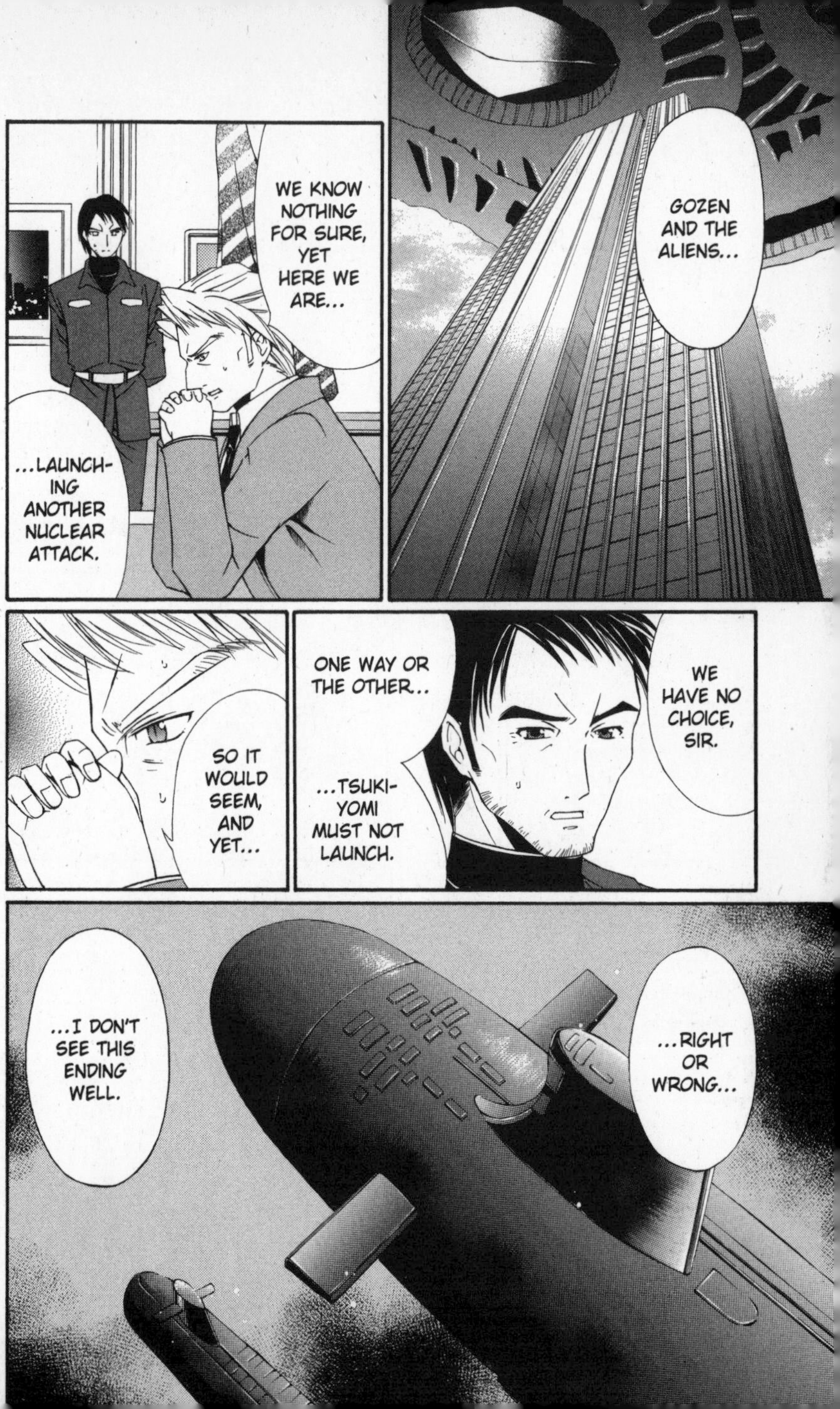
GOZEN AND THE ALIENS...
WE KNOW NOTHING FOR SURE, YET HERE WE ARE...
...LAUNCHING ANOTHER NUCLEAR ATTACK.
WE HAVE NO CHOICE, SIR.
ONE WAY OR THE OTHER...
...TSUKI-YOMI MUST NOT LAUNCH.
SO IT WOULD SEEM, AND YET...
...RIGHT OR WRONG...
...I DON'T SEE THIS ENDING WELL.

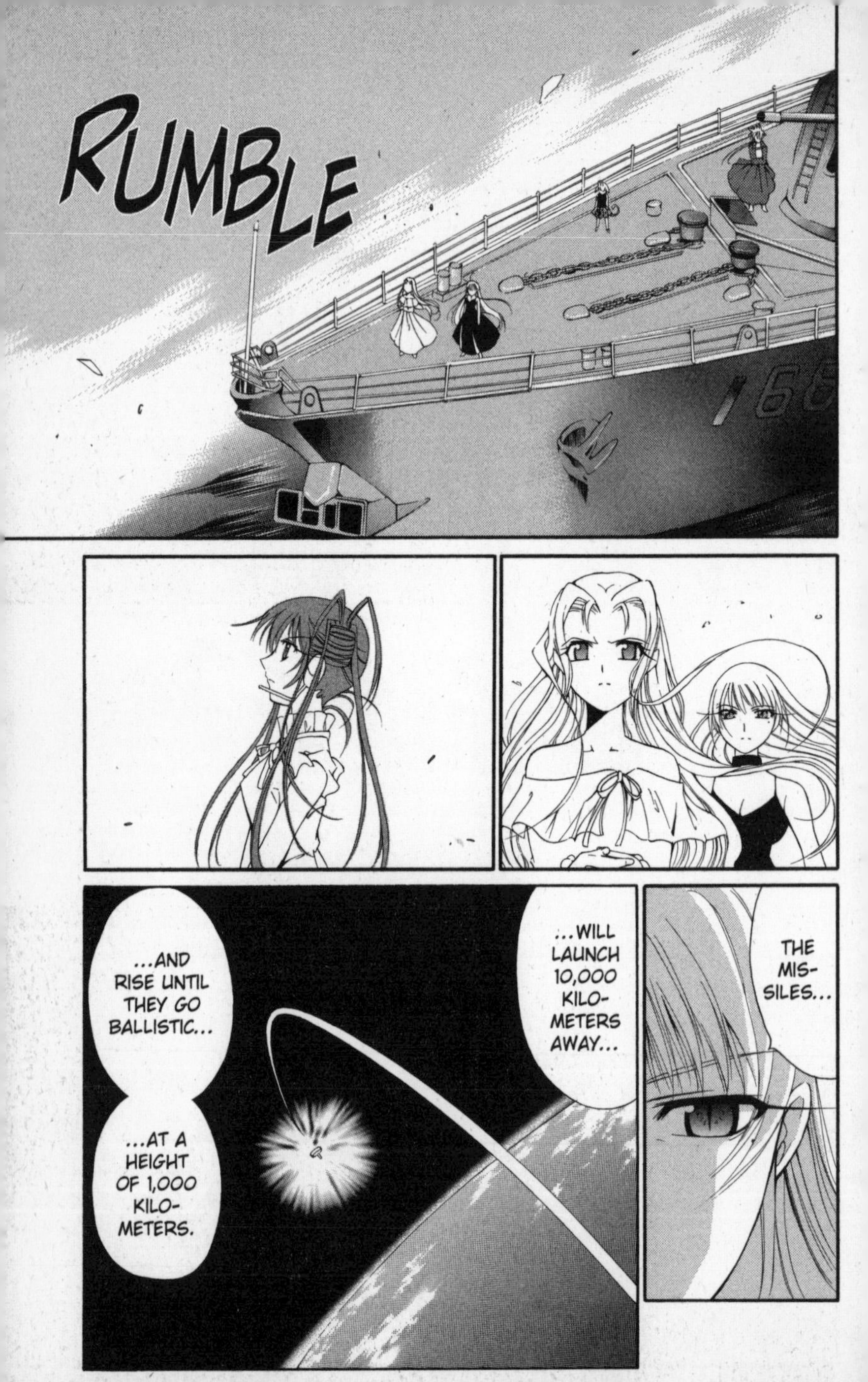
RUMBLE
THE MIS-SILES...
...WILL LAUNCH 10,000 KILO-METERS AWAY...
...AND RISE UNTIL THEY GO BALLISTIC...
...AT A HEIGHT OF 1,000 KILO-METERS.

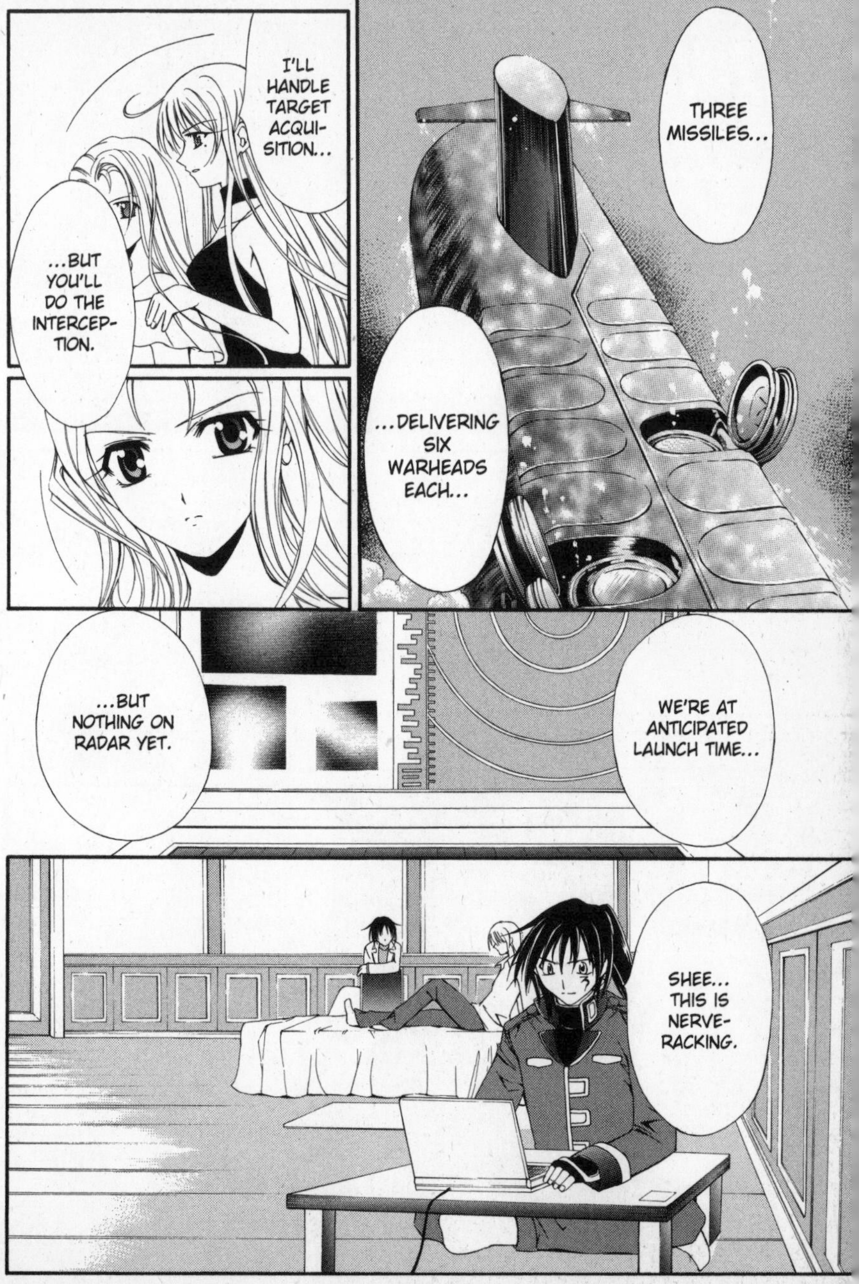
THREE MISSILES...
...DELIVERING SIX WARHEADS EACH...
I'LL HANDLE TARGET ACQUISITION...
...BUT YOU'LL DO THE INTERCEPTION.
WE'RE AT ANTICIPATED LAUNCH TIME...
...BUT NOTHING ON RADAR YET.
SHEE... THIS IS NERVE-RACKING.

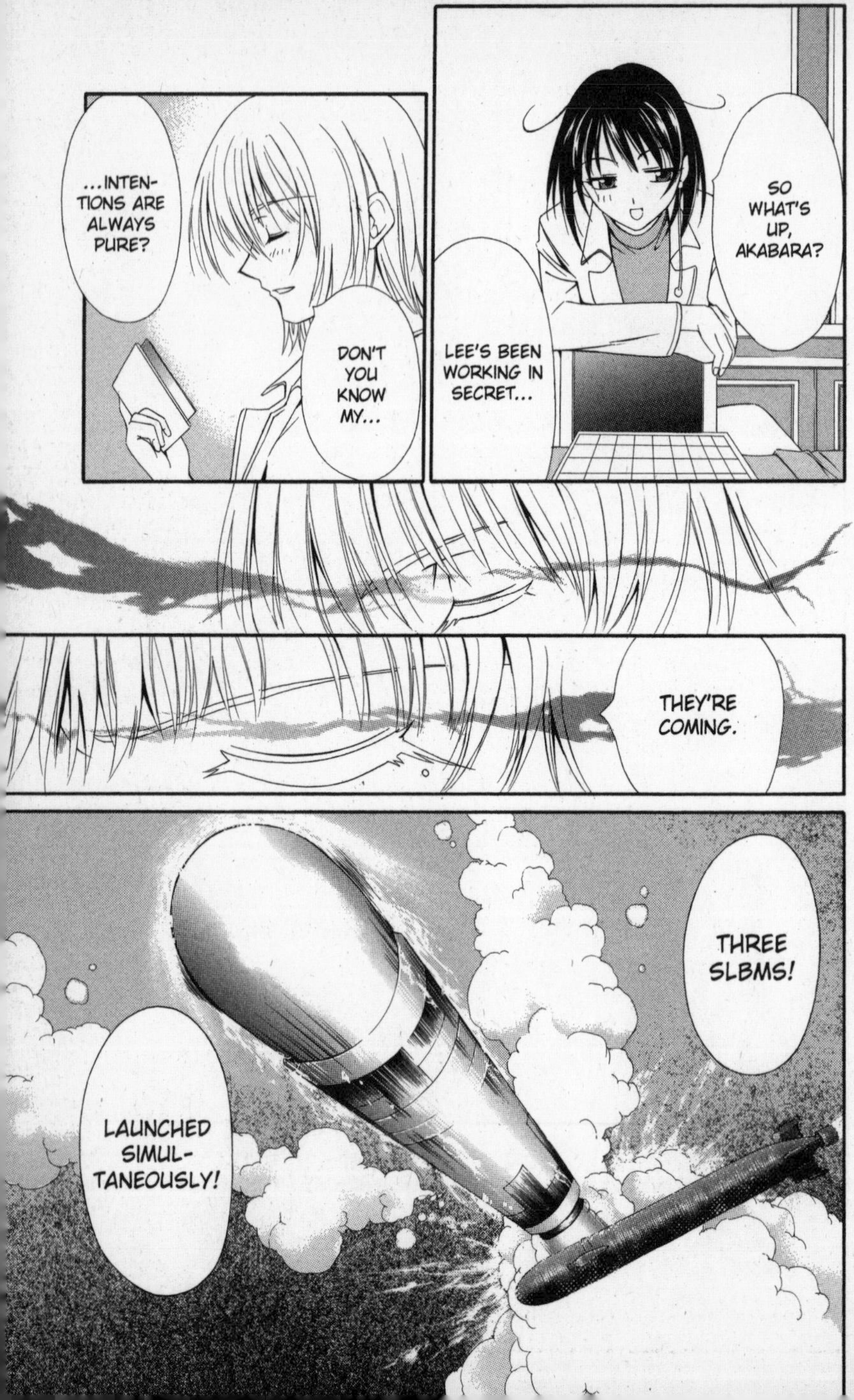
SO WHAT'S UP, AKABARA?
LEE'S BEEN WORKING IN SECRET...
DON'T YOU KNOW MY...
...INTEN-TIONS ARE ALWAYS PURE?
THEY'RE COMING.
THREE SLBMS!
LAUNCHED SIMUL-TANEOUSLY!

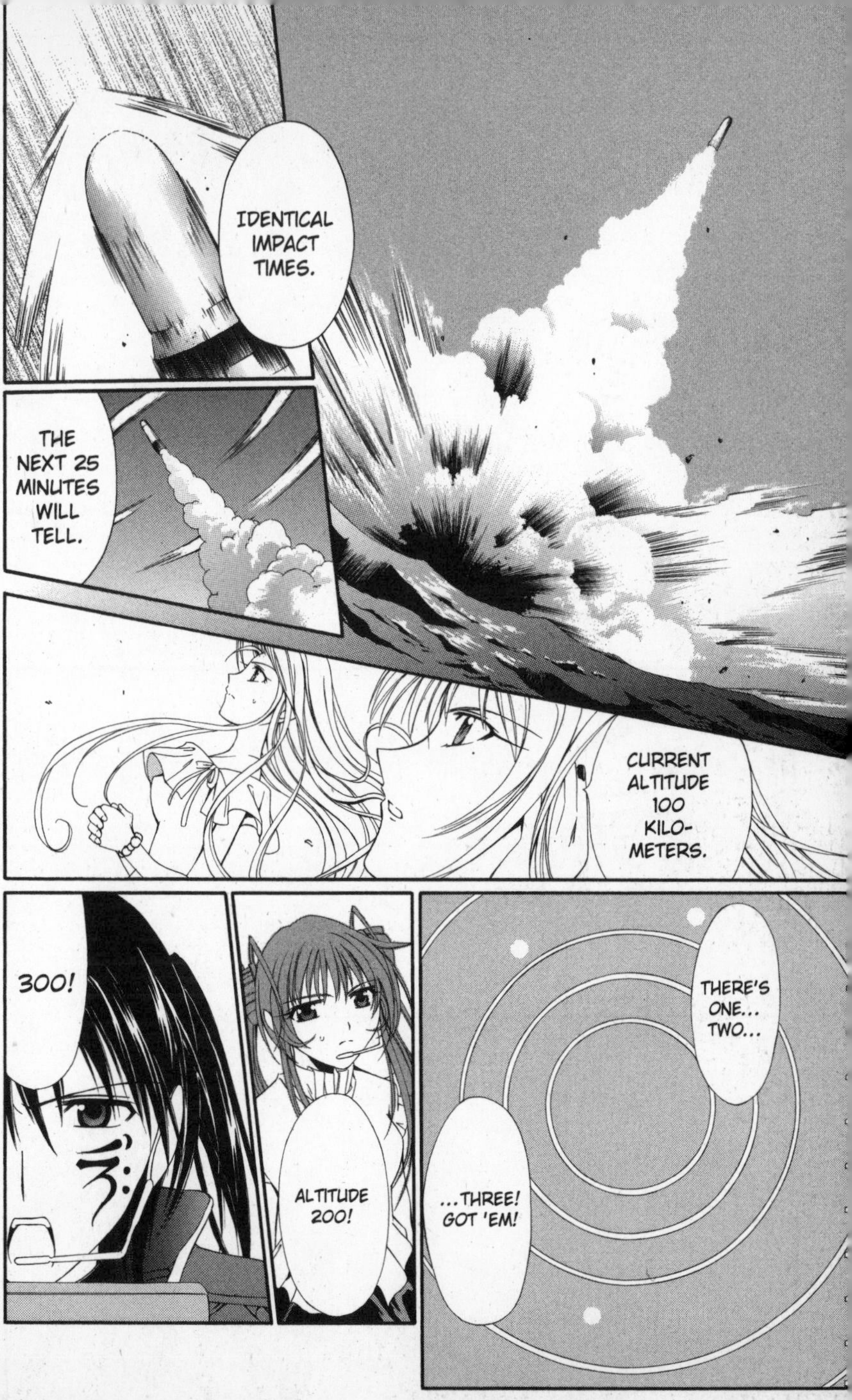
IDENTICAL IMPACT TIMES.
THE NEXT 25 MINUTES WILL TELL.
CURRENT ALTITUDE 100 KILO-METERS.
THERE'S ONE... TWO...
...THREE! GOT 'EM!
ALTITUDE 200!
300!

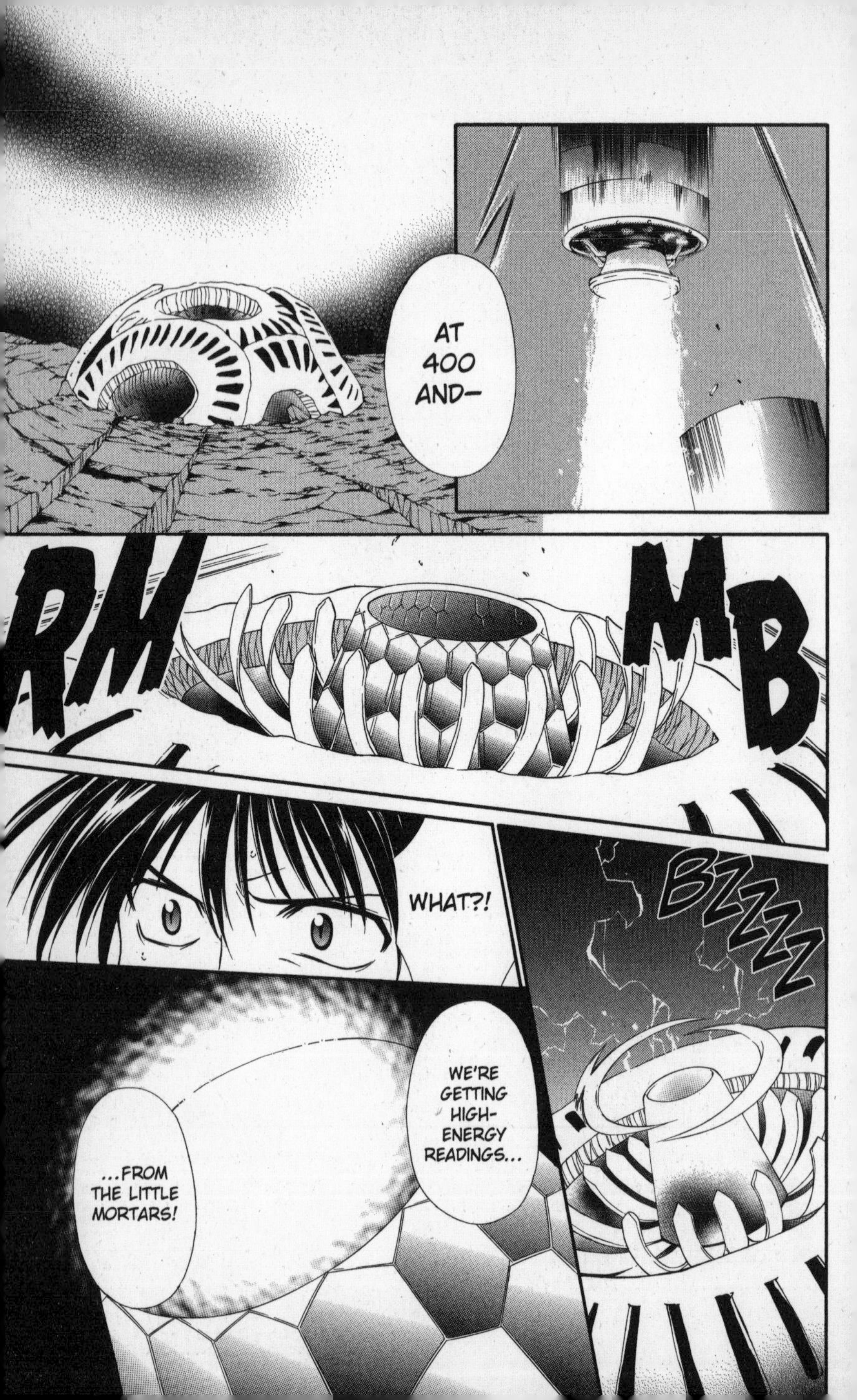
AT 400 AND—
RH
MB
BZZZZ
WHAT?!
WE'RE GETTING HIGH-ENERGY READINGS...
...FROM THE LITTLE MORTARS!

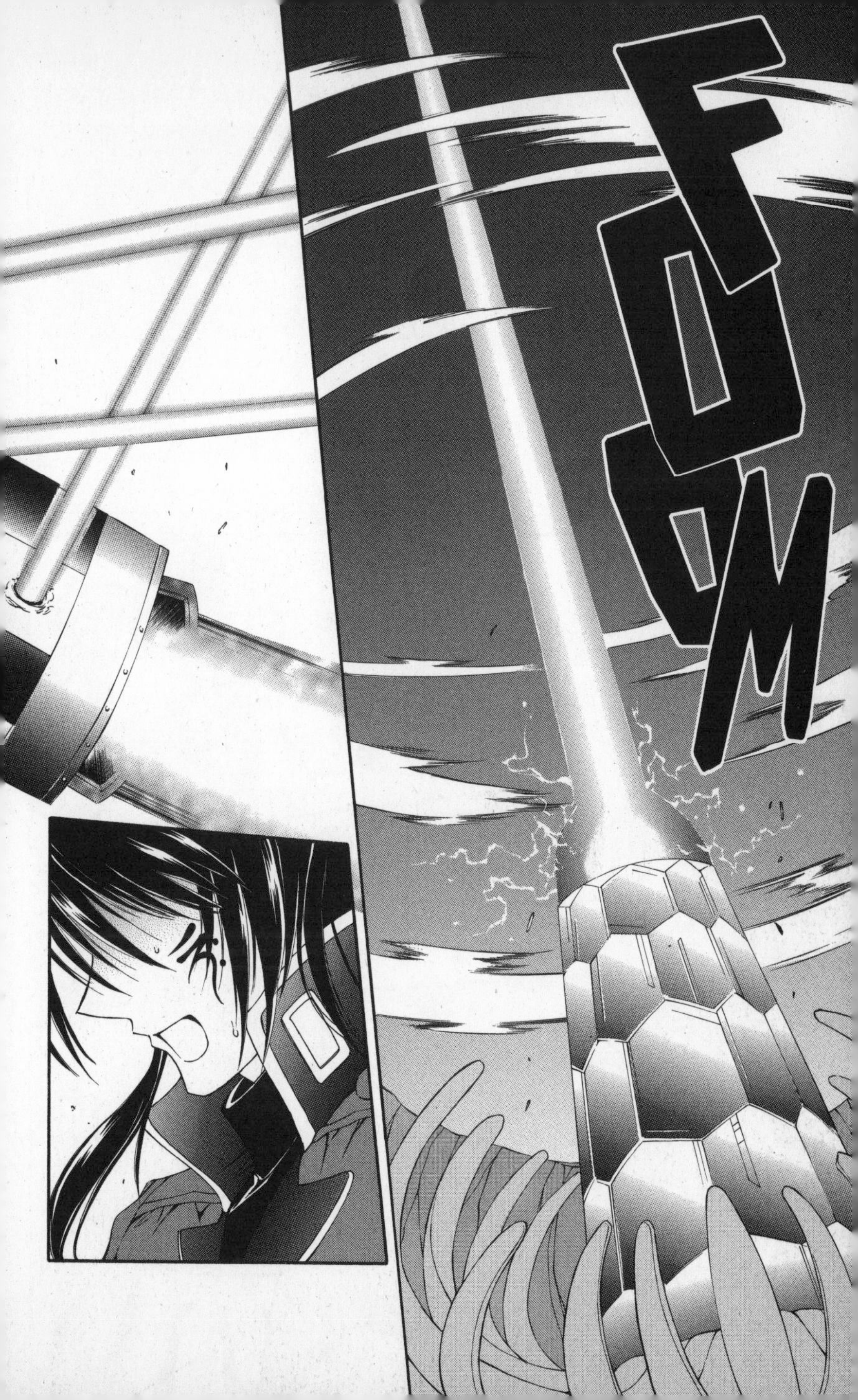
FOOM

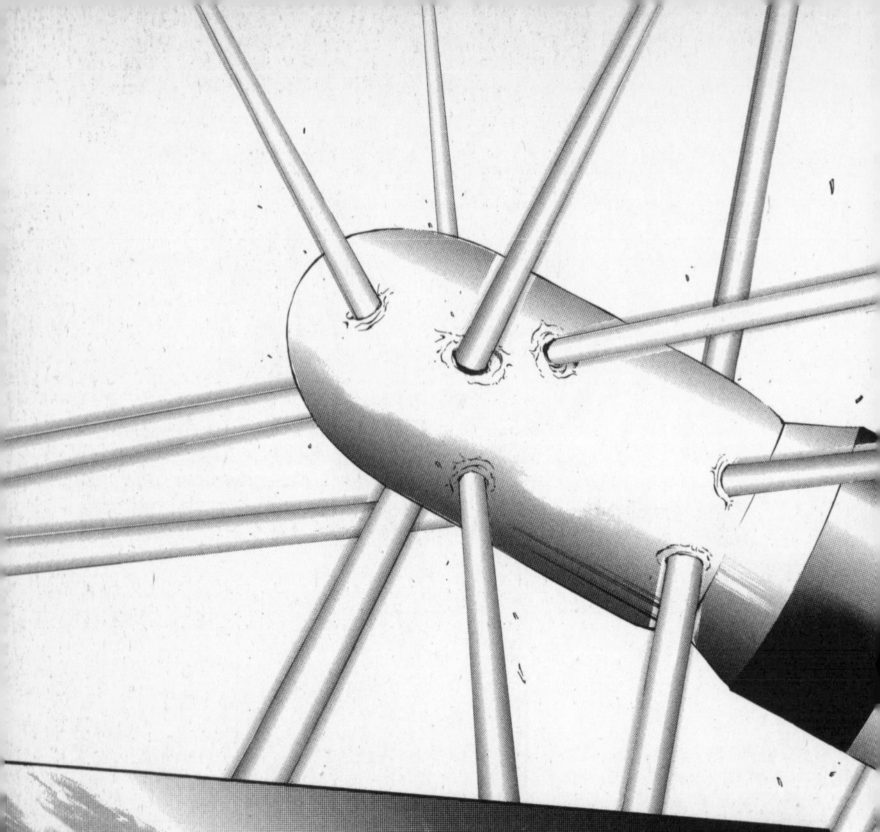
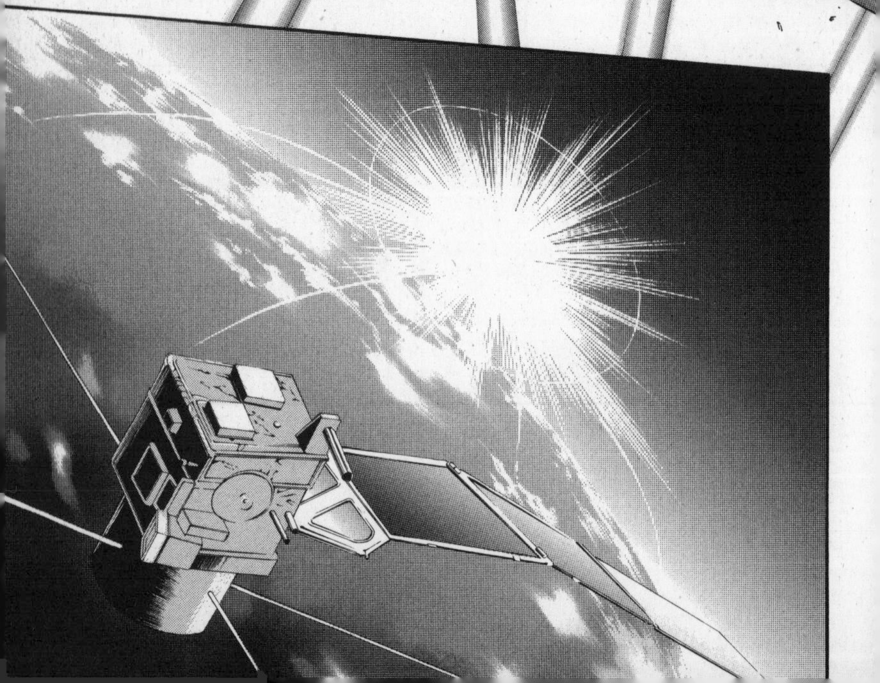

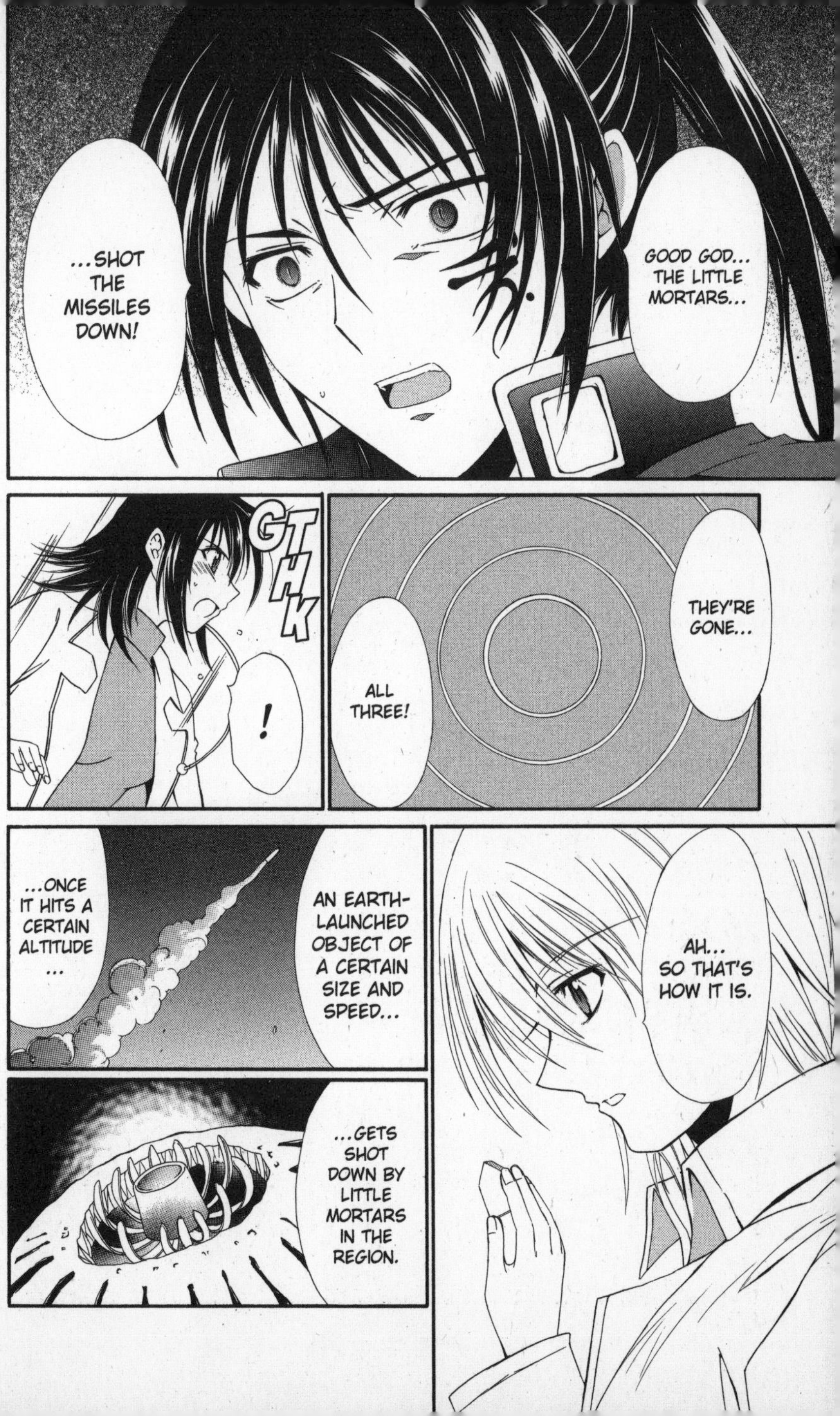
GOOD GOD... THE LITTLE MORTARS...
...SHOT THE MISSILES DOWN!
THEY'RE GONE...
ALL THREE!
GTHK
!
AH... SO THAT'S HOW IT IS.
AN EARTH-LAUNCHED OBJECT OF A CERTAIN SIZE AND SPEED...
...ONCE IT HITS A CERTAIN ALTITUDE...
...GETS SHOT DOWN BY LITTLE MORTARS IN THE REGION.

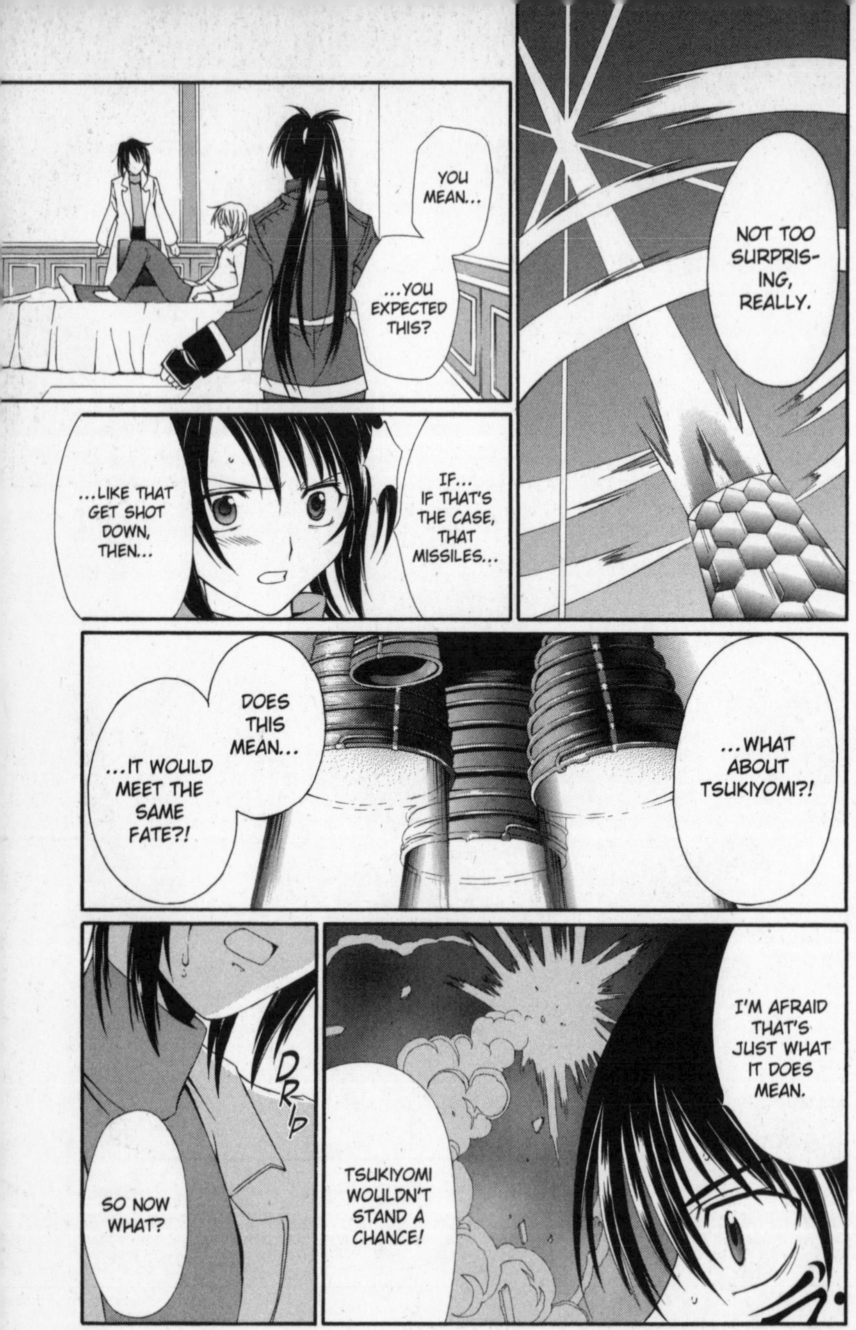
NOT TOO SURPRIS-ING, REALLY.
YOU MEAN...
...YOU EXPECTED THIS?
IF... IF THAT'S THE CASE, THAT MISSILES...
...LIKE THAT GET SHOT DOWN, THEN...
...WHAT ABOUT TSUKIYOMI?!
DOES THIS MEAN...
...IT WOULD MEET THE SAME FATE?!
I'M AFRAID THAT'S JUST WHAT IT DOES MEAN.
TSUKIYOMI WOULDN'T STAND A CHANCE!
DRIP
SO NOW WHAT?

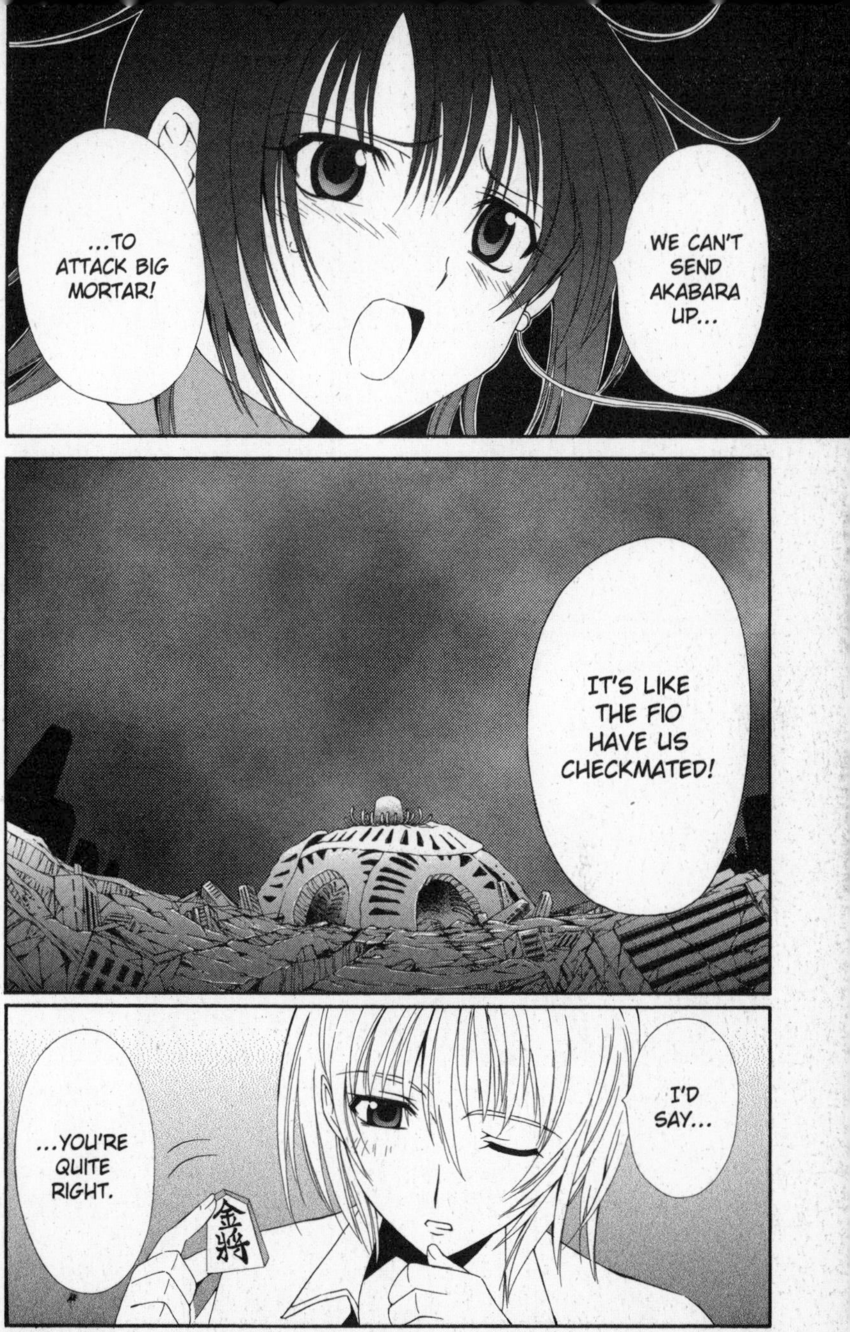
WE CAN'T SEND AKABARA UP...
...TO ATTACK BIG MORTAR!
IT'S LIKE THE FIO HAVE US CHECKMATED!
I'D SAY...
...YOU'RE QUITE RIGHT.
金将

THE RECORD OF A
FALLEN VAMPIRE

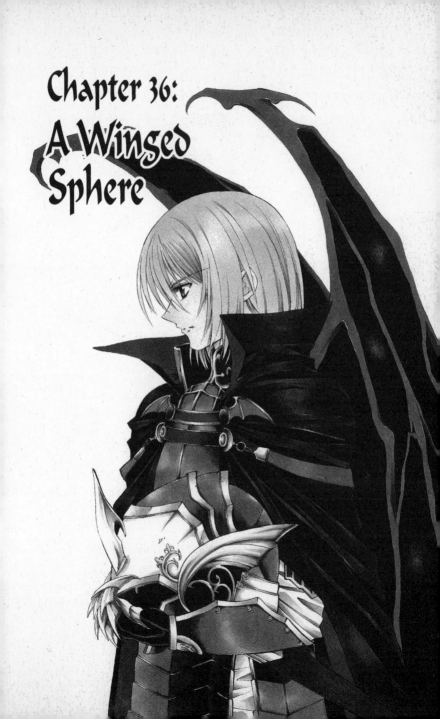

Chapter 36: A Winged Sphere

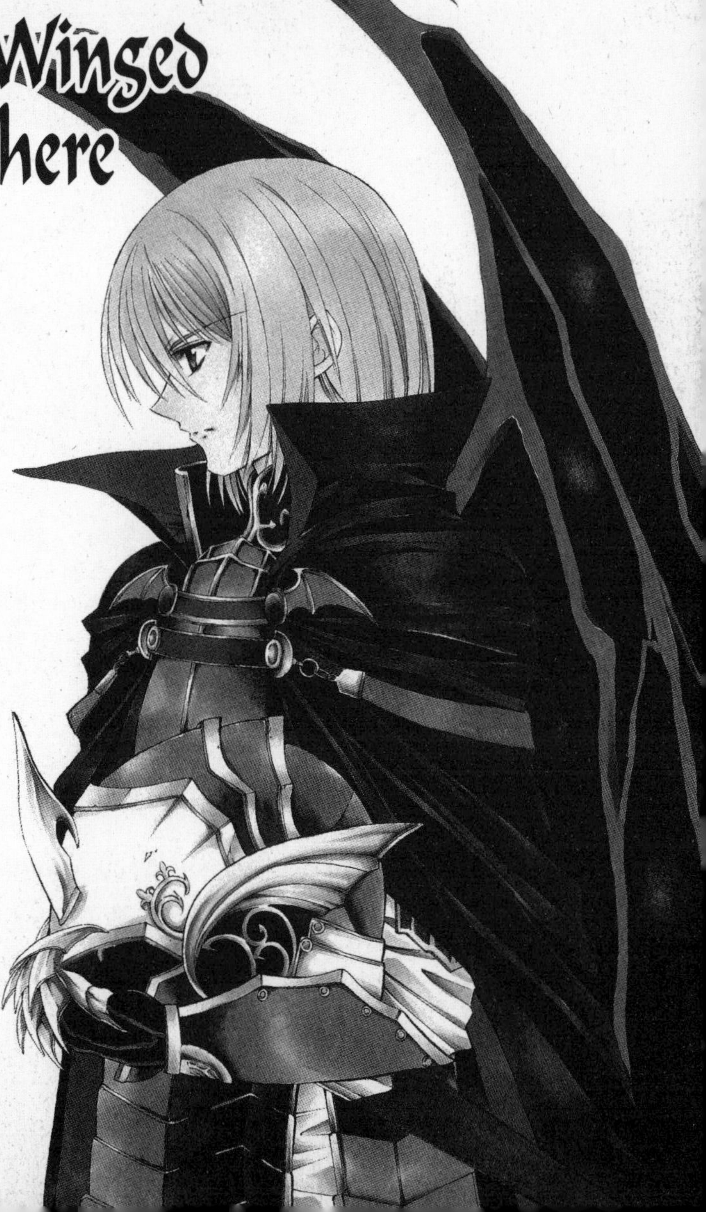

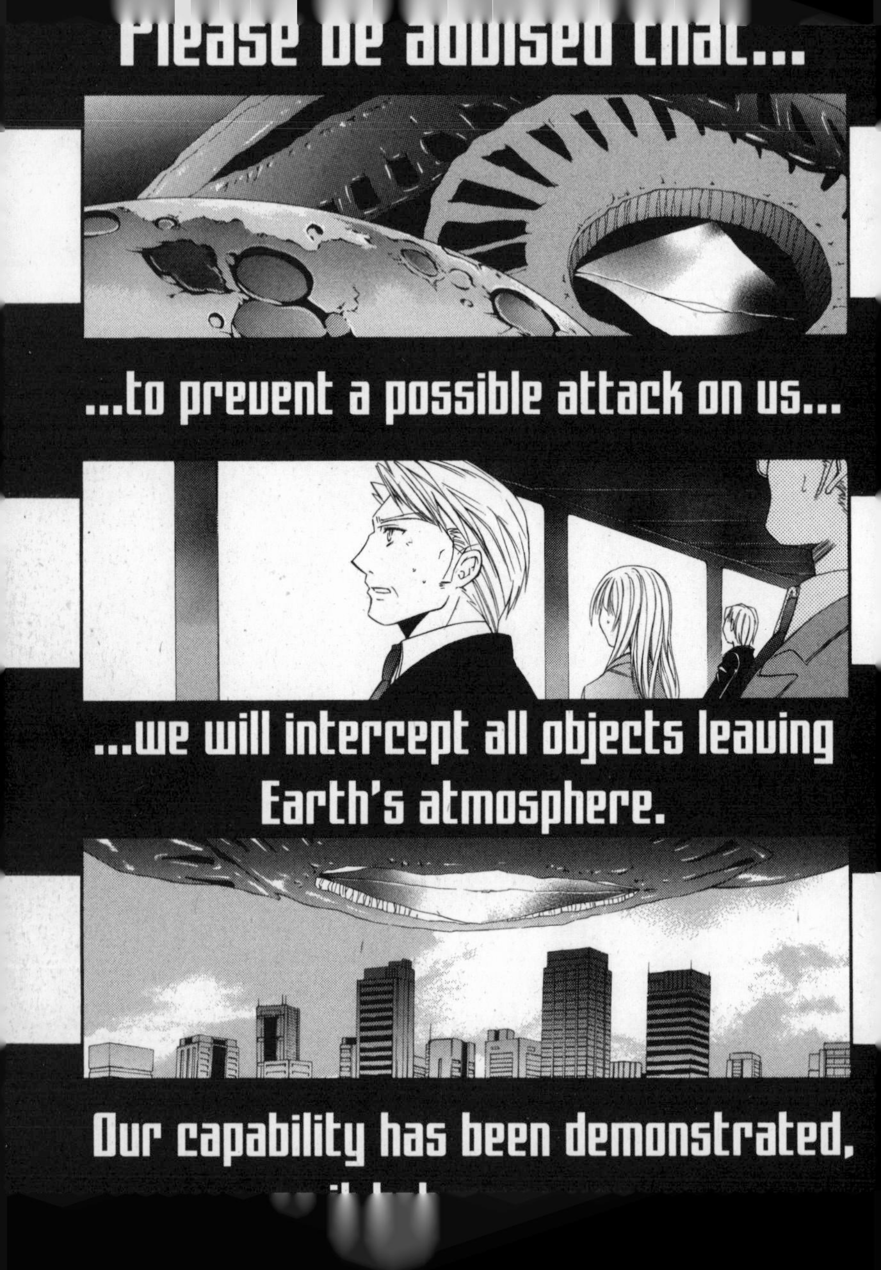
Please be advised that...
...to prevent a possible attack on us...
...we will intercept all objects leaving Earth's atmosphere.
Our capability has been demonstrated,

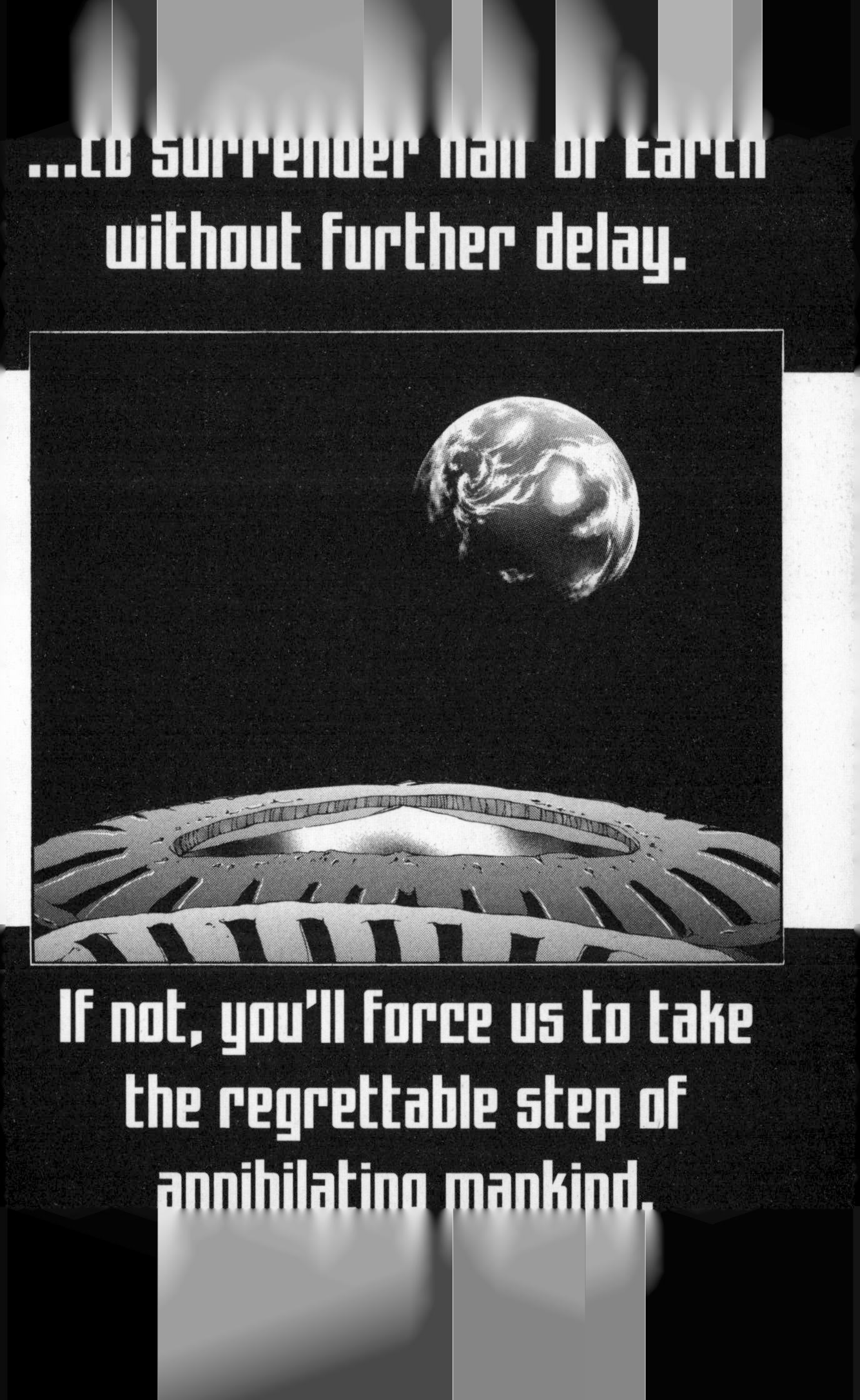
...to surrender half of Earth without further delay.
If not, you'll force us to take the regrettable step of annihilating mankind.

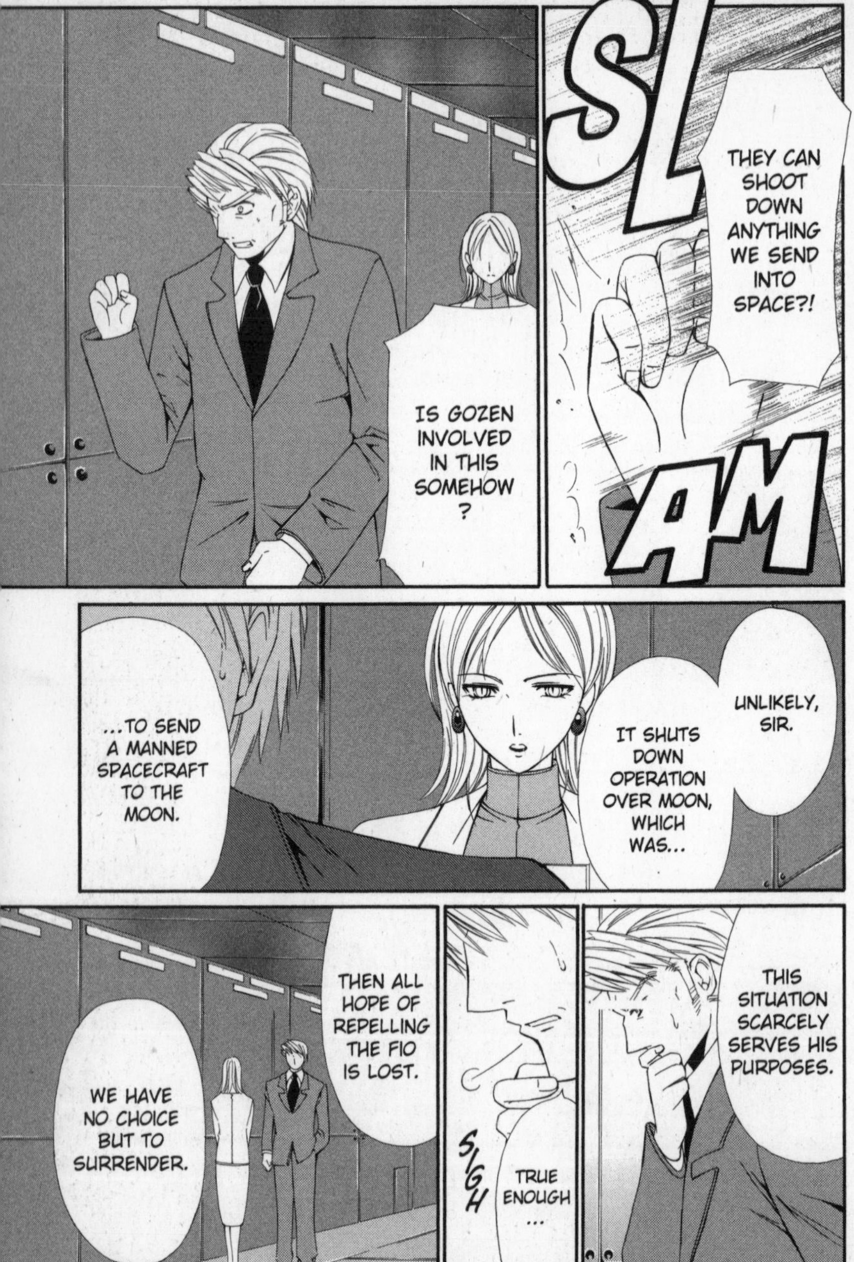
SLAM
THEY CAN SHOOT DOWN ANYTHING WE SEND INTO SPACE?!
IS GOZEN INVOLVED IN THIS SOMEHOW?
UNLIKELY, SIR.
IT SHUTS DOWN OPERATION OVER MOON, WHICH WAS...
...TO SEND A MANNED SPACECRAFT TO THE MOON.
THIS SITUATION SCARCELY SERVES HIS PURPOSES.
SIGH
TRUE ENOUGH...
THEN ALL HOPE OF REPELLING THE FIO IS LOST.
WE HAVE NO CHOICE BUT TO SURRENDER.

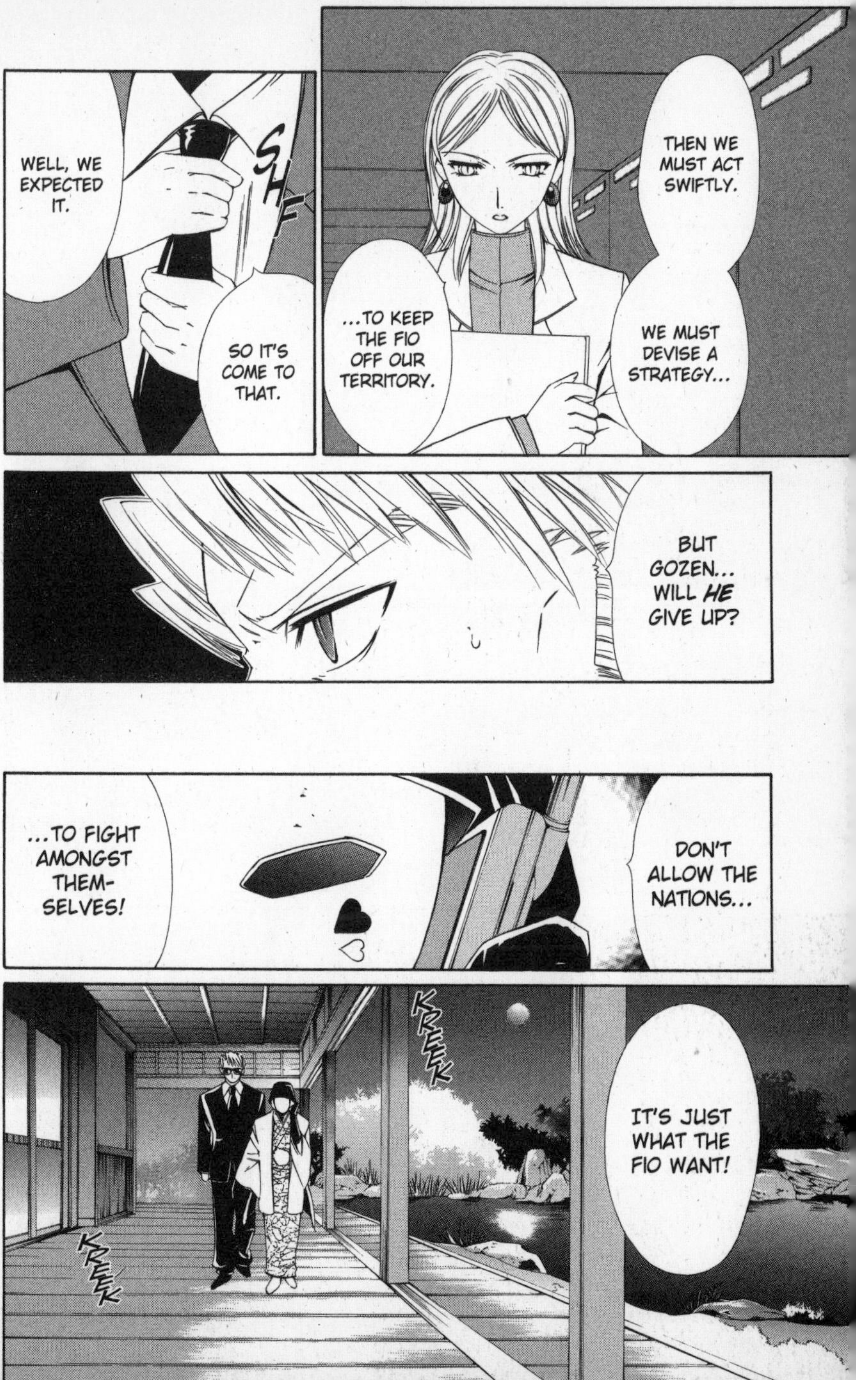
THEN WE MUST ACT SWIFTLY.
WE MUST DEVISE A STRATEGY...
...TO KEEP THE FIO OFF OUR TERRITORY.
SHF
SO IT'S COME TO THAT.
WELL, WE EXPECTED IT.
BUT GOZEN... WILL HE GIVE UP?
DON'T ALLOW THE NATIONS...
...TO FIGHT AMONGST THEM-SELVES!
KREEK
IT'S JUST WHAT THE FIO WANT!
KREEK

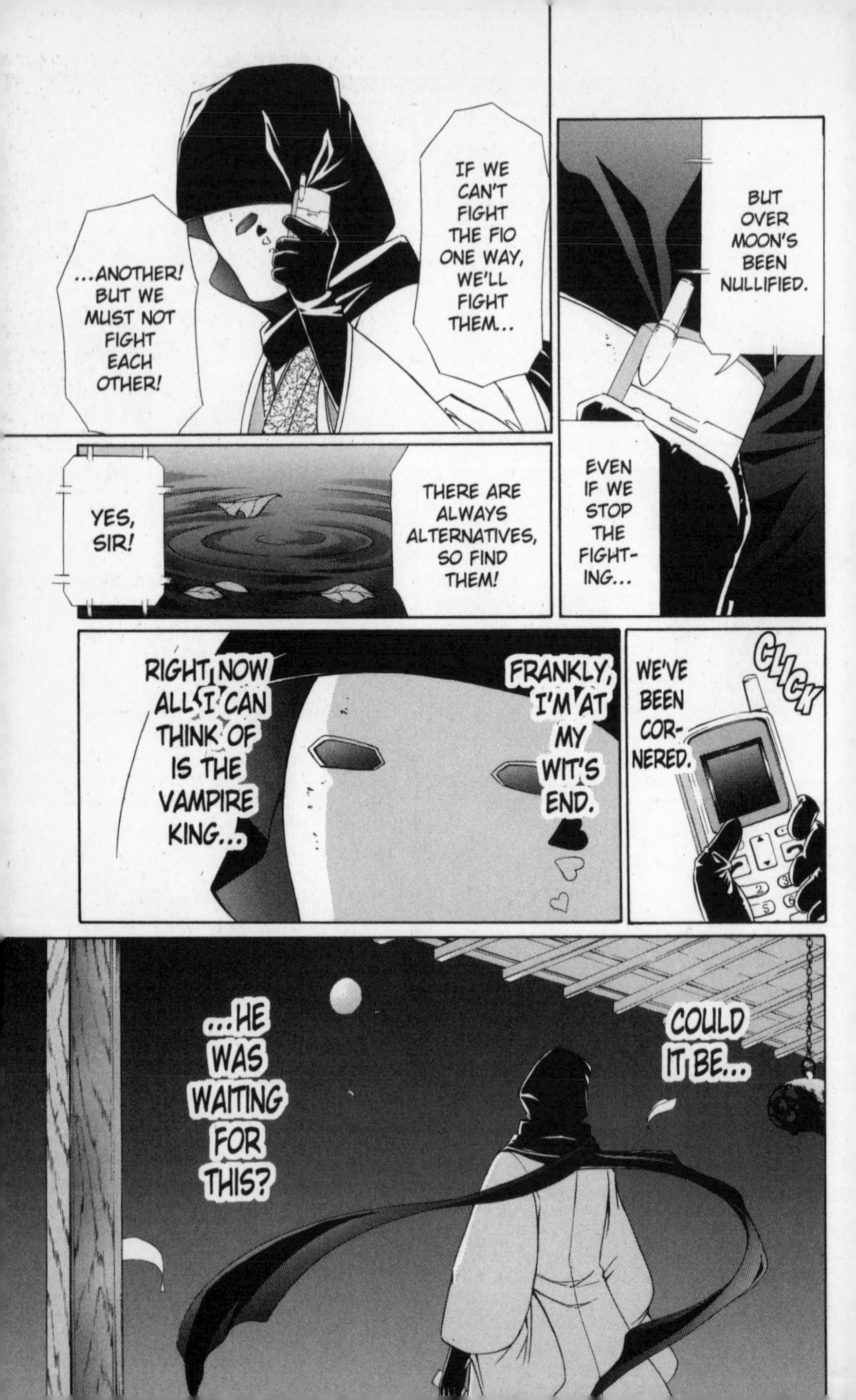
BUT OVER MOON'S BEEN NULLIFIED.
EVEN IF WE STOP THE FIGHT-ING...
IF WE CAN'T FIGHT THE FIO ONE WAY, WE'LL FIGHT THEM...
...ANOTHER! BUT WE MUST NOT FIGHT EACH OTHER!
THERE ARE ALWAYS ALTERNATIVES, SO FIND THEM!
YES, SIR!
CLICK
WE'VE BEEN COR-NERED.
FRANKLY, I'M AT MY WIT'S END.
RIGHT NOW ALL I CAN THINK OF IS THE VAMPIRE KING...
COULD IT BE...
...HE WAS WAITING FOR THIS?

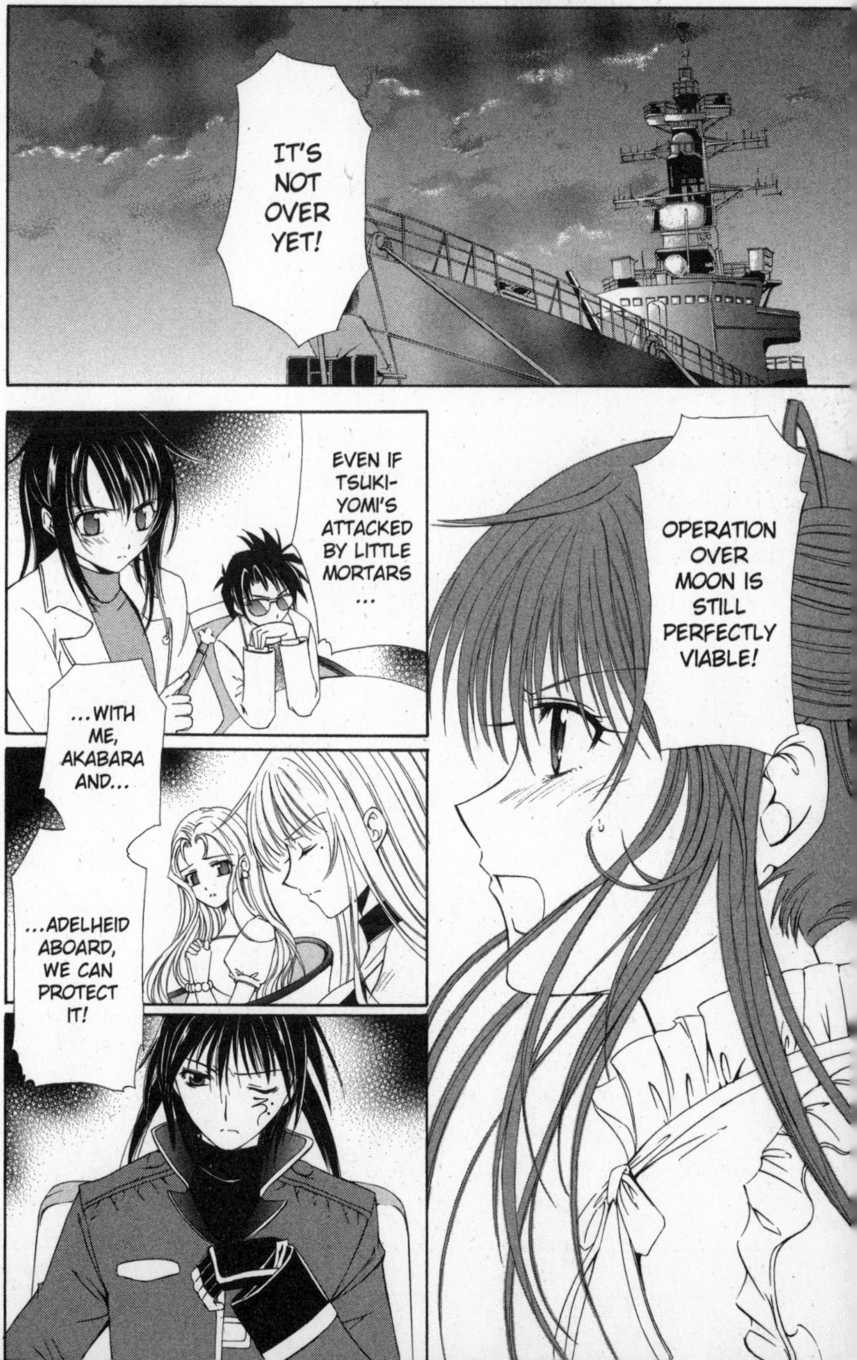
IT'S NOT OVER YET!
OPERATION OVER MOON IS STILL PERFECTLY VIABLE!
EVEN IF TSUKI-YOMI'S ATTACKED BY LITTLE MORTARS...
...WITH ME, AKABARA AND...
...ADELHEID ABOARD, WE CAN PROTECT IT!

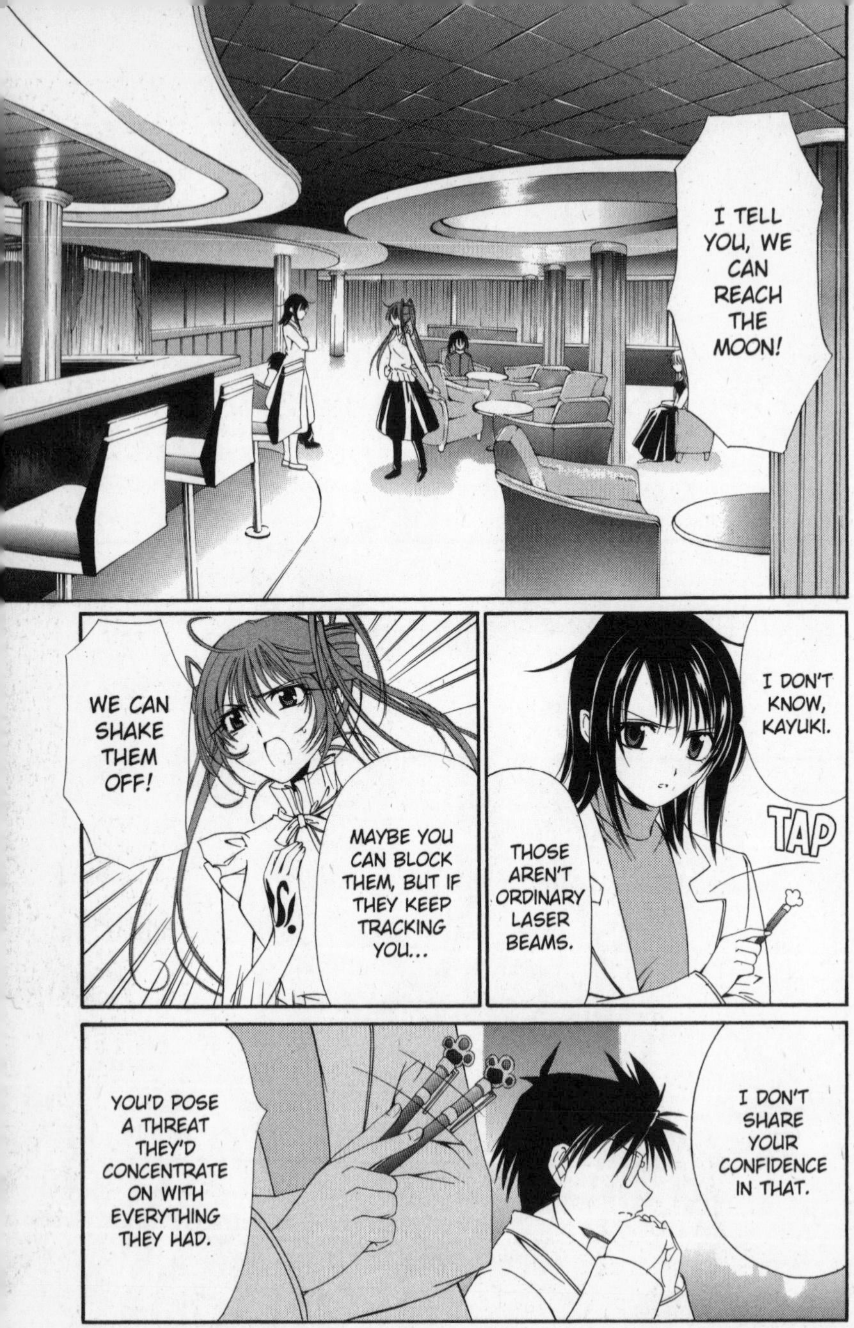
I TELL YOU, WE CAN REACH THE MOON!
I DON'T KNOW, KAYUKI.
TAP
THOSE AREN'T ORDINARY LASER BEAMS.
WE CAN SHAKE THEM OFF!
MAYBE YOU CAN BLOCK THEM, BUT IF THEY KEEP TRACKING YOU...
I DON'T SHARE YOUR CONFIDENCE IN THAT.
YOU'D POSE A THREAT THEY'D CONCENTRATE ON WITH EVERYTHING THEY HAD.

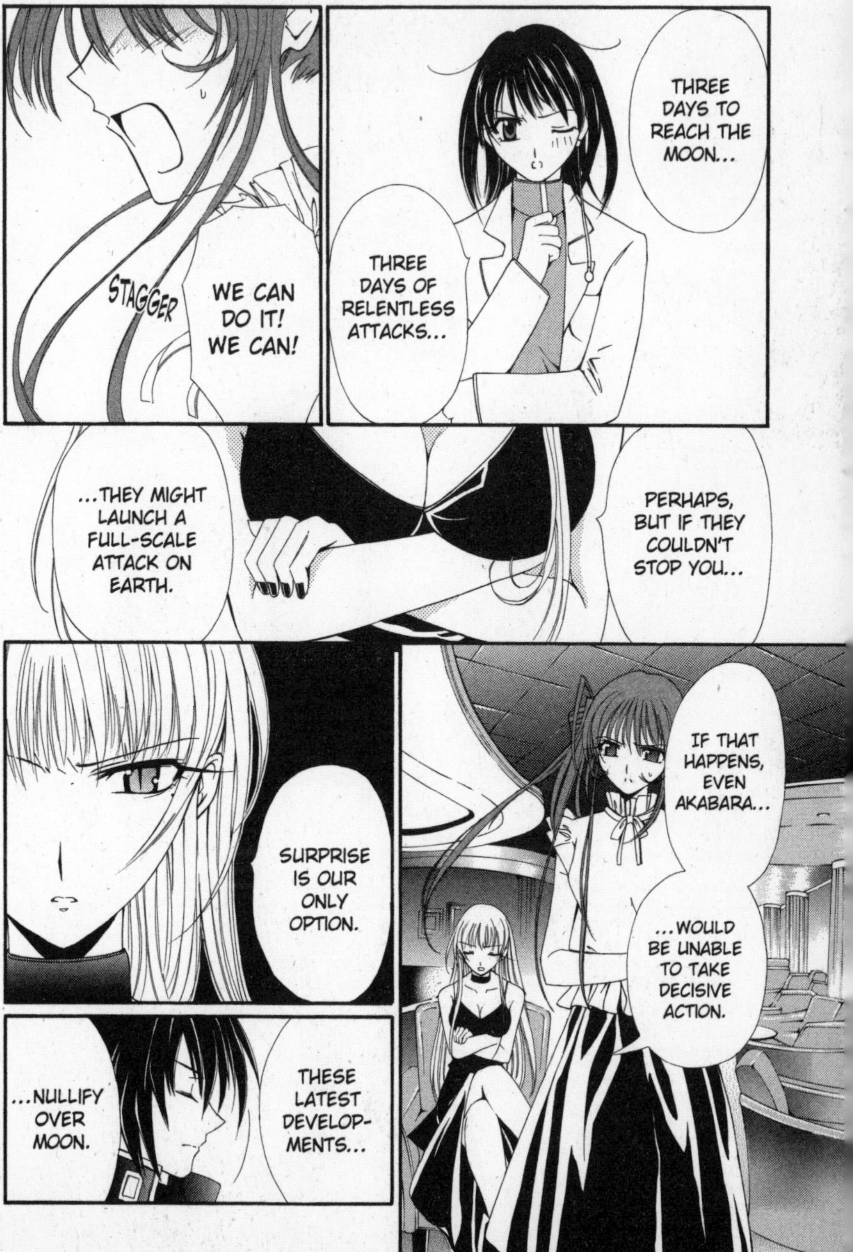
THREE DAYS TO REACH THE MOON...
THREE DAYS OF RELENTLESS ATTACKS...
STAGGER
WE CAN DO IT! WE CAN!
PERHAPS, BUT IF THEY COULDN'T STOP YOU...
...THEY MIGHT LAUNCH A FULL-SCALE ATTACK ON EARTH.
IF THAT HAPPENS, EVEN AKABARA...
...WOULD BE UNABLE TO TAKE DECISIVE ACTION.
SURPRISE IS OUR ONLY OPTION.
THESE LATEST DEVELOP-MENTS...
...NULLIFY OVER MOON.

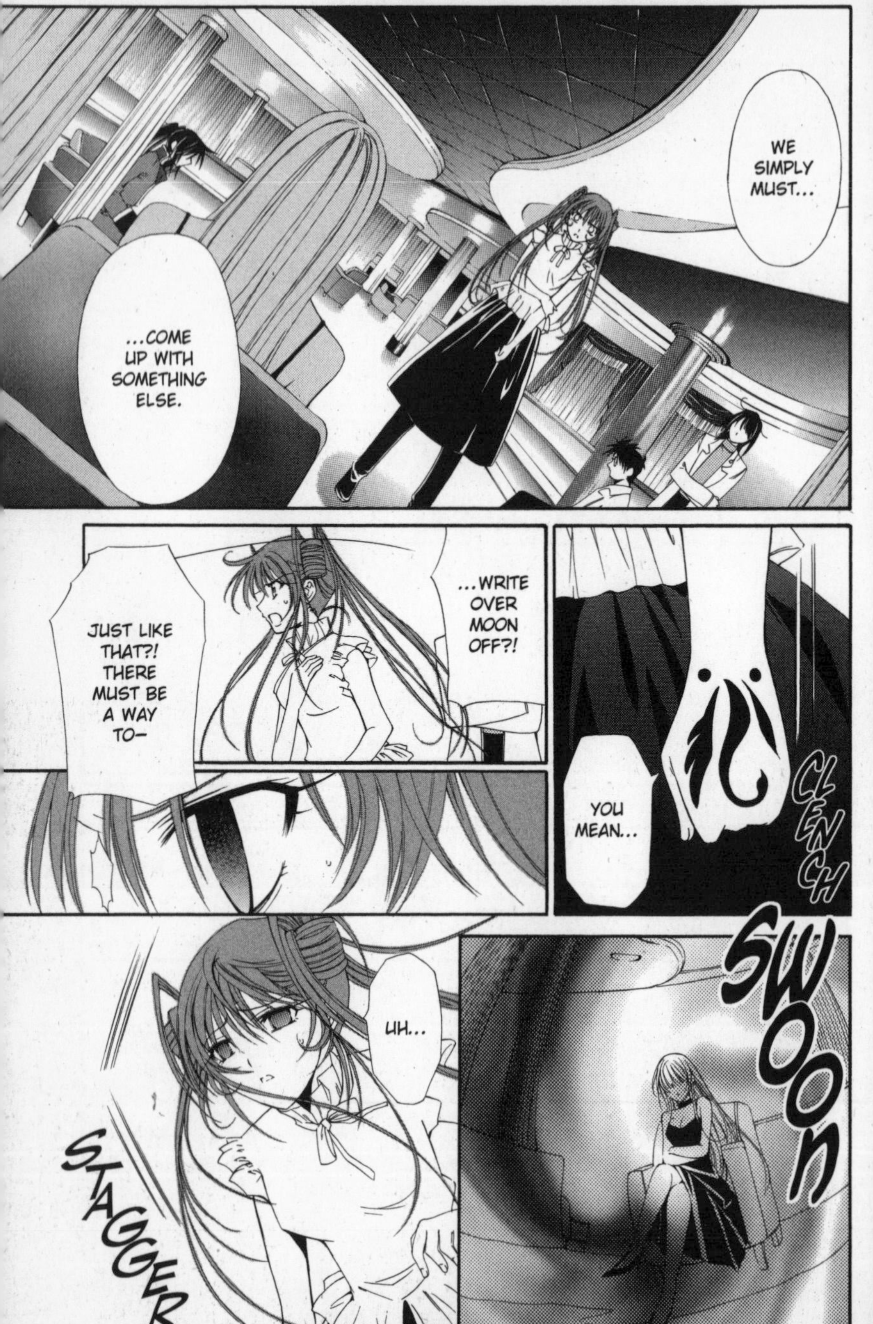
WE SIMPLY MUST...
...COME UP WITH SOMETHING ELSE.
YOU MEAN...
CLENCH
...WRITE OVER MOON OFF?!
JUST LIKE THAT?! THERE MUST BE A WAY TO—
SWOOON
UH...
STAGGER

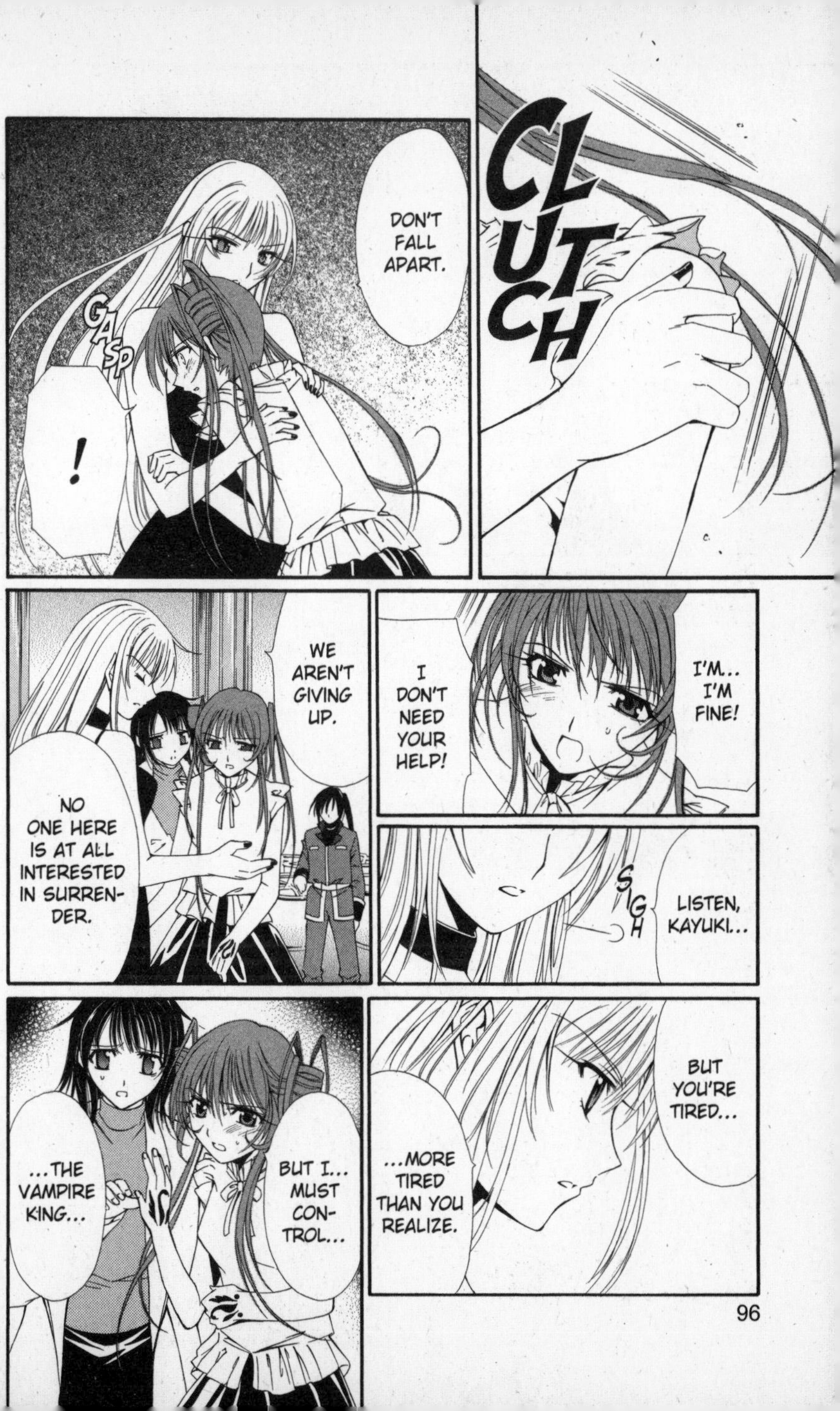
CLUTCH
DON'T FALL APART.
GASP
!
I'M... I'M FINE!
I DON'T NEED YOUR HELP!
SIGH
LISTEN, KAYUKI...
WE AREN'T GIVING UP.
NO ONE HERE IS AT ALL INTERESTED IN SURRENDER.
BUT YOU'RE TIRED...
...MORE TIRED THAN YOU REALIZE.
BUT I... MUST CONTROL...
...THE VAMPIRE KING...

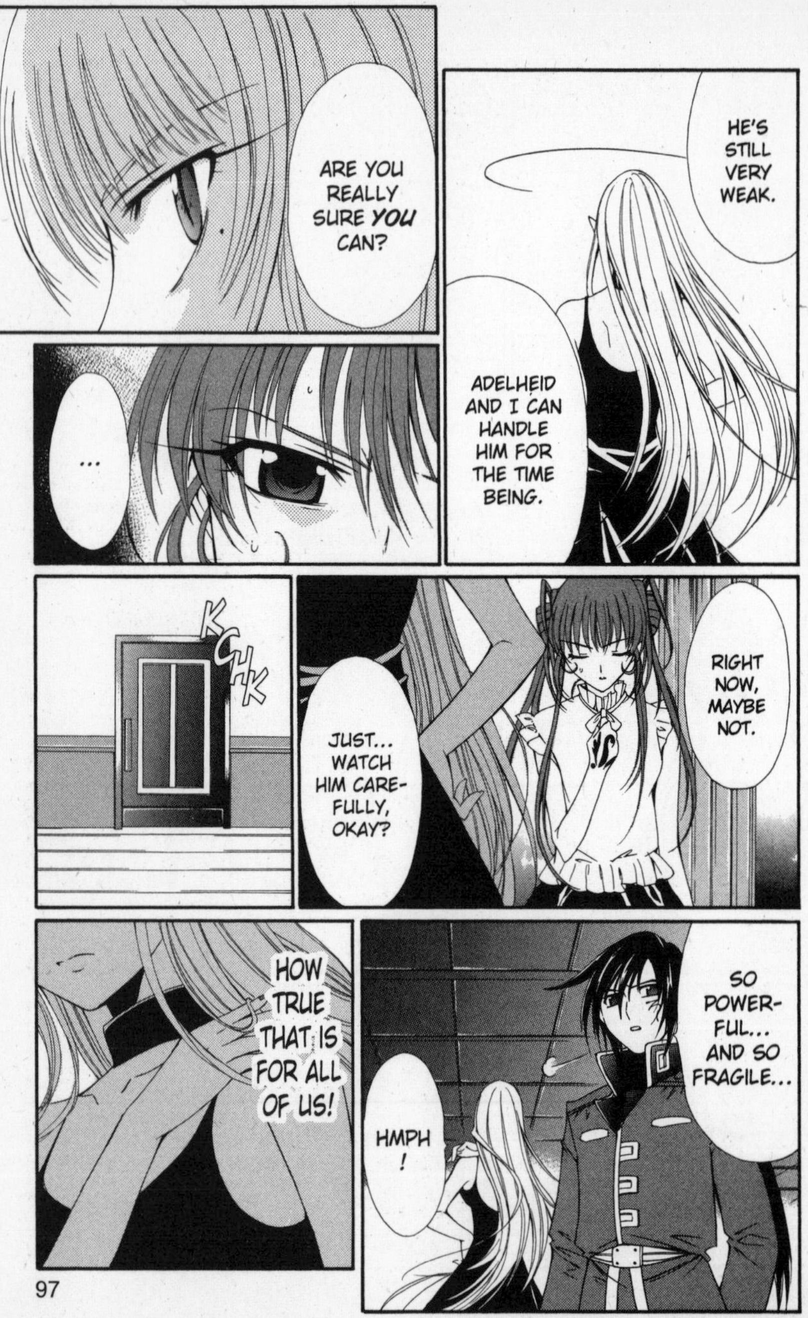
HE'S STILL VERY WEAK.
ADELHEID AND I CAN HANDLE HIM FOR THE TIME BEING.
ARE YOU REALLY SURE *YOU* CAN?
...
RIGHT NOW, MAYBE NOT.
JUST... WATCH HIM CAREFULLY, OKAY?
KCHK
SO POWERFUL... AND SO FRAGILE...
HMPH!
HOW TRUE THAT IS FOR ALL OF US!

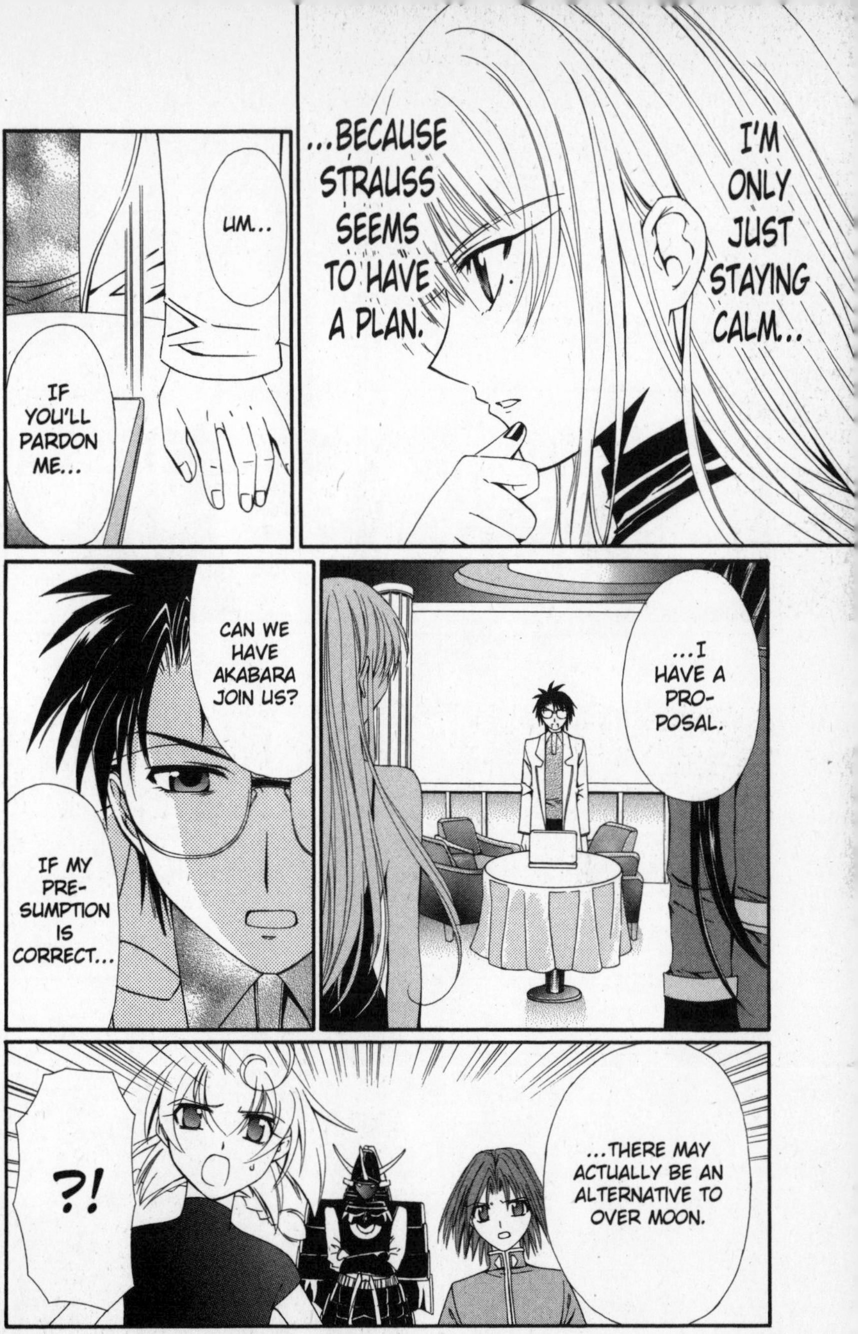
I'M ONLY JUST STAYING CALM...
...BECAUSE STRAUSS SEEMS TO HAVE A PLAN.
UM...
IF YOU'LL PARDON ME...
...I HAVE A PROPOSAL.
CAN WE HAVE AKABARA JOIN US?
IF MY PRESUMPTION IS CORRECT...
...THERE MAY ACTUALLY BE AN ALTERNATIVE TO OVER MOON.
?!

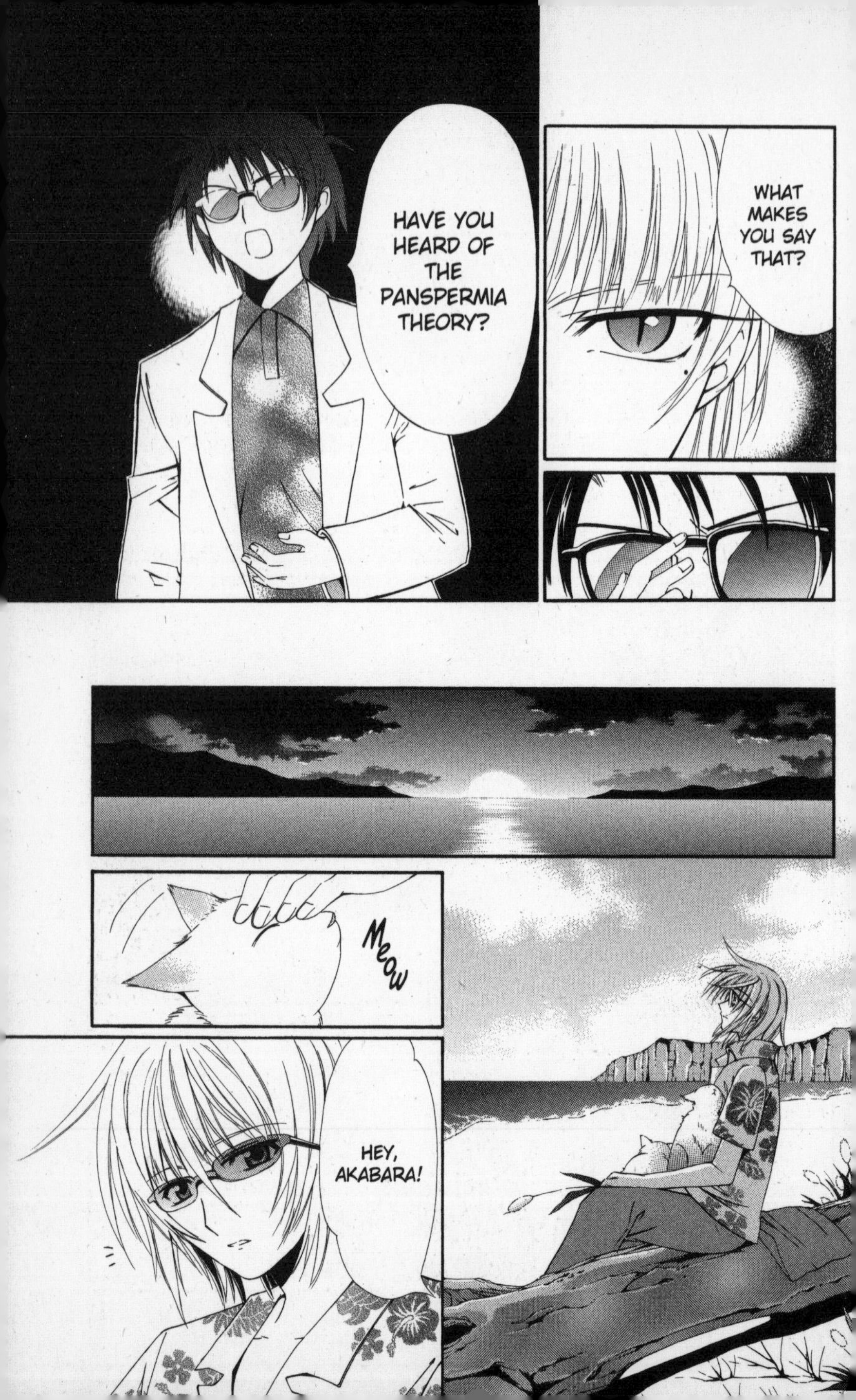
WHAT MAKES YOU SAY THAT?
HAVE YOU HEARD OF THE PANSPERMIA THEORY?
Meow
HEY, AKABARA!

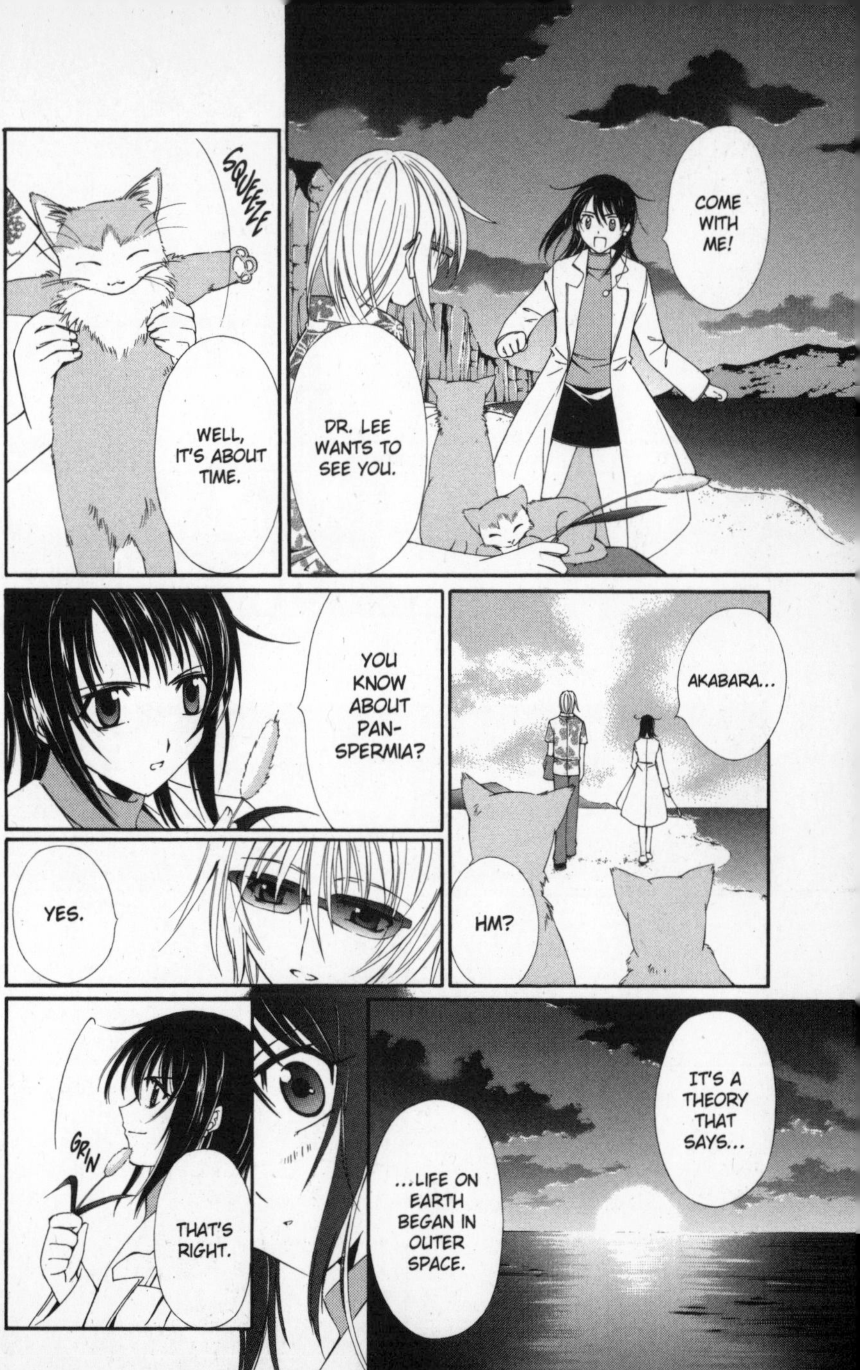
COME WITH ME!
DR. LEE WANTS TO SEE YOU.
SQUEEZE
WELL, IT'S ABOUT TIME.
AKABARA...
HM?
YOU KNOW ABOUT PAN-SPERMIA?
YES.
IT'S A THEORY THAT SAYS...
...LIFE ON EARTH BEGAN IN OUTER SPACE.
GRIN
THAT'S RIGHT.

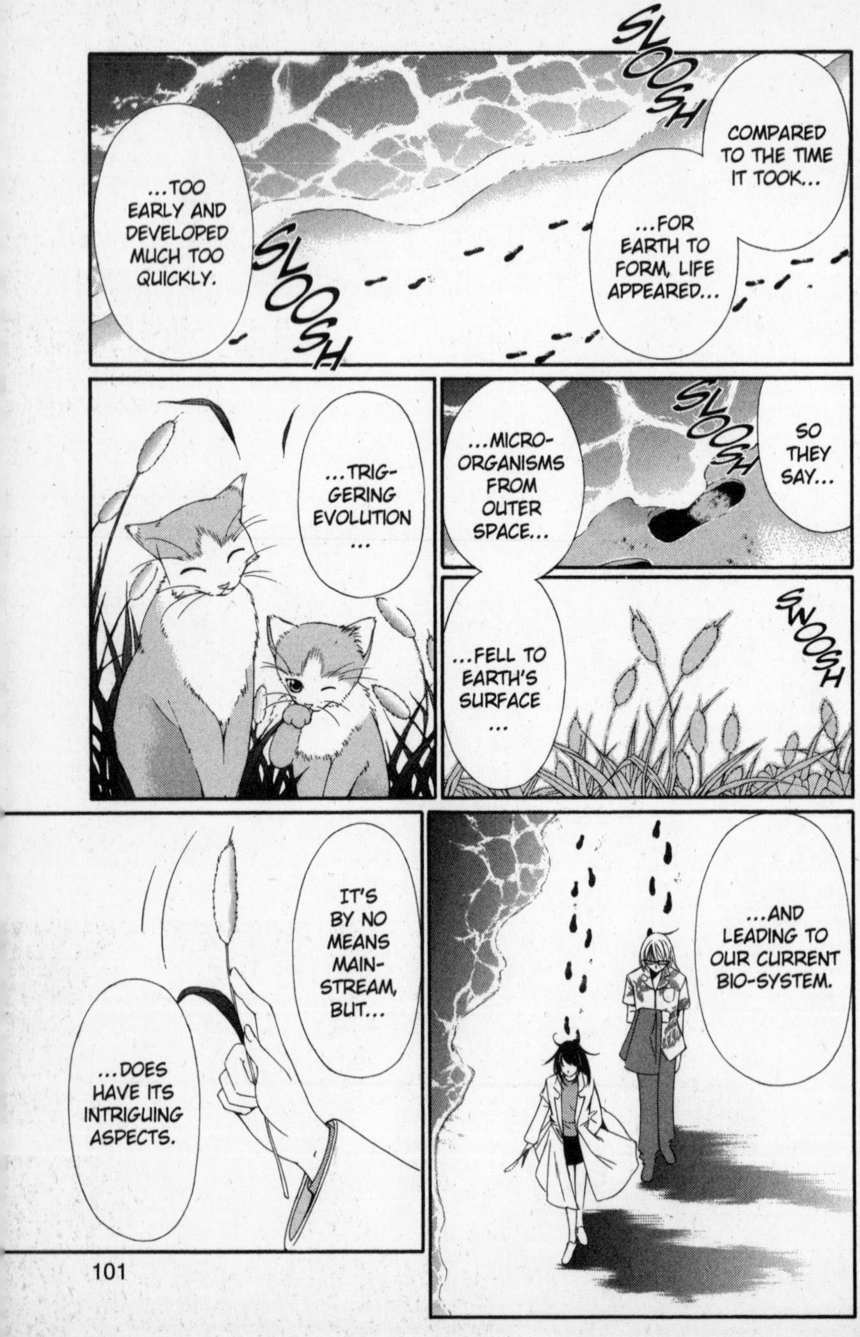
SLOOSH
COMPARED TO THE TIME IT TOOK...
...FOR EARTH TO FORM, LIFE APPEARED...
SLOOSH
...TOO EARLY AND DEVELOPED MUCH TOO QUICKLY.
SO THEY SAY...
SLOOSH
...MICRO-ORGANISMS FROM OUTER SPACE...
SWOOSH
...FELL TO EARTH'S SURFACE...
...TRIG-GERING EVOLUTION...
...AND LEADING TO OUR CURRENT BIO-SYSTEM.
IT'S BY NO MEANS MAIN-STREAM, BUT...
...DOES HAVE ITS INTRIGUING ASPECTS.

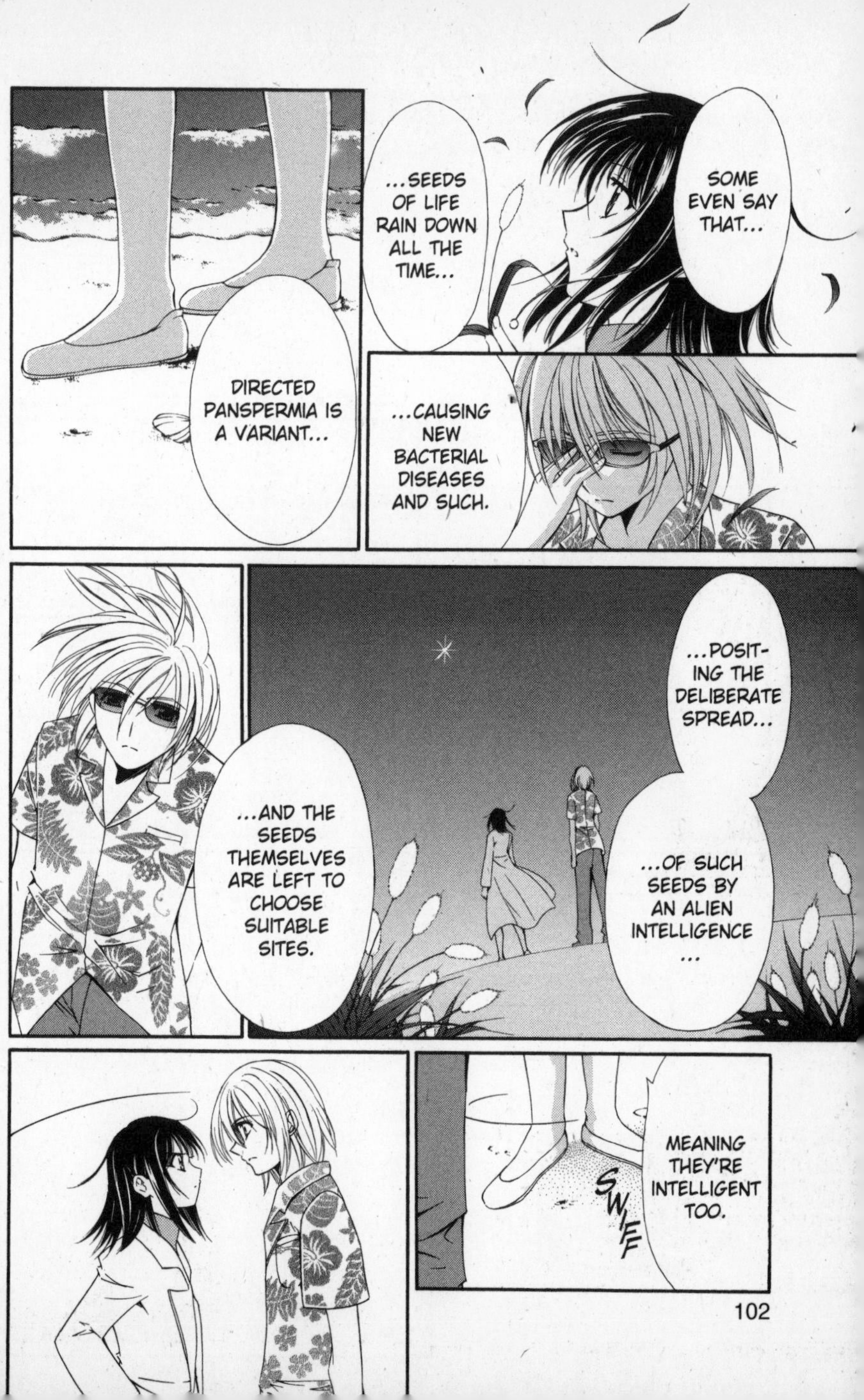
SOME EVEN SAY THAT...
...SEEDS OF LIFE RAIN DOWN ALL THE TIME...
...CAUSING NEW BACTERIAL DISEASES AND SUCH.
DIRECTED PANSPERMIA IS A VARIANT...
...POSIT-ING THE DELIBERATE SPREAD...
...OF SUCH SEEDS BY AN ALIEN INTELLIGENCE...
...AND THE SEEDS THEMSELVES ARE LEFT TO CHOOSE SUITABLE SITES.
SWIFF
MEANING THEY'RE INTELLIGENT TOO.

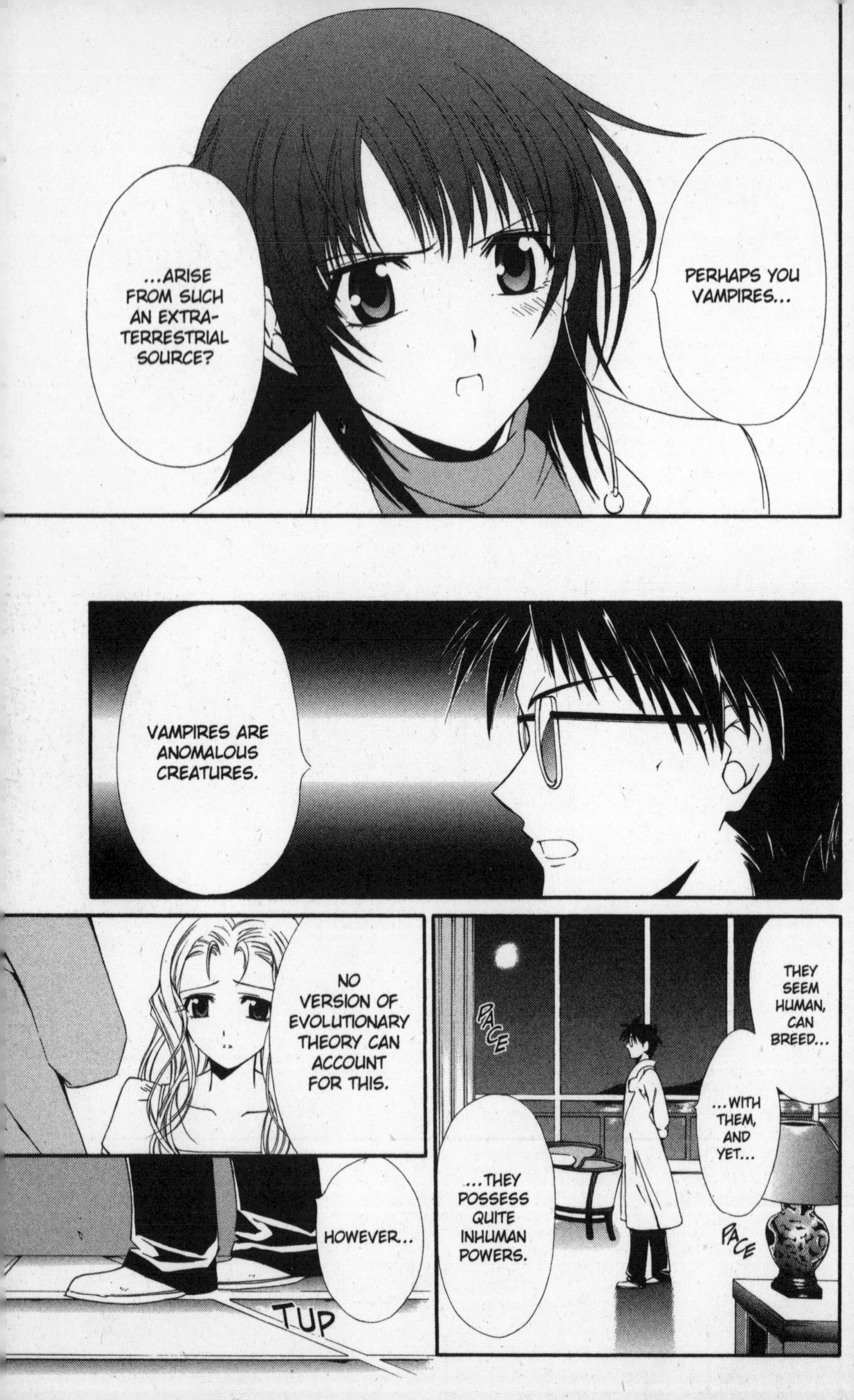
PERHAPS YOU VAMPIRES...
...ARISE FROM SUCH AN EXTRA-TERRESTRIAL SOURCE?
VAMPIRES ARE ANOMALOUS CREATURES.
THEY SEEM HUMAN, CAN BREED...
...WITH THEM, AND YET...
PACE
PACE
...THEY POSSESS QUITE INHUMAN POWERS.
NO VERSION OF EVOLUTIONARY THEORY CAN ACCOUNT FOR THIS.
HOWEVER...
TUP

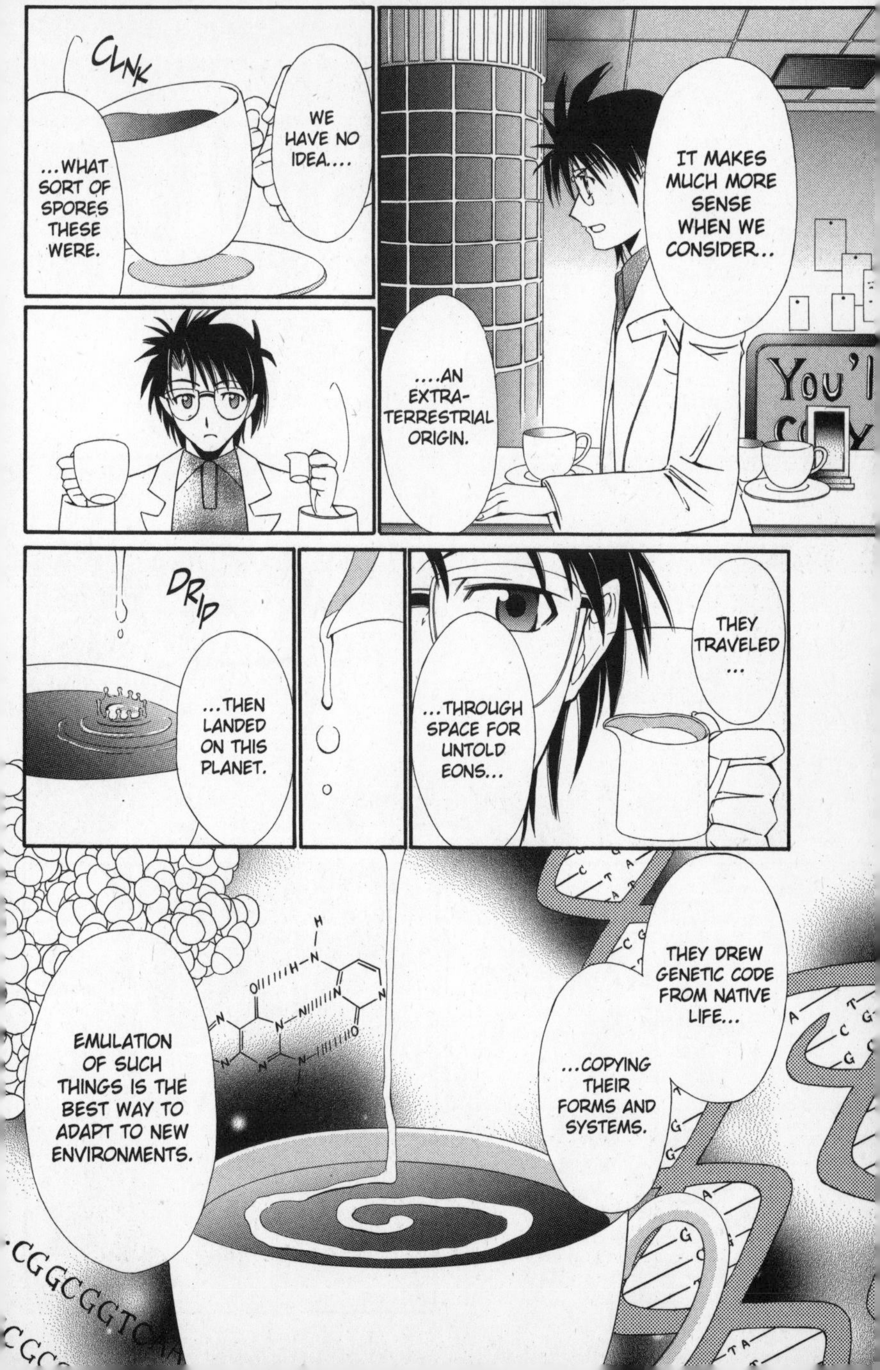
IT MAKES MUCH MORE SENSE WHEN WE CONSIDER...
....AN EXTRA-TERRESTRIAL ORIGIN.
CLNK
WE HAVE NO IDEA....
...WHAT SORT OF SPORES THESE WERE.
THEY TRAVELED...
...THROUGH SPACE FOR UNTOLD EONS...
DRIP
...THEN LANDED ON THIS PLANET.
THEY DREW GENETIC CODE FROM NATIVE LIFE...
...COPYING THEIR FORMS AND SYSTEMS.
EMULATION OF SUCH THINGS IS THE BEST WAY TO ADAPT TO NEW ENVIRONMENTS.

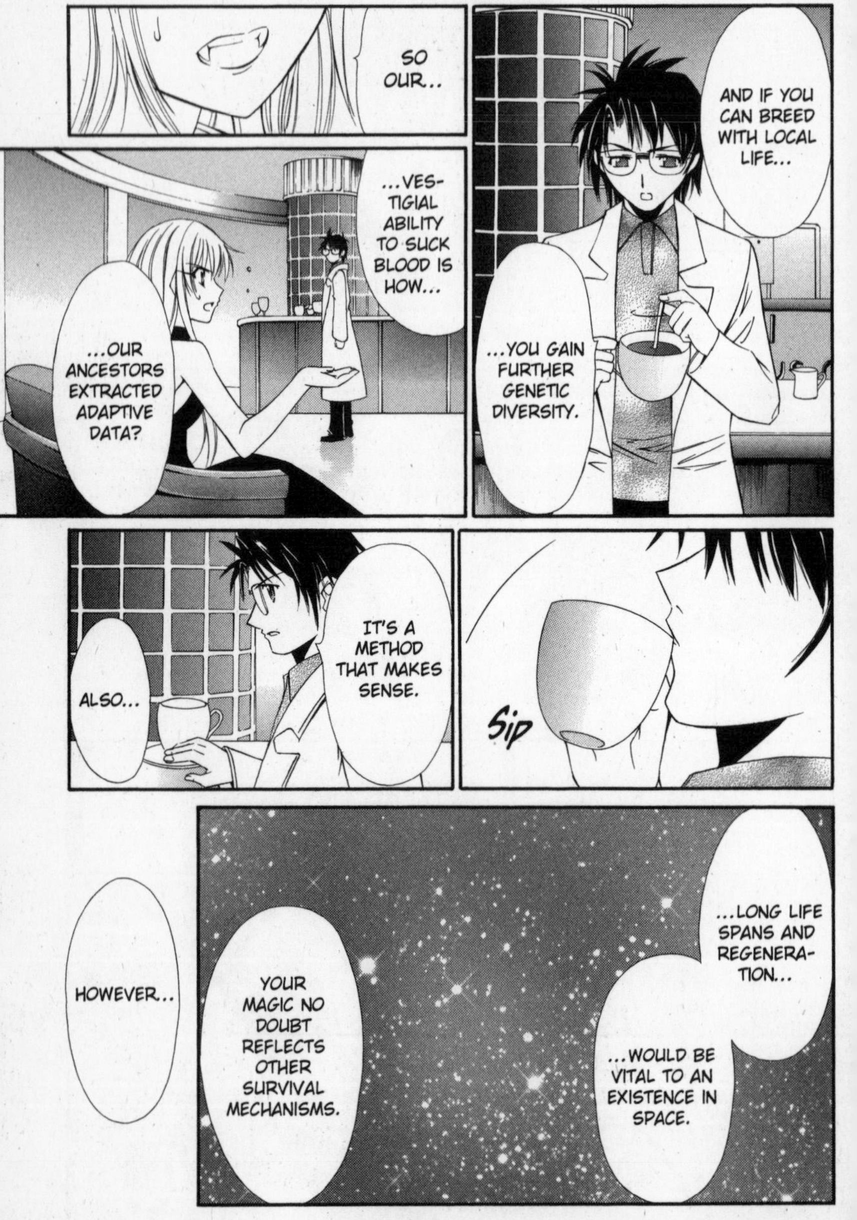
AND IF YOU CAN BREED WITH LOCAL LIFE...
...YOU GAIN FURTHER GENETIC DIVERSITY.
SO OUR...
...VES-TIGIAL ABILITY TO SUCK BLOOD IS HOW...
...OUR ANCESTORS EXTRACTED ADAPTIVE DATA?
Sip
IT'S A METHOD THAT MAKES SENSE.
ALSO...
...LONG LIFE SPANS AND REGENERA-TION...
...WOULD BE VITAL TO AN EXISTENCE IN SPACE.
YOUR MAGIC NO DOUBT REFLECTS OTHER SURVIVAL MECHANISMS.
HOWEVER...

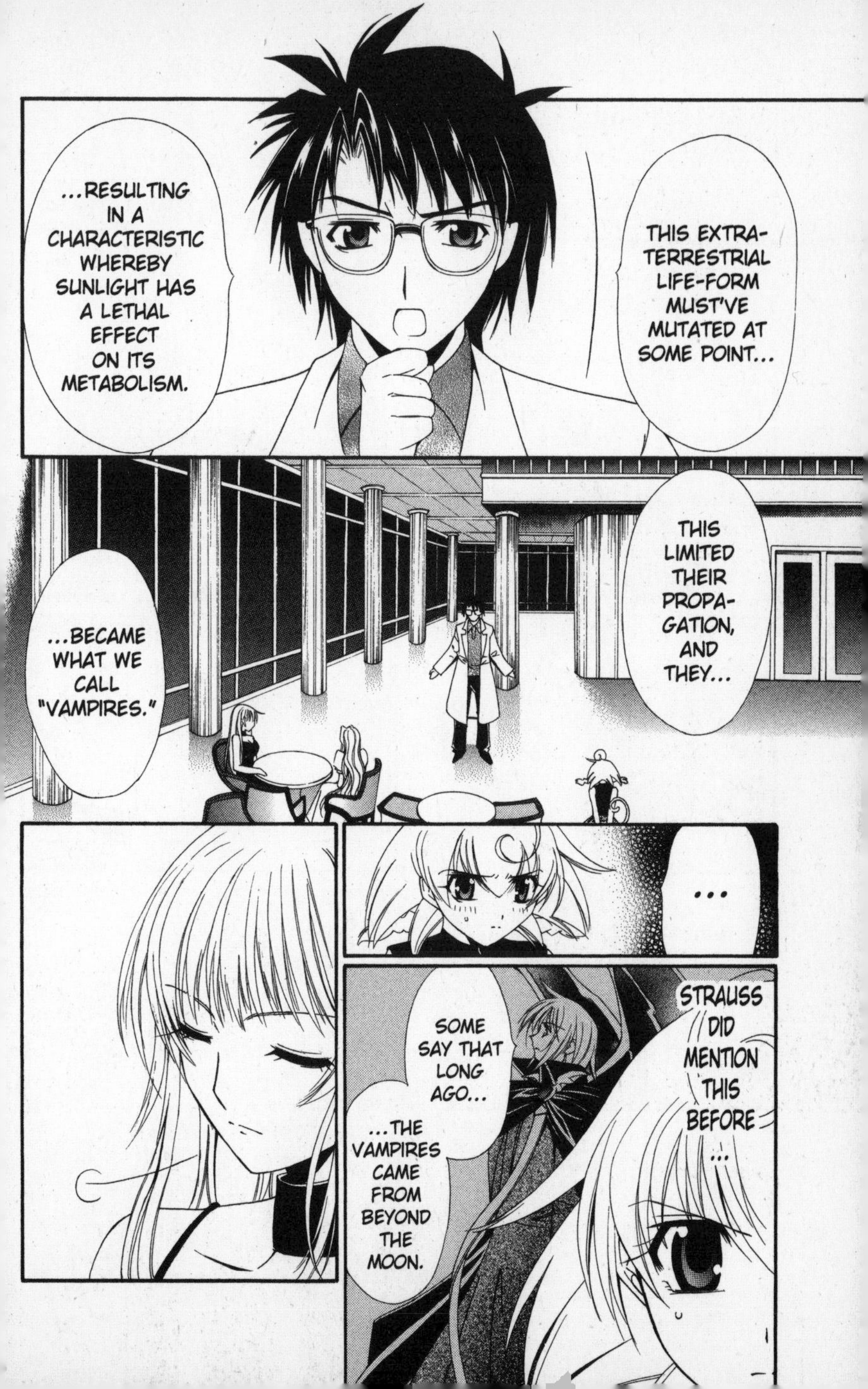
THIS EXTRA-TERRESTRIAL LIFE-FORM MUST'VE MUTATED AT SOME POINT...
...RESULTING IN A CHARACTERISTIC WHEREBY SUNLIGHT HAS A LETHAL EFFECT ON ITS METABOLISM.
THIS LIMITED THEIR PROPAGATION, AND THEY...
...BECAME WHAT WE CALL "VAMPIRES."
...
STRAUSS DID MENTION THIS BEFORE...
SOME SAY THAT LONG AGO...
...THE VAMPIRES CAME FROM BEYOND THE MOON.

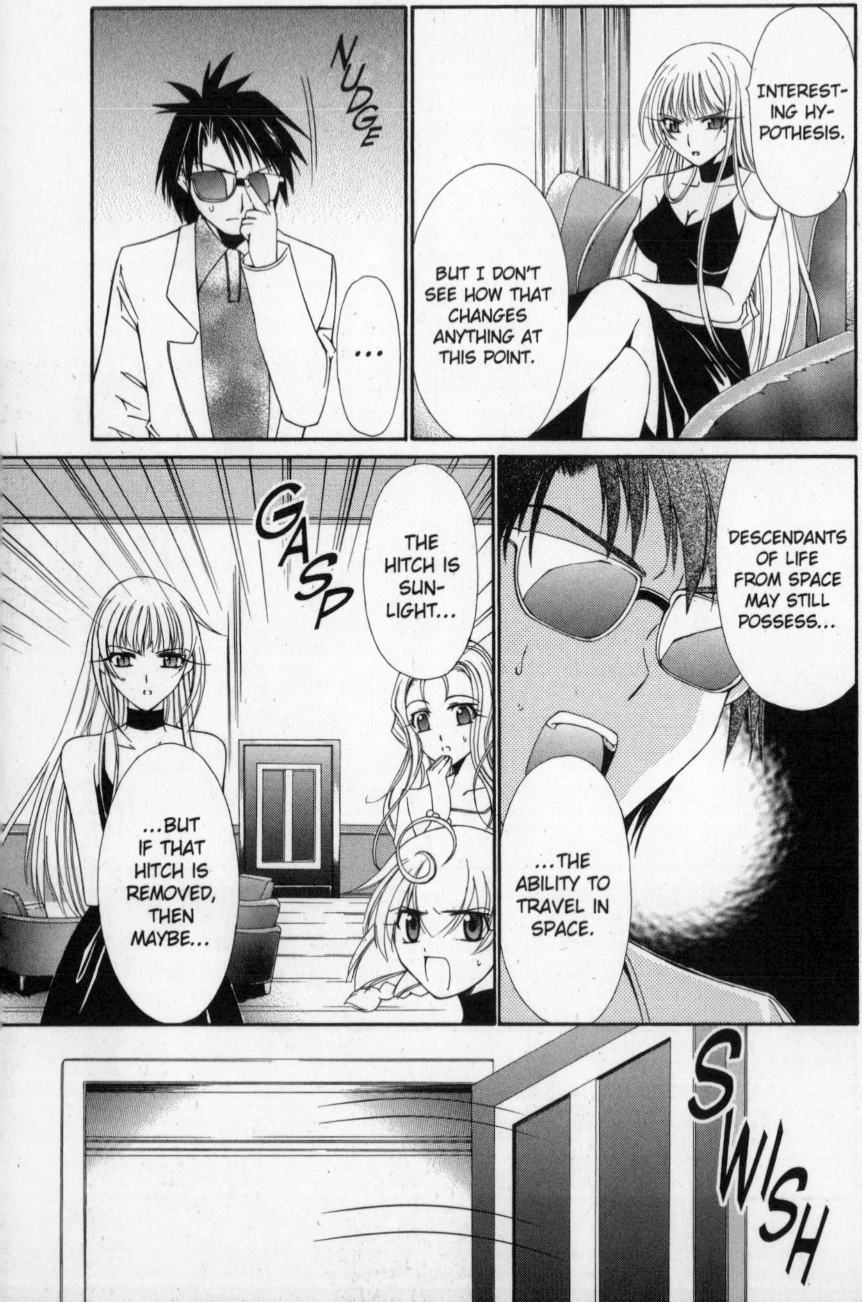
INTEREST-ING HY-POTHESIS.
BUT I DON'T SEE HOW THAT CHANGES ANYTHING AT THIS POINT.
NUDGE
...
DESCENDANTS OF LIFE FROM SPACE MAY STILL POSSESS...
...THE ABILITY TO TRAVEL IN SPACE.
THE HITCH IS SUN-LIGHT...
GASP
...BUT IF THAT HITCH IS REMOVED, THEN MAYBE...
SWISH

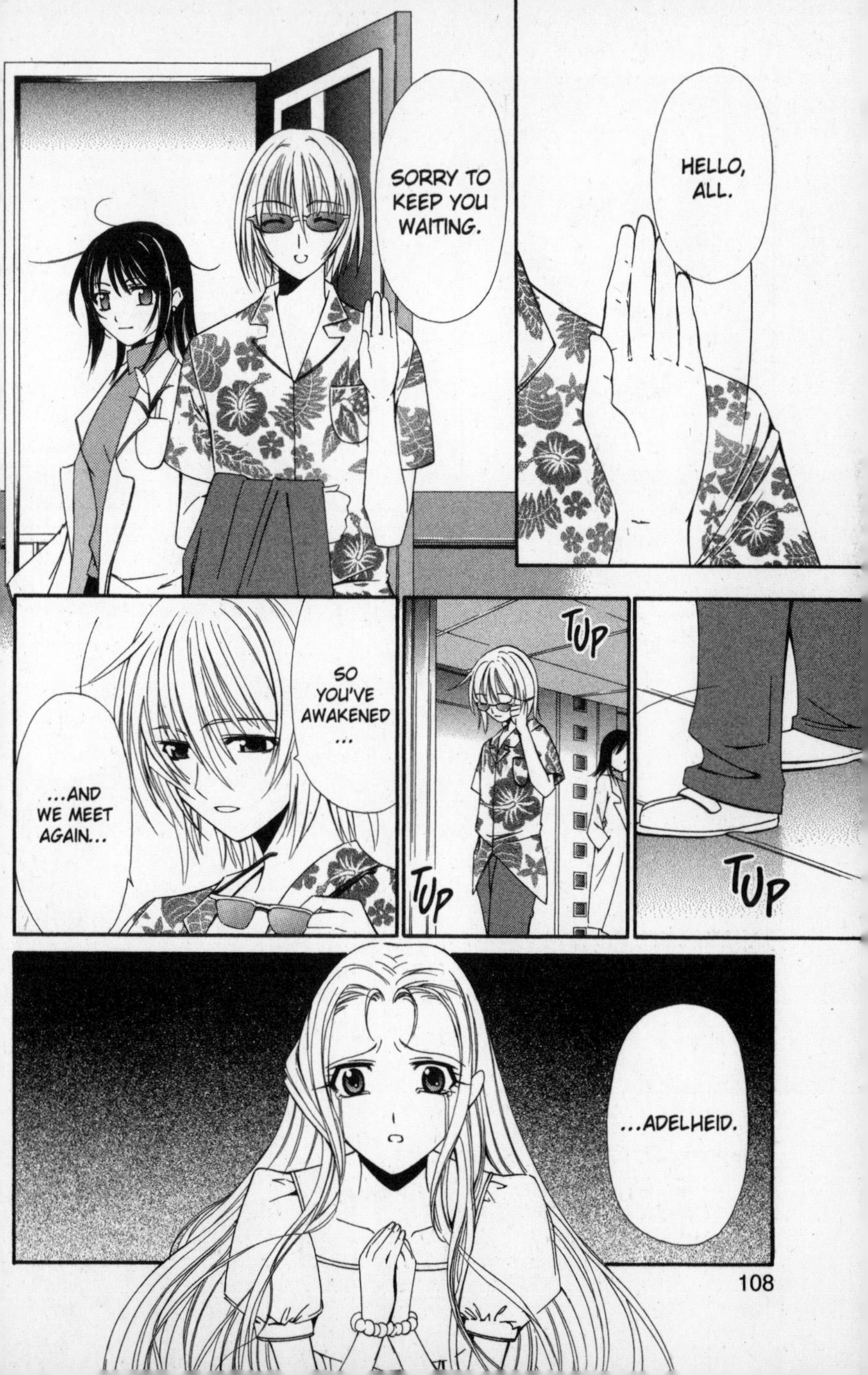
HELLO, ALL.
SORRY TO KEEP YOU WAITING.
TUP
TUP
TUP
SO YOU'VE AWAKENED ...
...AND WE MEET AGAIN...
...ADELHEID.

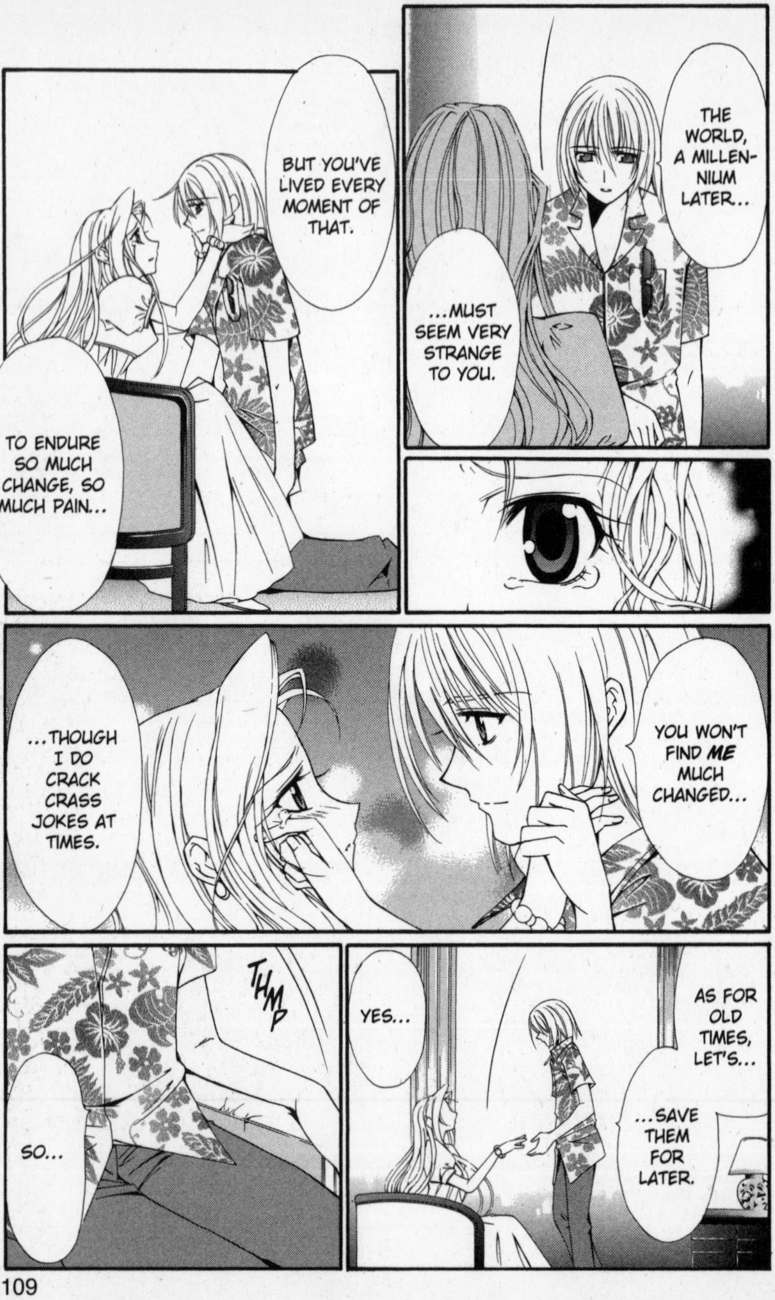
THE WORLD, A MILLENNIUM LATER...
...MUST SEEM VERY STRANGE TO YOU.
BUT YOU'VE LIVED EVERY MOMENT OF THAT.
TO ENDURE SO MUCH CHANGE, SO MUCH PAIN...
YOU WON'T FIND *ME* MUCH CHANGED...
...THOUGH I DO CRACK CRASS JOKES AT TIMES.
AS FOR OLD TIMES, LET'S...
...SAVE THEM FOR LATER.
YES...
THMP
SO...

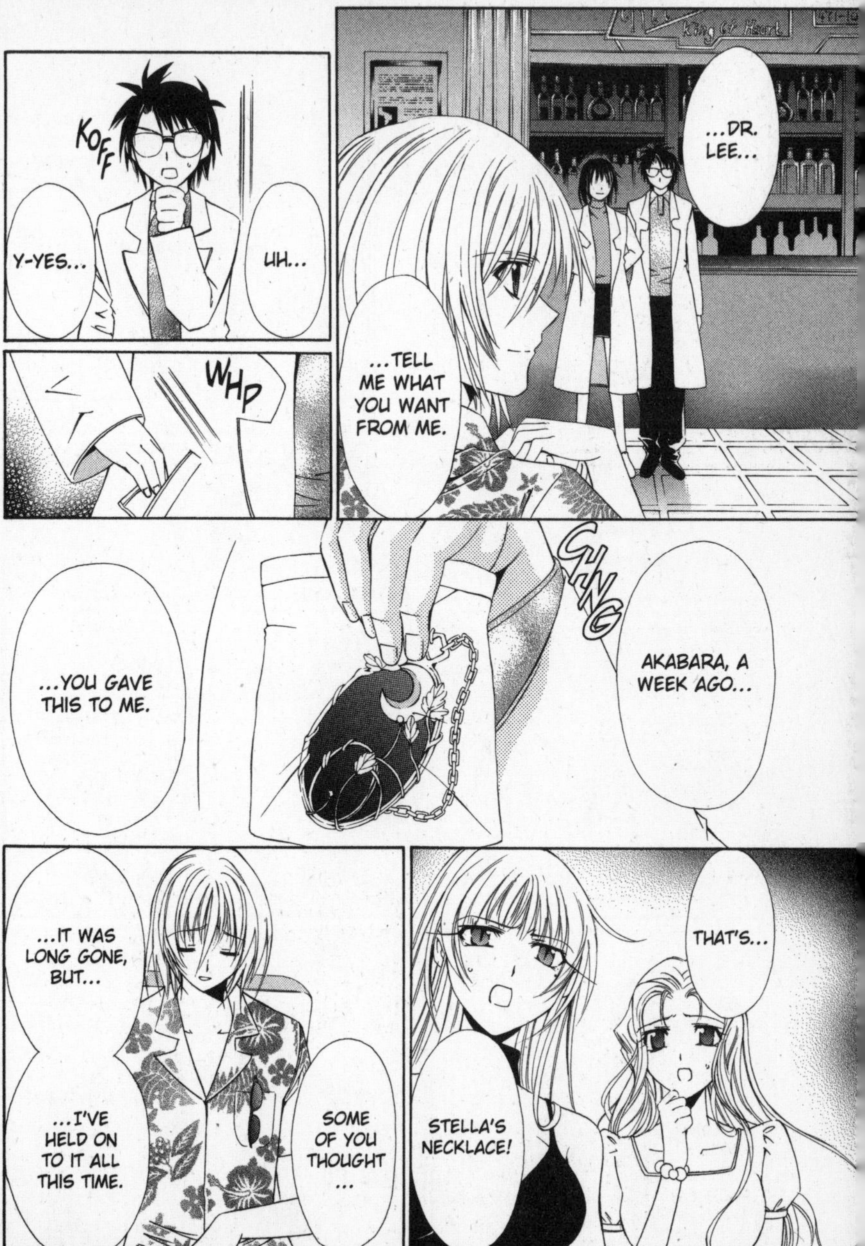
...DR. LEE...
...TELL ME WHAT YOU WANT FROM ME.
UH...
KOFF
Y-YES...
WHP
CHING
AKABARA, A WEEK AGO...
...YOU GAVE THIS TO ME.
THAT'S...
STELLA'S NECKLACE!
SOME OF YOU THOUGHT ...
...IT WAS LONG GONE, BUT...
...I'VE HELD ON TO IT ALL THIS TIME.

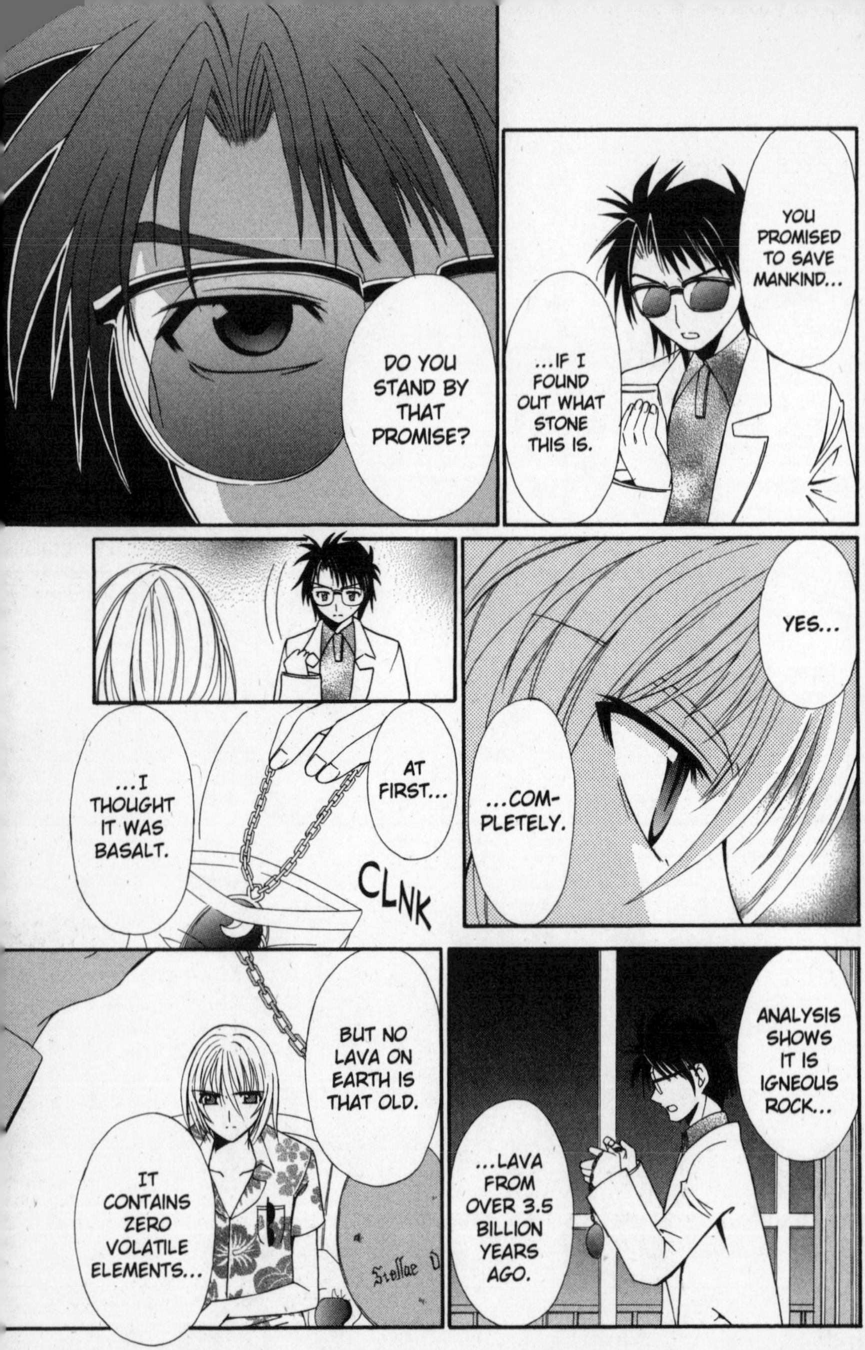
YOU PROMISED TO SAVE MANKIND...
...IF I FOUND OUT WHAT STONE THIS IS.
DO YOU STAND BY THAT PROMISE?
YES...
...COM-PLETELY.
AT FIRST...
...I THOUGHT IT WAS BASALT.
CLNK
ANALYSIS SHOWS IT IS IGNEOUS ROCK...
...LAVA FROM OVER 3.5 BILLION YEARS AGO.
BUT NO LAVA ON EARTH IS THAT OLD.
IT CONTAINS ZERO VOLATILE ELEMENTS...

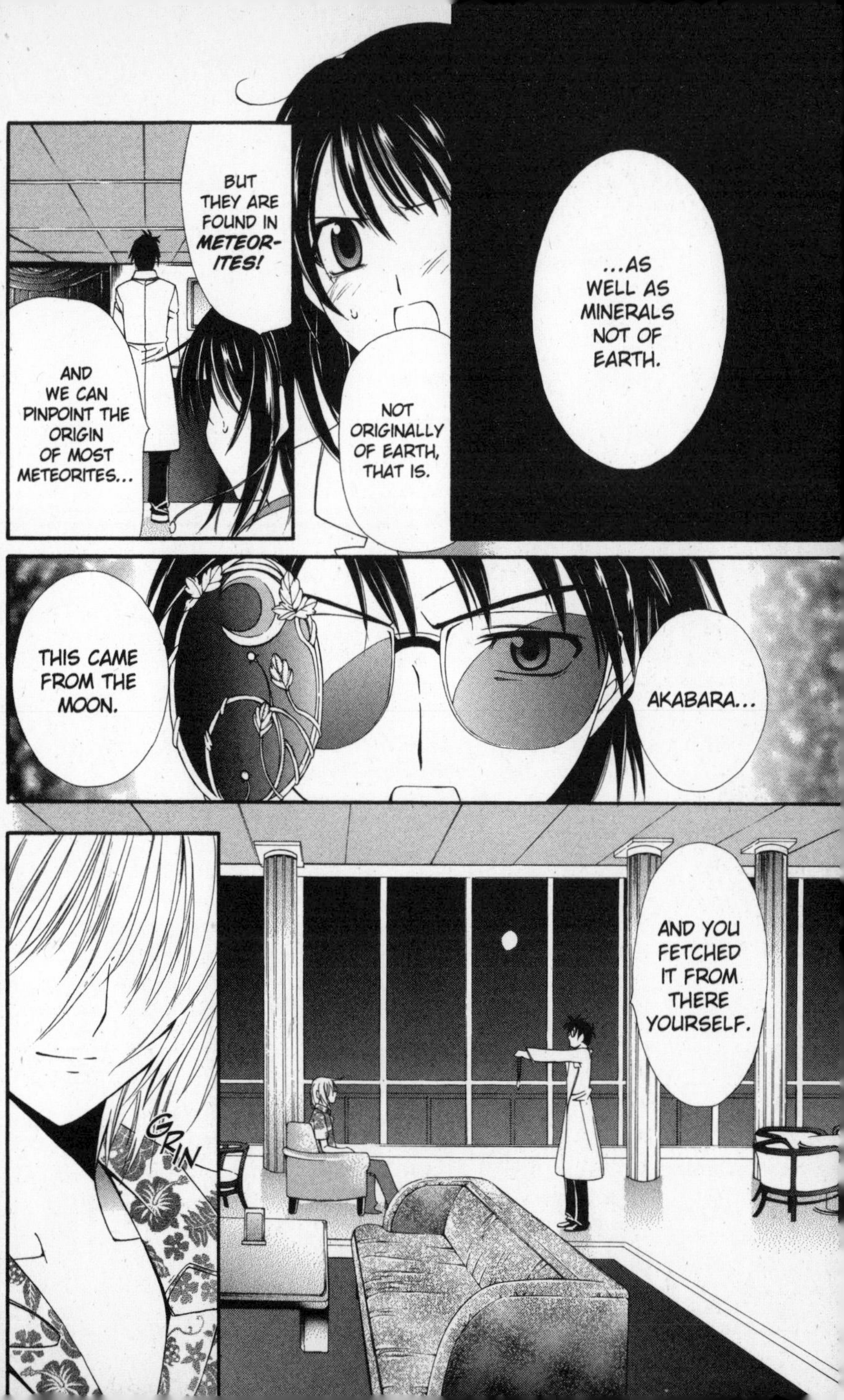
...AS WELL AS MINERALS NOT OF EARTH.
NOT ORIGINALLY OF EARTH, THAT IS.
BUT THEY ARE FOUND IN *METEORITES!*
AND WE CAN PINPOINT THE ORIGIN OF MOST METEORITES...
AKABARA...
THIS CAME FROM THE MOON.
AND YOU FETCHED IT FROM THERE YOURSELF.
GRIN

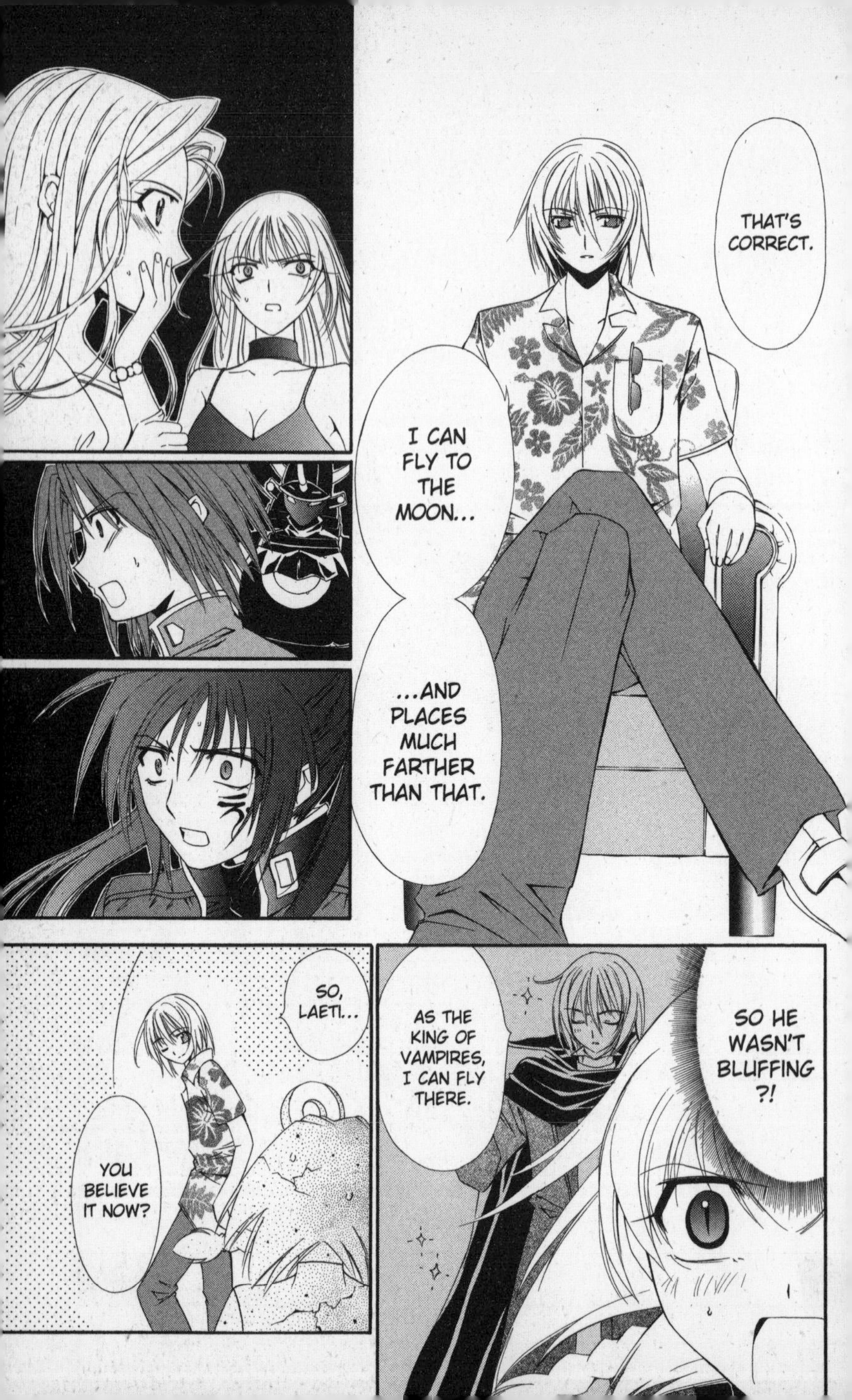
THAT'S CORRECT.
I CAN FLY TO THE MOON...
...AND PLACES MUCH FARTHER THAN THAT.
AS THE KING OF VAMPIRES, I CAN FLY THERE.
SO HE WASN'T BLUFFING?!
SO, LAETI...
YOU BELIEVE IT NOW?

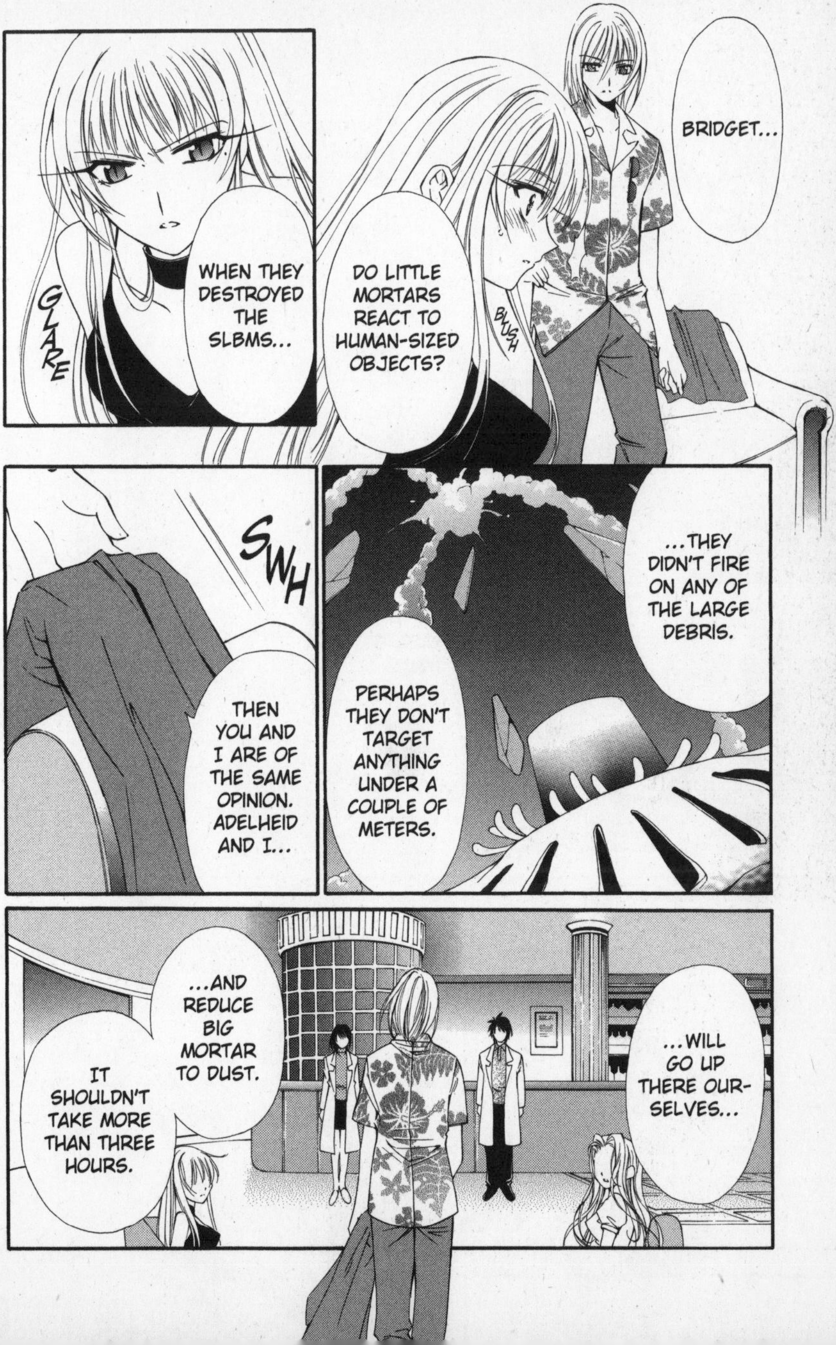
BRIDGET...
DO LITTLE MORTARS REACT TO HUMAN-SIZED OBJECTS?
BLUSH
WHEN THEY DESTROYED THE SLBMS...
GLARE
...THEY DIDN'T FIRE ON ANY OF THE LARGE DEBRIS.
PERHAPS THEY DON'T TARGET ANYTHING UNDER A COUPLE OF METERS.
SWH
THEN YOU AND I ARE OF THE SAME OPINION. ADELHEID AND I...
...WILL GO UP THERE OURSELVES...
...AND REDUCE BIG MORTAR TO DUST.
IT SHOULDN'T TAKE MORE THAN THREE HOURS.

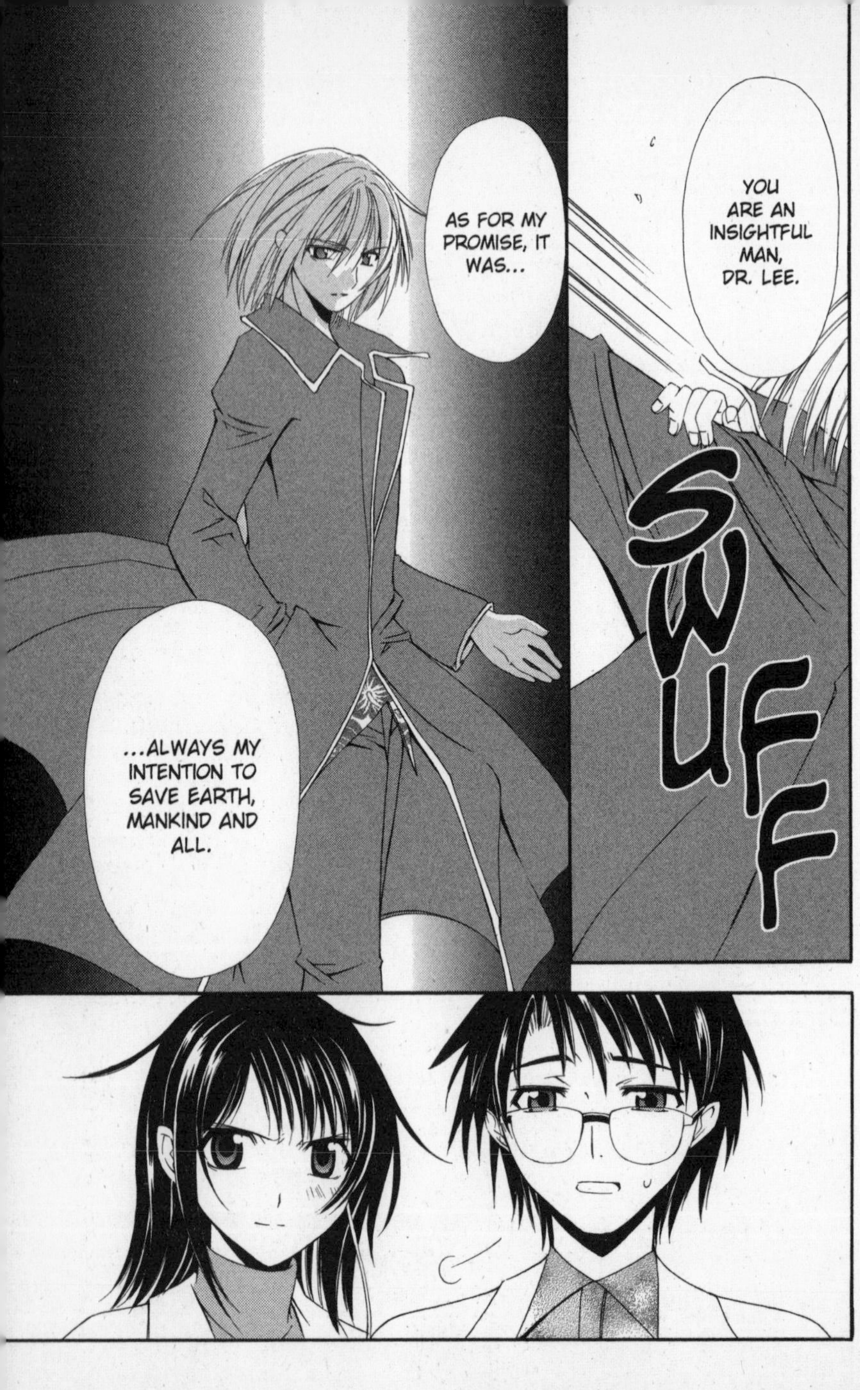
YOU ARE AN INSIGHTFUL MAN, DR. LEE.
SWUFF
AS FOR MY PROMISE, IT WAS...
...ALWAYS MY INTENTION TO SAVE EARTH, MANKIND AND ALL.

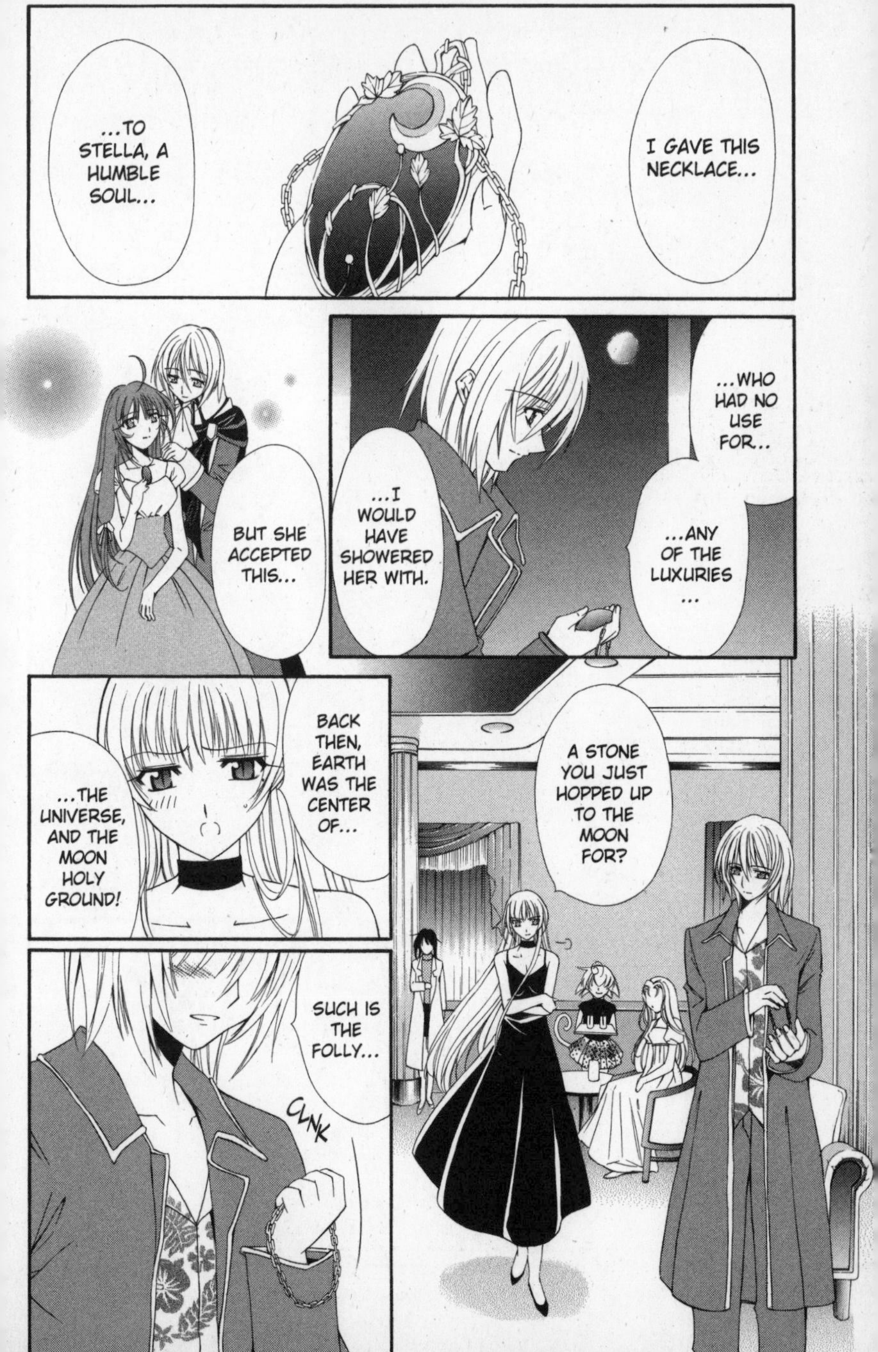
I GAVE THIS NECKLACE...
...TO STELLA, A HUMBLE SOUL...
...WHO HAD NO USE FOR...
...ANY OF THE LUXURIES ...
...I WOULD HAVE SHOWERED HER WITH.
BUT SHE ACCEPTED THIS...
A STONE YOU JUST HOPPED UP TO THE MOON FOR?
BACK THEN, EARTH WAS THE CENTER OF...
...THE UNIVERSE, AND THE MOON HOLY GROUND!
SUCH IS THE FOLLY...
CLNK

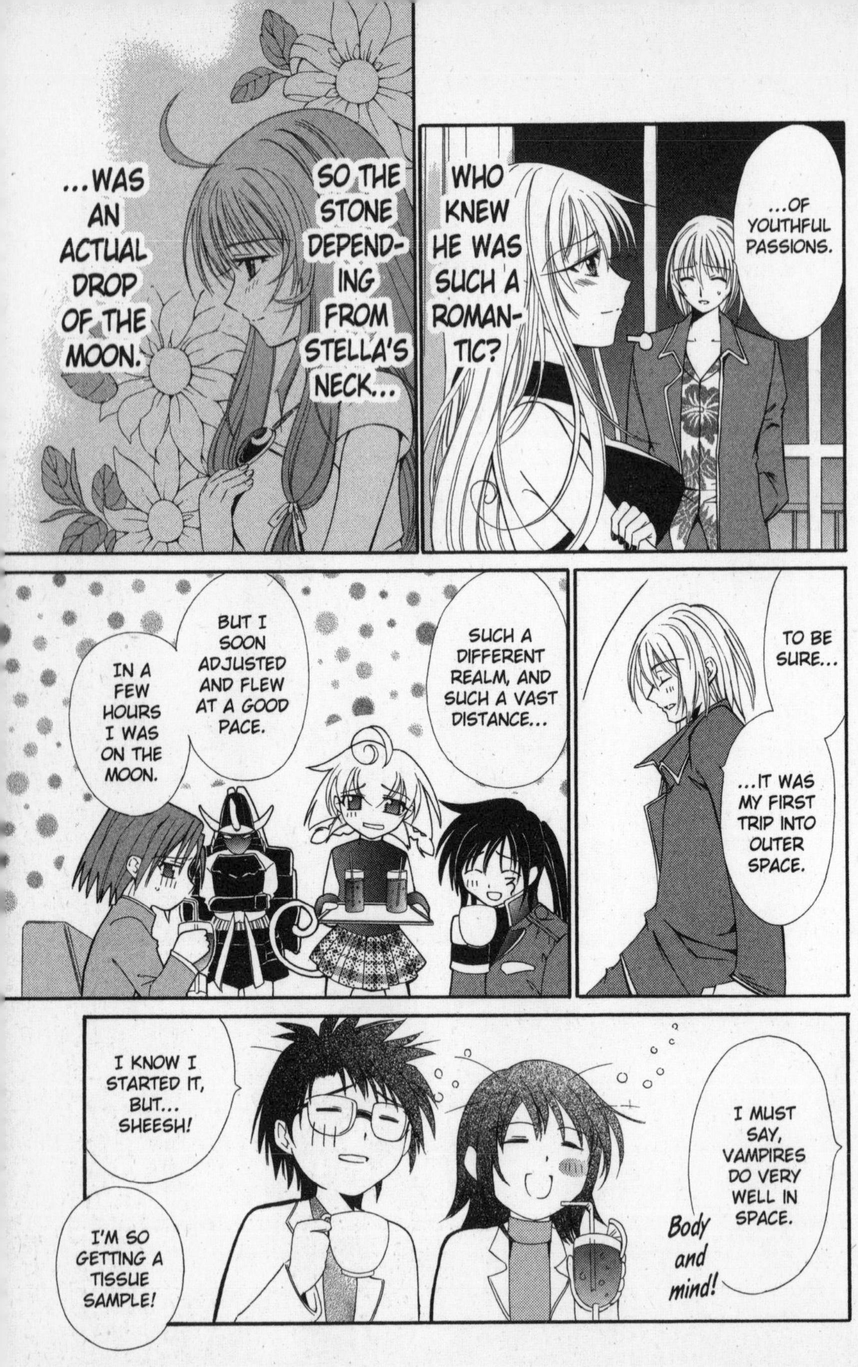
...OF YOUTHFUL PASSIONS.
WHO KNEW HE WAS SUCH A ROMAN-TIC?
SO THE STONE DEPEND-ING FROM STELLA'S NECK...
...WAS AN ACTUAL DROP OF THE MOON.
TO BE SURE...
...IT WAS MY FIRST TRIP INTO OUTER SPACE.
SUCH A DIFFERENT REALM, AND SUCH A VAST DISTANCE...
BUT I SOON ADJUSTED AND FLEW AT A GOOD PACE.
IN A FEW HOURS I WAS ON THE MOON.
I MUST SAY, VAMPIRES DO VERY WELL IN SPACE.
Body and mind!
I KNOW I STARTED IT, BUT... SHEESH!
I'M SO GETTING A TISSUE SAMPLE!

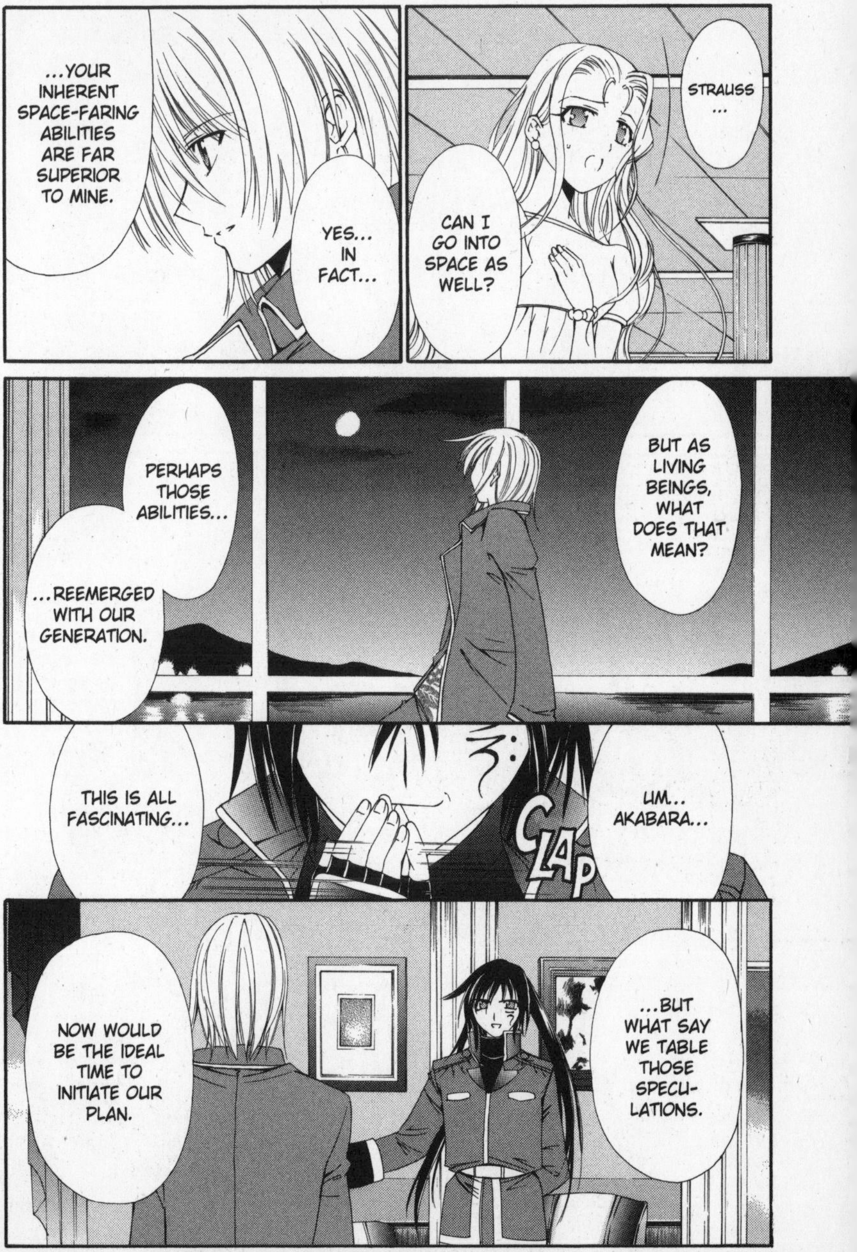
STRAUSS ...
CAN I GO INTO SPACE AS WELL?
YES... IN FACT...
...YOUR INHERENT SPACE-FARING ABILITIES ARE FAR SUPERIOR TO MINE.
BUT AS LIVING BEINGS, WHAT DOES THAT MEAN?
PERHAPS THOSE ABILITIES...
...REEMERGED WITH OUR GENERATION.
UM... AKABARA...
CLAP
THIS IS ALL FASCINATING...
...BUT WHAT SAY WE TABLE THOSE SPECU-LATIONS.
NOW WOULD BE THE IDEAL TIME TO INITIATE OUR PLAN.

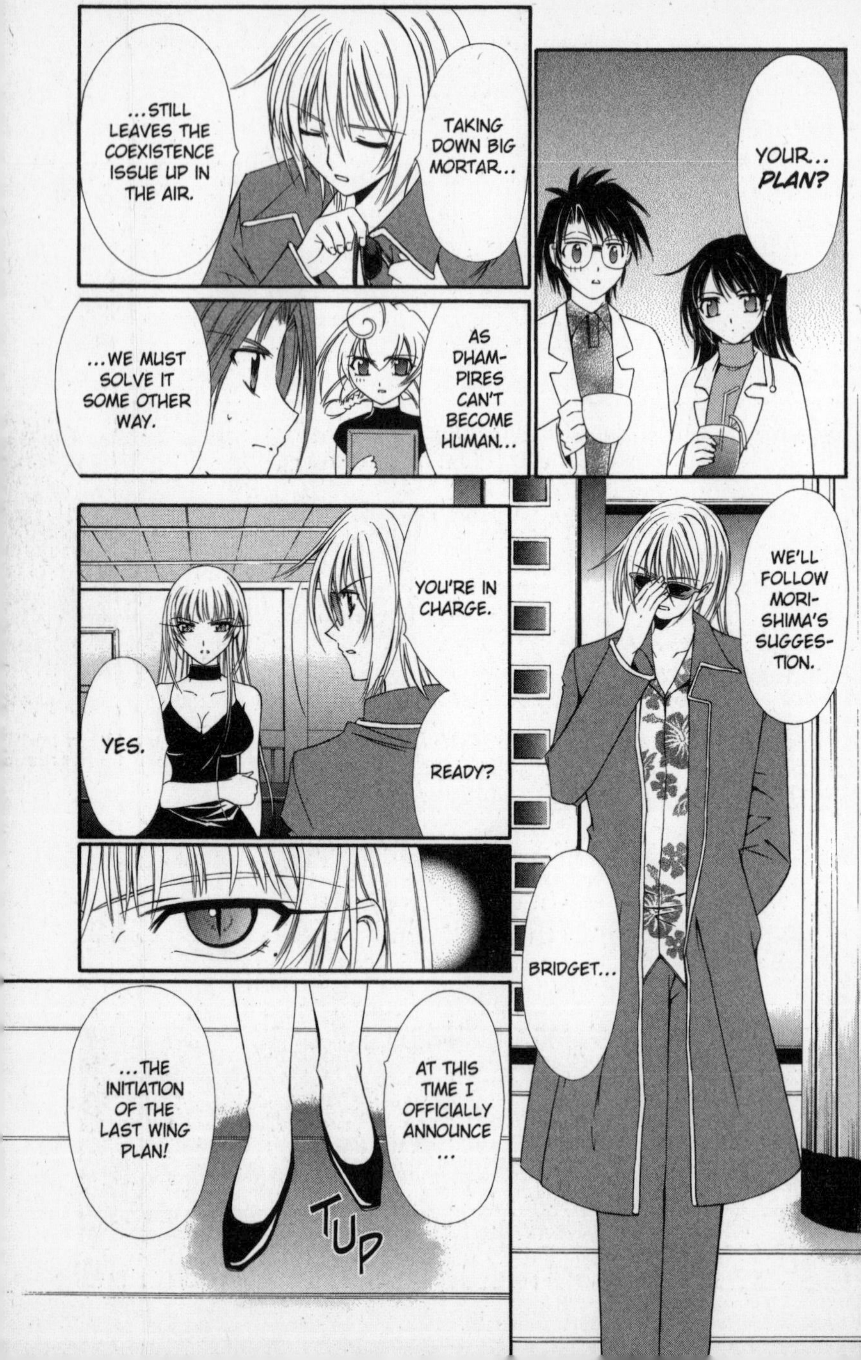
YOUR... PLAN?
TAKING DOWN BIG MORTAR...
...STILL LEAVES THE COEXISTENCE ISSUE UP IN THE AIR.
AS DHAMPIRES CAN'T BECOME HUMAN...
...WE MUST SOLVE IT SOME OTHER WAY.
WE'LL FOLLOW MORISHIMA'S SUGGESTION.
BRIDGET...
YOU'RE IN CHARGE.
READY?
YES.
AT THIS TIME I OFFICIALLY ANNOUNCE...
...THE INITIATION OF THE LAST WING PLAN!
TUP

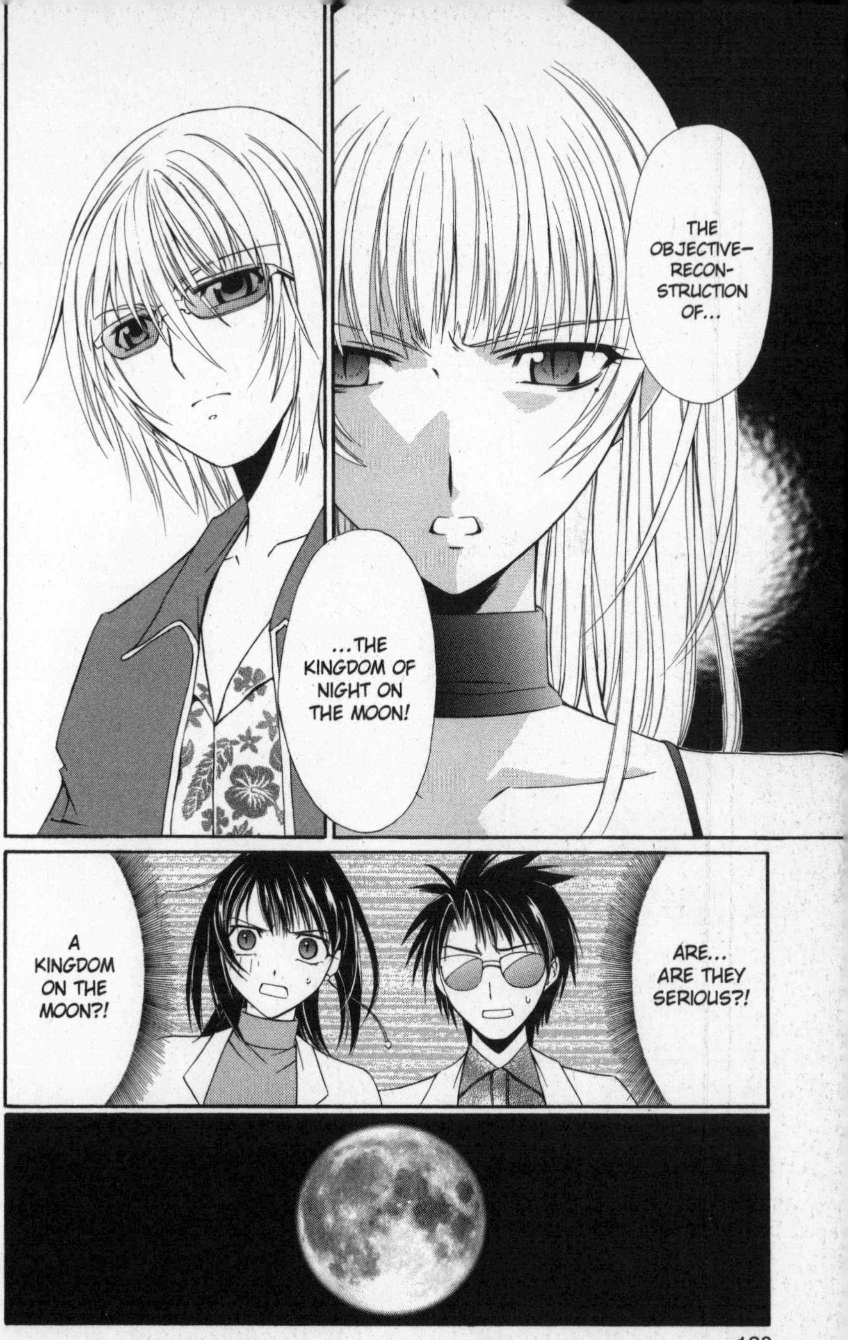
THE OBJECTIVE— RECON-STRUCTION OF...
...THE KINGDOM OF NIGHT ON THE MOON!
ARE... ARE THEY SERIOUS?!
A KINGDOM ON THE MOON?!

THE RECORD OF A

FALLEN VAMPIRE

THE RECORD OF A

FALLEN VAMPIRE

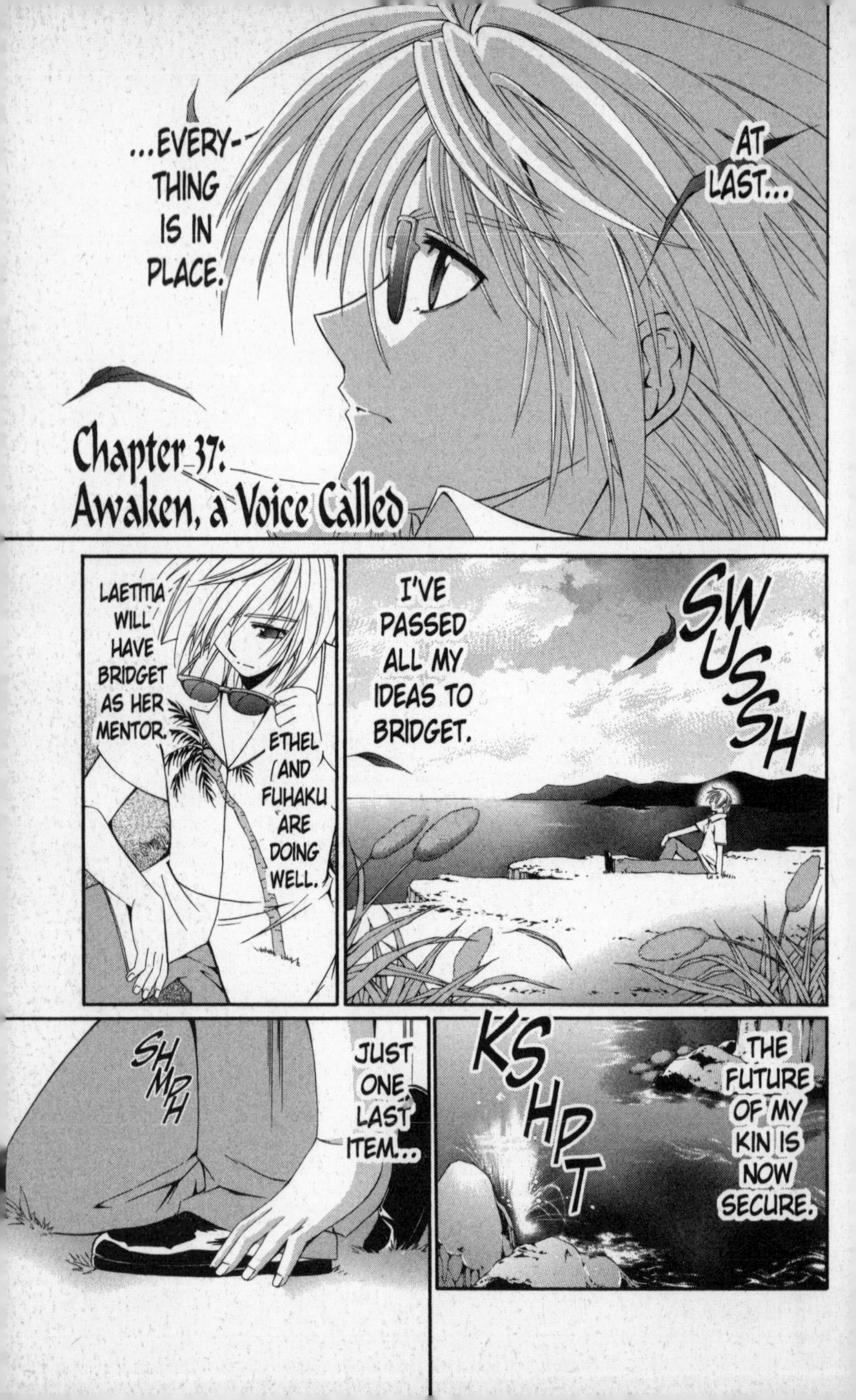
AT LAST...
...EVERYTHING IS IN PLACE.
Chapter 37: Awaken, a Voice Called
I'VE PASSED ALL MY IDEAS TO BRIDGET.
SWUSSH
LAETITIA WILL HAVE BRIDGET AS HER MENTOR.
ETHEL AND FUHAKU ARE DOING WELL.
THE FUTURE OF MY KIN IS NOW SECURE.
KSHPT
JUST ONE LAST ITEM...
SHMPH

Chapter 37: Awaken, a Voice Called

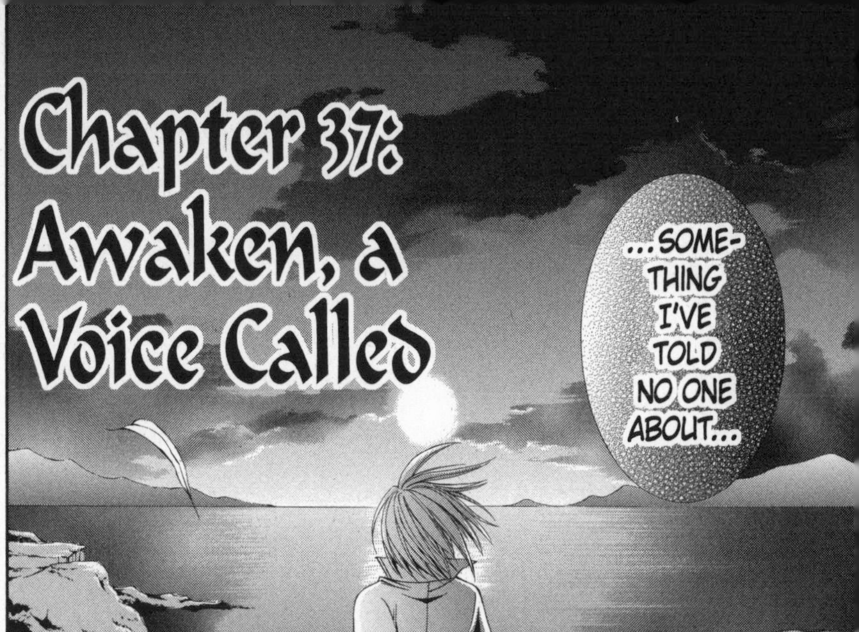
...SOME-THING I'VE TOLD NO ONE ABOUT...
...A SECRET I MUST TAKE TO MY GRAVE.

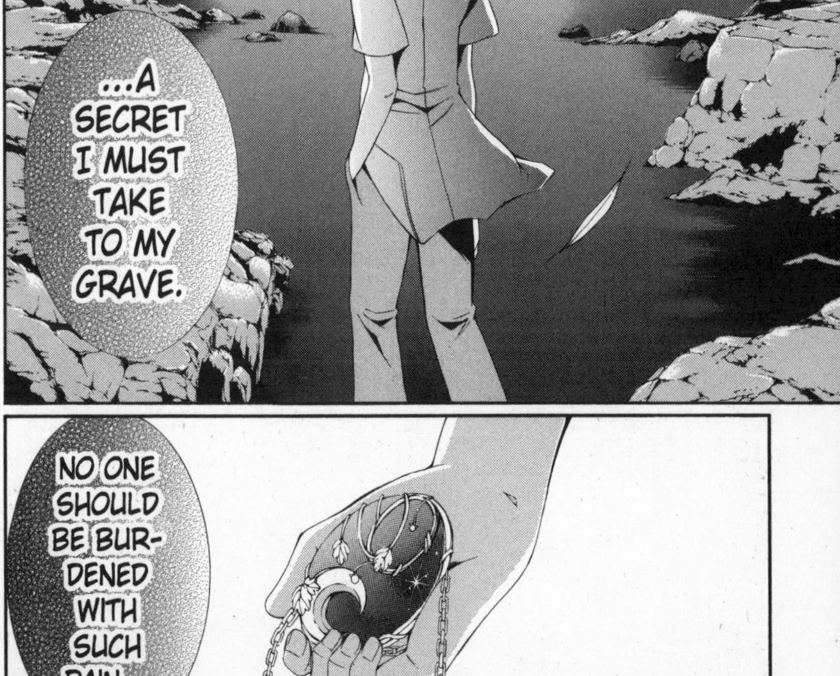
NO ONE SHOULD BE BUR-DENED WITH SUCH PAIN...

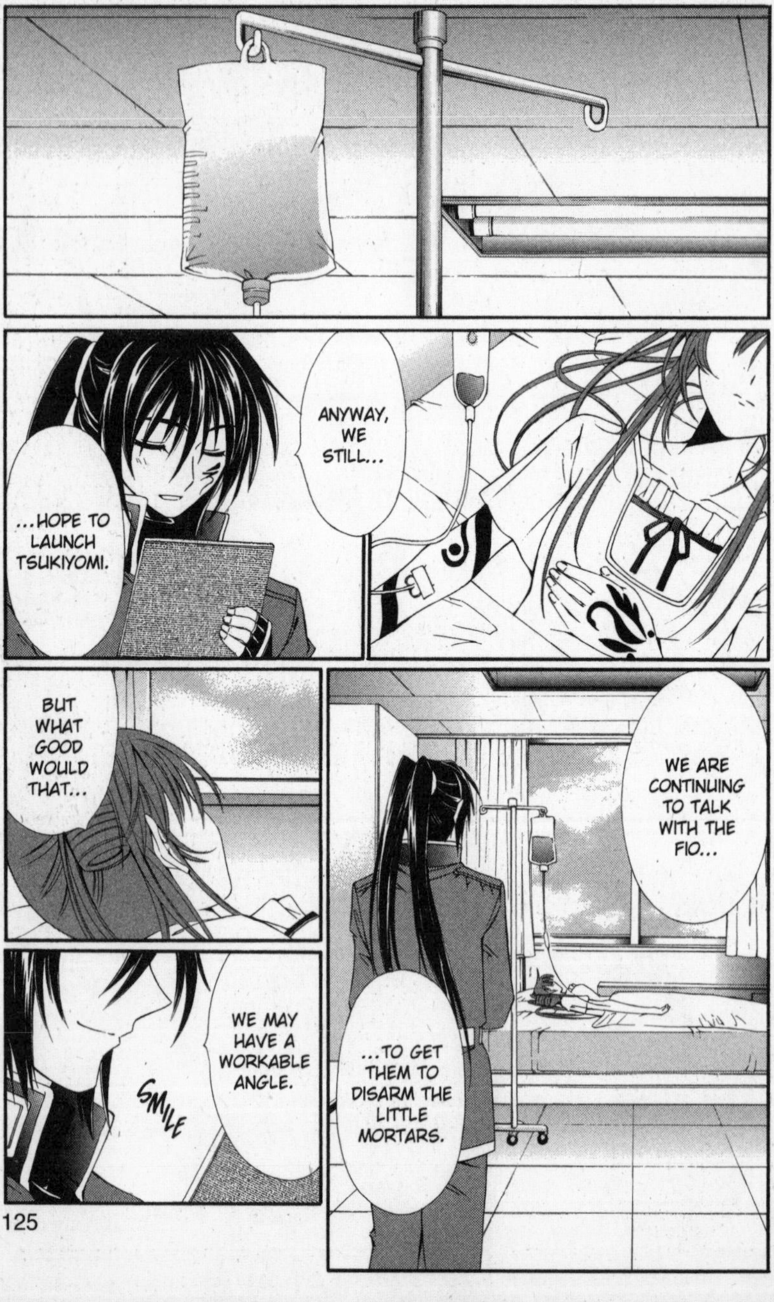
ANYWAY, WE STILL...
...HOPE TO LAUNCH TSUKIYOMI.
WE ARE CONTINUING TO TALK WITH THE FIO...
...TO GET THEM TO DISARM THE LITTLE MORTARS.
BUT WHAT GOOD WOULD THAT...
WE MAY HAVE A WORKABLE ANGLE.
SMILE

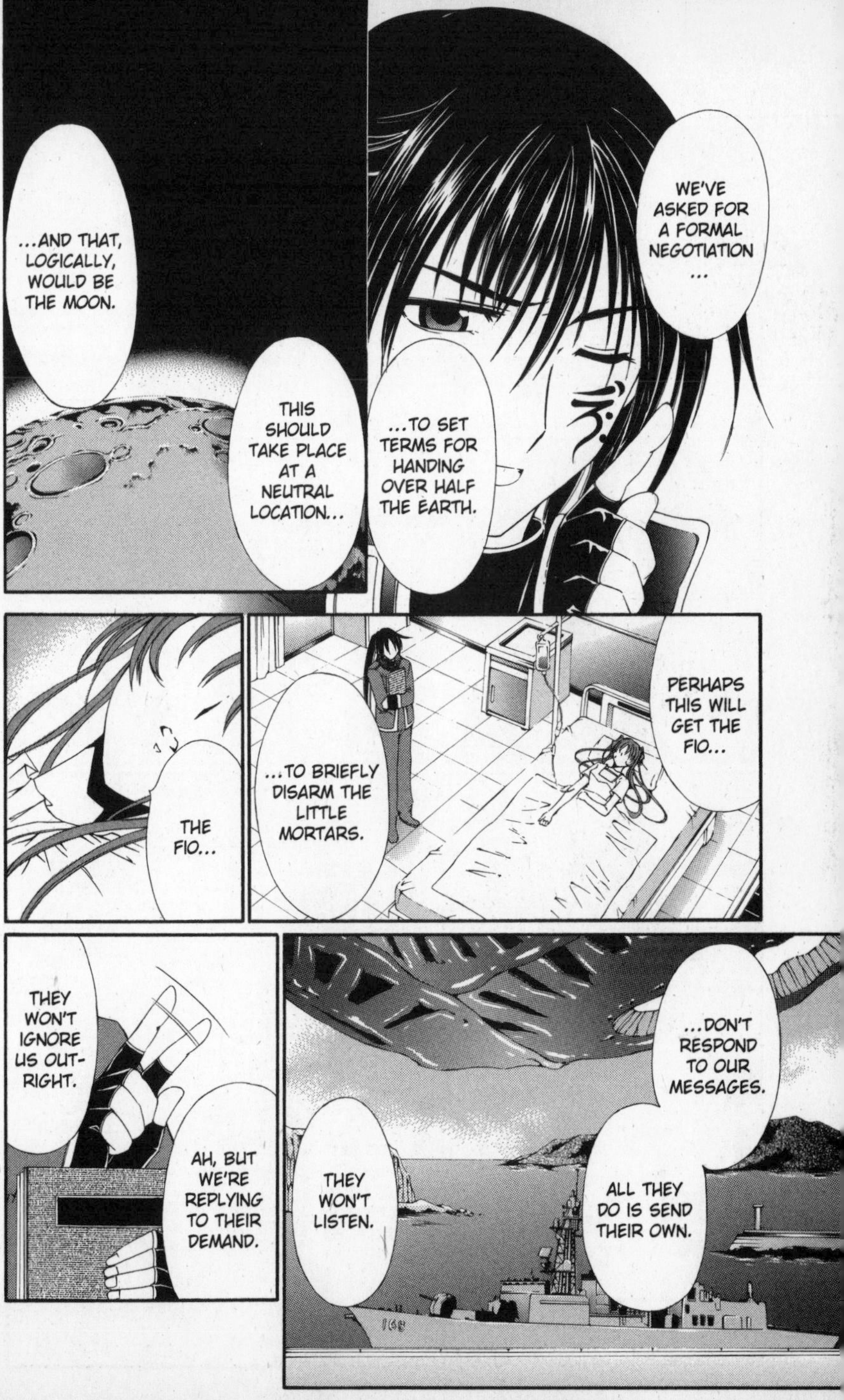
WE'VE ASKED FOR A FORMAL NEGOTIATION ...
...TO SET TERMS FOR HANDING OVER HALF THE EARTH.
THIS SHOULD TAKE PLACE AT A NEUTRAL LOCATION...
...AND THAT, LOGICALLY, WOULD BE THE MOON.
PERHAPS THIS WILL GET THE FIO...
...TO BRIEFLY DISARM THE LITTLE MORTARS.
THE FIO...
...DON'T RESPOND TO OUR MESSAGES.
ALL THEY DO IS SEND THEIR OWN.
THEY WON'T LISTEN.
THEY WON'T IGNORE US OUT-RIGHT.
AH, BUT WE'RE REPLYING TO THEIR DEMAND.

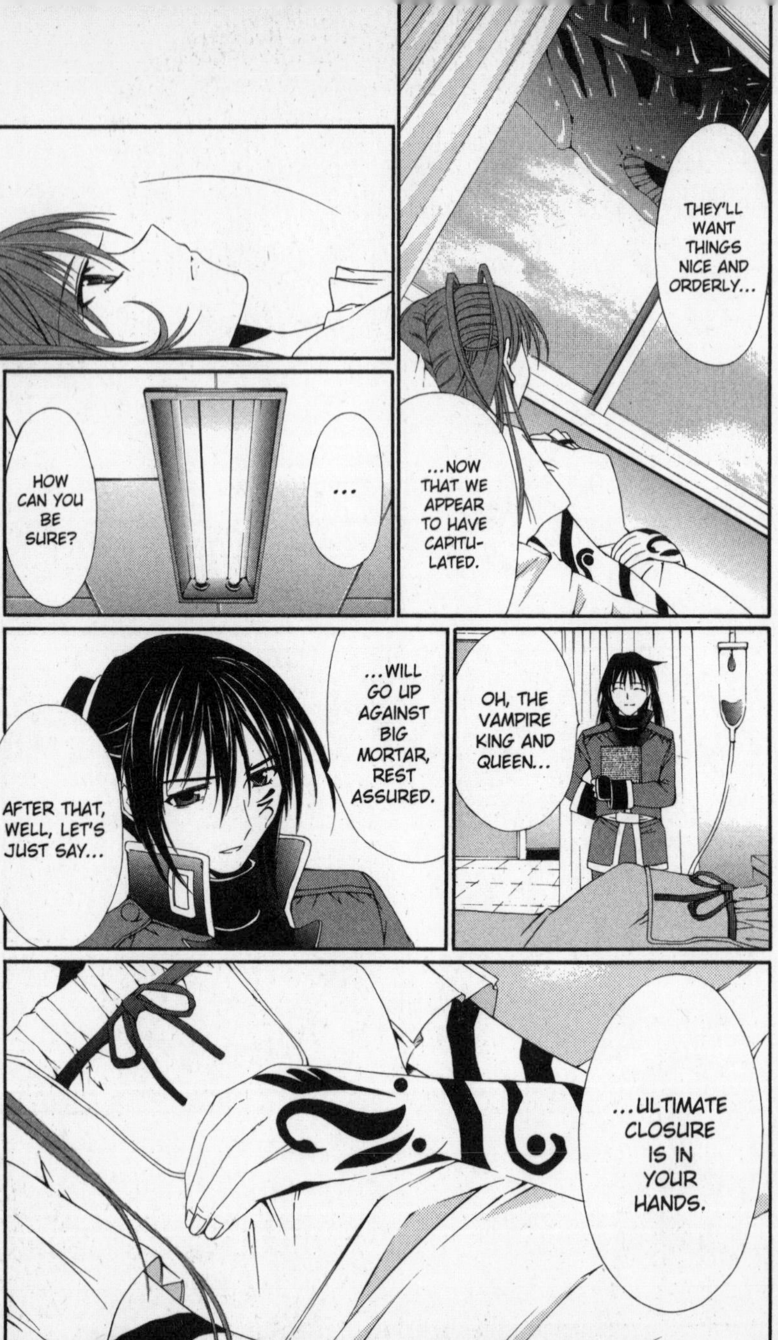
THEY'LL WANT THINGS NICE AND ORDERLY...
...NOW THAT WE APPEAR TO HAVE CAPITULATED.
...
HOW CAN YOU BE SURE?
OH, THE VAMPIRE KING AND QUEEN...
...WILL GO UP AGAINST BIG MORTAR, REST ASSURED.
AFTER THAT, WELL, LET'S JUST SAY...
...ULTIMATE CLOSURE IS IN YOUR HANDS.

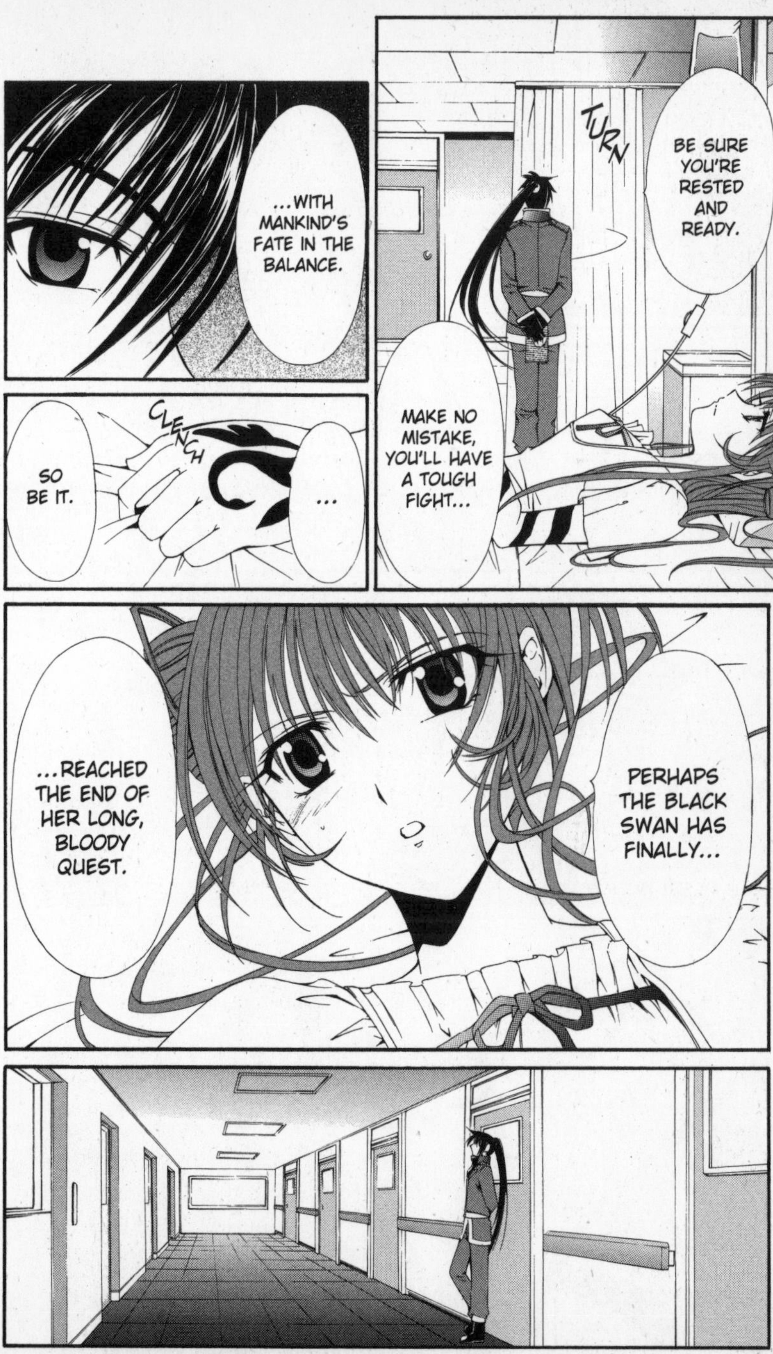
TURN
BE SURE YOU'RE RESTED AND READY.
MAKE NO MISTAKE, YOU'LL HAVE A TOUGH FIGHT...
...WITH MANKIND'S FATE IN THE BALANCE.
...
CLENCH
SO BE IT.
PERHAPS THE BLACK SWAN HAS FINALLY...
...REACHED THE END OF HER LONG, BLOODY QUEST.

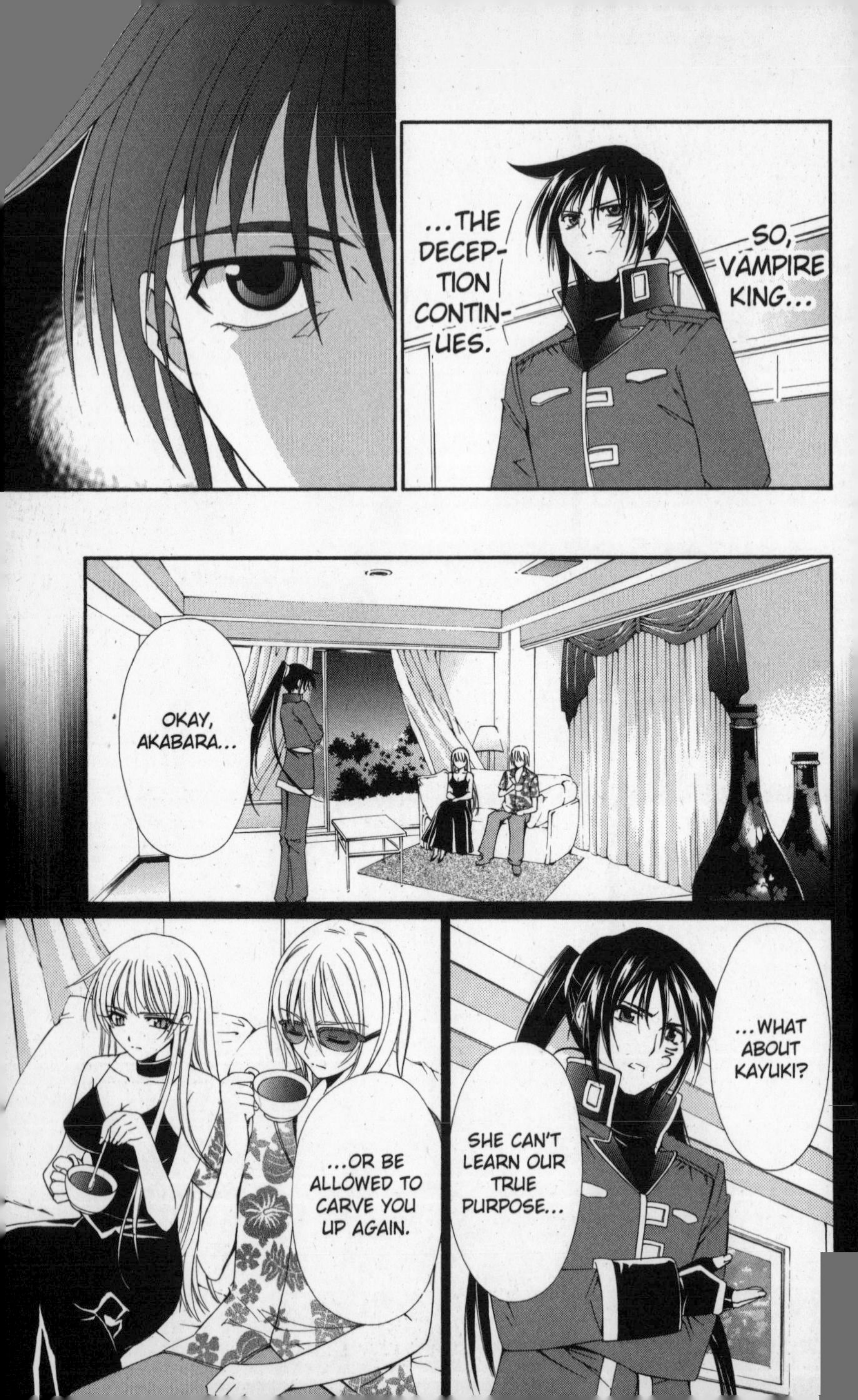
SO, VAMPIRE KING...
...THE DECEPTION CONTINUES.
OKAY, AKABARA...
...WHAT ABOUT KAYUKI?
SHE CAN'T LEARN OUR TRUE PURPOSE...
...OR BE ALLOWED TO CARVE YOU UP AGAIN.

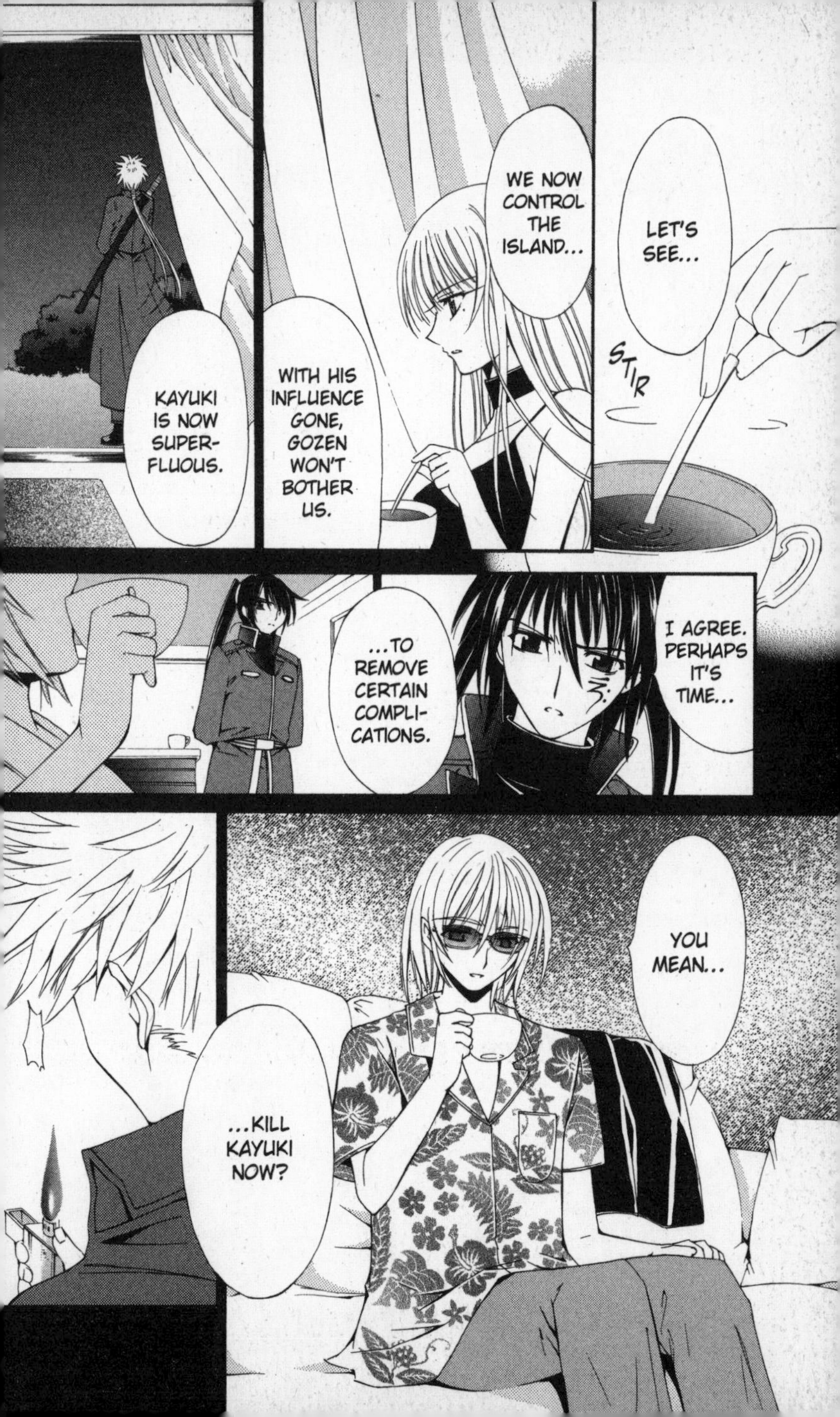
LET'S SEE...
STIR
WE NOW CONTROL THE ISLAND...
WITH HIS INFLUENCE GONE, GOZEN WON'T BOTHER US.
KAYUKI IS NOW SUPER-FLUOUS.
I AGREE. PERHAPS IT'S TIME...
...TO REMOVE CERTAIN COMPLI-CATIONS.
YOU MEAN...
...KILL KAYUKI NOW?

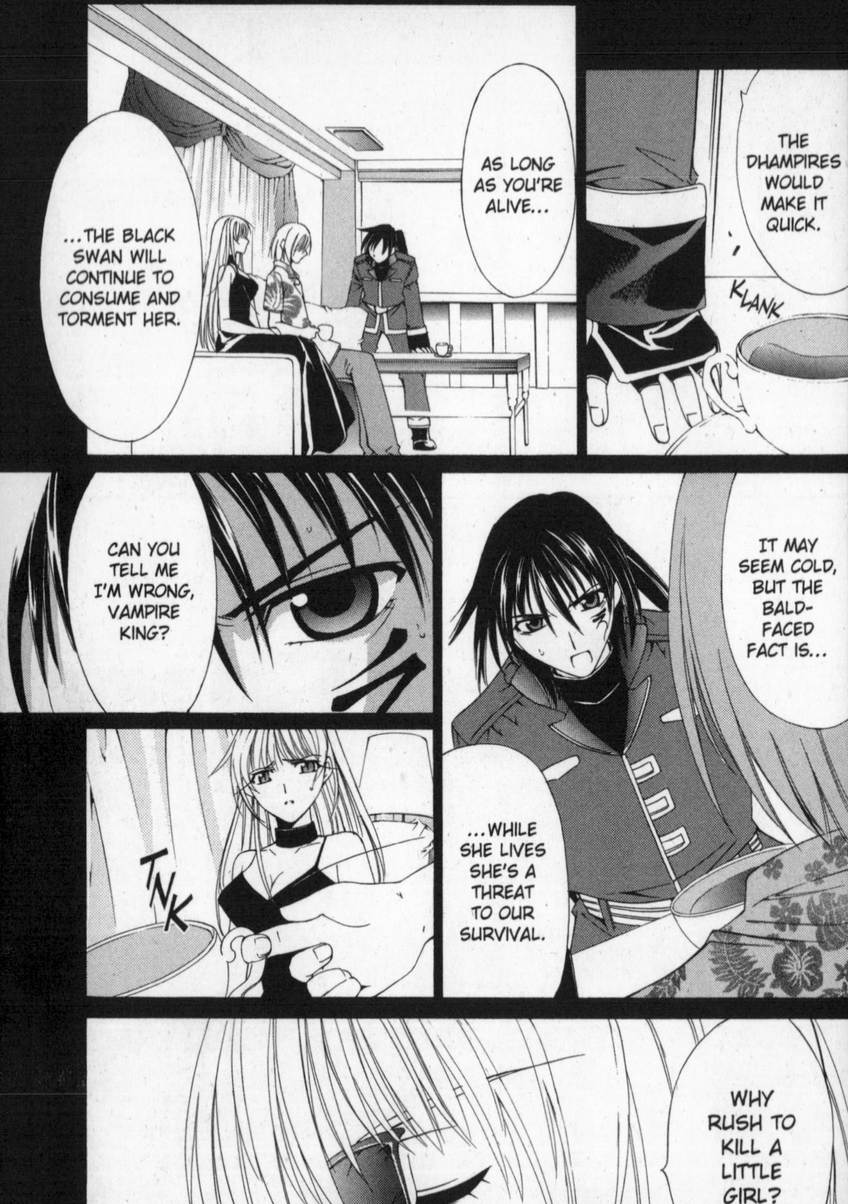
THE DHAMPIRES WOULD MAKE IT QUICK.
KLANK
AS LONG AS YOU'RE ALIVE...
...THE BLACK SWAN WILL CONTINUE TO CONSUME AND TORMENT HER.
IT MAY SEEM COLD, BUT THE BALD-FACED FACT IS...
...WHILE SHE LIVES SHE'S A THREAT TO OUR SURVIVAL.
CAN YOU TELL ME I'M WRONG, VAMPIRE KING?
TNK
WHY RUSH TO KILL A LITTLE GIRL?

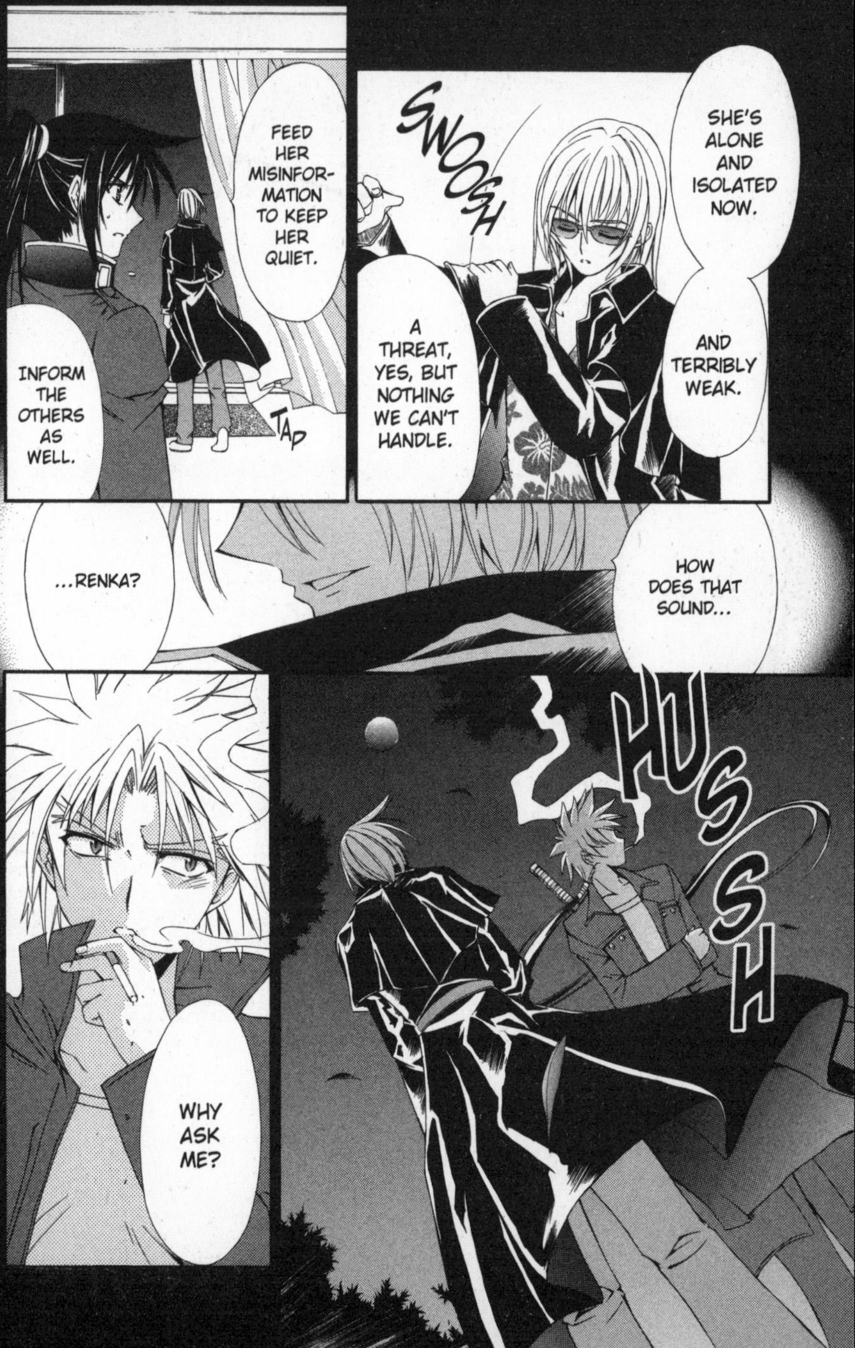
SWOOSH
SHE'S ALONE AND ISOLATED NOW.
AND TERRIBLY WEAK.
A THREAT, YES, BUT NOTHING WE CAN'T HANDLE.
FEED HER MISINFORMATION TO KEEP HER QUIET.
INFORM THE OTHERS AS WELL.
TAP
HOW DOES THAT SOUND...
...RENKA?
HUSSH
WHY ASK ME?

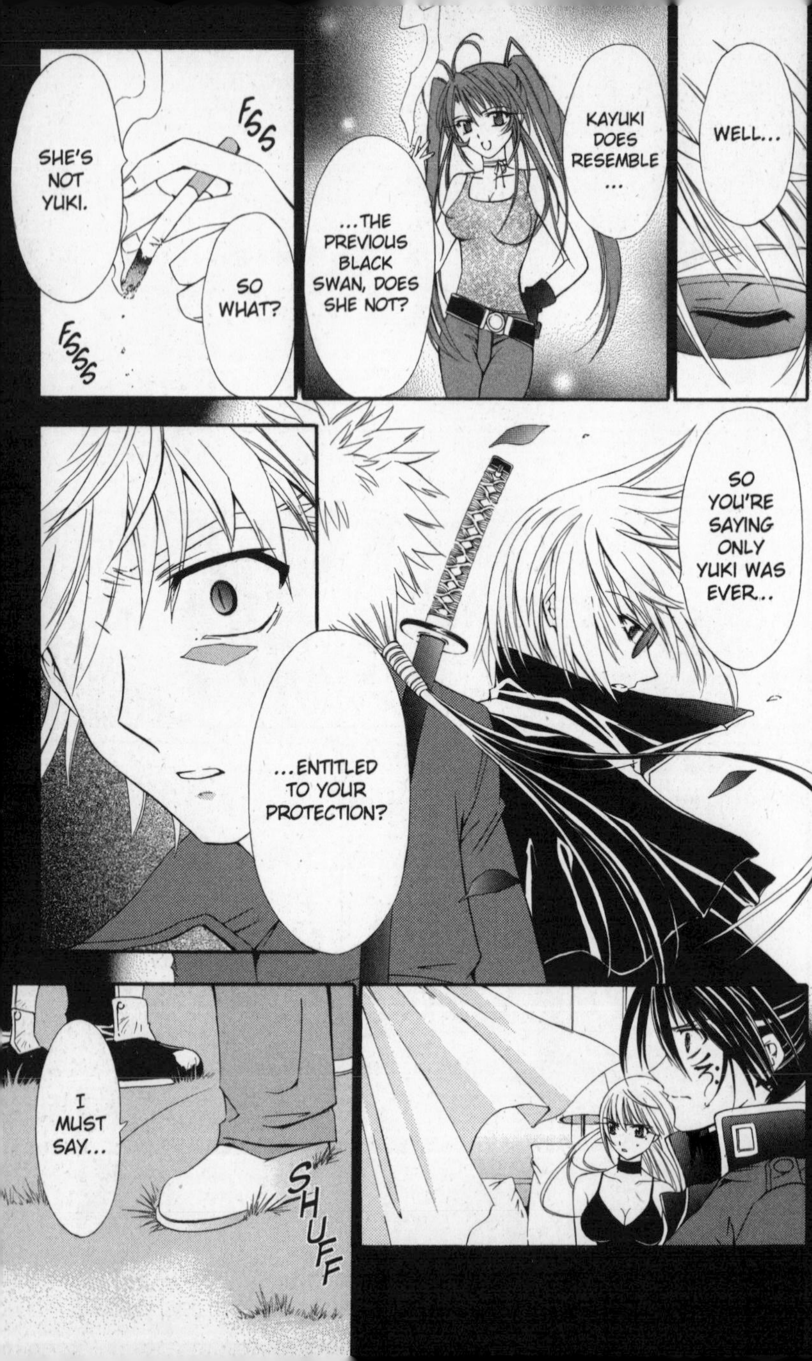
WELL...
KAYUKI DOES RESEMBLE ...
...THE PREVIOUS BLACK SWAN, DOES SHE NOT?
SHE'S NOT YUKI.
SO WHAT?
FSS
FSSS
SO YOU'RE SAYING ONLY YUKI WAS EVER...
...ENTITLED TO YOUR PROTECTION?
I MUST SAY...
SHUFF

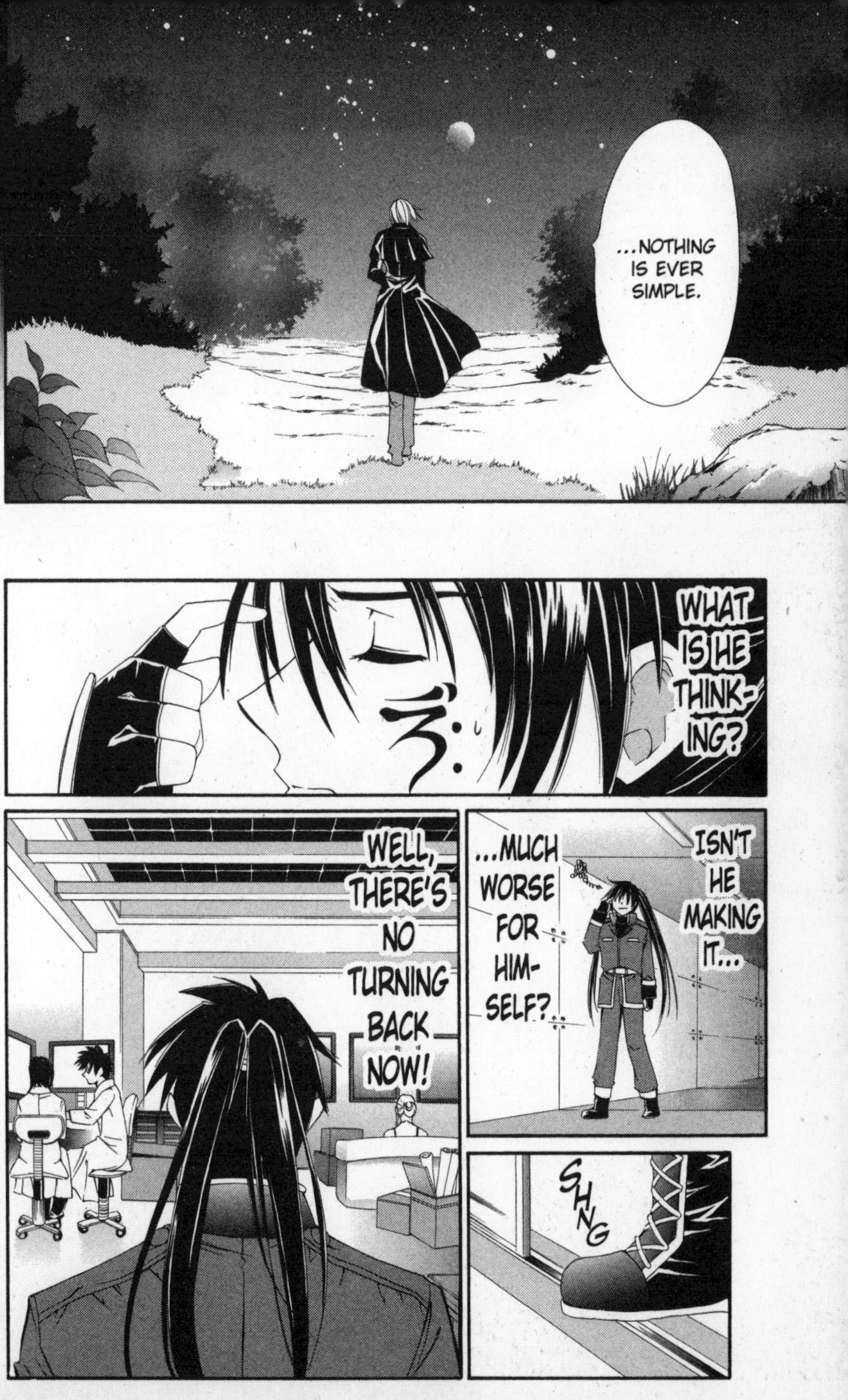
...NOTHING IS EVER SIMPLE.
WHAT IS HE THINK-ING?
ISN'T HE MAKING IT...
...MUCH WORSE FOR HIM-SELF?
SHNG
WELL, THERE'S NO TURNING BACK NOW!

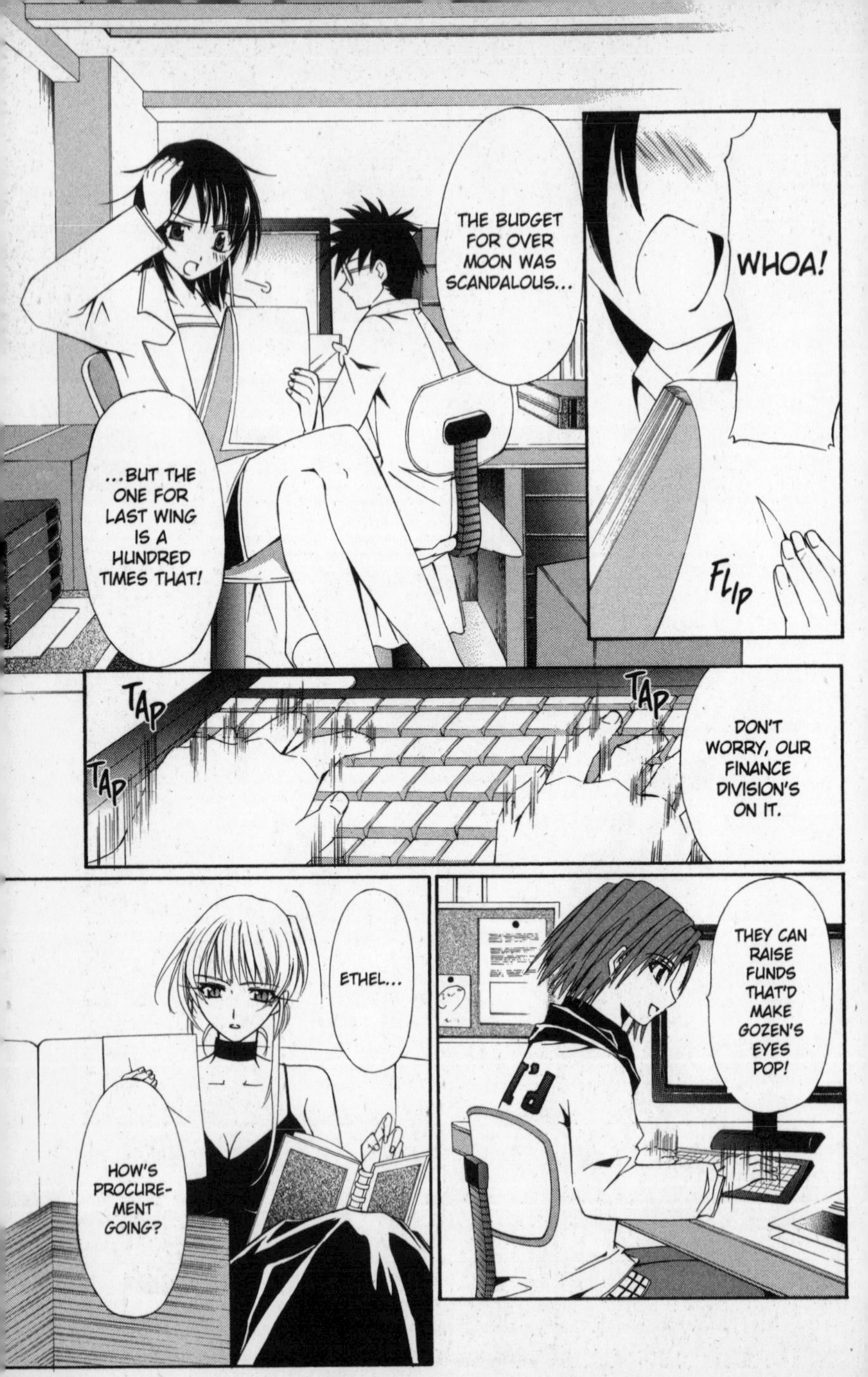
WHOA!
FLIP
THE BUDGET FOR OVER MOON WAS SCANDALOUS...
...BUT THE ONE FOR LAST WING IS A HUNDRED TIMES THAT!
DON'T WORRY, OUR FINANCE DIVISION'S ON IT.
TAP
TAP
TAP
THEY CAN RAISE FUNDS THAT'D MAKE GOZEN'S EYES POP!
ETHEL...
HOW'S PROCURE-MENT GOING?

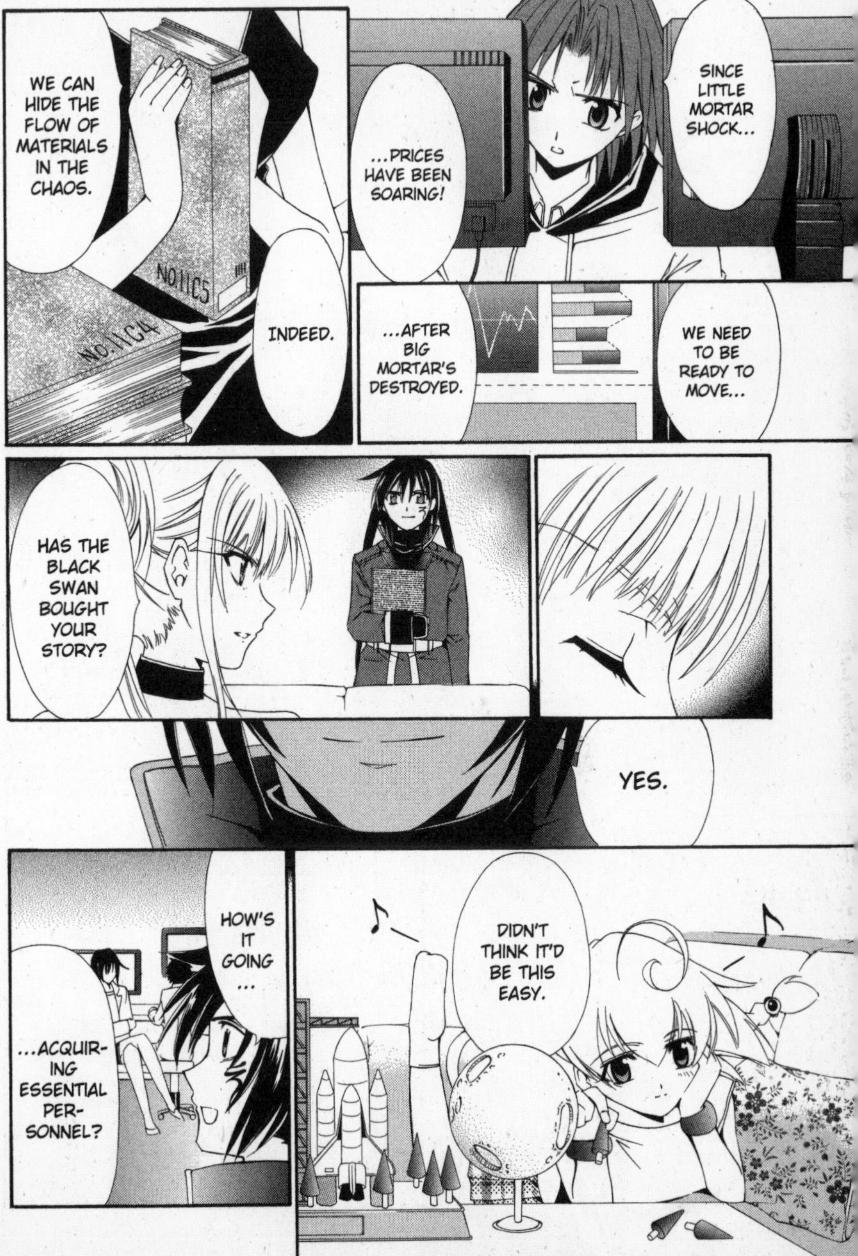
SINCE LITTLE MORTAR SHOCK...
...PRICES HAVE BEEN SOARING!
WE NEED TO BE READY TO MOVE...
...AFTER BIG MORTAR'S DESTROYED.
WE CAN HIDE THE FLOW OF MATERIALS IN THE CHAOS.
NO.11C5
NO.11C4
INDEED.
HAS THE BLACK SWAN BOUGHT YOUR STORY?
YES.
DIDN'T THINK IT'D BE THIS EASY.
HOW'S IT GOING ...
...ACQUIR-ING ESSENTIAL PER-SONNEL?

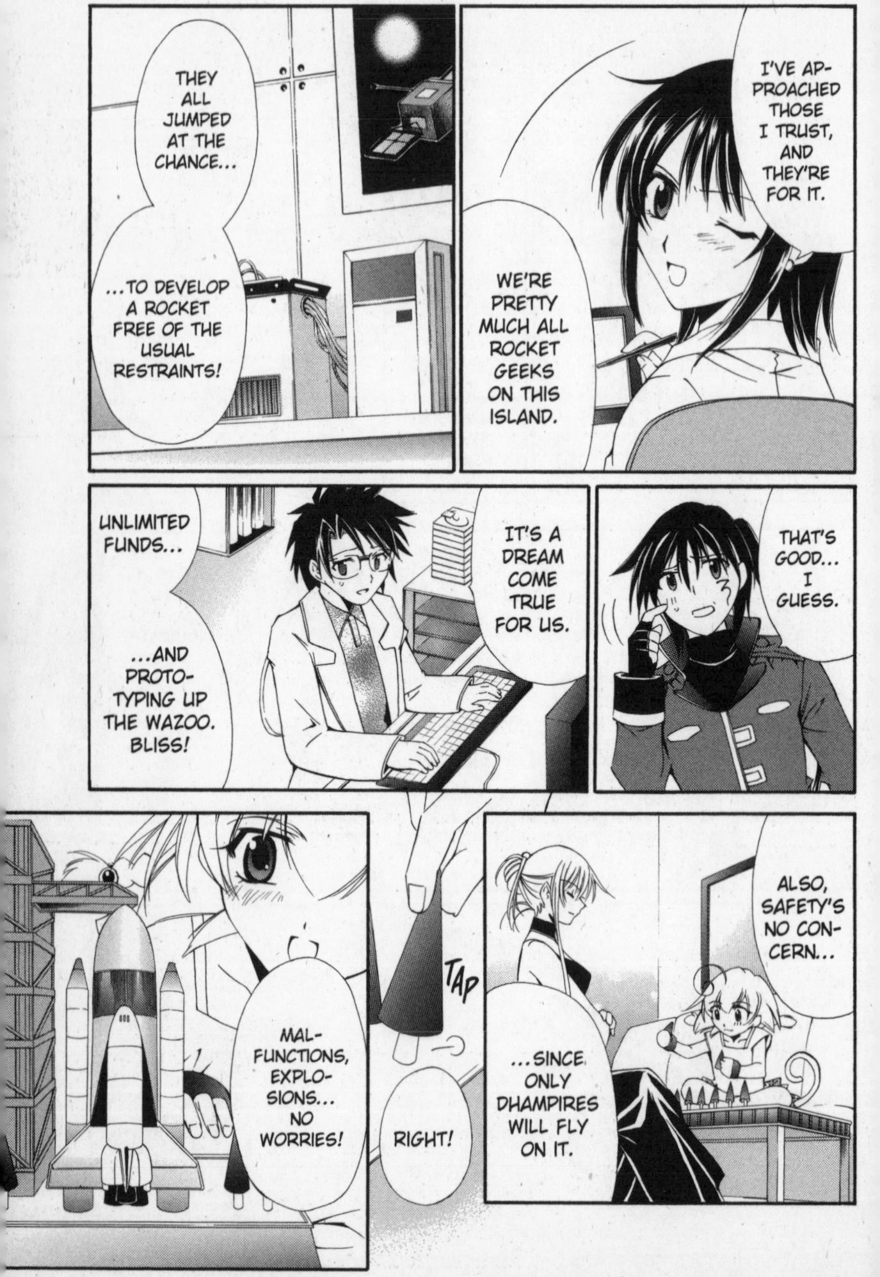
I'VE AP-PROACHED THOSE I TRUST, AND THEY'RE FOR IT.
WE'RE PRETTY MUCH ALL ROCKET GEEKS ON THIS ISLAND.
THEY ALL JUMPED AT THE CHANCE...
...TO DEVELOP A ROCKET FREE OF THE USUAL RESTRAINTS!
THAT'S GOOD... I GUESS.
IT'S A DREAM COME TRUE FOR US.
UNLIMITED FUNDS...
...AND PROTO-TYPING UP THE WAZOO. BLISS!
ALSO, SAFETY'S NO CON-CERN...
...SINCE ONLY DHAMPIRES WILL FLY ON IT.
TAP
MAL-FUNCTIONS, EXPLO-SIONS... NO WORRIES!
RIGHT!

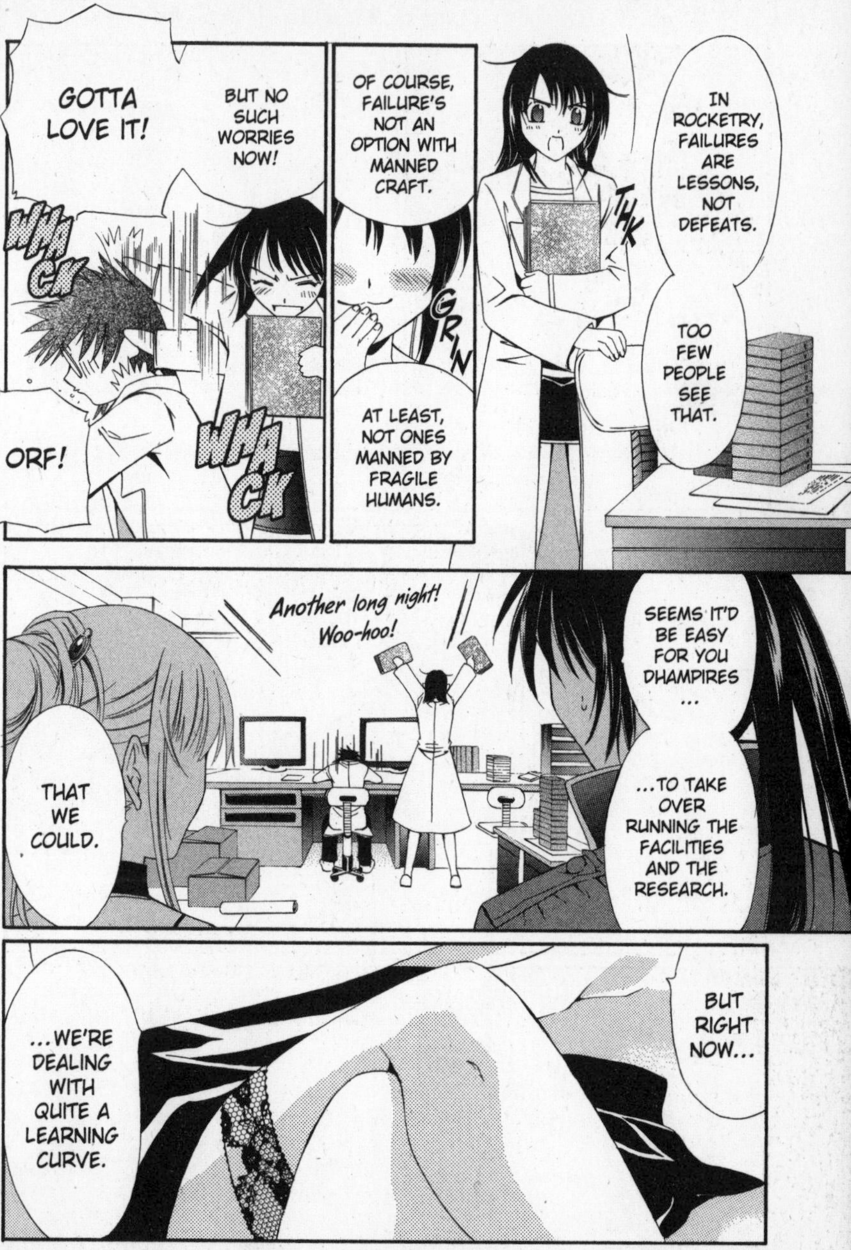
IN ROCKETRY, FAILURES ARE LESSONS, NOT DEFEATS.
THK
TOO FEW PEOPLE SEE THAT.
OF COURSE, FAILURE'S NOT AN OPTION WITH MANNED CRAFT.
GRIN
AT LEAST, NOT ONES MANNED BY FRAGILE HUMANS.
BUT NO SUCH WORRIES NOW!
WHACK
GOTTA LOVE IT!
WHACK
ORF!
SEEMS IT'D BE EASY FOR YOU DHAMPIRES...
...TO TAKE OVER RUNNING THE FACILITIES AND THE RESEARCH.
Another long night! Woo-hoo!
THAT WE COULD.
BUT RIGHT NOW...
...WE'RE DEALING WITH QUITE A LEARNING CURVE.

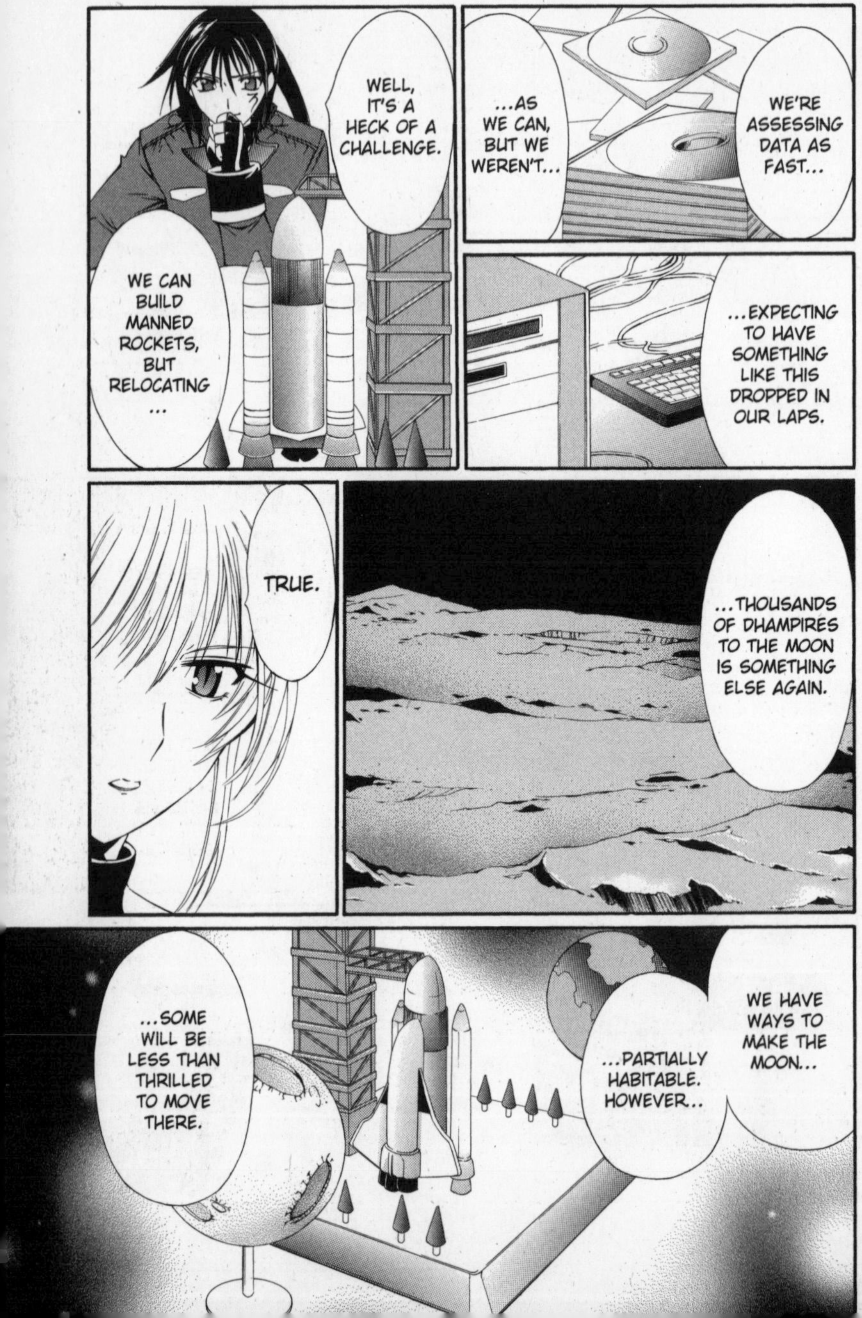
WE'RE ASSESSING DATA AS FAST...
...AS WE CAN, BUT WE WEREN'T...
...EXPECTING TO HAVE SOMETHING LIKE THIS DROPPED IN OUR LAPS.
WELL, IT'S A HECK OF A CHALLENGE.
WE CAN BUILD MANNED ROCKETS, BUT RELOCATING ...
...THOUSANDS OF DHAMPIRES TO THE MOON IS SOMETHING ELSE AGAIN.
TRUE.
WE HAVE WAYS TO MAKE THE MOON...
...PARTIALLY HABITABLE. HOWEVER...
...SOME WILL BE LESS THAN THRILLED TO MOVE THERE.

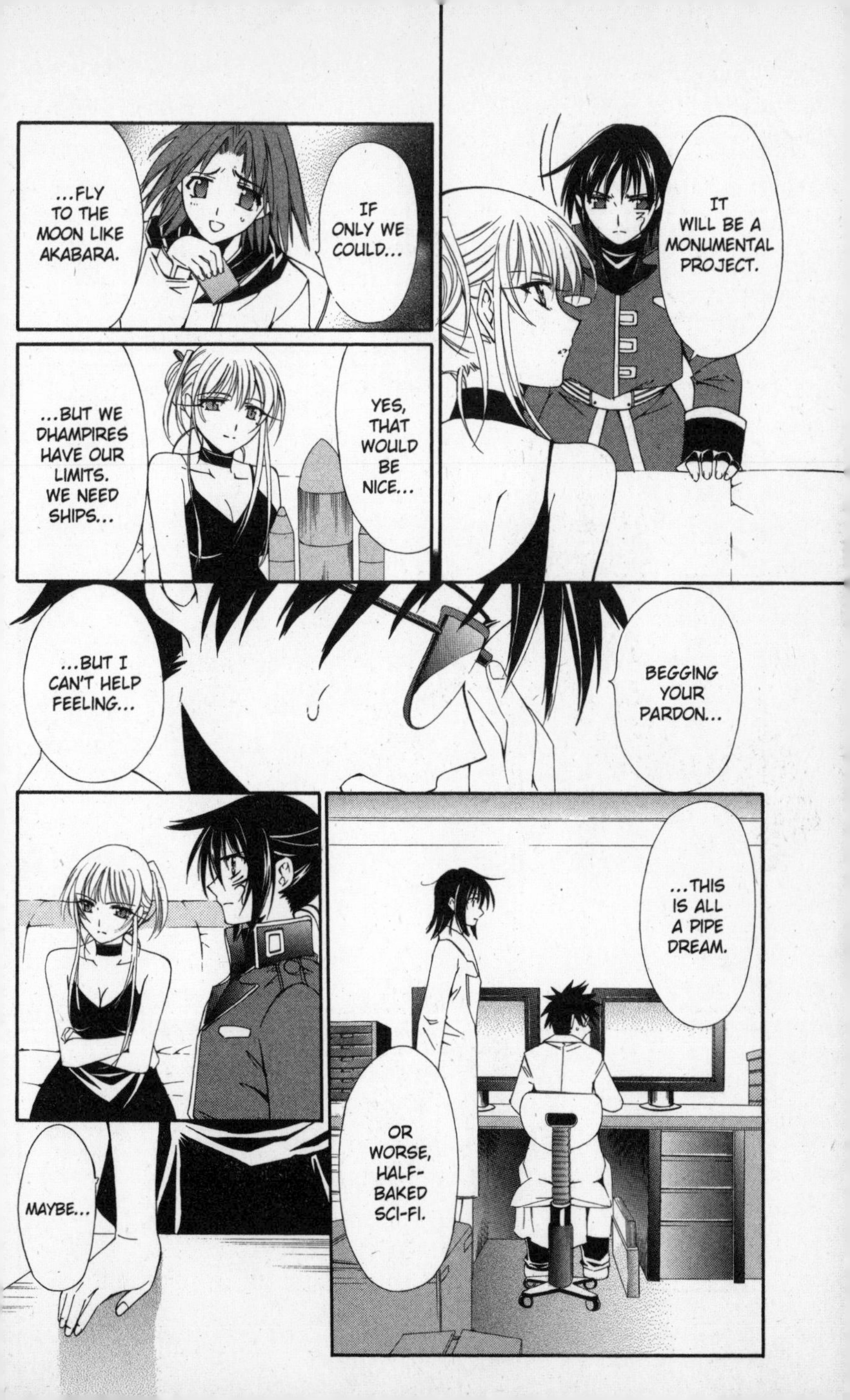
IT WILL BE A MONUMENTAL PROJECT.
IF ONLY WE COULD...
...FLY TO THE MOON LIKE AKABARA.
YES, THAT WOULD BE NICE...
...BUT WE DHAMPIRES HAVE OUR LIMITS. WE NEED SHIPS...
BEGGING YOUR PARDON...
...BUT I CAN'T HELP FEELING...
...THIS IS ALL A PIPE DREAM.
OR WORSE, HALF-BAKED SCI-FI.
MAYBE...

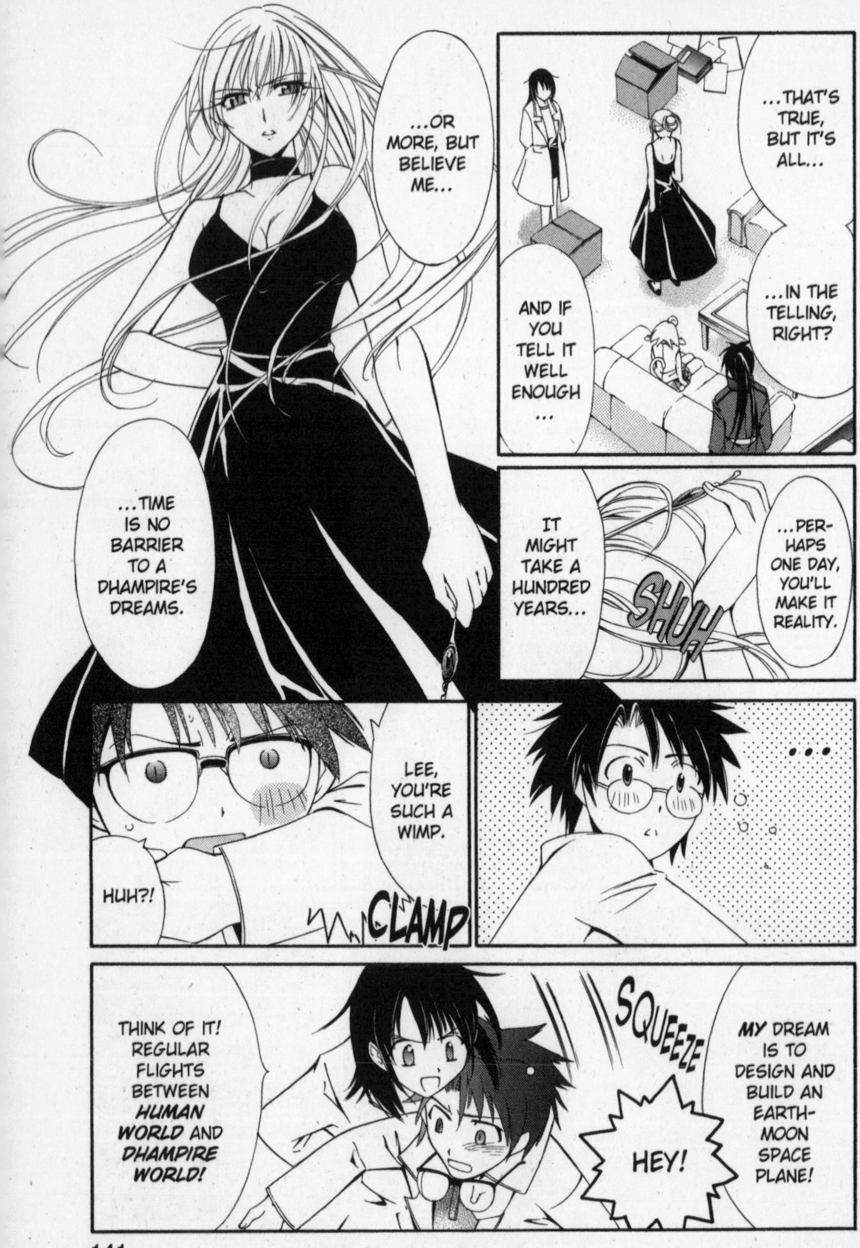
...THAT'S TRUE, BUT IT'S ALL...
...IN THE TELLING, RIGHT?
AND IF YOU TELL IT WELL ENOUGH...
...PER-HAPS ONE DAY, YOU'LL MAKE IT REALITY.
IT MIGHT TAKE A HUNDRED YEARS...
SHUH
...OR MORE, BUT BELIEVE ME...
...TIME IS NO BARRIER TO A DHAMPIRE'S DREAMS.
...
LEE, YOU'RE SUCH A WIMP.
HUH?!
CLAMP
MY DREAM IS TO DESIGN AND BUILD AN EARTH-MOON SPACE PLANE!
SQUEEZE
HEY!
THINK OF IT! REGULAR FLIGHTS BETWEEN ***HUMAN WORLD*** AND ***DHAMPIRE WORLD!***

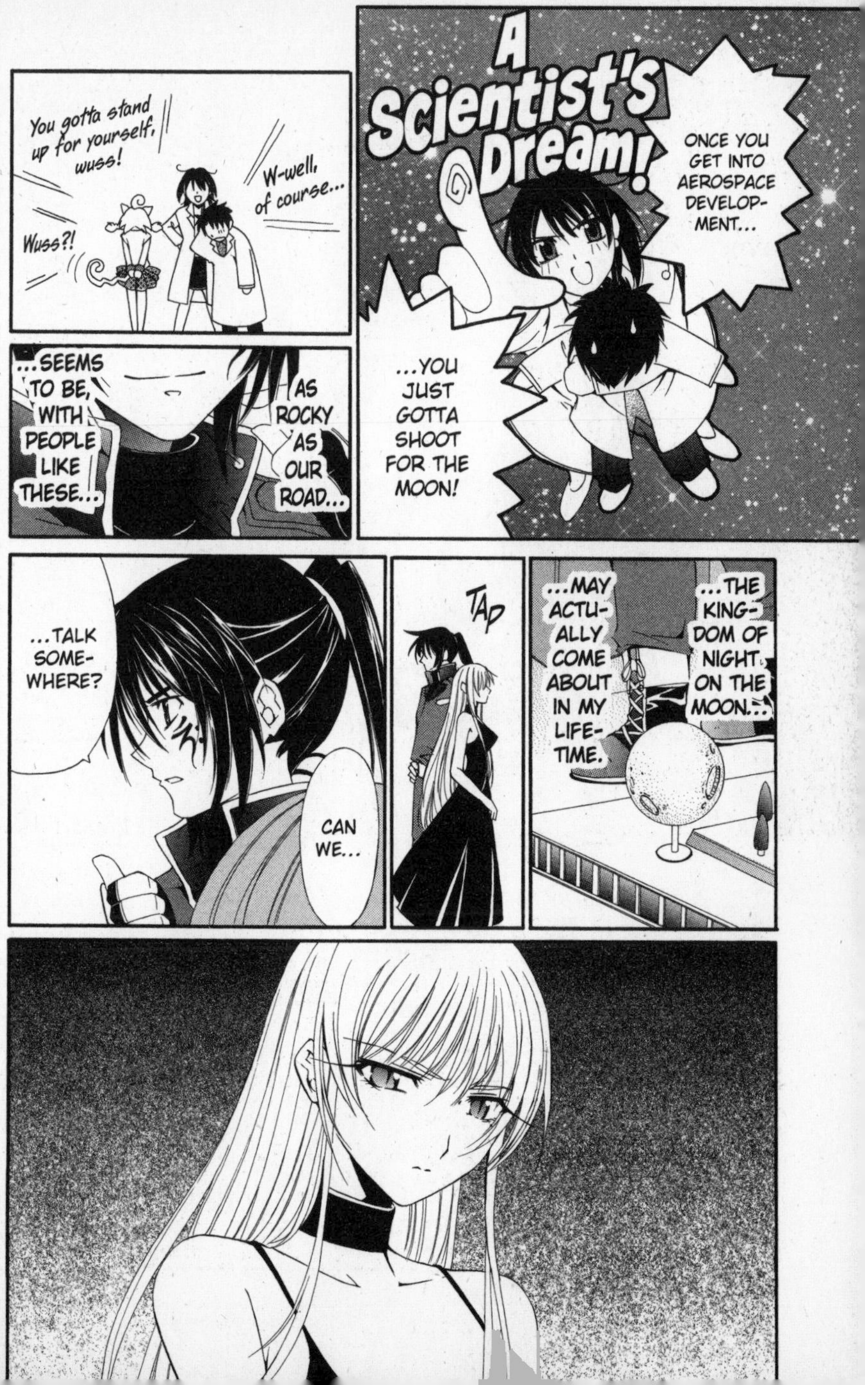
A Scientist's Dream!
ONCE YOU GET INTO AEROSPACE DEVELOPMENT...
...YOU JUST GOTTA SHOOT FOR THE MOON!
You gotta stand up for yourself, wuss!
W-well, of course...
Wuss?!
AS ROCKY AS OUR ROAD...
...SEEMS TO BE, WITH PEOPLE LIKE THESE...
...THE KINGDOM OF NIGHT ON THE MOON...
...MAY ACTUALLY COME ABOUT IN MY LIFETIME.
TAP
CAN WE...
...TALK SOMEWHERE?

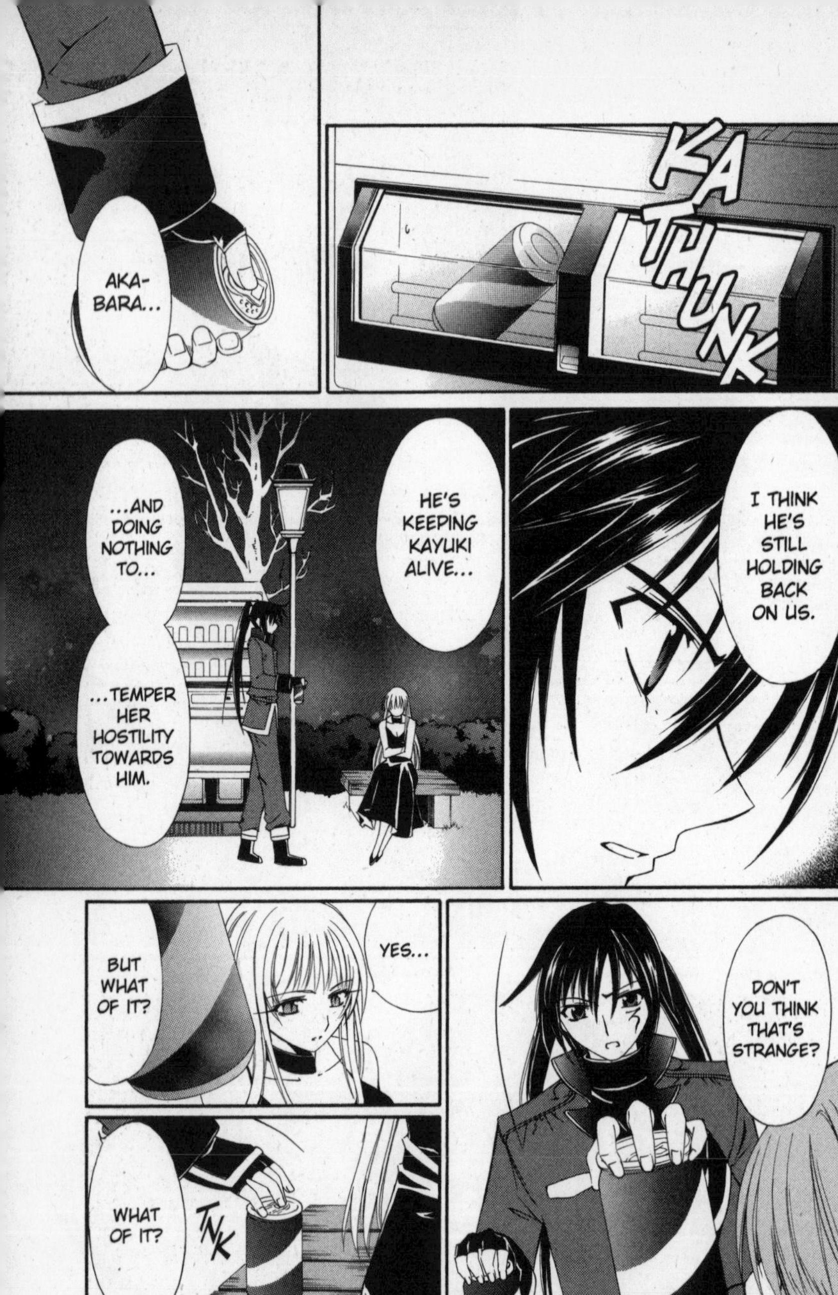
KA THUNK
AKA-BARA...
I THINK HE'S STILL HOLDING BACK ON US.
HE'S KEEPING KAYUKI ALIVE...
...AND DOING NOTHING TO...
...TEMPER HER HOSTILITY TOWARDS HIM.
DON'T YOU THINK THAT'S STRANGE?
YES...
BUT WHAT OF IT?
WHAT OF IT?
TNK

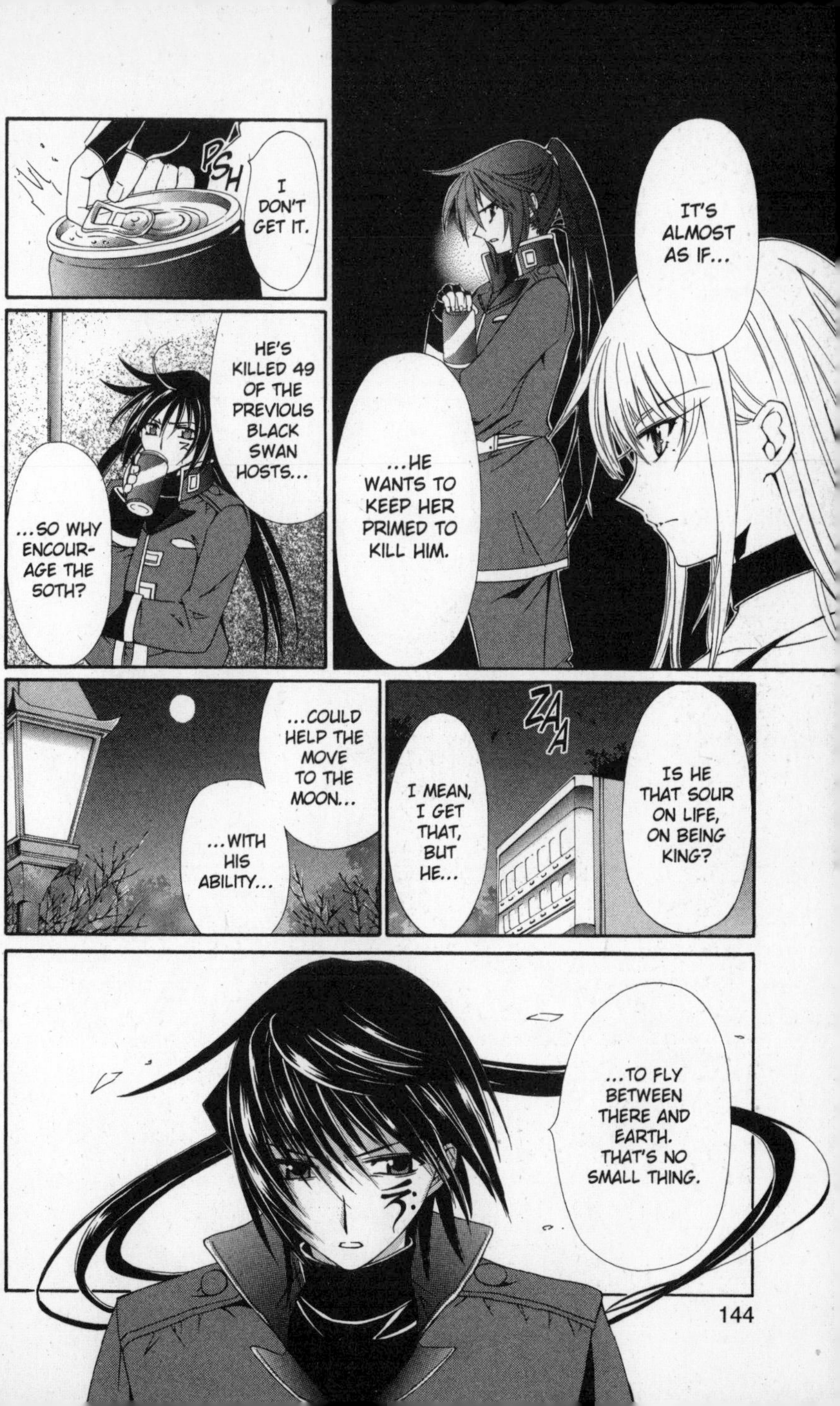
PSH
I DON'T GET IT.
HE'S KILLED 49 OF THE PREVIOUS BLACK SWAN HOSTS...
...SO WHY ENCOURAGE THE SOTH?
IT'S ALMOST AS IF...
...HE WANTS TO KEEP HER PRIMED TO KILL HIM.
ZAA
IS HE THAT SOUR ON LIFE, ON BEING KING?
I MEAN, I GET THAT, BUT HE...
...COULD HELP THE MOVE TO THE MOON...
...WITH HIS ABILITY...
...TO FLY BETWEEN THERE AND EARTH. THAT'S NO SMALL THING.

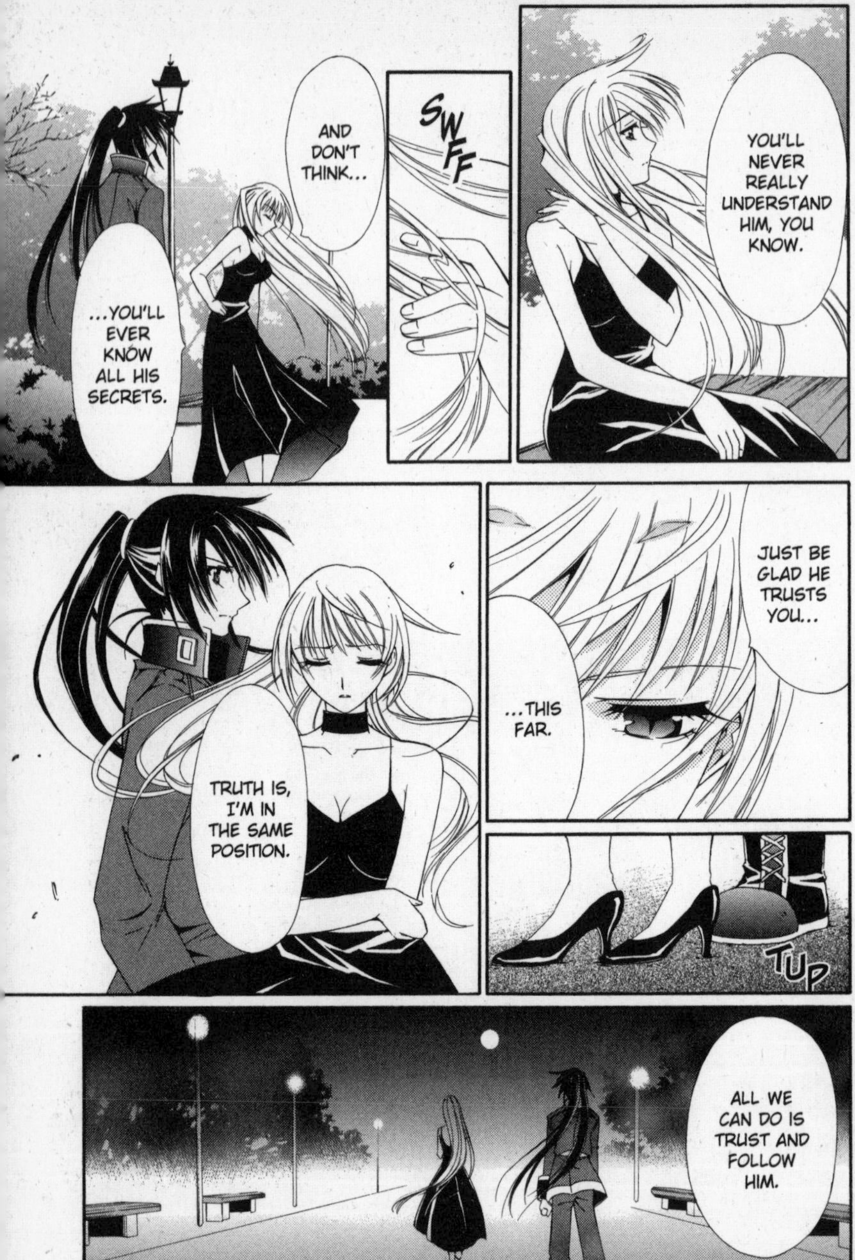
YOU'LL NEVER REALLY UNDERSTAND HIM, YOU KNOW.
SWFF
AND DON'T THINK...
...YOU'LL EVER KNOW ALL HIS SECRETS.
JUST BE GLAD HE TRUSTS YOU...
...THIS FAR.
TUP
TRUTH IS, I'M IN THE SAME POSITION.
ALL WE CAN DO IS TRUST AND FOLLOW HIM.

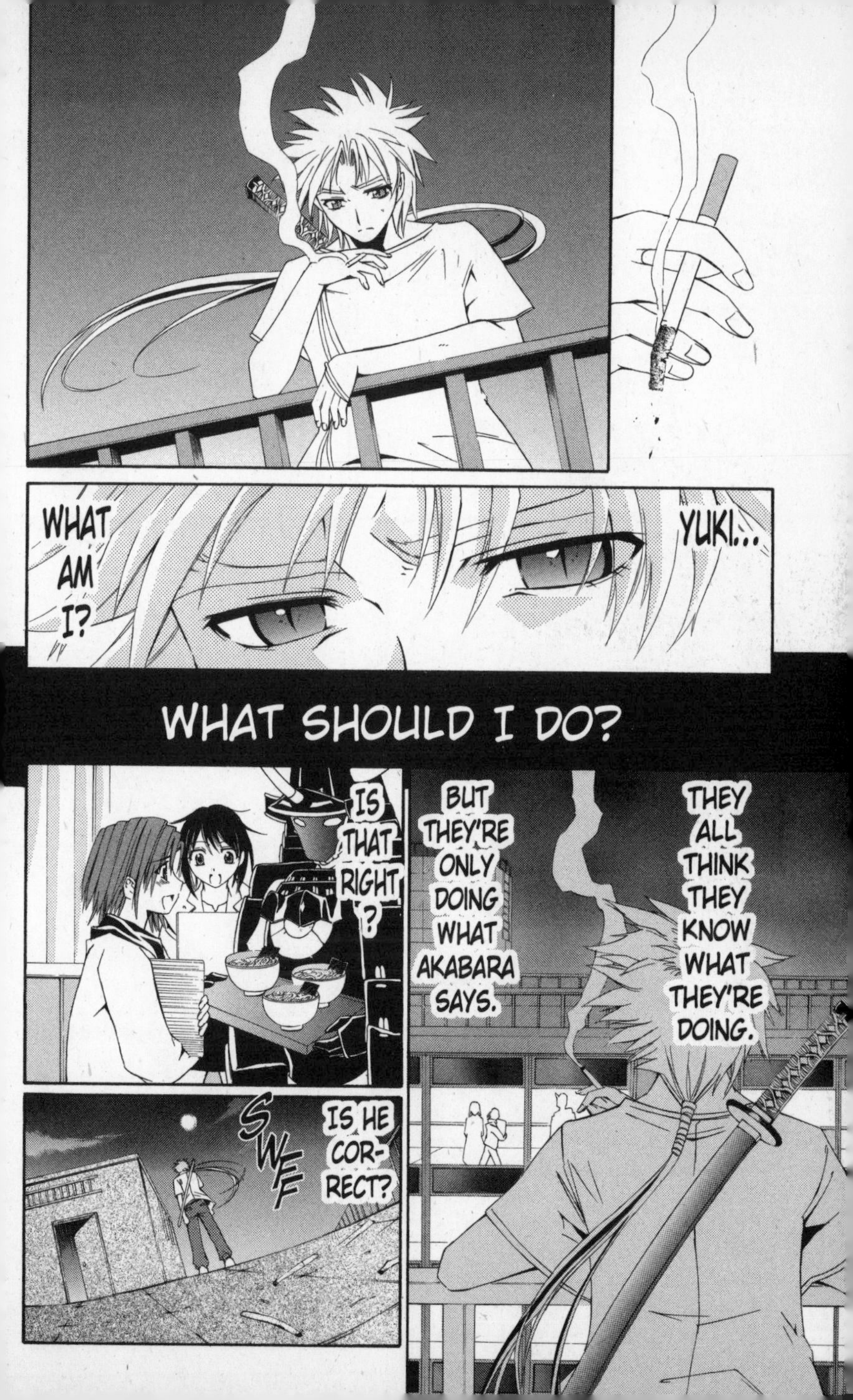
YUKI...
WHAT AM I?
WHAT SHOULD I DO?
THEY ALL THINK THEY KNOW WHAT THEY'RE DOING.
BUT THEY'RE ONLY DOING WHAT AKABARA SAYS.
IS THAT RIGHT?
IS HE COR-RECT?
SWF

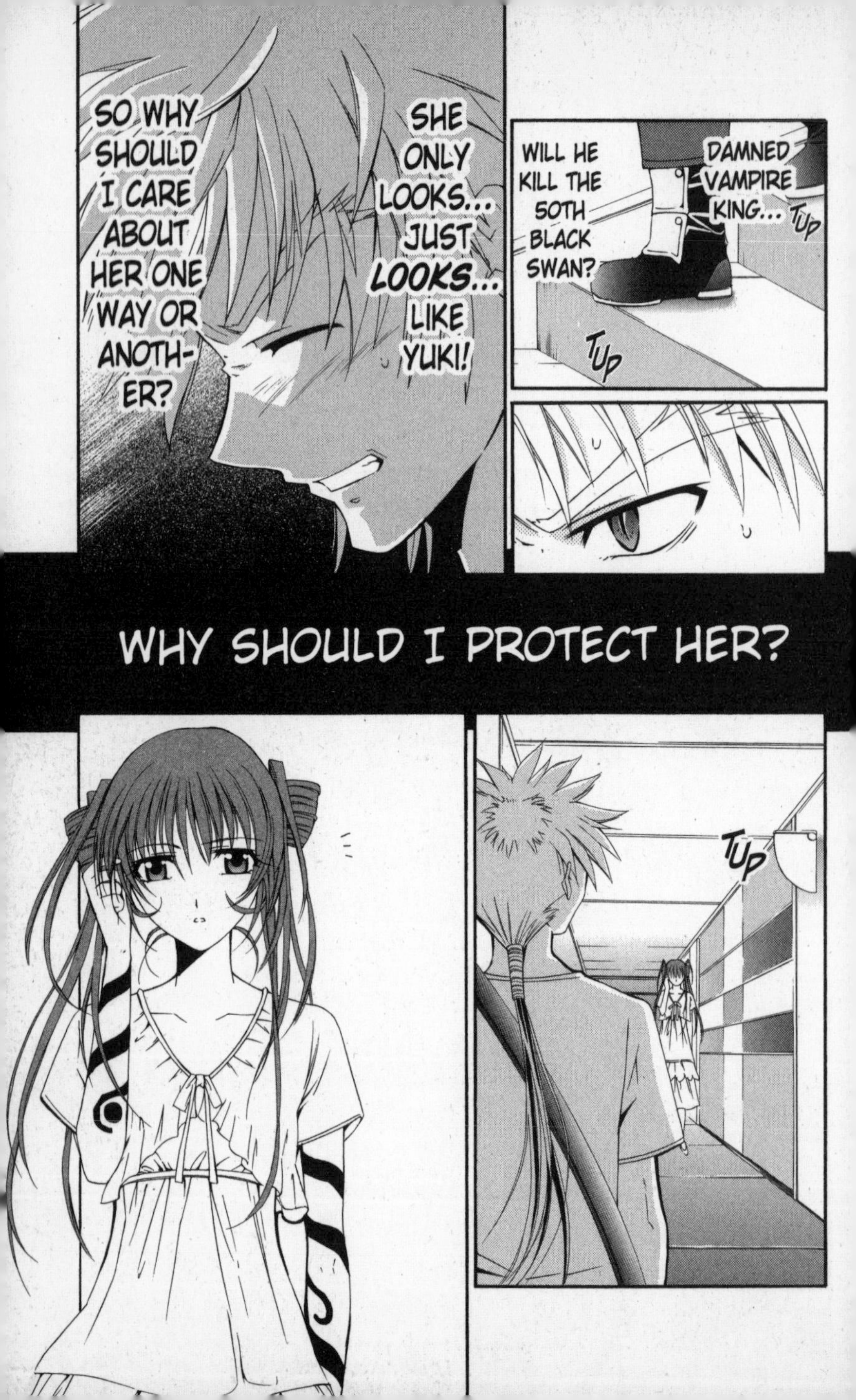
DAMNED VAMPIRE KING...
TUP
WILL HE KILL THE 50TH BLACK SWAN?
TUP
SHE ONLY LOOKS... JUST **LOOKS**... LIKE YUKI!
SO WHY SHOULD I CARE ABOUT HER ONE WAY OR ANOTH-ER?
WHY SHOULD I PROTECT HER?
TUP

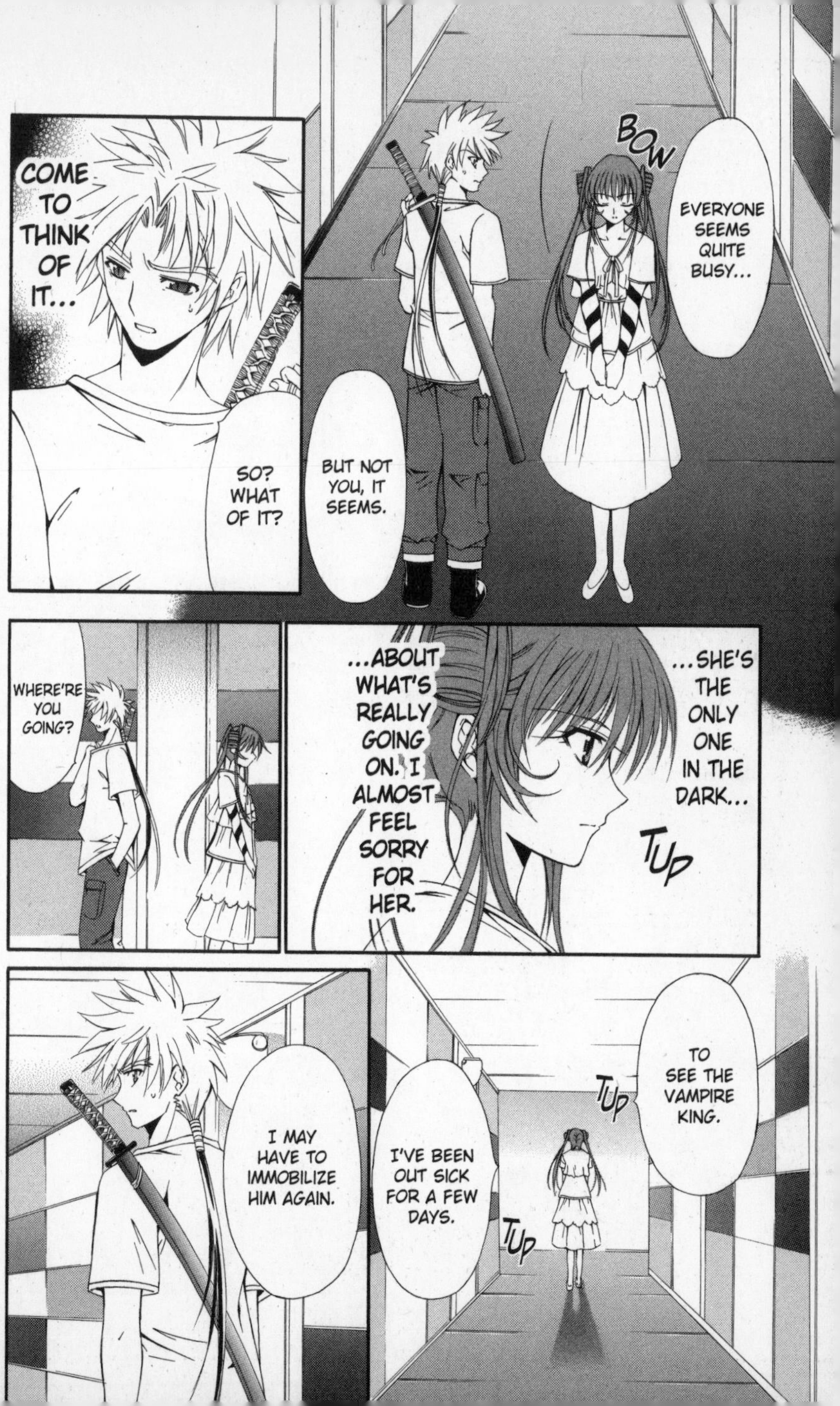
BOW
EVERYONE SEEMS QUITE BUSY...
BUT NOT YOU, IT SEEMS.
SO? WHAT OF IT?
COME TO THINK OF IT...
...SHE'S THE ONLY ONE IN THE DARK...
...ABOUT WHAT'S REALLY GOING ON. I ALMOST FEEL SORRY FOR HER.
TUP
WHERE'RE YOU GOING?
TO SEE THE VAMPIRE KING.
TUP
TUP
I'VE BEEN OUT SICK FOR A FEW DAYS.
I MAY HAVE TO IMMOBILIZE HIM AGAIN.

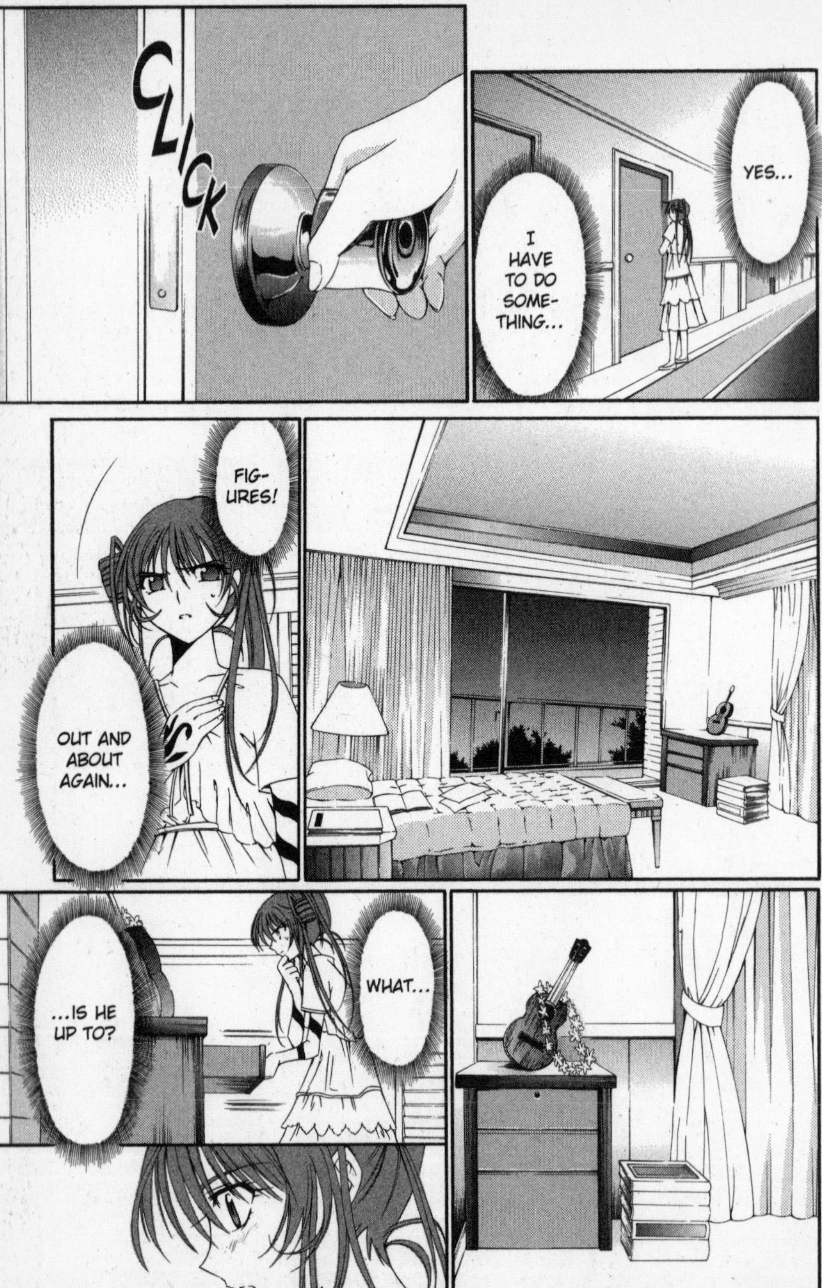
YES...
I HAVE TO DO SOME-THING...
CLICK
FIG-URES!
OUT AND ABOUT AGAIN...
WHAT...
...IS HE UP TO?

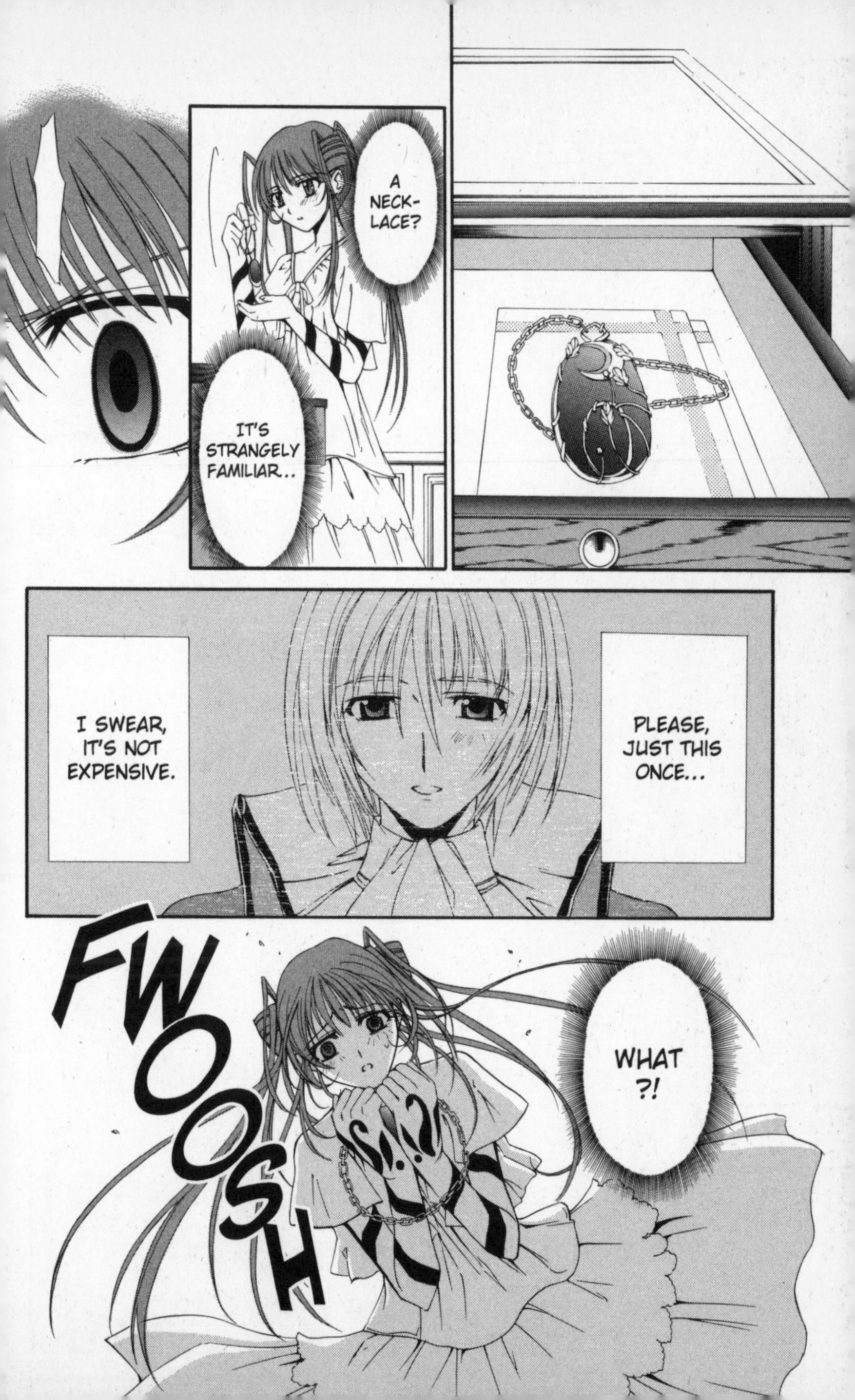
A NECK-LACE?
IT'S STRANGELY FAMILIAR...
PLEASE, JUST THIS ONCE...
I SWEAR, IT'S NOT EXPENSIVE.
WHAT ?!
FWOOSH

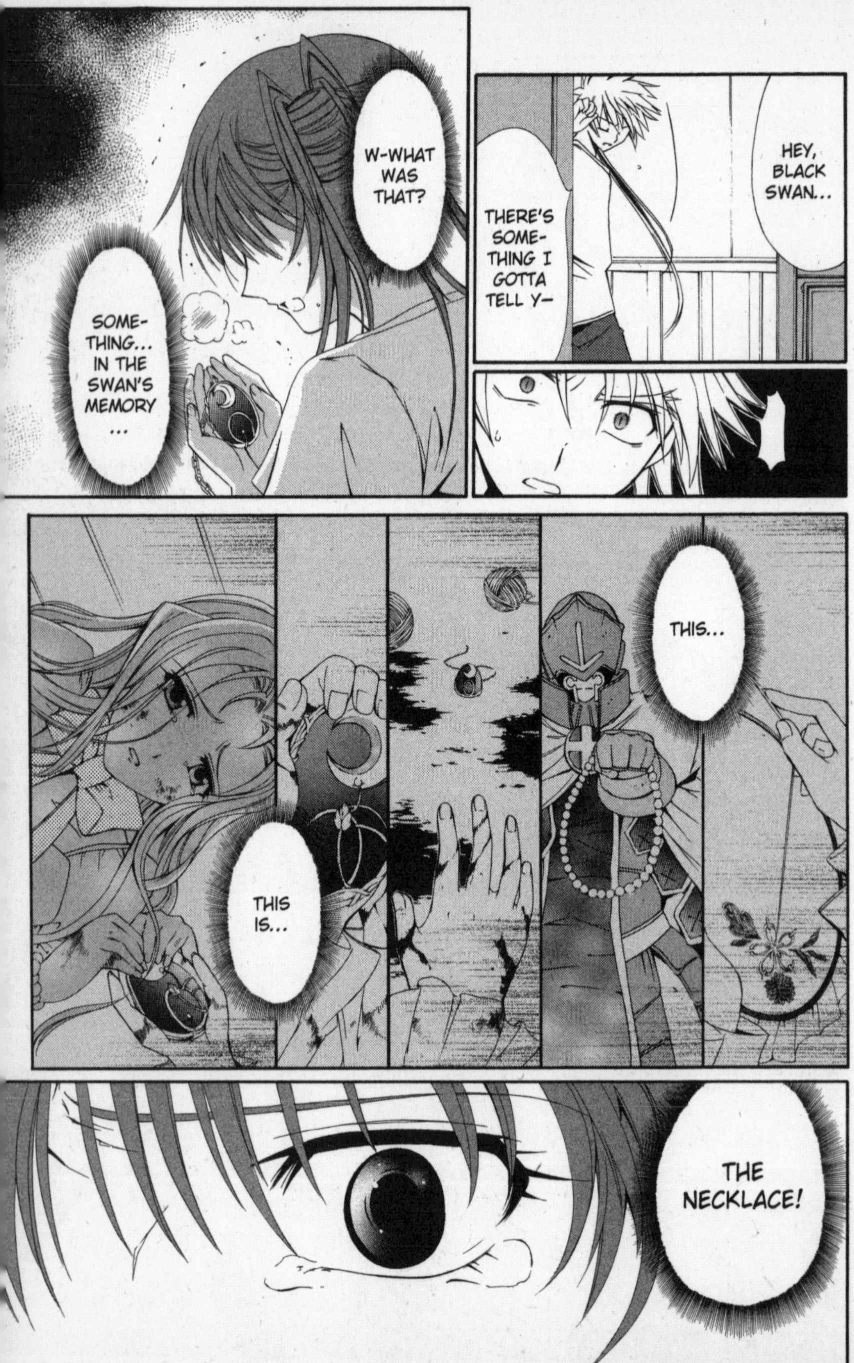
HEY, BLACK SWAN...
THERE'S SOME-THING I GOTTA TELL Y—
W-WHAT WAS THAT?
SOME-THING... IN THE SWAN'S MEMORY ...
THIS...
THIS IS...
THE NECKLACE!

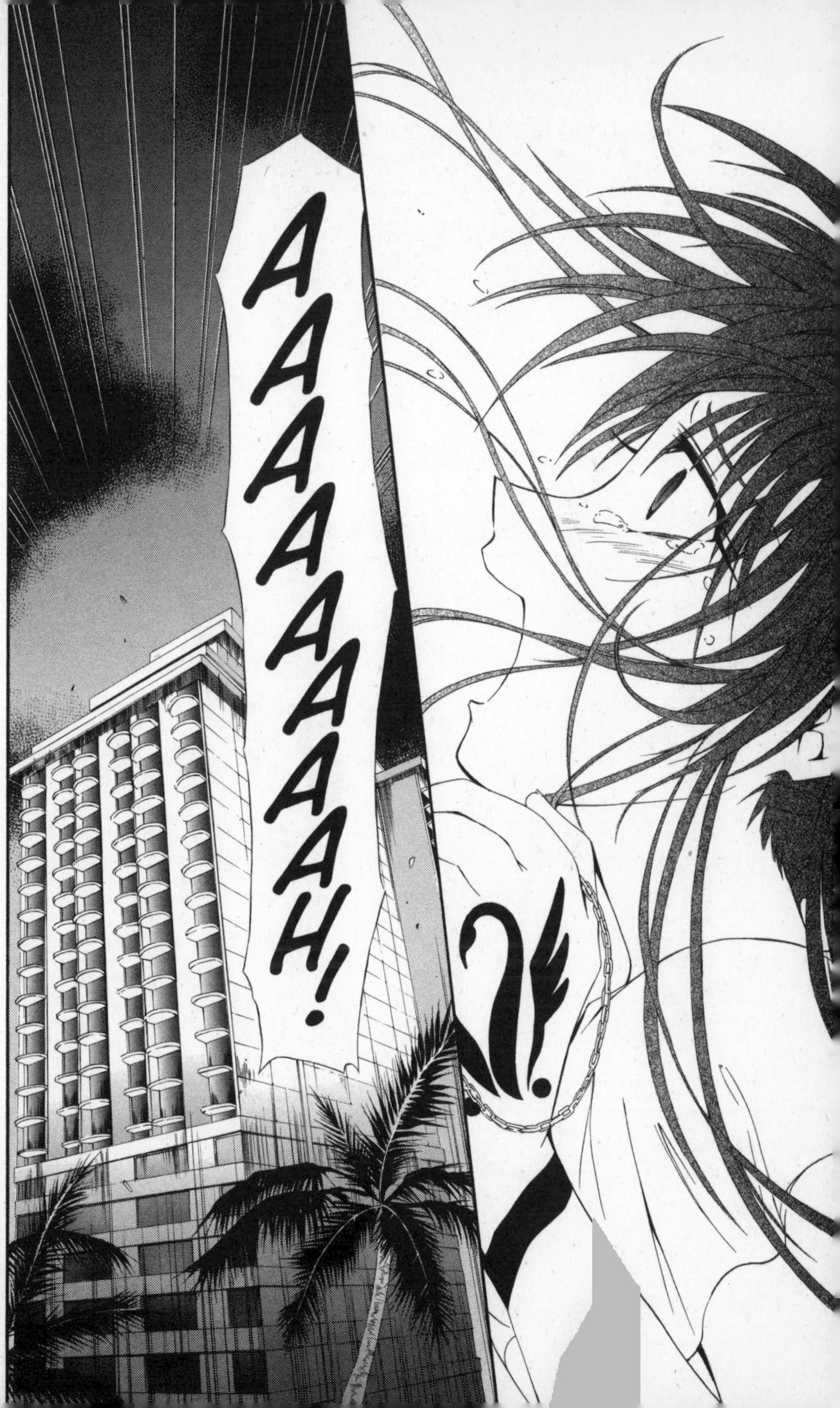
AAAAAAAAH!
?!

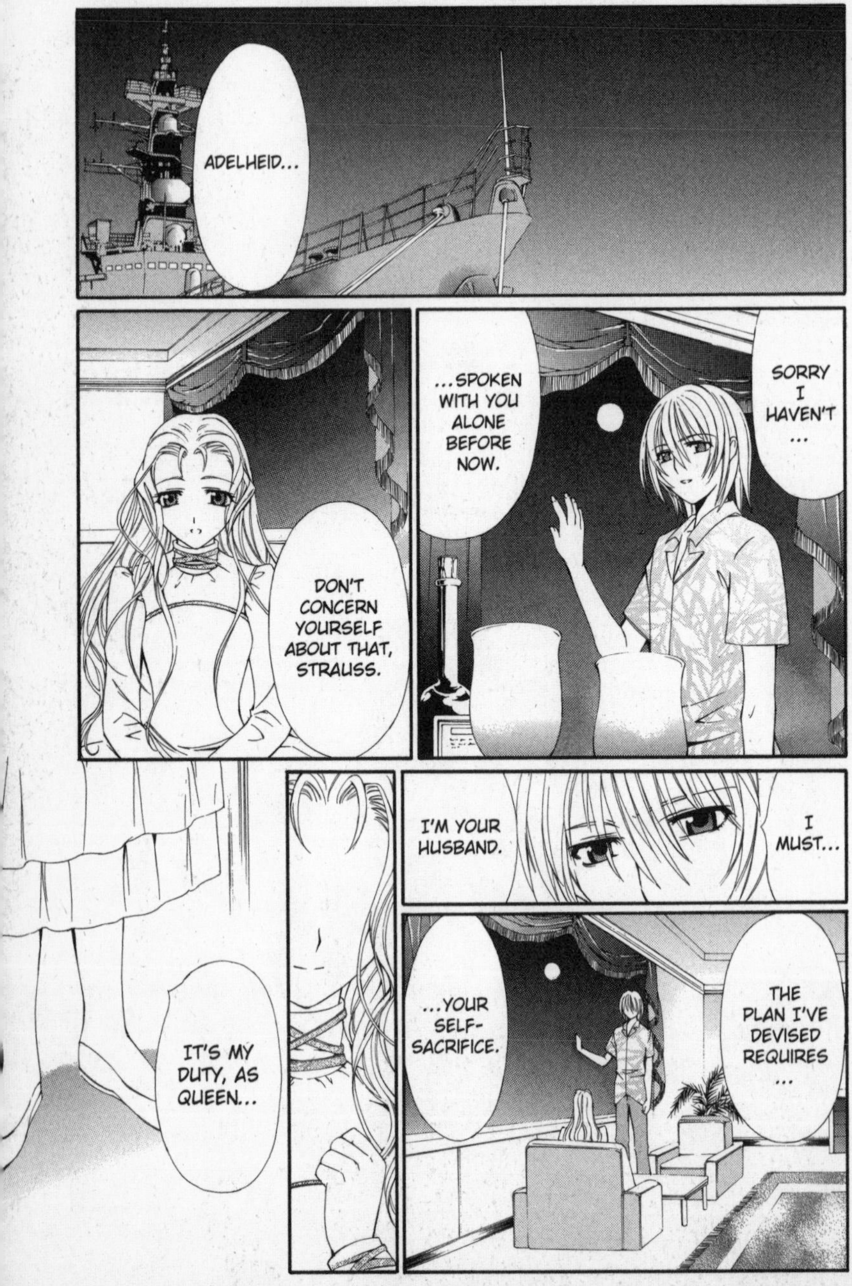
ADELHEID...
SORRY I HAVEN'T...
...SPOKEN WITH YOU ALONE BEFORE NOW.
DON'T CONCERN YOURSELF ABOUT THAT, STRAUSS.
I MUST...
I'M YOUR HUSBAND.
THE PLAN I'VE DEVISED REQUIRES...
...YOUR SELF-SACRIFICE.
IT'S MY DUTY, AS QUEEN...

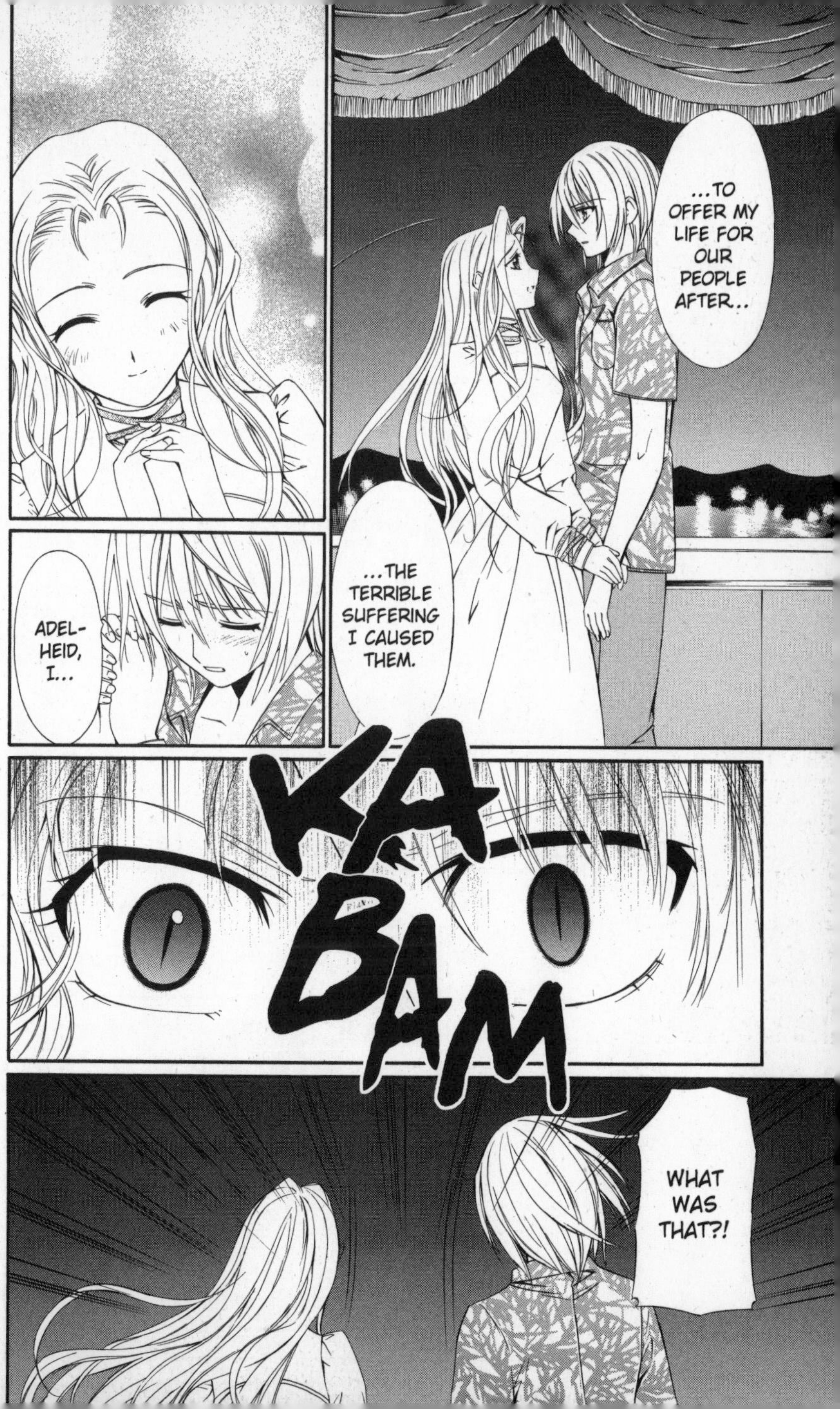
...TO OFFER MY LIFE FOR OUR PEOPLE AFTER...
...THE TERRIBLE SUFFERING I CAUSED THEM.
ADEL-HEID, I...
KA BAM
WHAT WAS THAT?!

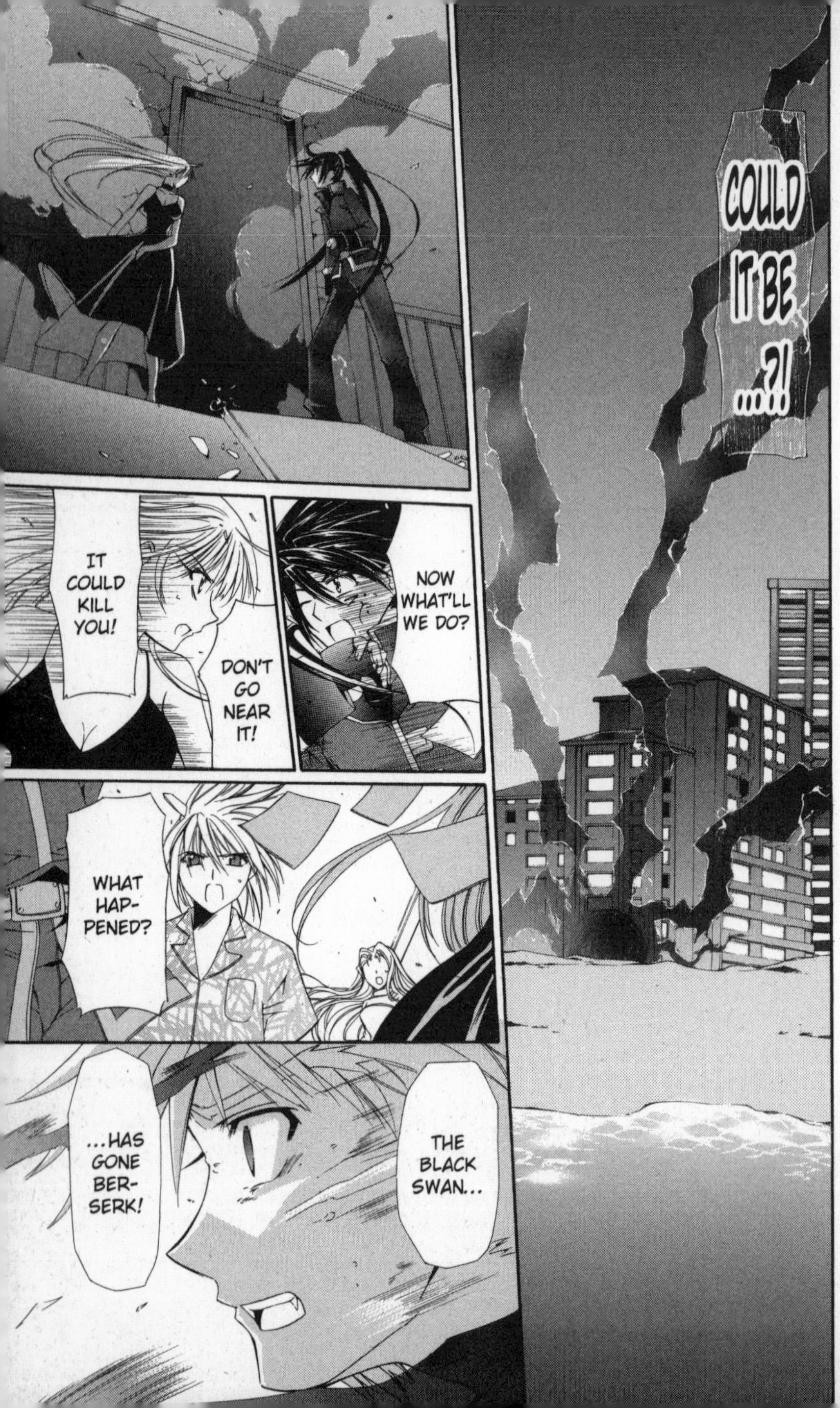
COULD IT BE ...?!
NOW WHAT'LL WE DO?
DON'T GO NEAR IT!
IT COULD KILL YOU!
WHAT HAP-PENED?
THE BLACK SWAN...
...HAS GONE BER-SERK!

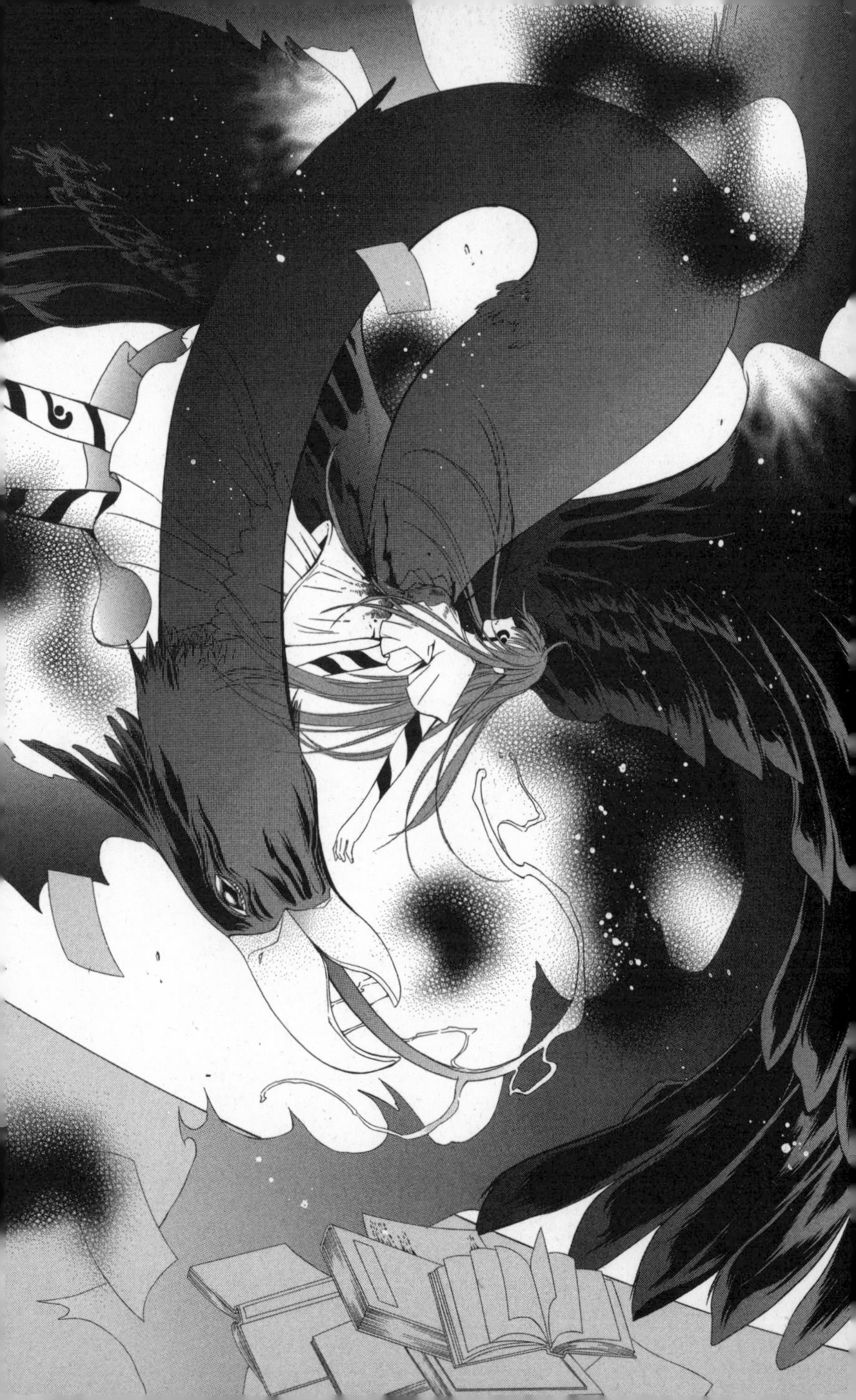

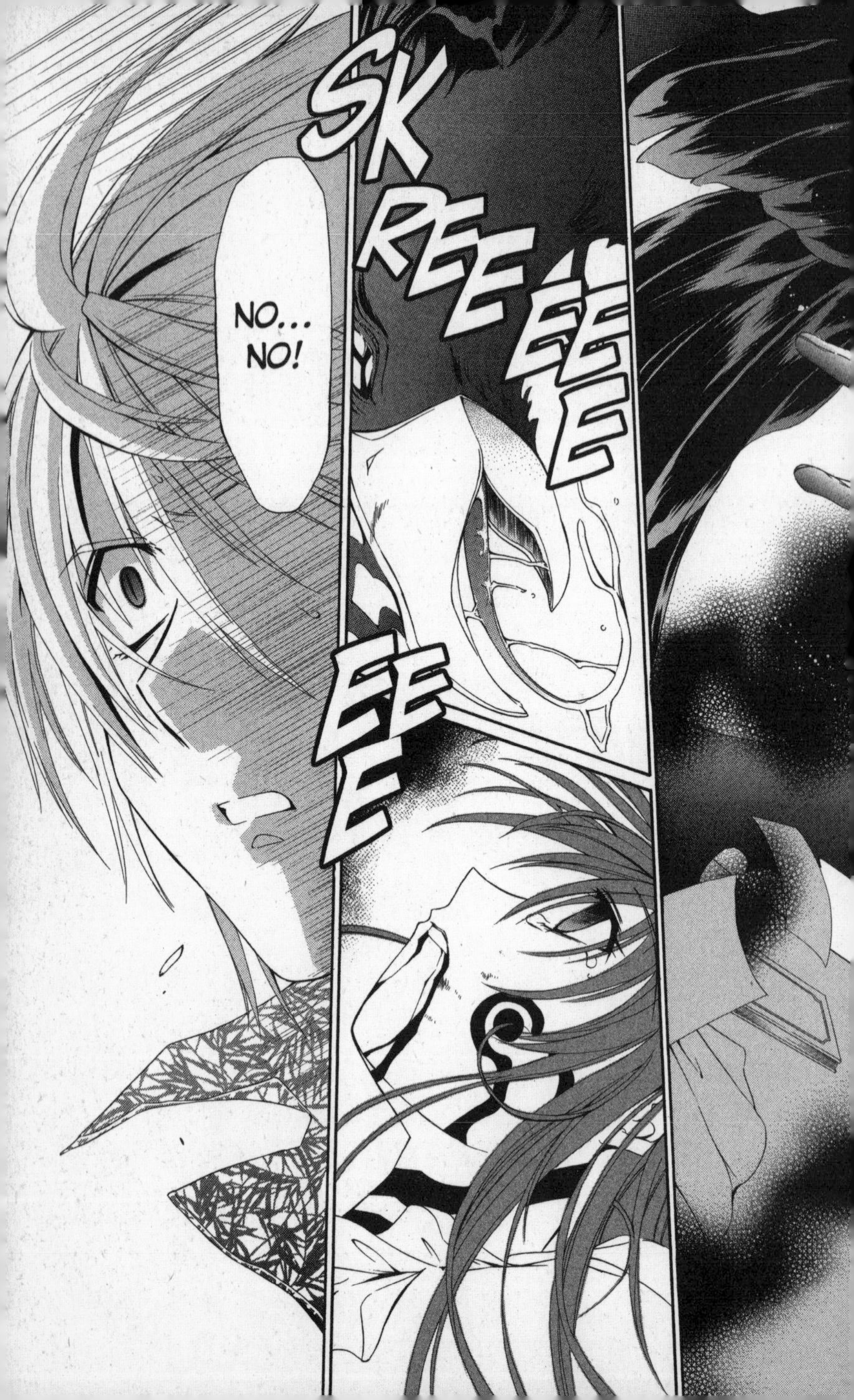
SKREEEEEEEEEE
NO... NO!

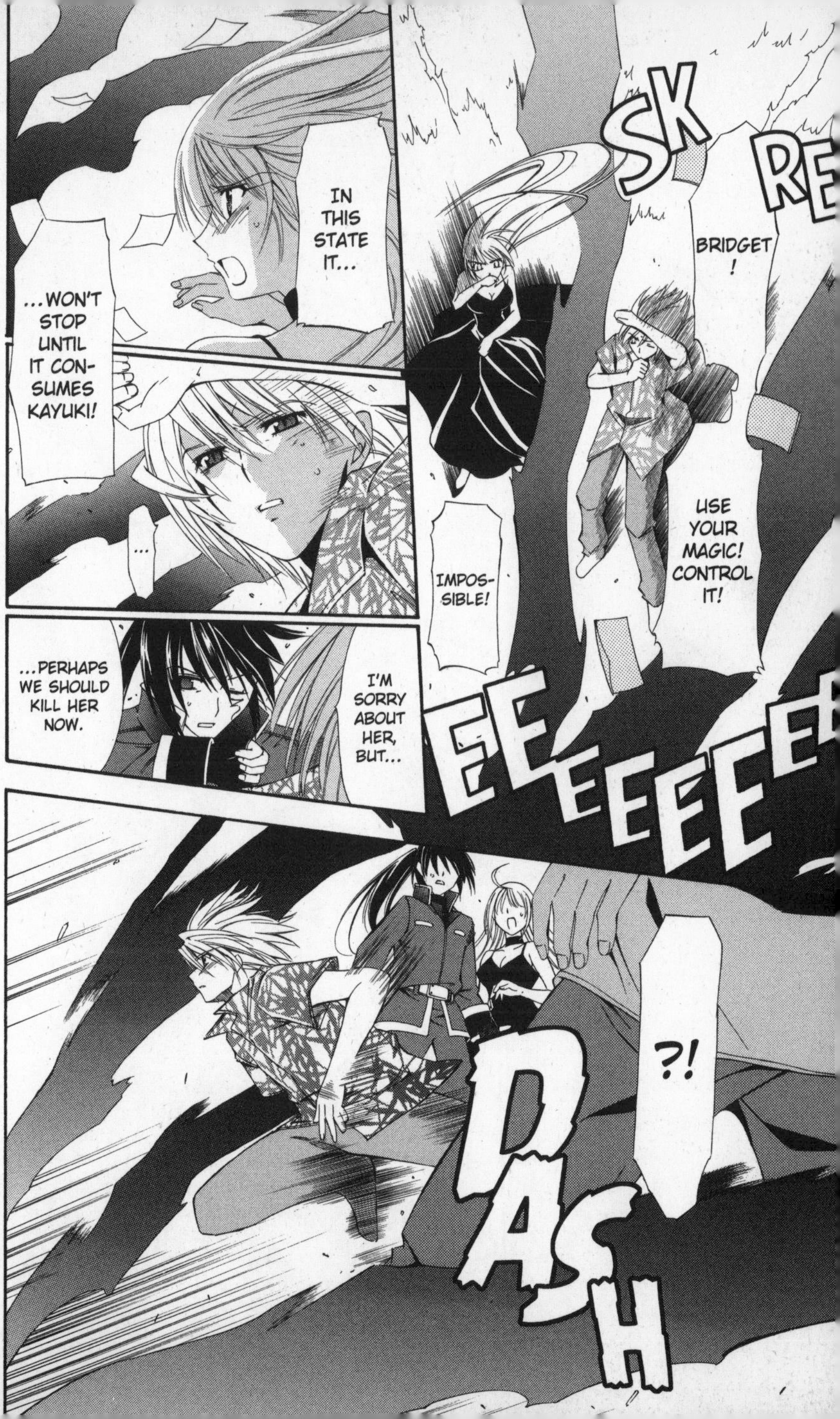
SKREEEEEEEEE
BRIDGET!
USE YOUR MAGIC! CONTROL IT!
IMPOSSIBLE!
IN THIS STATE IT...
...WON'T STOP UNTIL IT CONSUMES KAYUKI!
...
I'M SORRY ABOUT HER, BUT...
...PERHAPS WE SHOULD KILL HER NOW.
?!
DASH

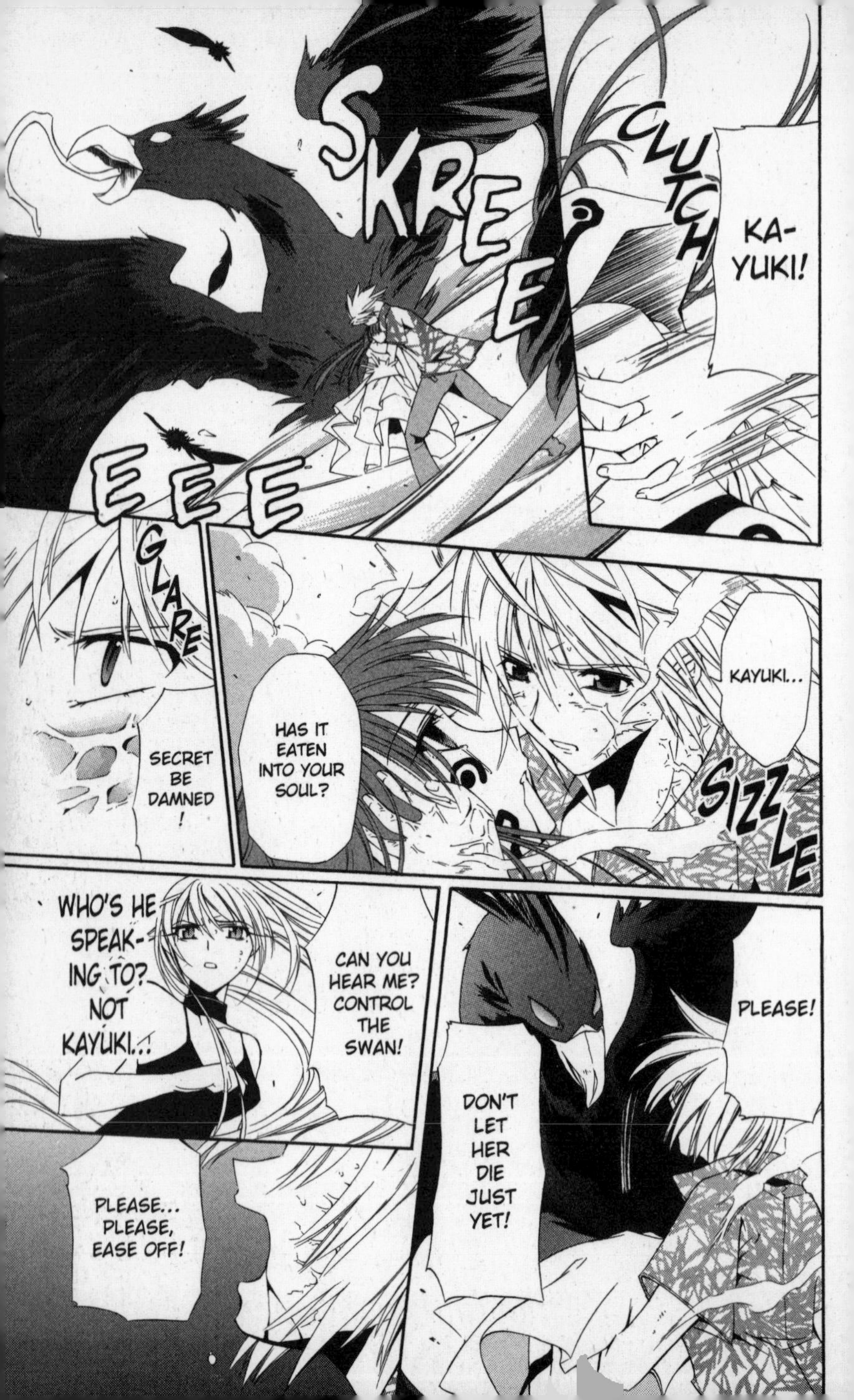
CLUTCH
KA-YUKI!
SKREEEEEE
KAYUKI...
SIZZLE
HAS IT EATEN INTO YOUR SOUL?
GLARE
SECRET BE DAMNED!
PLEASE!
DON'T LET HER DIE JUST YET!
CAN YOU HEAR ME? CONTROL THE SWAN!
WHO'S HE SPEAK-ING TO? NOT KAYUKI...
PLEASE... PLEASE, EASE OFF!

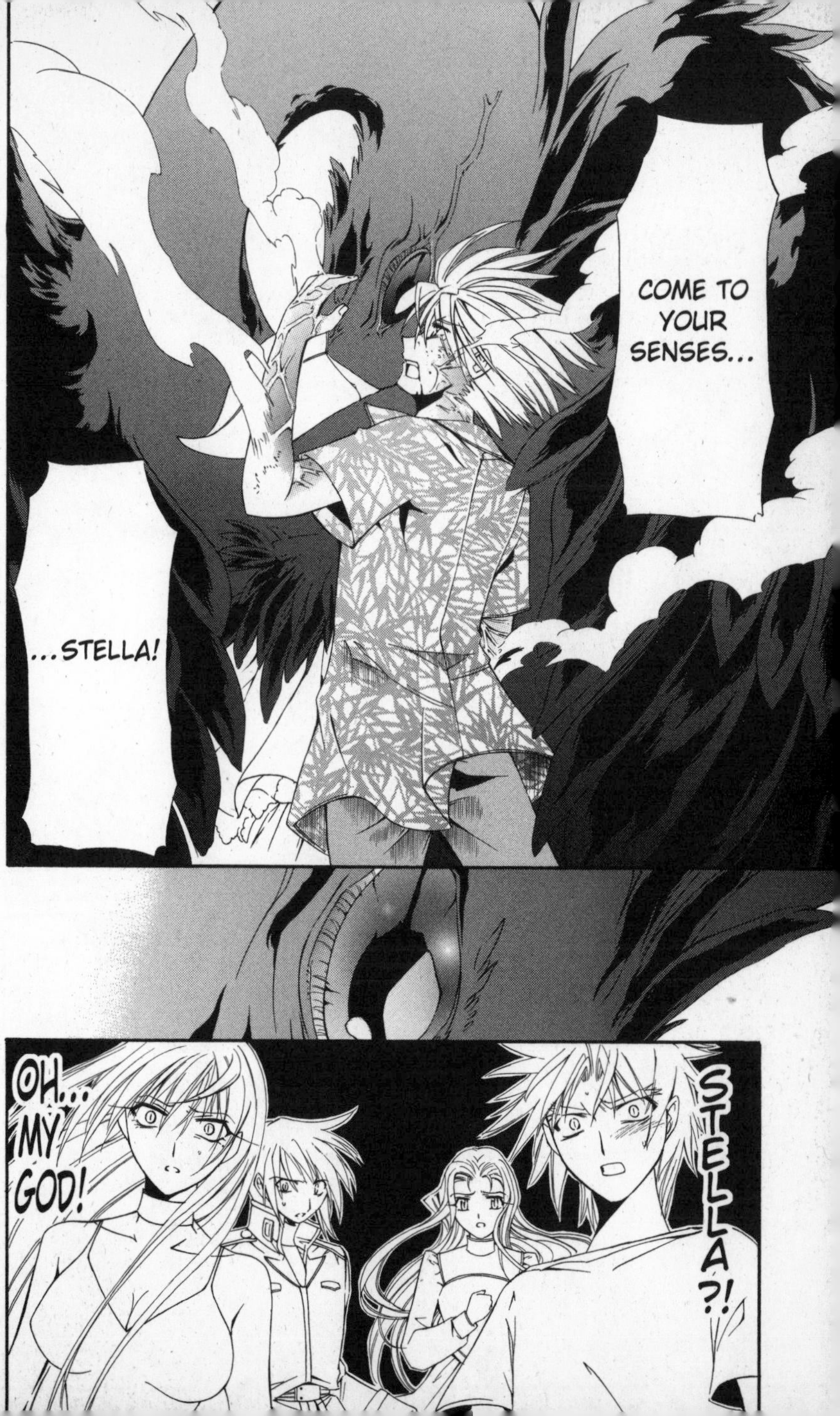
COME TO YOUR SENSES...
...STELLA!
STELLA?!
OH... MY GOD!

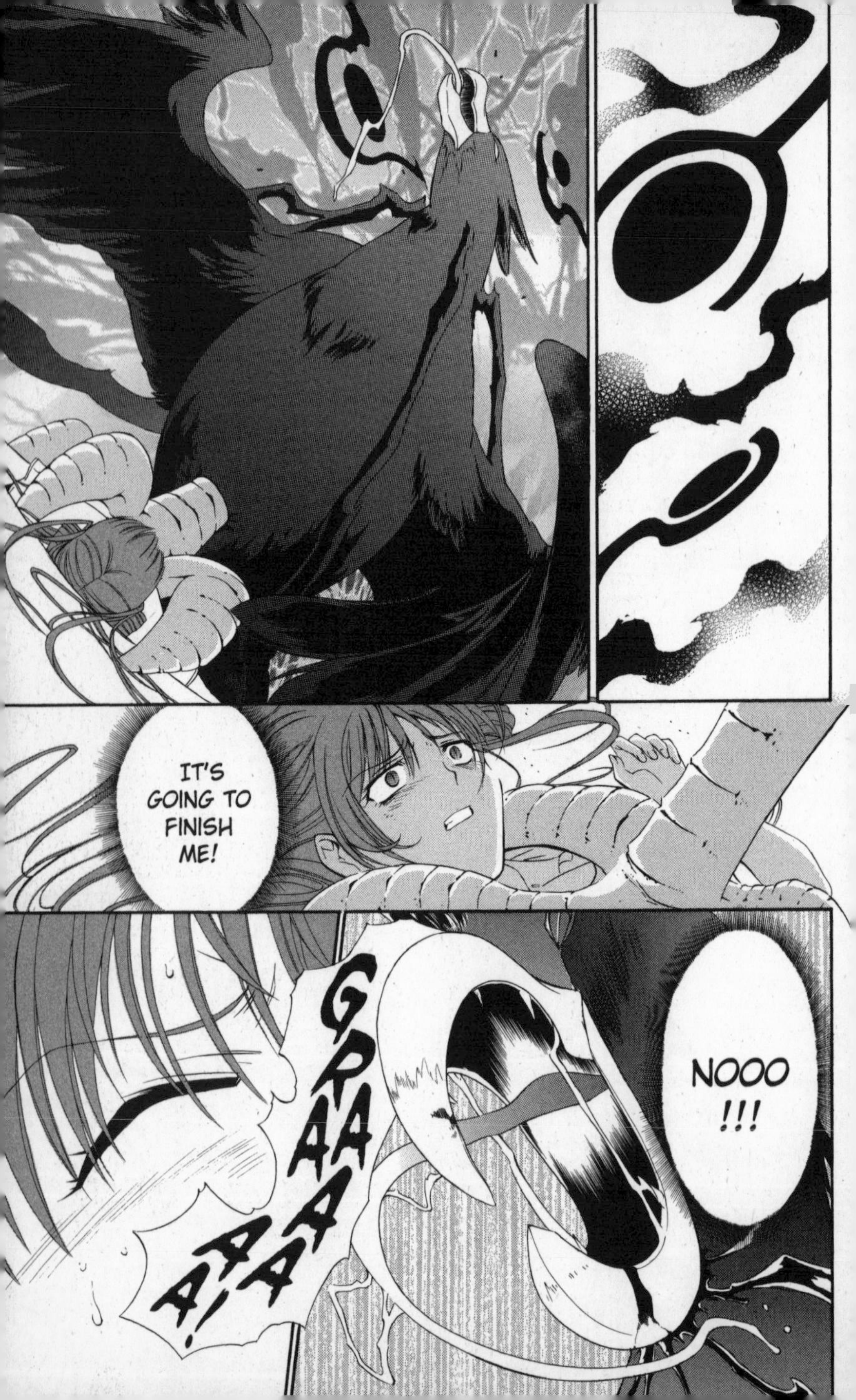
IT'S GOING TO FINISH ME!
NOOO !!!
GRAAAAAAAA!

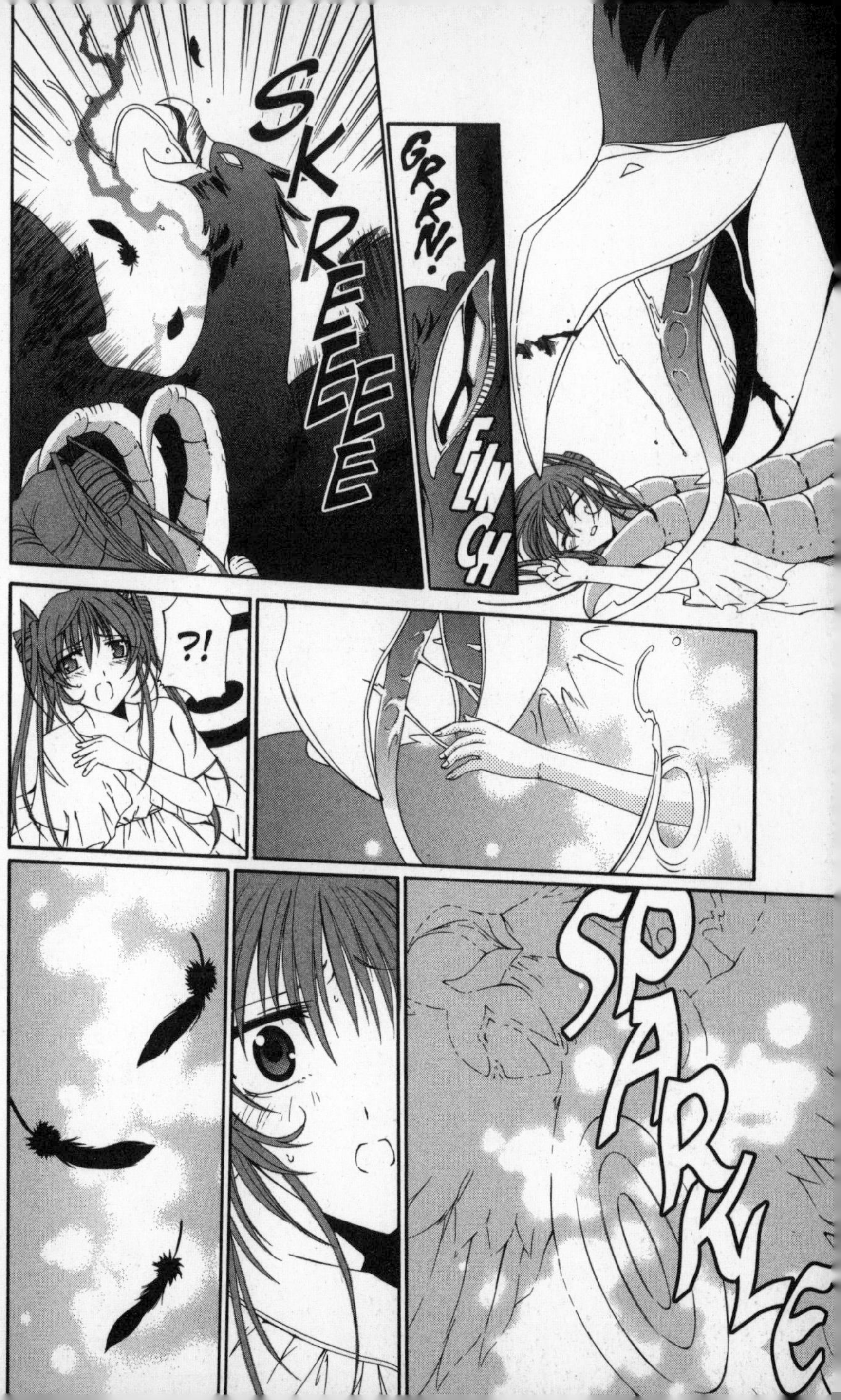
GRRRN!
FLINCH
SKREEEEE
?!
SPARKLE

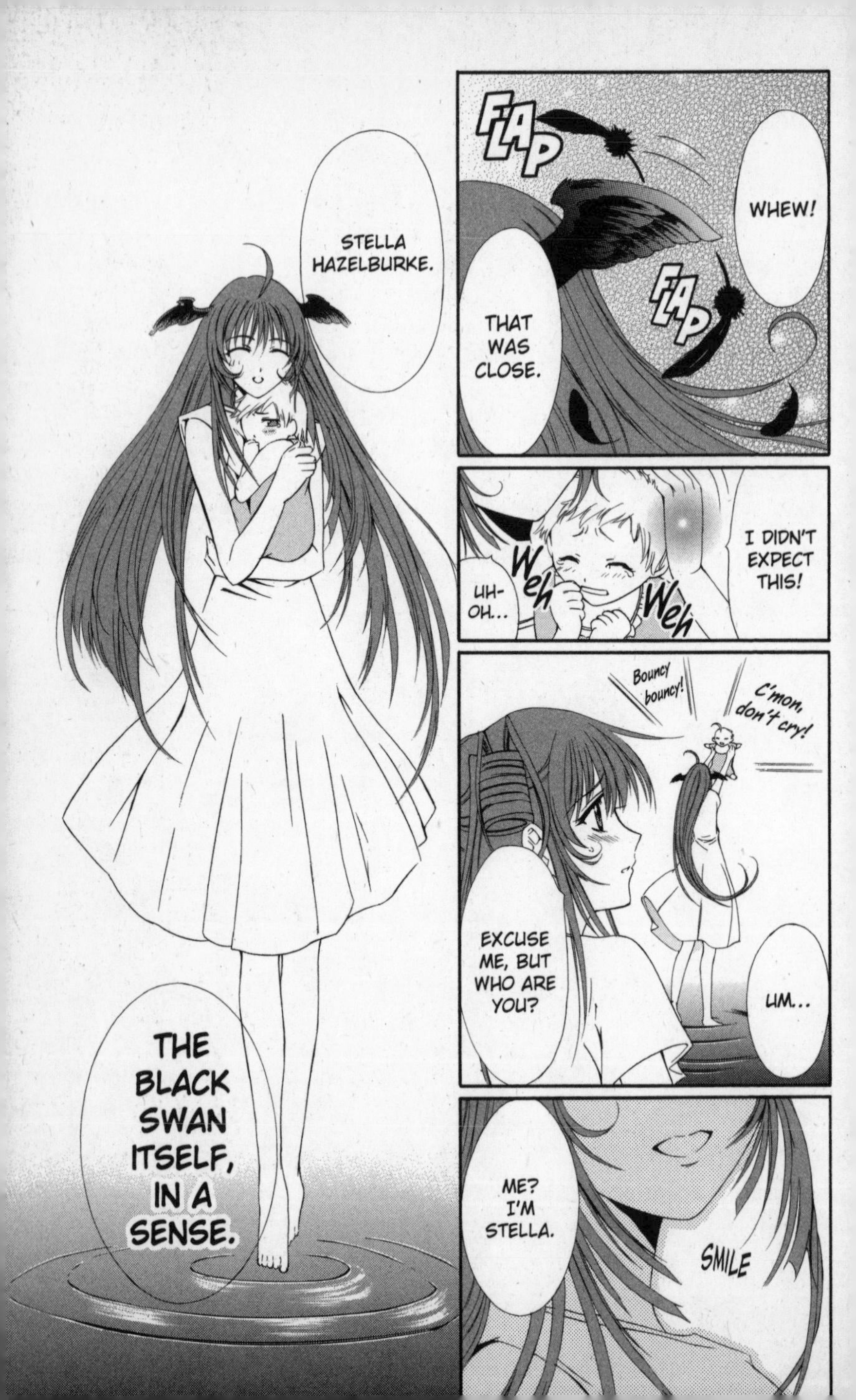
WHEW!
FLAP
FLAP
THAT WAS CLOSE.
I DIDN'T EXPECT THIS!
Weh
Weh
UH-OH...
C'mon, don't cry!
Bouncy bouncy!
UM...
EXCUSE ME, BUT WHO ARE YOU?
ME? I'M STELLA.
SMILE
STELLA HAZELBURKE.
THE BLACK SWAN ITSELF, IN A SENSE.

THE RECORD OF A
FALLEN VAMPIRE

Chapter 38: The Unabsolved

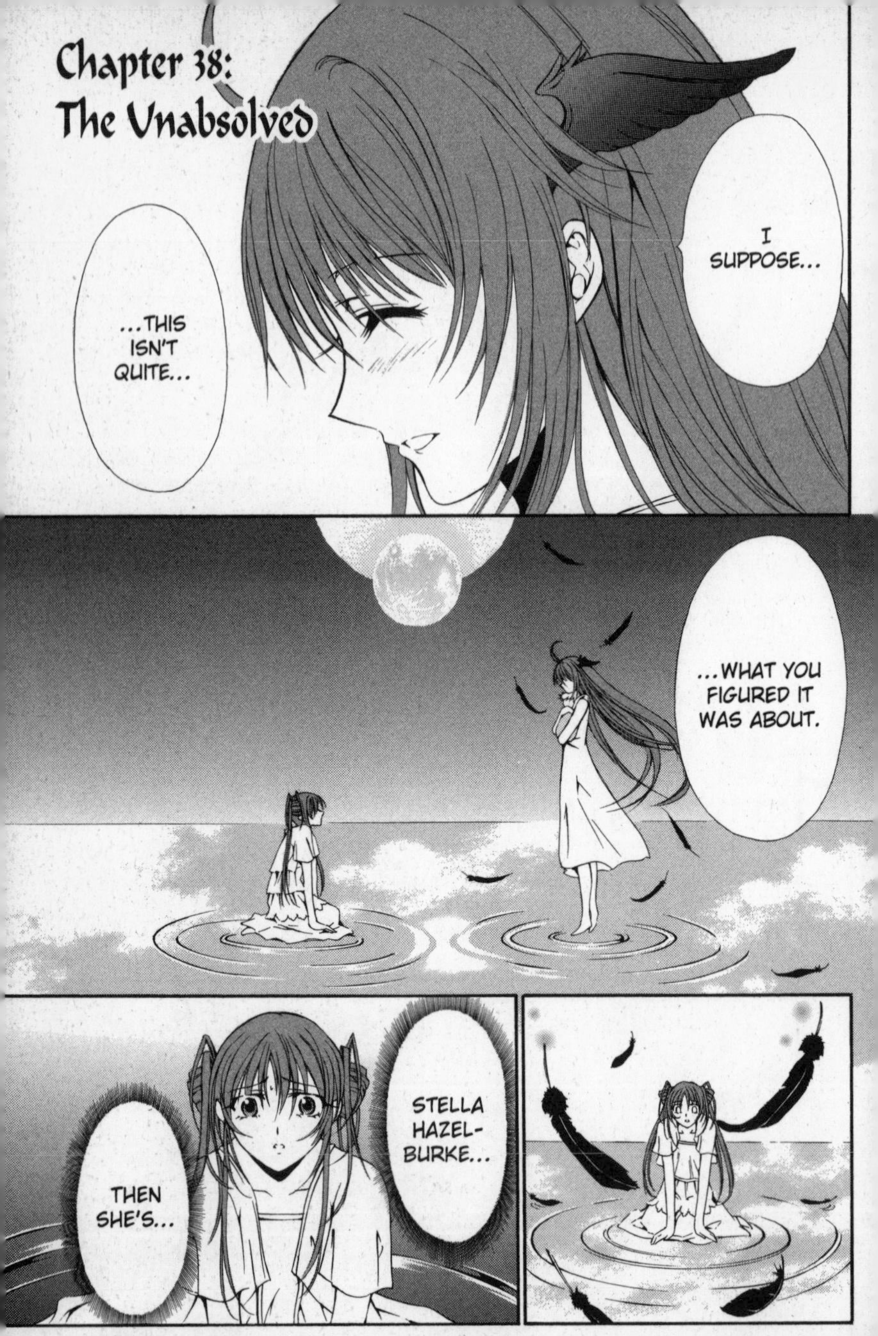
I SUPPOSE...
...THIS ISN'T QUITE...
...WHAT YOU FIGURED IT WAS ABOUT.
STELLA HAZEL-BURKE...
THEN SHE'S...

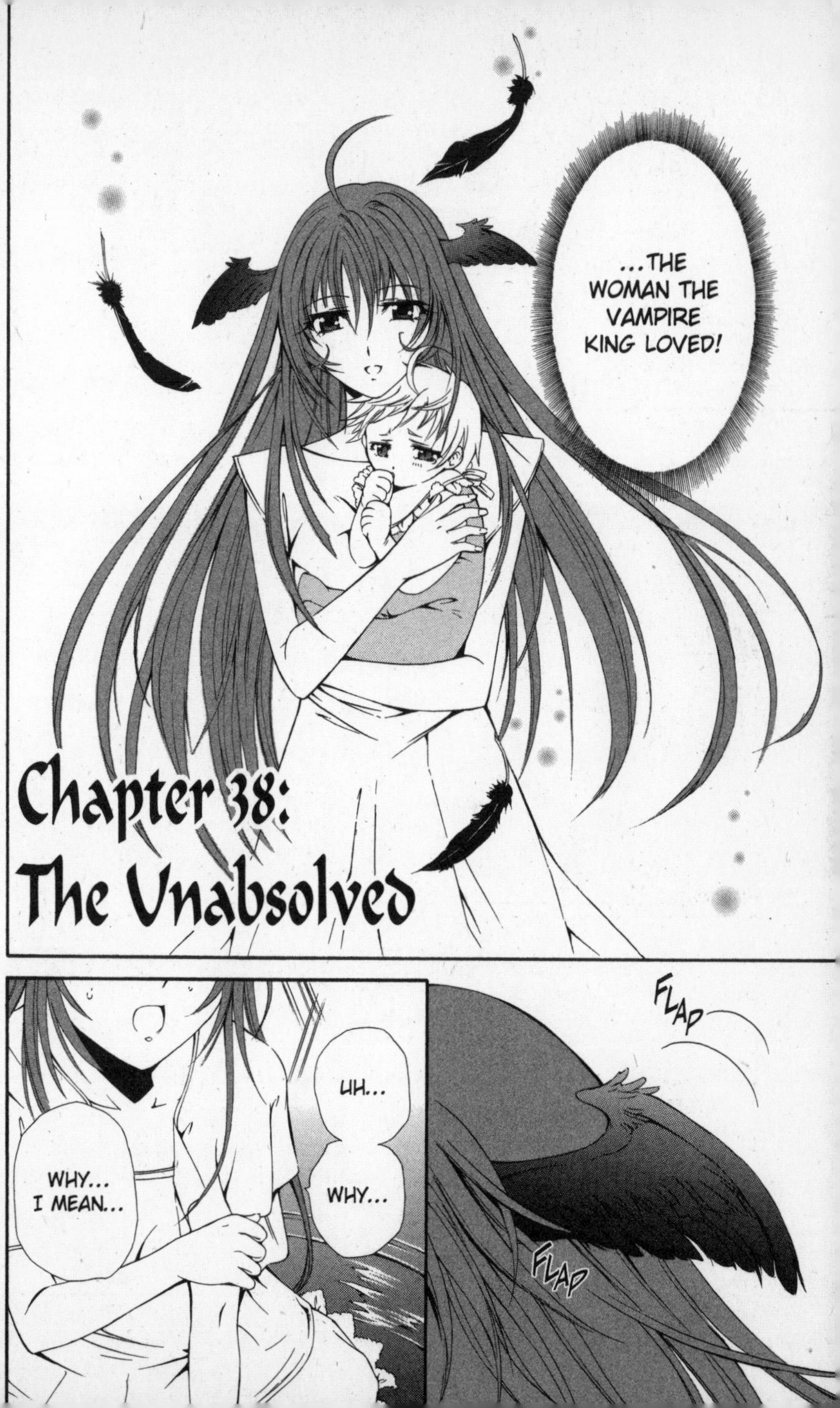
...THE WOMAN THE VAMPIRE KING LOVED!
Chapter 38:
The Unabsolved
FLAP
FLAP
UH...
WHY...
WHY...
I MEAN...

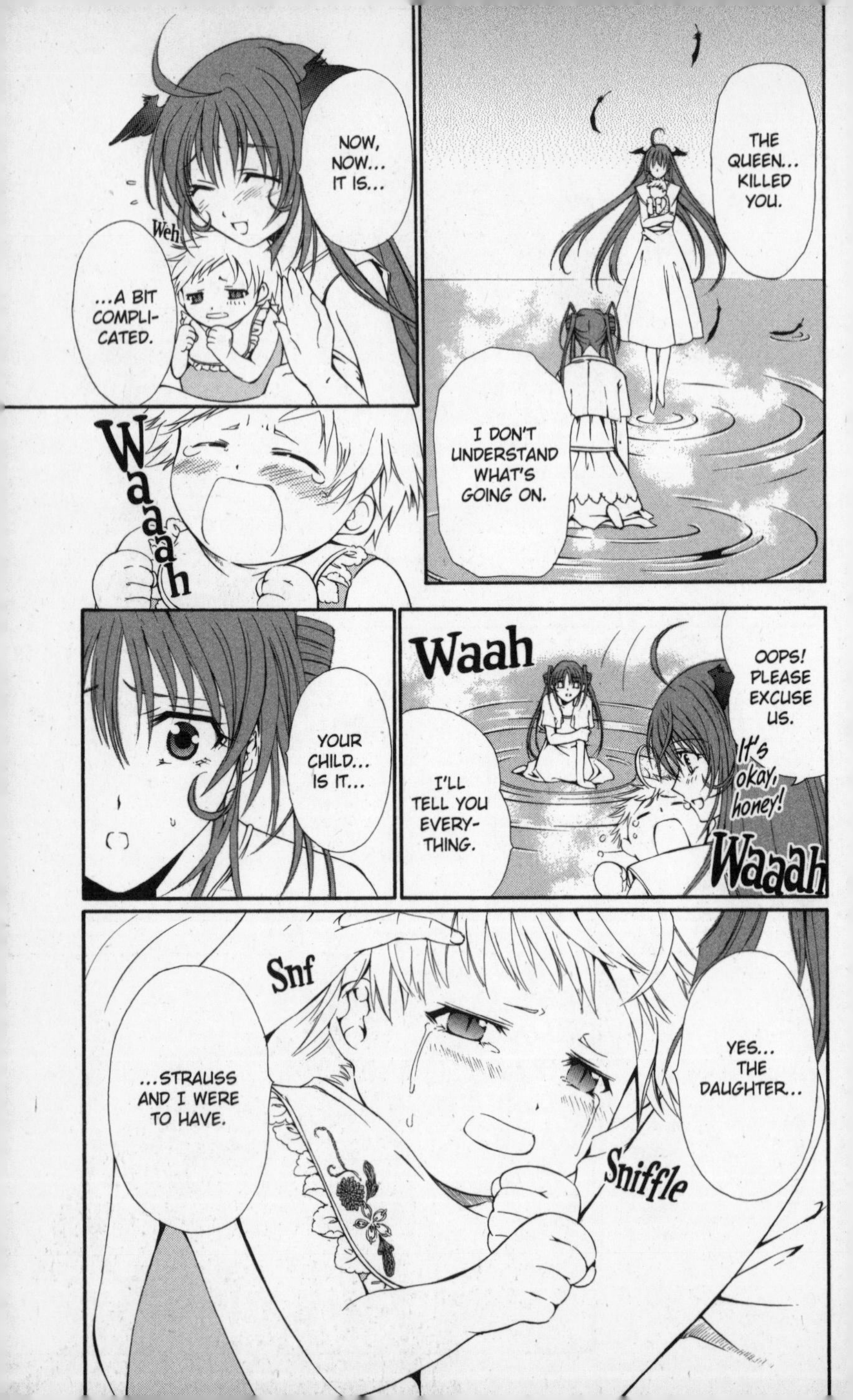
THE QUEEN... KILLED YOU.
I DON'T UNDERSTAND WHAT'S GOING ON.
NOW, NOW... IT IS...
Weh
...A BIT COMPLICATED.
Waaaah
OOPS! PLEASE EXCUSE US.
It's okay, honey!
Waah
I'LL TELL YOU EVERYTHING.
Waaah
YOUR CHILD... IS IT...
YES... THE DAUGHTER...
Snf
Sniffle
...STRAUSS AND I WERE TO HAVE.

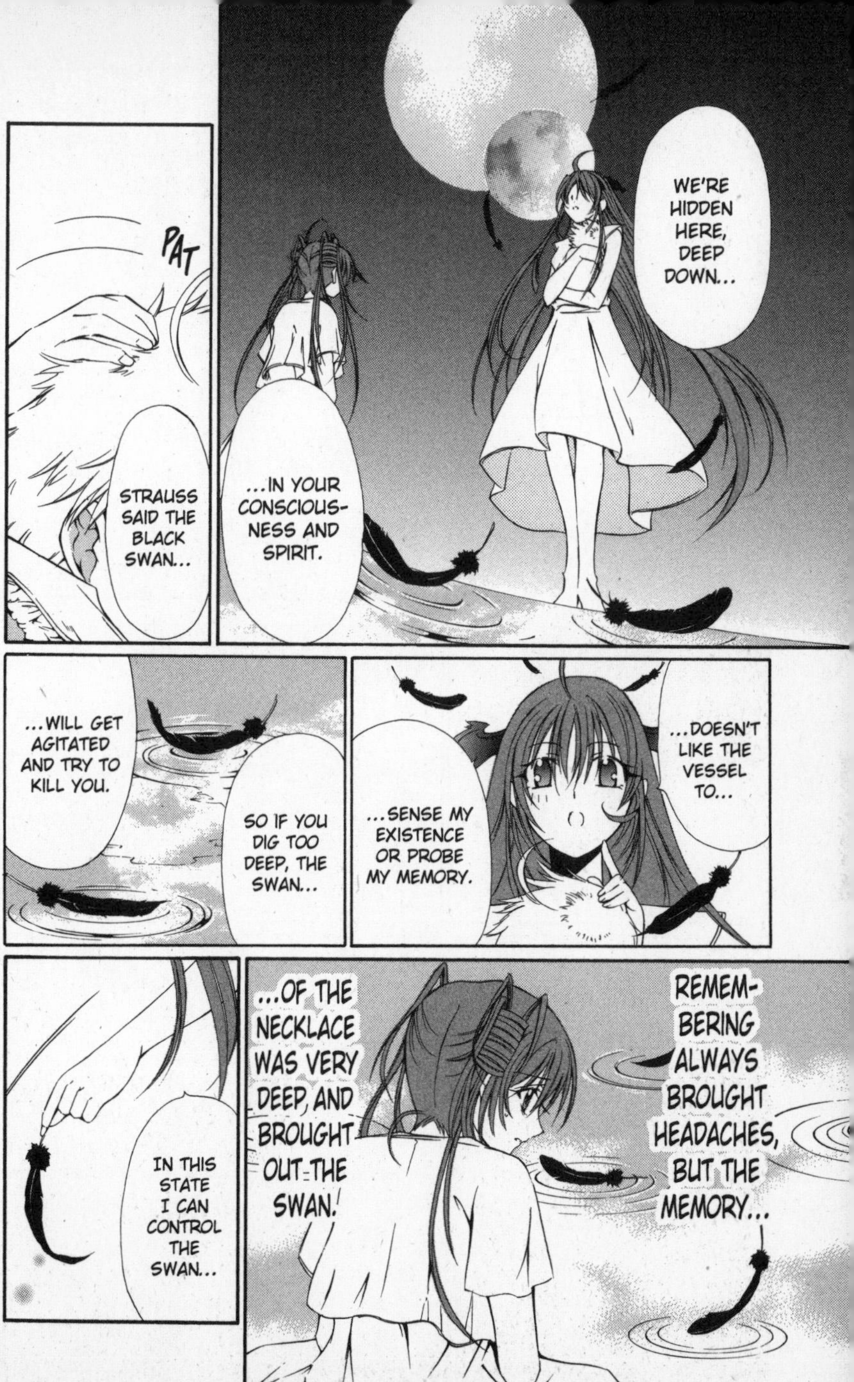
WE'RE HIDDEN HERE, DEEP DOWN...
...IN YOUR CONSCIOUSNESS AND SPIRIT.
PAT
STRAUSS SAID THE BLACK SWAN...
...DOESN'T LIKE THE VESSEL TO...
...SENSE MY EXISTENCE OR PROBE MY MEMORY.
SO IF YOU DIG TOO DEEP, THE SWAN...
...WILL GET AGITATED AND TRY TO KILL YOU.
REMEM-BERING ALWAYS BROUGHT HEADACHES, BUT THE MEMORY...
...OF THE NECKLACE WAS VERY DEEP, AND BROUGHT OUT THE SWAN.
IN THIS STATE I CAN CONTROL THE SWAN...

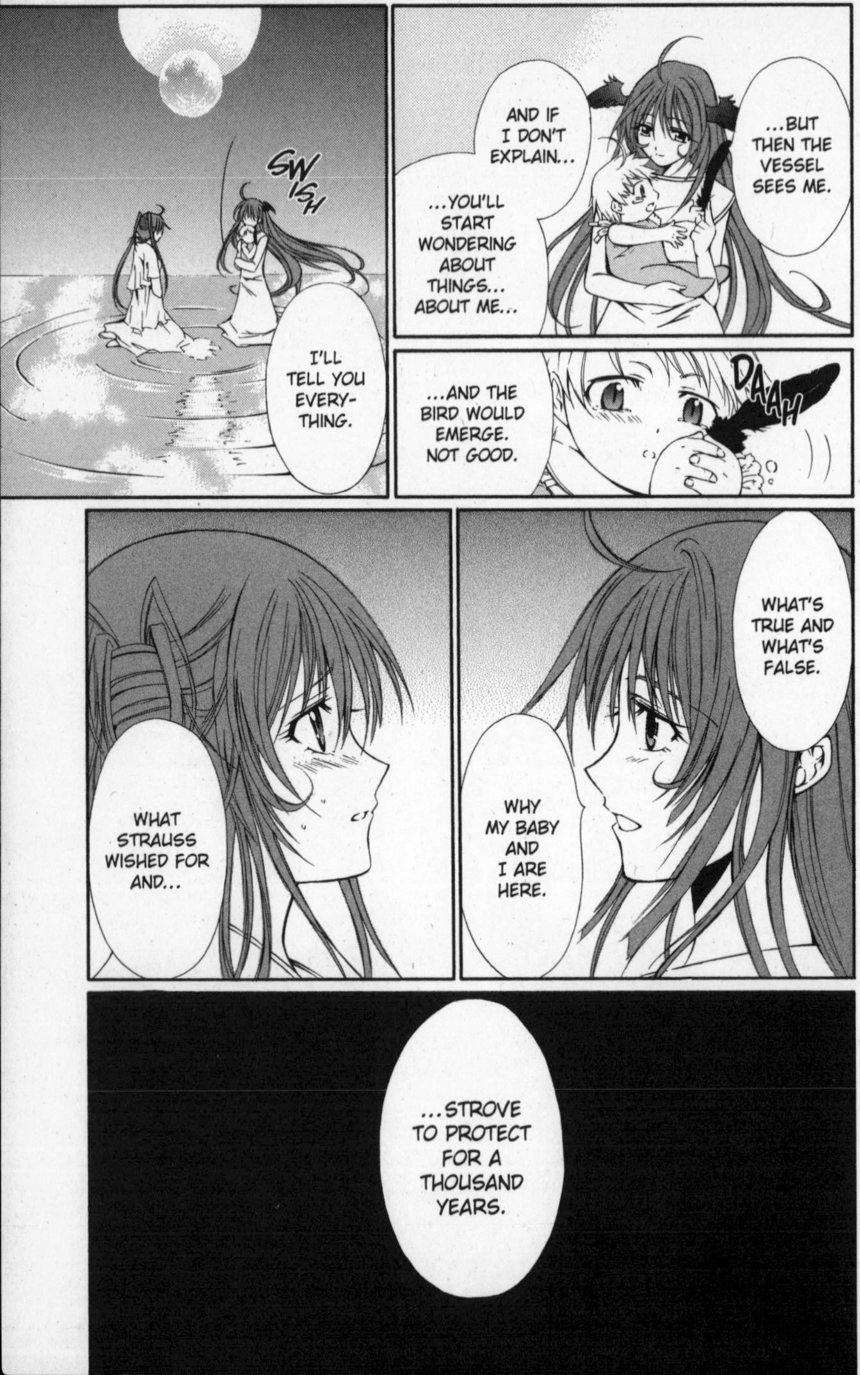
...BUT THEN THE VESSEL SEES ME.
AND IF I DON'T EXPLAIN...
...YOU'LL START WONDERING ABOUT THINGS... ABOUT ME...
DAAAH
...AND THE BIRD WOULD EMERGE. NOT GOOD.
SWISH
I'LL TELL YOU EVERY-THING.
WHAT'S TRUE AND WHAT'S FALSE.
WHY MY BABY AND I ARE HERE.
WHAT STRAUSS WISHED FOR AND...
...STROVE TO PROTECT FOR A THOUSAND YEARS.

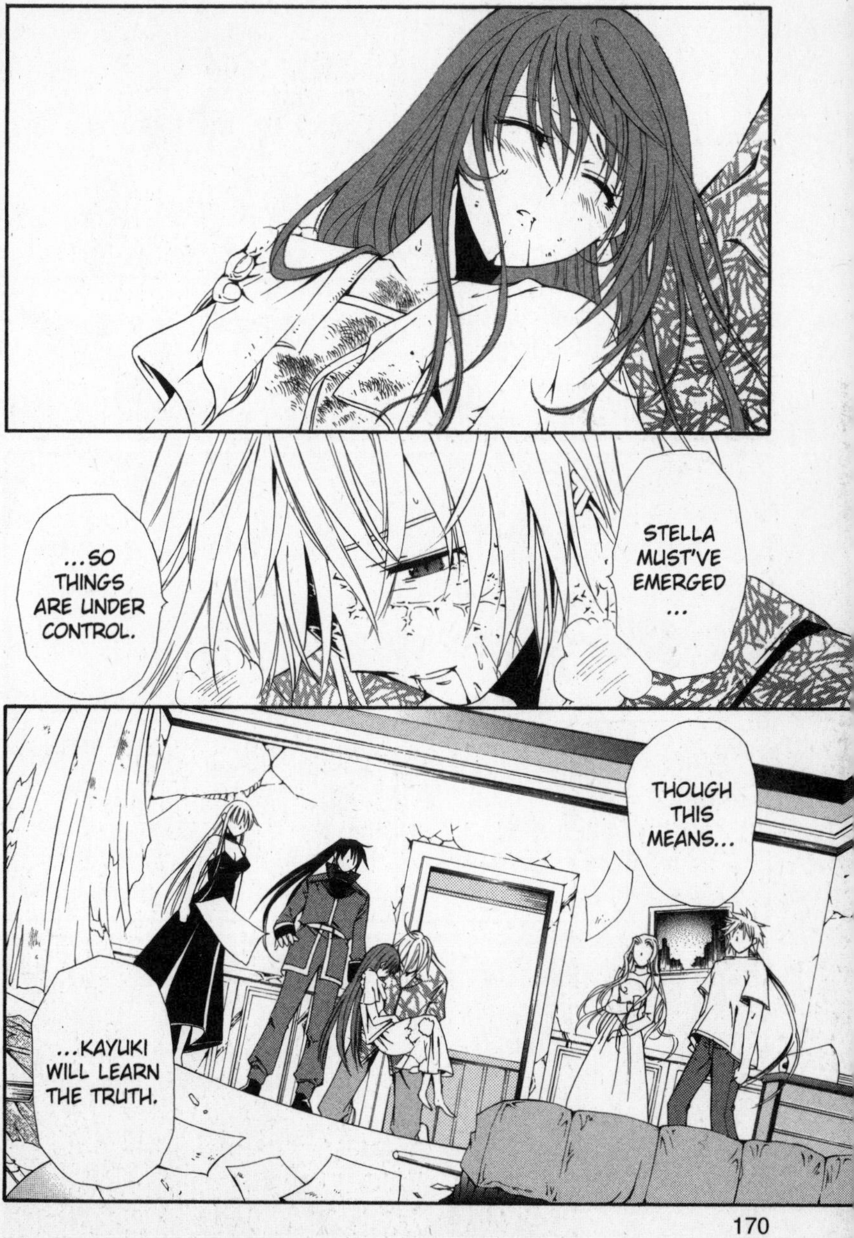
STELLA MUST'VE EMERGED ...
...SO THINGS ARE UNDER CONTROL.
THOUGH THIS MEANS...
...KAYUKI WILL LEARN THE TRUTH.

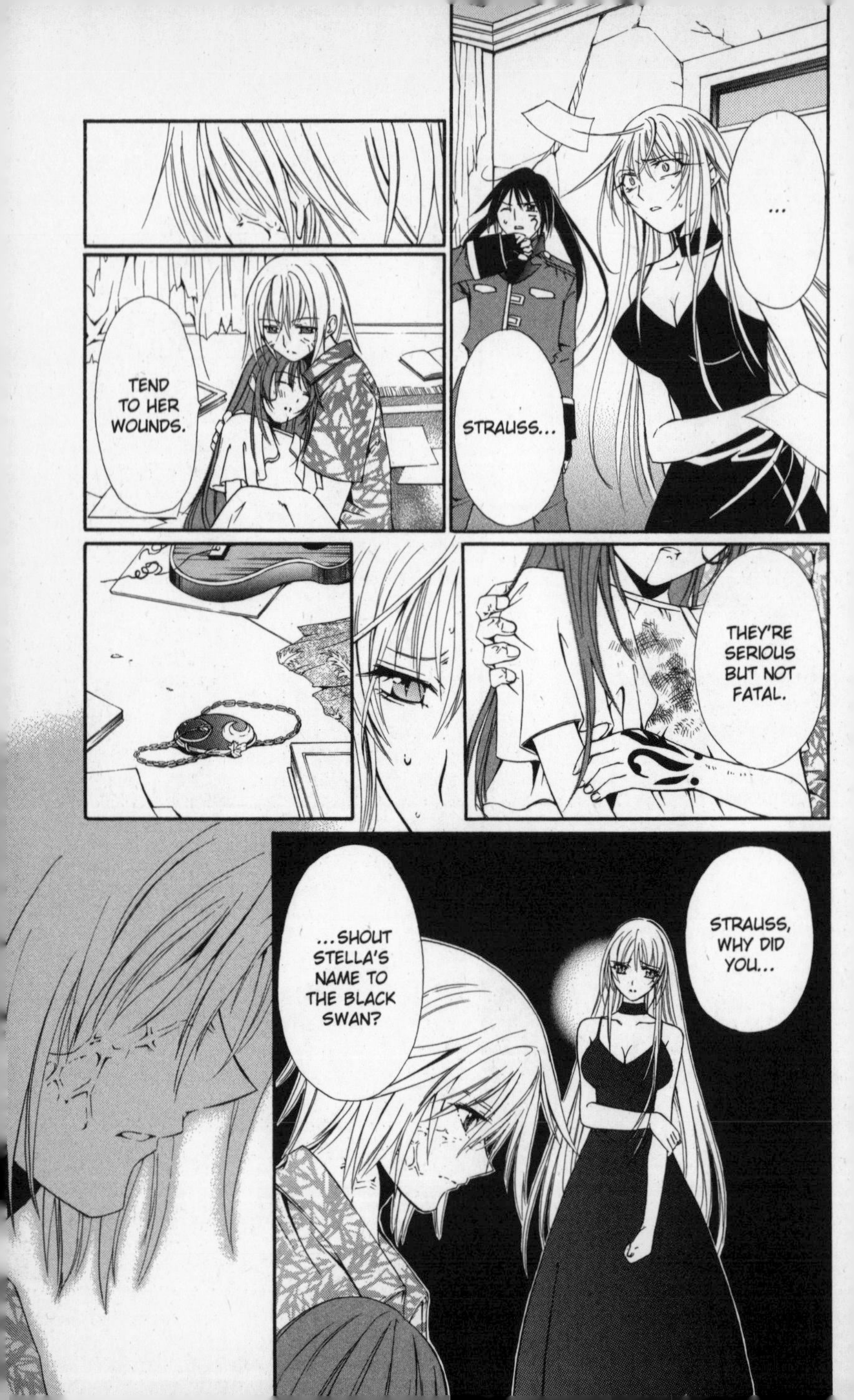
...
STRAUSS...
TEND TO HER WOUNDS.
THEY'RE SERIOUS BUT NOT FATAL.
STRAUSS, WHY DID YOU...
...SHOUT STELLA'S NAME TO THE BLACK SWAN?

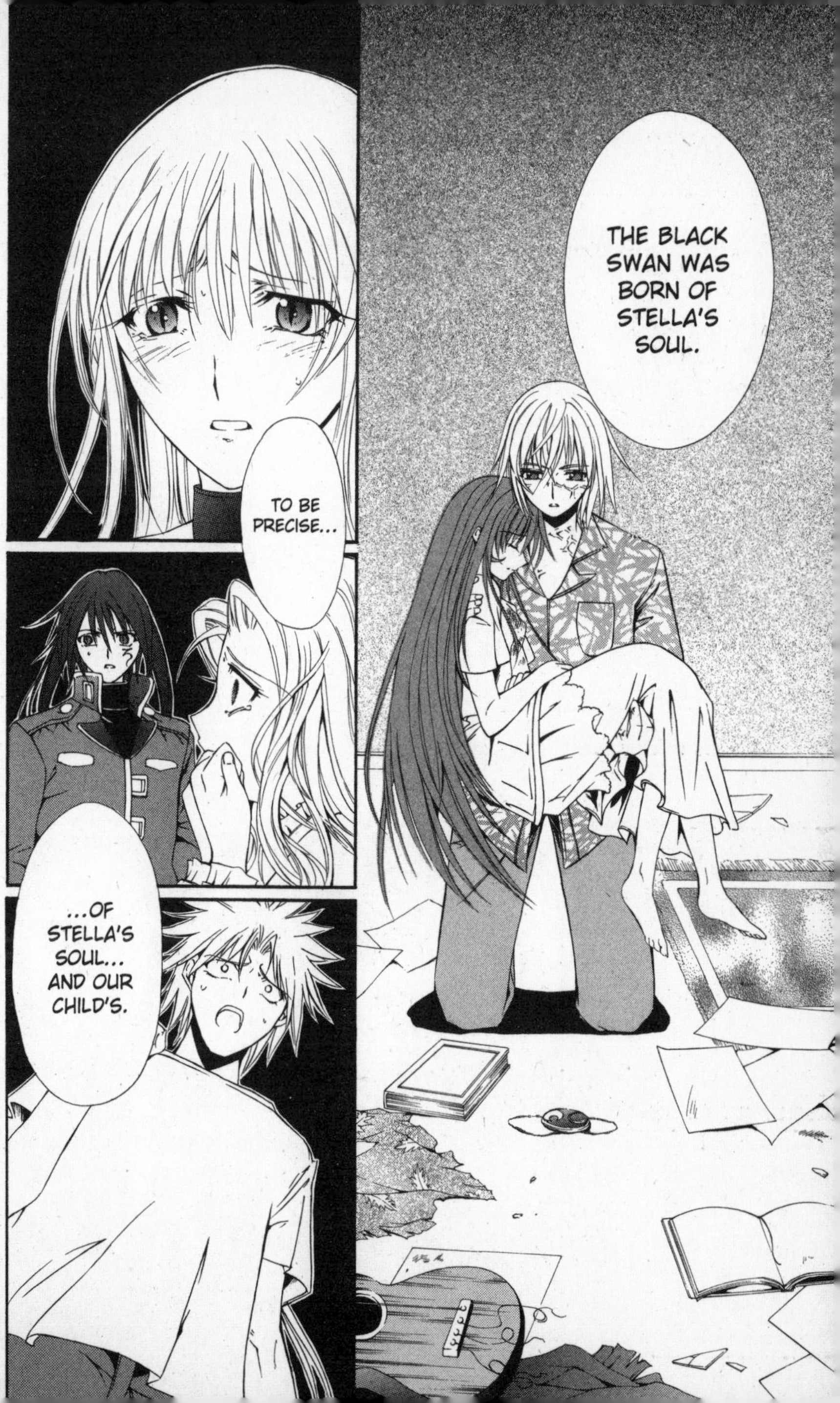
THE BLACK SWAN WAS BORN OF STELLA'S SOUL.
TO BE PRECISE...
...OF STELLA'S SOUL... AND OUR CHILD'S.

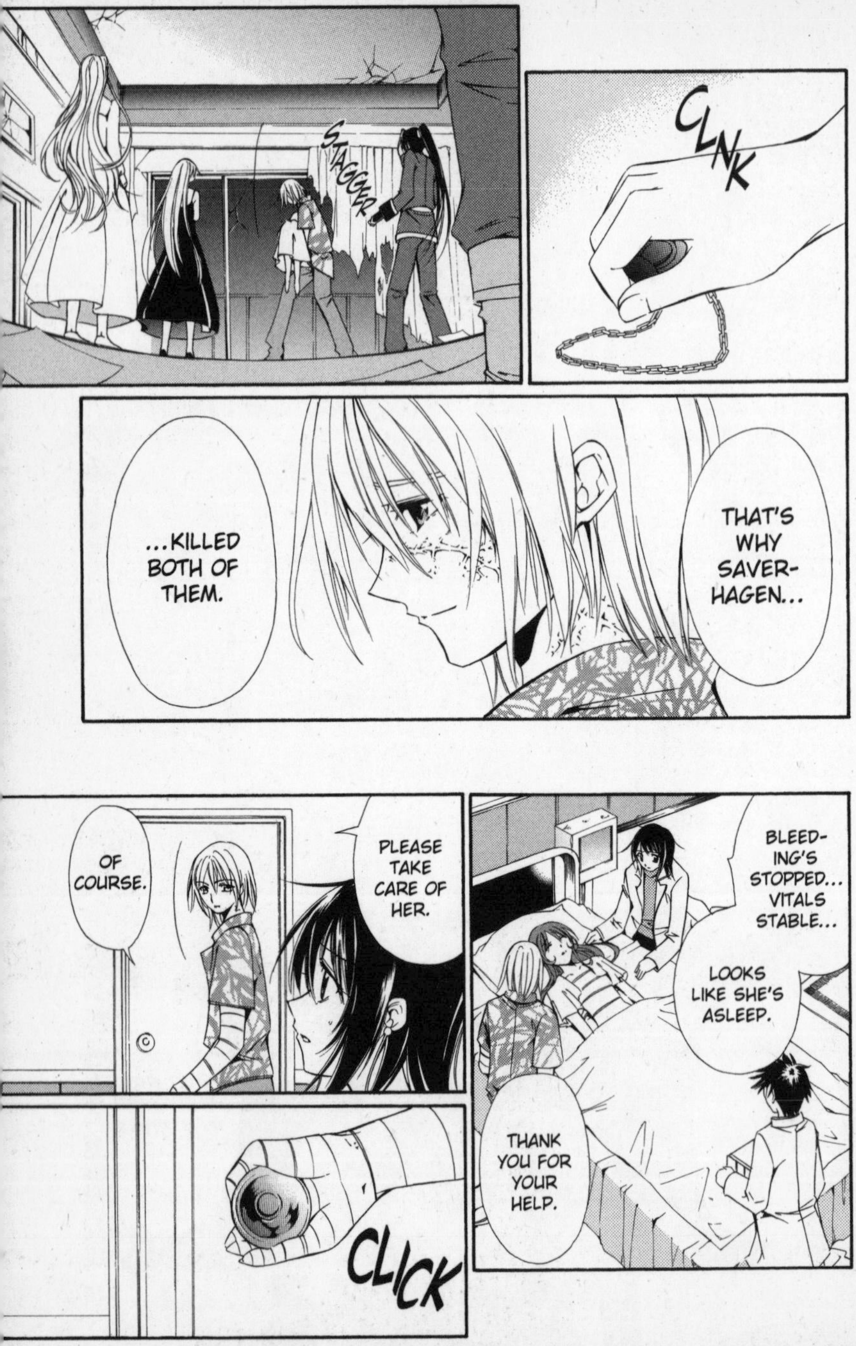
CLNK
STAGGER
THAT'S WHY SAVER-HAGEN...
...KILLED BOTH OF THEM.
BLEED-ING'S STOPPED... VITALS STABLE...
LOOKS LIKE SHE'S ASLEEP.
THANK YOU FOR YOUR HELP.
PLEASE TAKE CARE OF HER.
OF COURSE.
CLICK

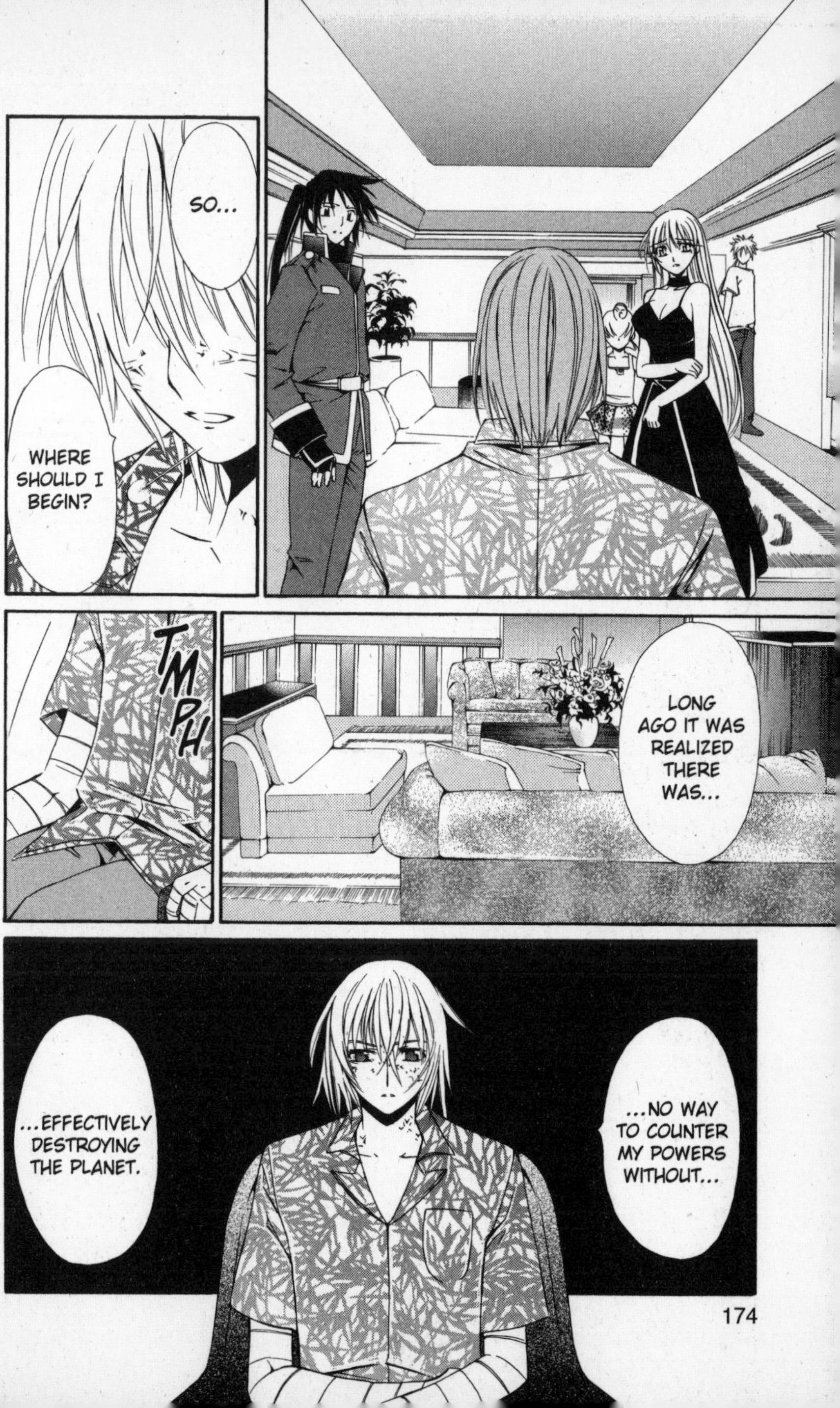
SO...
WHERE SHOULD I BEGIN?
LONG AGO IT WAS REALIZED THERE WAS...
TMPH
...NO WAY TO COUNTER MY POWERS WITHOUT...
...EFFECTIVELY DESTROYING THE PLANET.

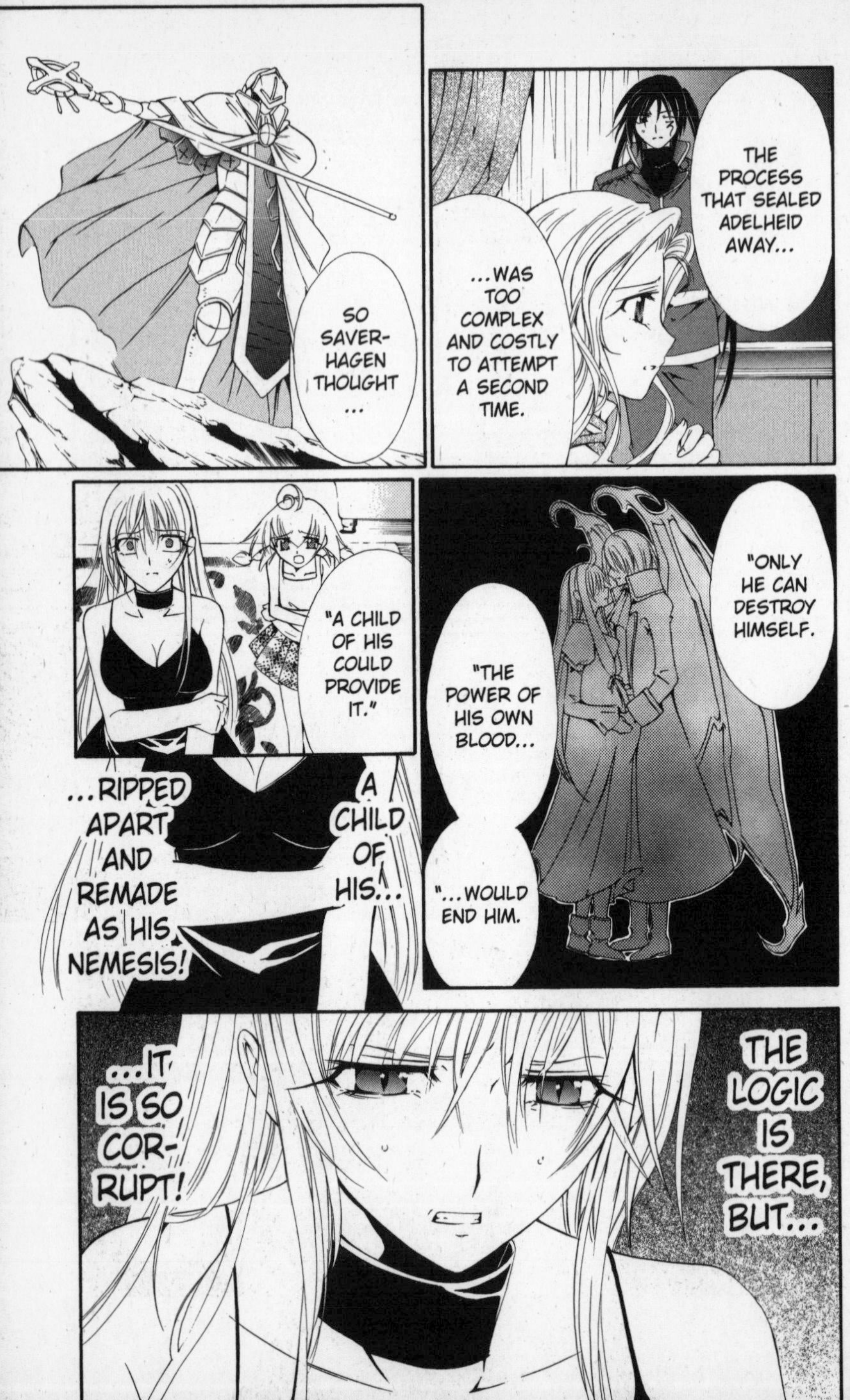
THE PROCESS THAT SEALED ADELHEID AWAY...
...WAS TOO COMPLEX AND COSTLY TO ATTEMPT A SECOND TIME.
SO SAVER-HAGEN THOUGHT...
"ONLY HE CAN DESTROY HIMSELF.
"THE POWER OF HIS OWN BLOOD...
"...WOULD END HIM.
"A CHILD OF HIS COULD PROVIDE IT."
A CHILD OF HIS...
...RIPPED APART AND REMADE AS HIS NEMESIS!
THE LOGIC IS THERE, BUT...
...IT IS SO COR-RUPT!

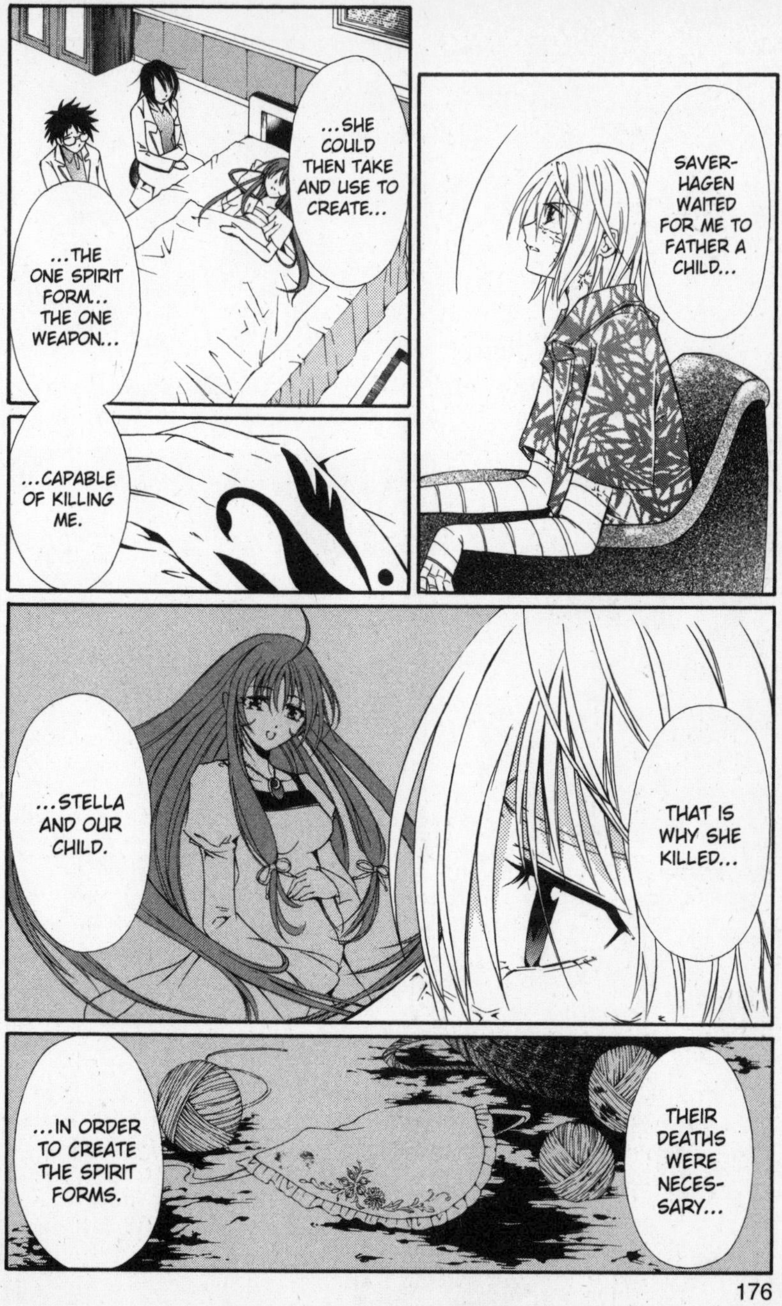
SAVER-HAGEN WAITED FOR ME TO FATHER A CHILD...
...SHE COULD THEN TAKE AND USE TO CREATE...
...THE ONE SPIRIT FORM... THE ONE WEAPON...
...CAPABLE OF KILLING ME.
THAT IS WHY SHE KILLED...
...STELLA AND OUR CHILD.
THEIR DEATHS WERE NECES-SARY...
...IN ORDER TO CREATE THE SPIRIT FORMS.

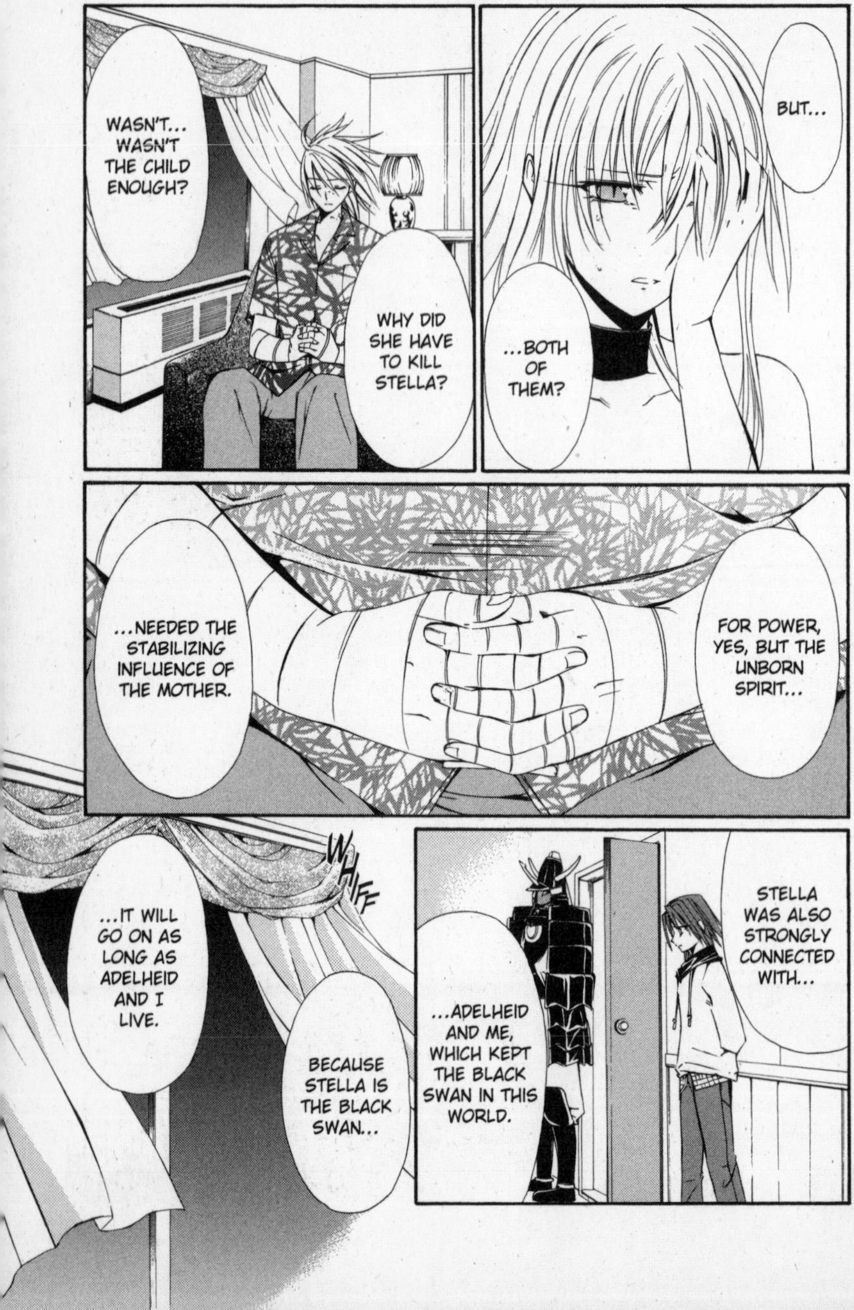
BUT...
...BOTH OF THEM?
WASN'T... WASN'T THE CHILD ENOUGH?
WHY DID SHE HAVE TO KILL STELLA?
FOR POWER, YES, BUT THE UNBORN SPIRIT...
...NEEDED THE STABILIZING INFLUENCE OF THE MOTHER.
STELLA WAS ALSO STRONGLY CONNECTED WITH...
...ADELHEID AND ME, WHICH KEPT THE BLACK SWAN IN THIS WORLD.
BECAUSE STELLA IS THE BLACK SWAN...
...IT WILL GO ON AS LONG AS ADELHEID AND I LIVE.
WHIFF

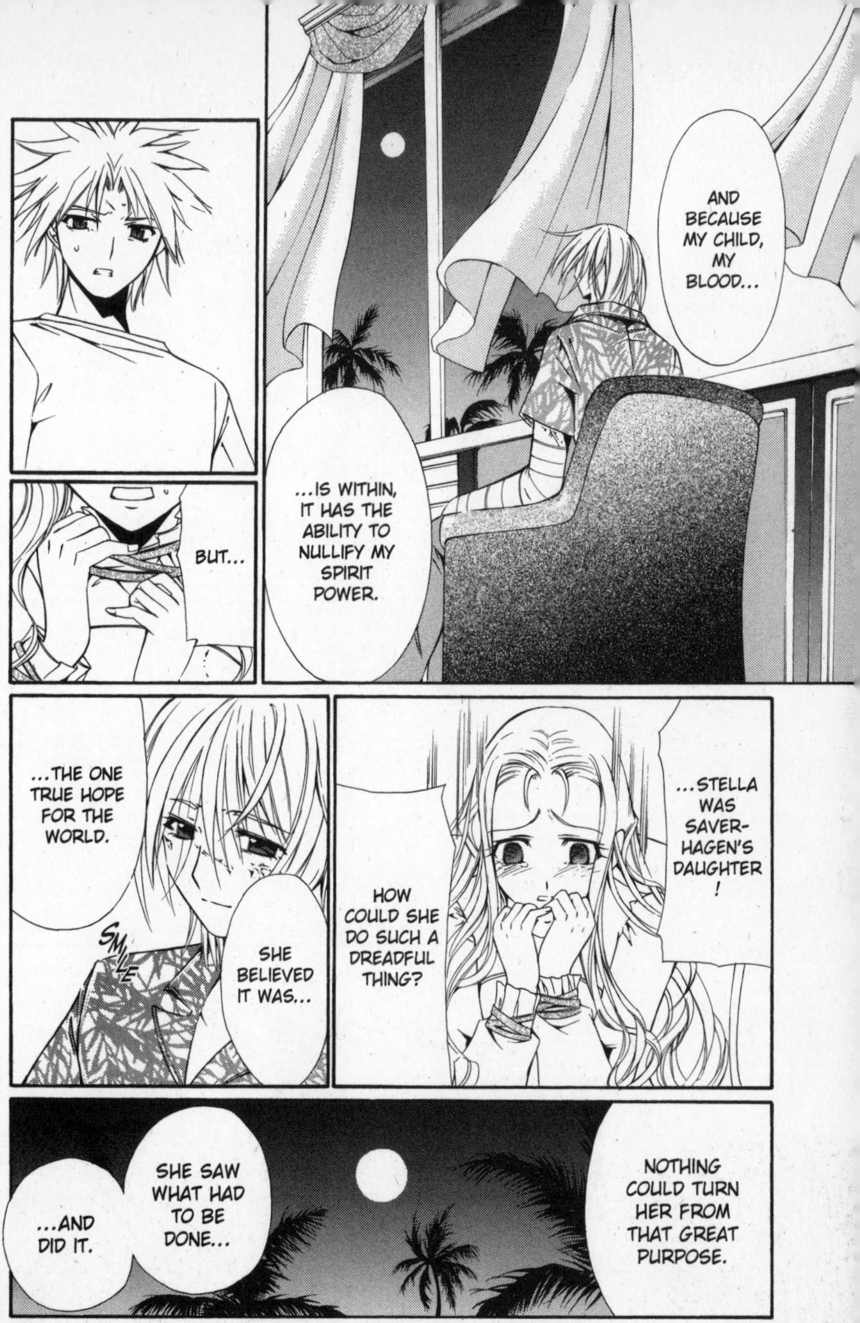
AND BECAUSE MY CHILD, MY BLOOD...
...IS WITHIN, IT HAS THE ABILITY TO NULLIFY MY SPIRIT POWER.
BUT...
...STELLA WAS SAVER-HAGEN'S DAUGHTER!
HOW COULD SHE DO SUCH A DREADFUL THING?
SHE BELIEVED IT WAS...
...THE ONE TRUE HOPE FOR THE WORLD.
SMILE
NOTHING COULD TURN HER FROM THAT GREAT PURPOSE.
SHE SAW WHAT HAD TO BE DONE...
...AND DID IT.

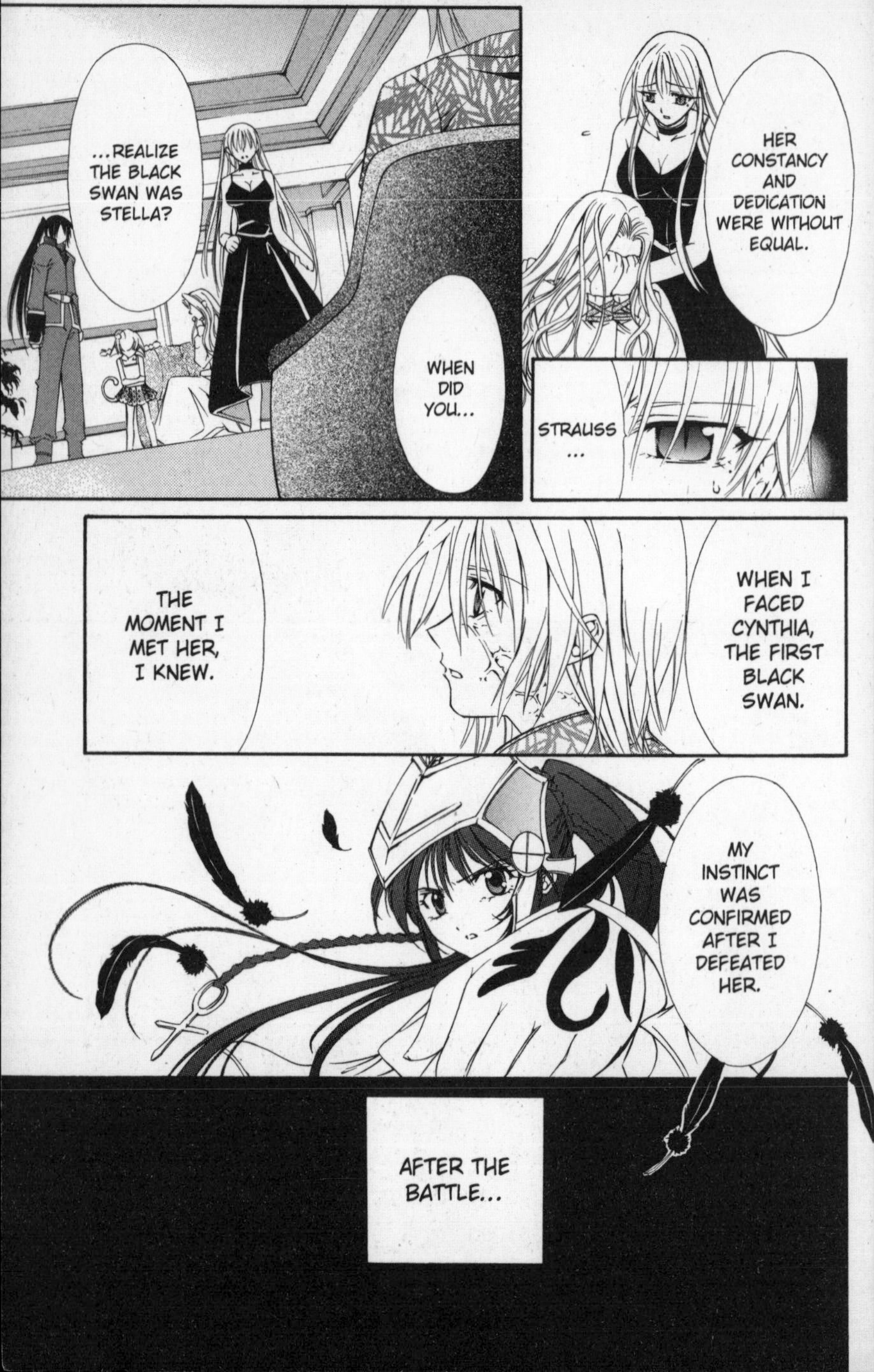
HER CONSTANCY AND DEDICATION WERE WITHOUT EQUAL.
STRAUSS...
WHEN DID YOU...
...REALIZE THE BLACK SWAN WAS STELLA?
WHEN I FACED CYNTHIA, THE FIRST BLACK SWAN.
THE MOMENT I MET HER, I KNEW.
MY INSTINCT WAS CONFIRMED AFTER I DEFEATED HER.
AFTER THE BATTLE...

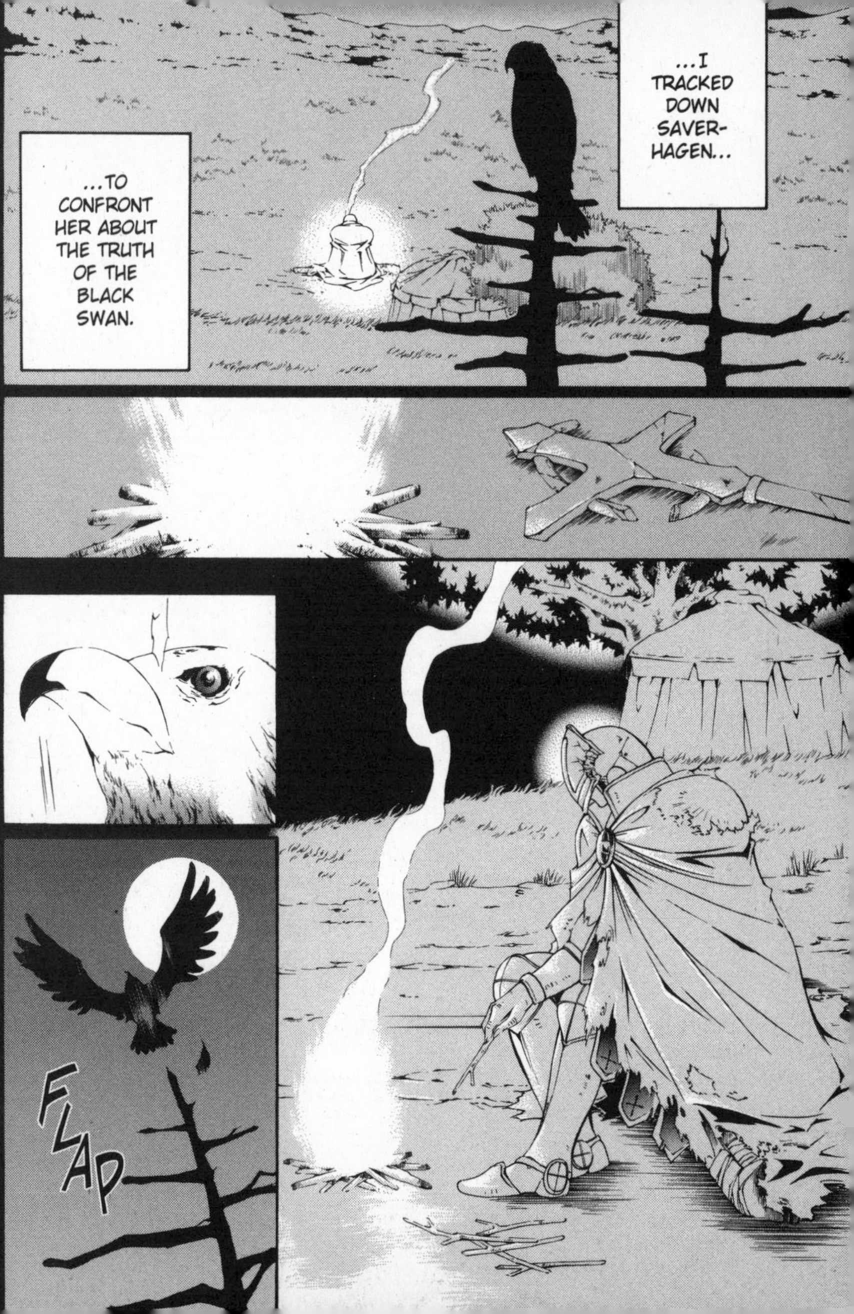
...I TRACKED DOWN SAVER-HAGEN...
...TO CONFRONT HER ABOUT THE TRUTH OF THE BLACK SWAN.
FLAP

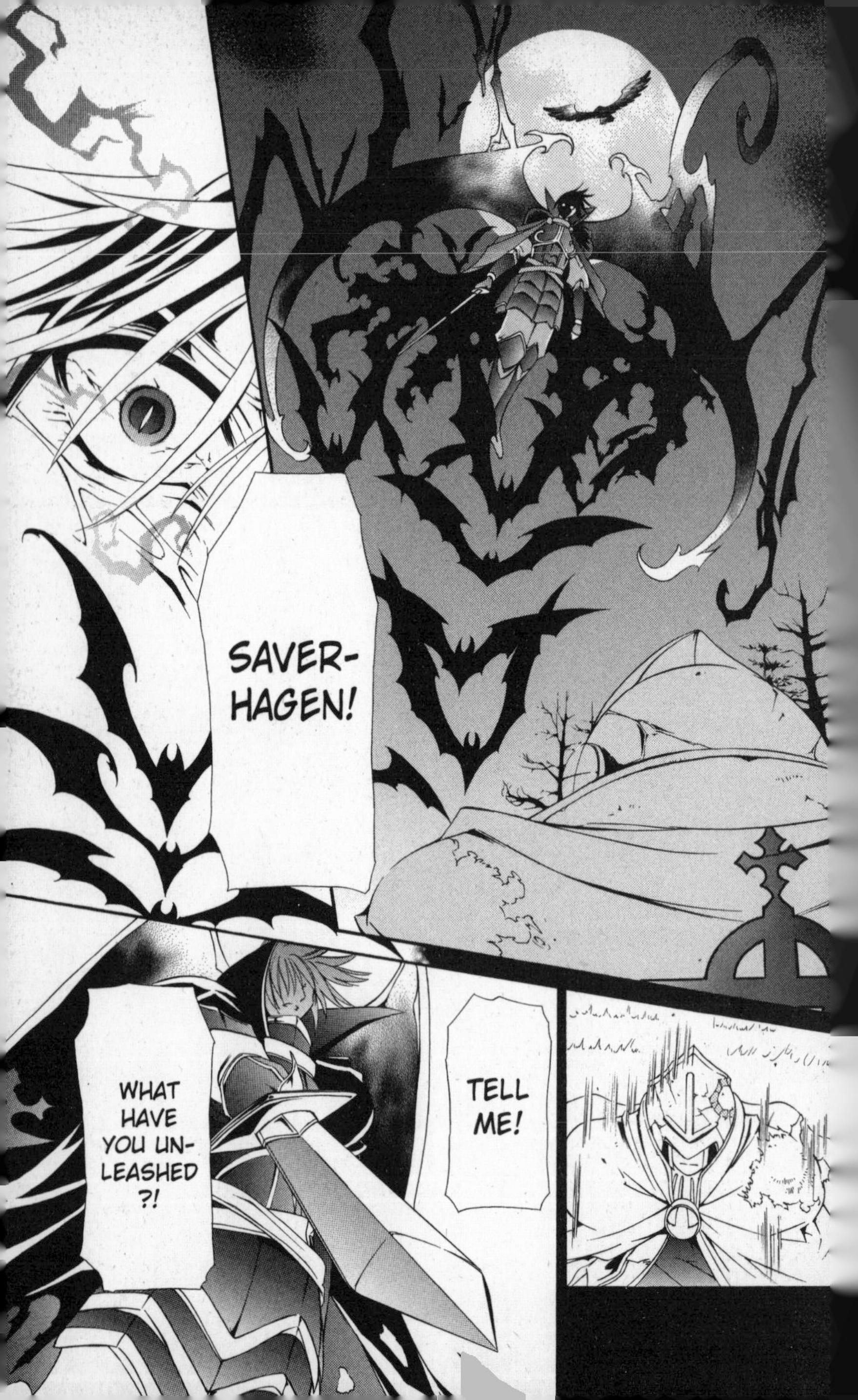
SAVER-HAGEN!
TELL ME!
WHAT HAVE YOU UN-LEASHED ?!

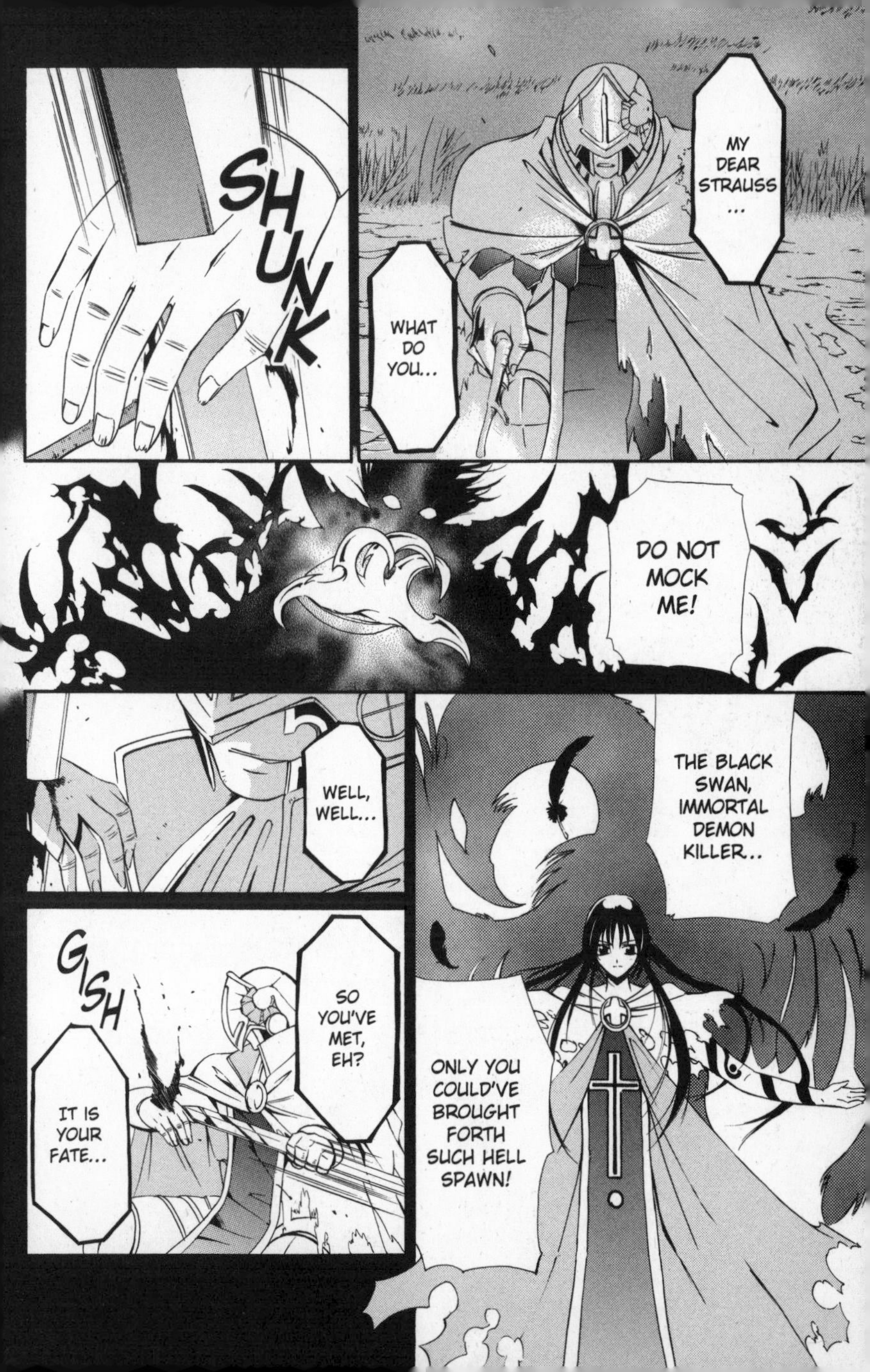
MY DEAR STRAUSS ...
WHAT DO YOU...
SHUNK
DO NOT MOCK ME!
THE BLACK SWAN, IMMORTAL DEMON KILLER...
ONLY YOU COULD'VE BROUGHT FORTH SUCH HELL SPAWN!
WELL, WELL...
SO YOU'VE MET, EH?
GISH
IT IS YOUR FATE...

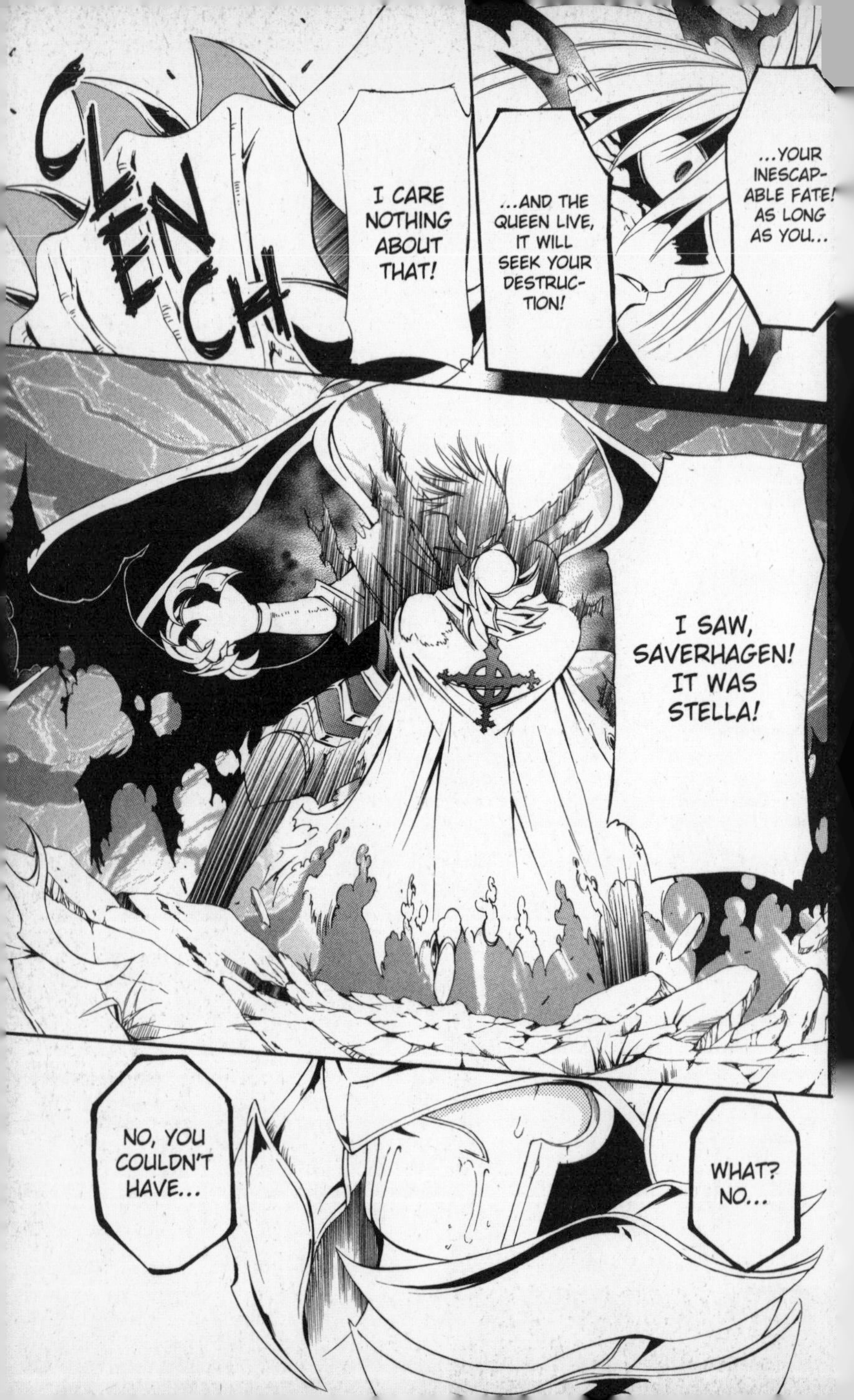
...YOUR INESCAPABLE FATE! AS LONG AS YOU...
...AND THE QUEEN LIVE, IT WILL SEEK YOUR DESTRUCTION!
I CARE NOTHING ABOUT THAT!
CLENCH
I SAW, SAVERHAGEN! IT WAS STELLA!
WHAT? NO...
NO, YOU COULDN'T HAVE...

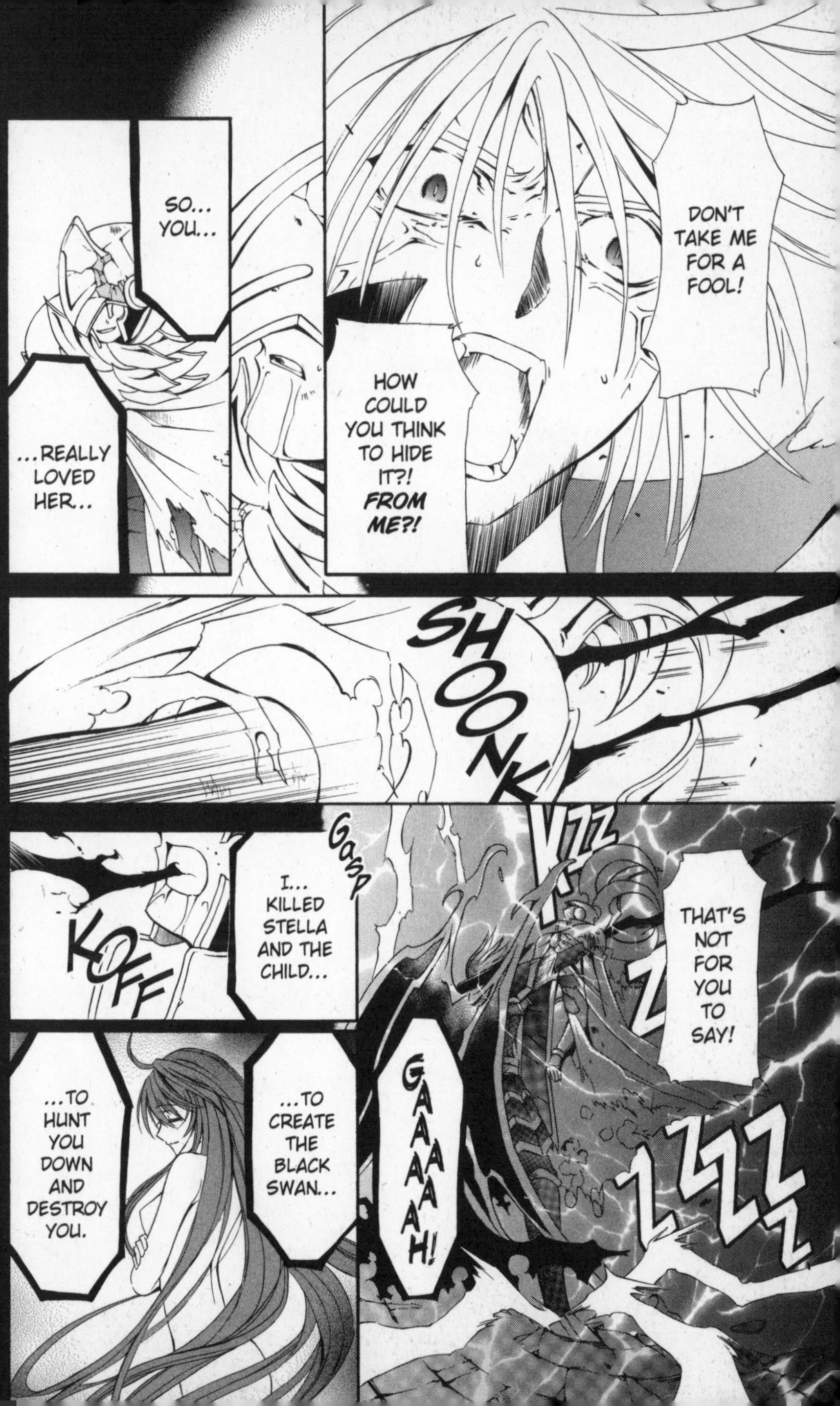
DON'T TAKE ME FOR A FOOL!
HOW COULD YOU THINK TO HIDE IT?! *FROM ME?!*
SO... YOU...
...REALLY LOVED HER...
SHOONK
KZZZ
THAT'S NOT FOR YOU TO SAY!
Z
GAAAAAAH!
ZZZZ
Gasp
I... KILLED STELLA AND THE CHILD...
KOFF
...TO CREATE THE BLACK SWAN...
...TO HUNT YOU DOWN AND DESTROY YOU.

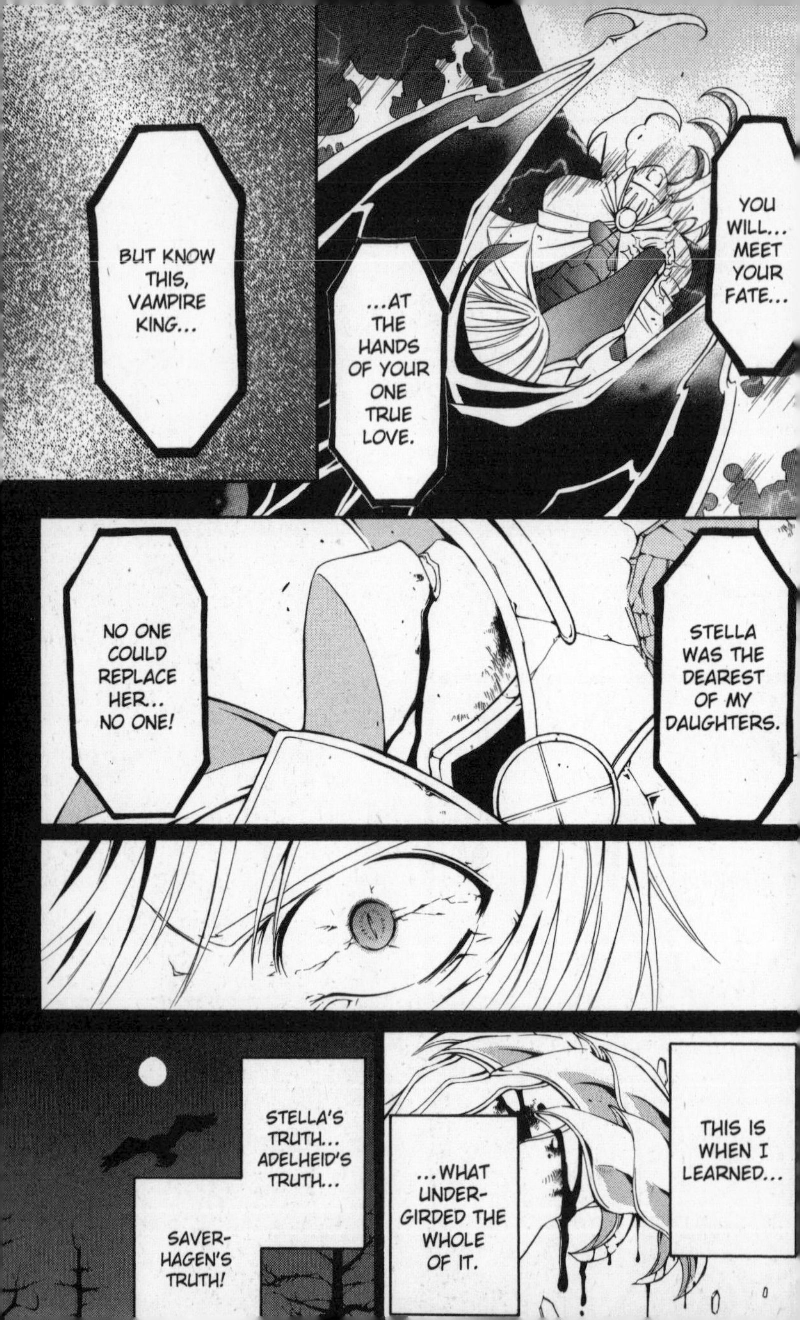
YOU WILL... MEET YOUR FATE...
...AT THE HANDS OF YOUR ONE TRUE LOVE.
BUT KNOW THIS, VAMPIRE KING...
STELLA WAS THE DEAREST OF MY DAUGHTERS.
NO ONE COULD REPLACE HER... NO ONE!
THIS IS WHEN I LEARNED...
...WHAT UNDER-GIRDED THE WHOLE OF IT.
STELLA'S TRUTH... ADELHEID'S TRUTH...
SAVER-HAGEN'S TRUTH!

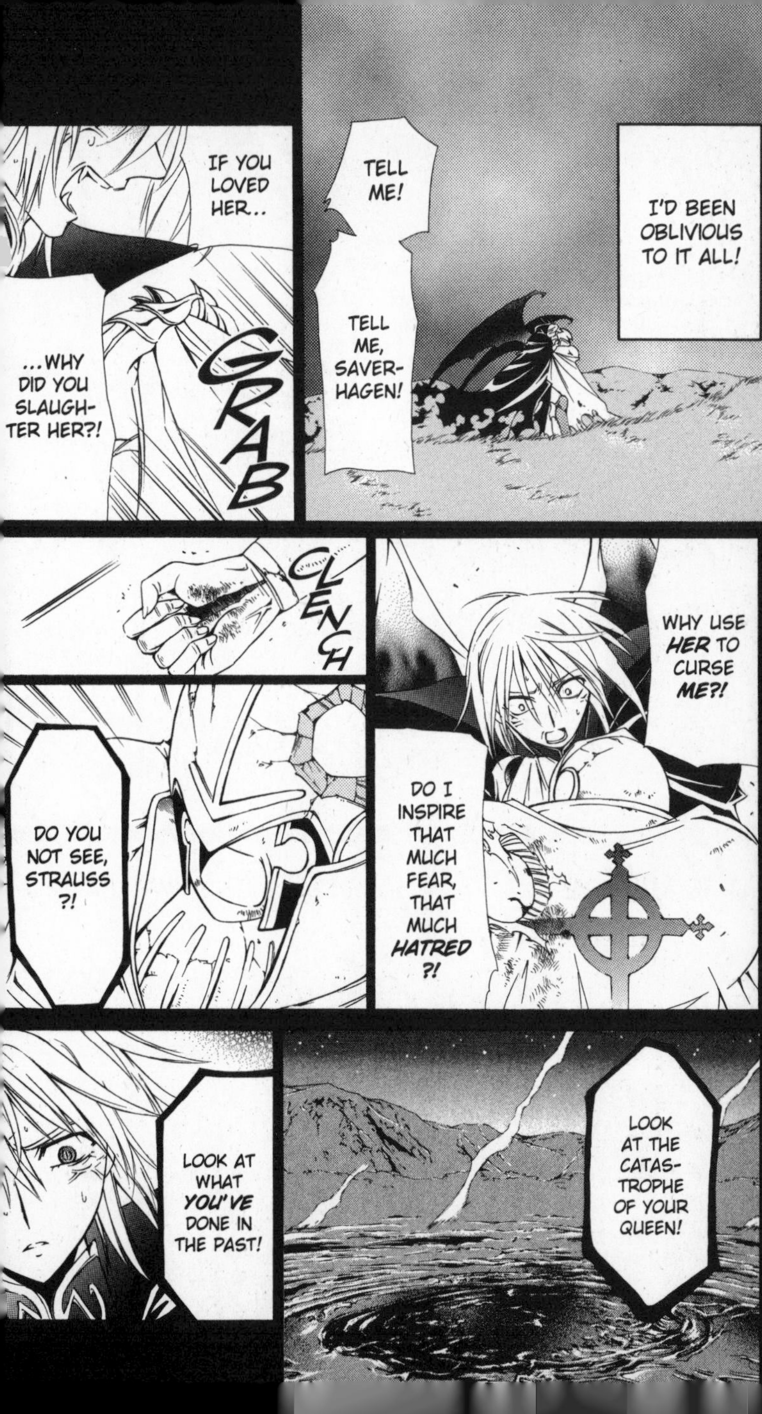
I'D BEEN OBLIVIOUS TO IT ALL!
TELL ME!
TELL ME, SAVER-HAGEN!
IF YOU LOVED HER...
GRAB
...WHY DID YOU SLAUGH-TER HER?!
WHY USE *HER* TO CURSE *ME?!*
DO I INSPIRE THAT MUCH FEAR, THAT MUCH *HATRED* ?!
CLENCH
DO YOU NOT SEE, STRAUSS ?!
LOOK AT THE CATAS-TROPHE OF YOUR QUEEN!
LOOK AT WHAT *YOU'VE* DONE IN THE PAST!

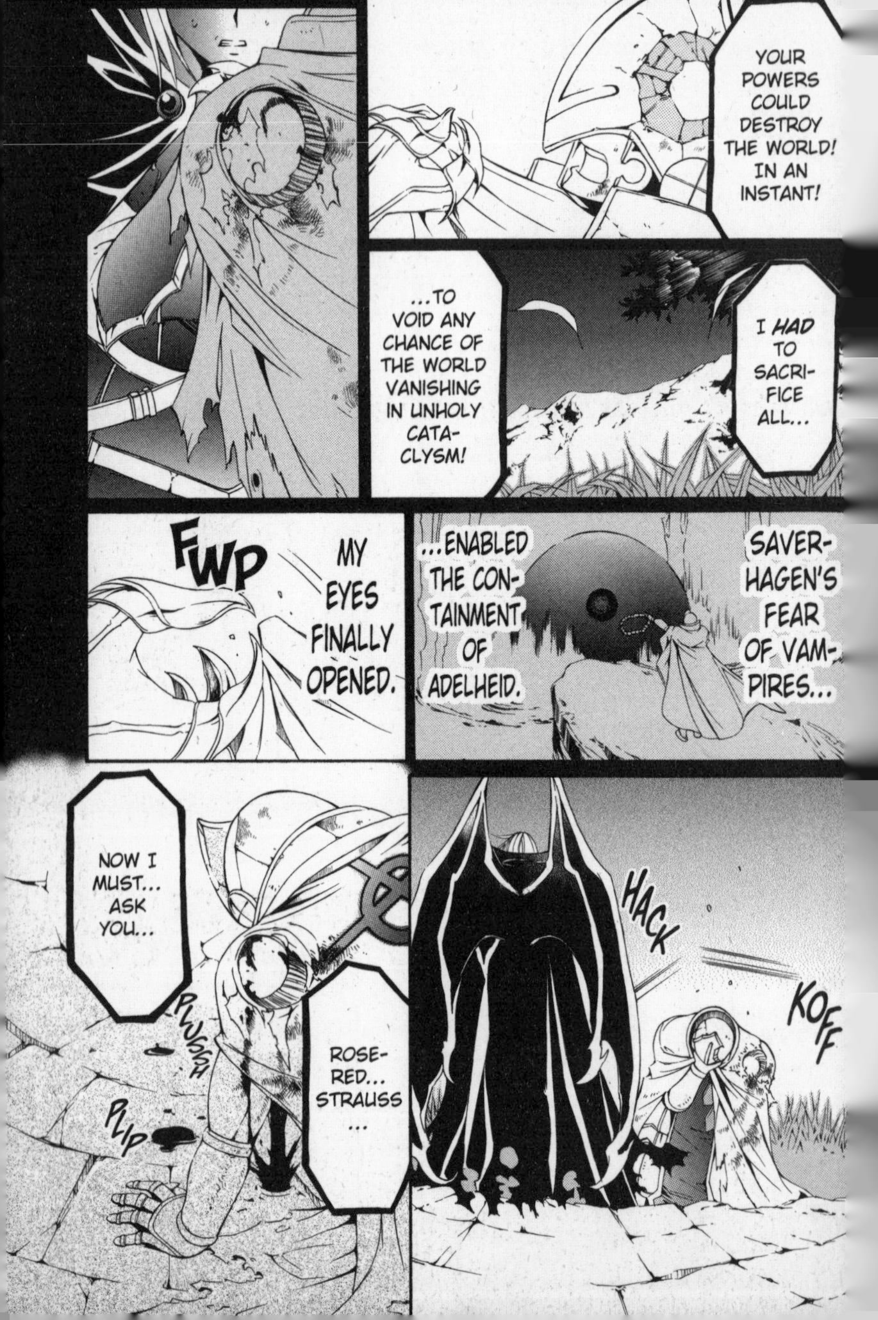
YOUR POWERS COULD DESTROY THE WORLD! IN AN INSTANT!
I *HAD* TO SACRI-FICE ALL...
...TO VOID ANY CHANCE OF THE WORLD VANISHING IN UNHOLY CATA-CLYSM!
SAVER-HAGEN'S FEAR OF VAM-PIRES...
...ENABLED THE CON-TAINMENT OF ADELHEID.
FWP
MY EYES FINALLY OPENED.
HACK
KOFF
NOW I MUST... ASK YOU...
PLUSSH
ROSE-RED... STRAUSS ...
PLIP

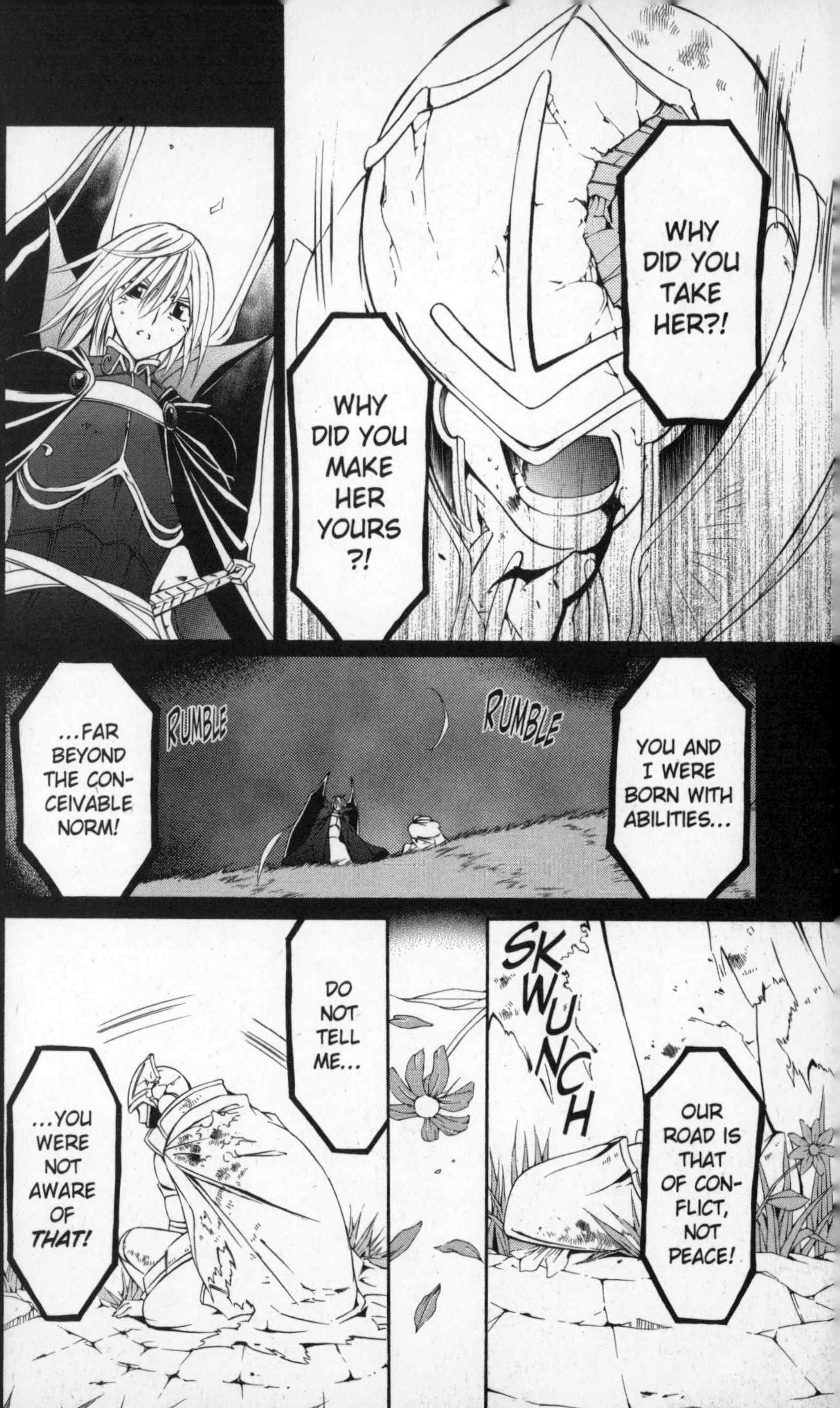
WHY DID YOU TAKE HER?!
WHY DID YOU MAKE HER YOURS ?!
YOU AND I WERE BORN WITH ABILITIES...
RUMBLE
RUMBLE
...FAR BEYOND THE CON-CEIVABLE NORM!
SKWUNCH
OUR ROAD IS THAT OF CON-FLICT, NOT PEACE!
DO NOT TELL ME...
...YOU WERE NOT AWARE OF *THAT!*

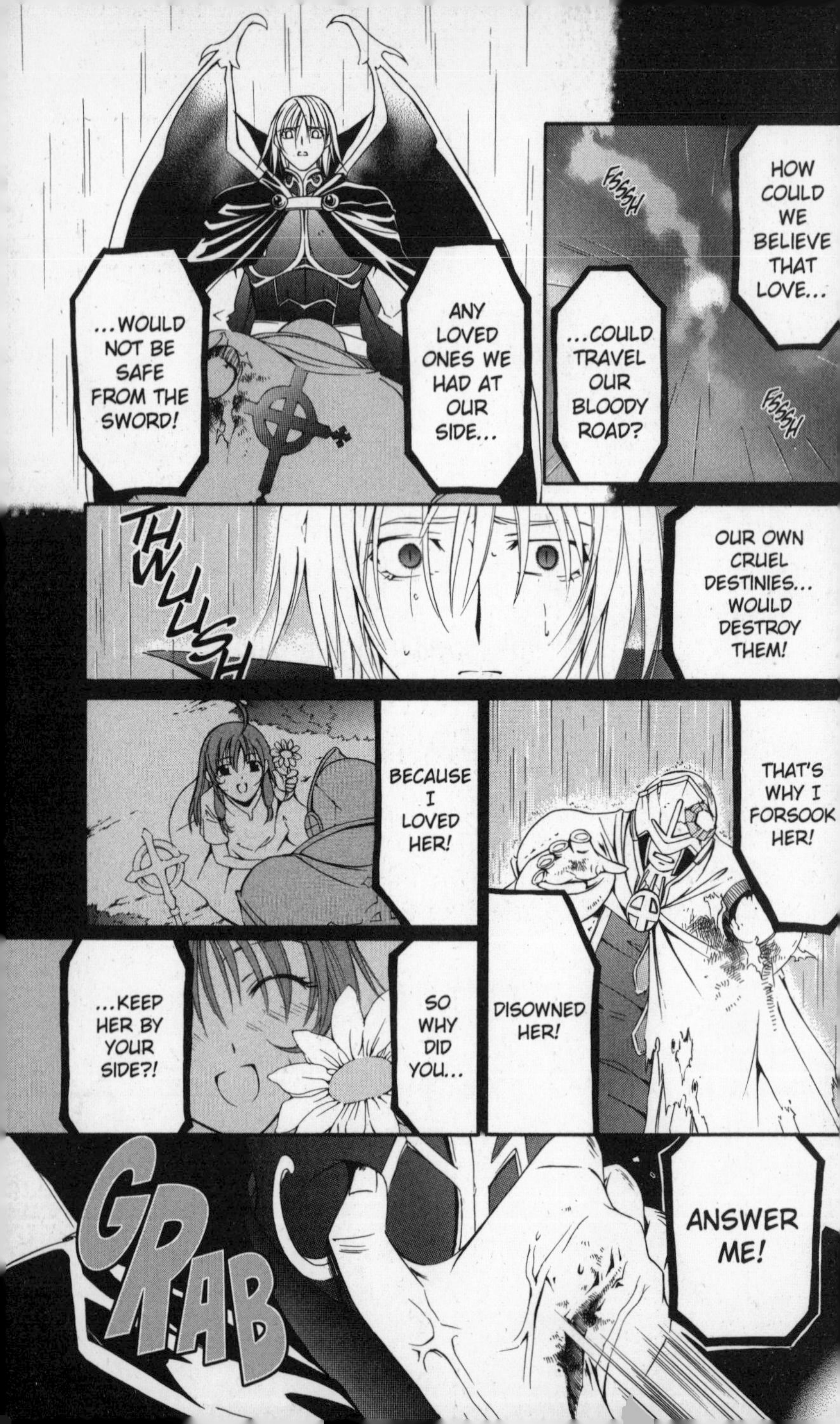

HOW COULD WE BELIEVE THAT LOVE...
FSSSH
...COULD TRAVEL OUR BLOODY ROAD?
FSSSH
ANY LOVED ONES WE HAD AT OUR SIDE...
...WOULD NOT BE SAFE FROM THE SWORD!
OUR OWN CRUEL DESTINIES... WOULD DESTROY THEM!
THWUSH
THAT'S WHY I FORSOOK HER!
BECAUSE I LOVED HER!
DISOWNED HER!
SO WHY DID YOU...
...KEEP HER BY YOUR SIDE?!
ANSWER ME!
GRAB

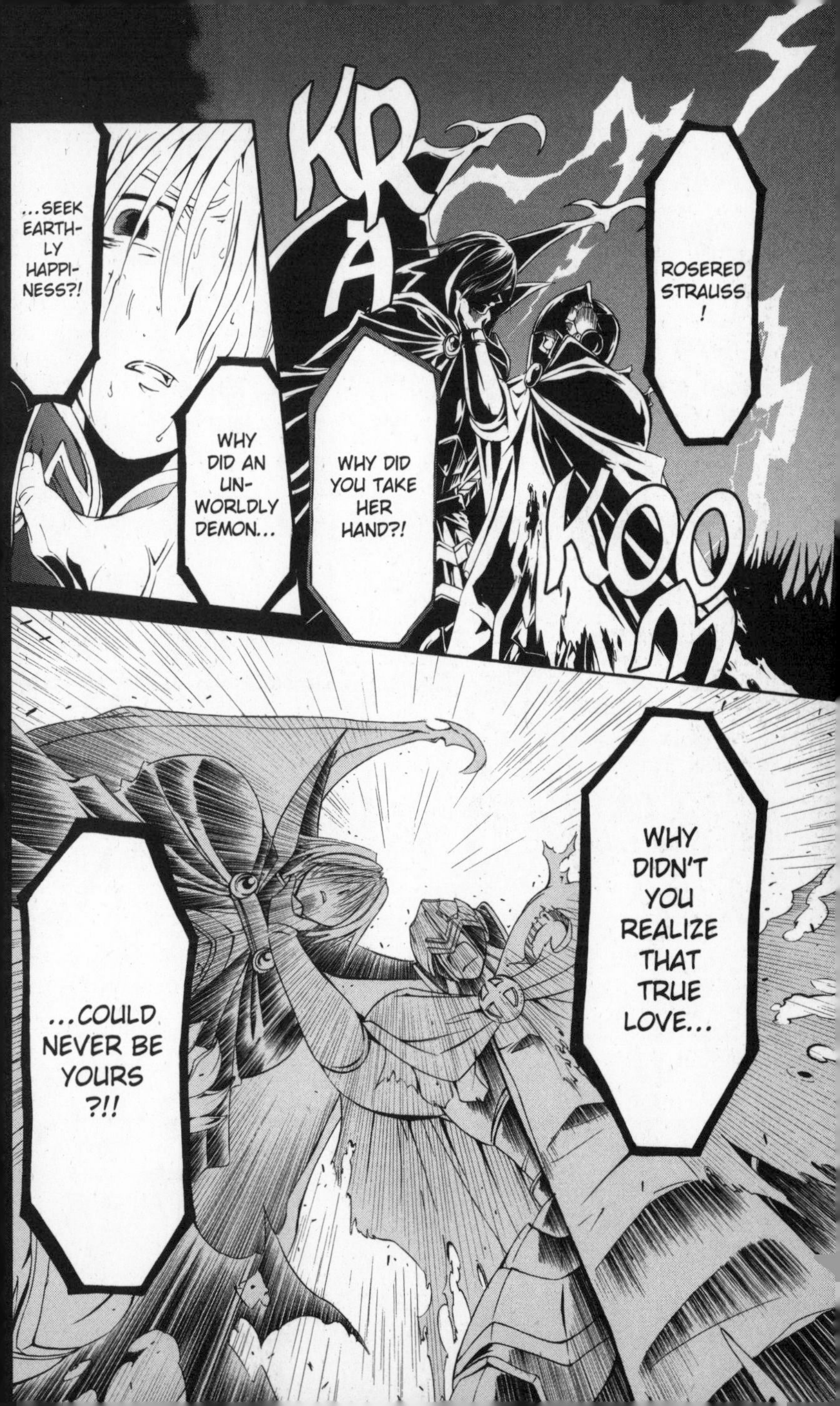
ROSERED STRAUSS!
KRA
KOOM
WHY DID YOU TAKE HER HAND?!
WHY DID AN UN-WORLDLY DEMON...
...SEEK EARTH-LY HAPPI-NESS?!
WHY DIDN'T YOU REALIZE THAT TRUE LOVE...
...COULD NEVER BE YOURS?!!

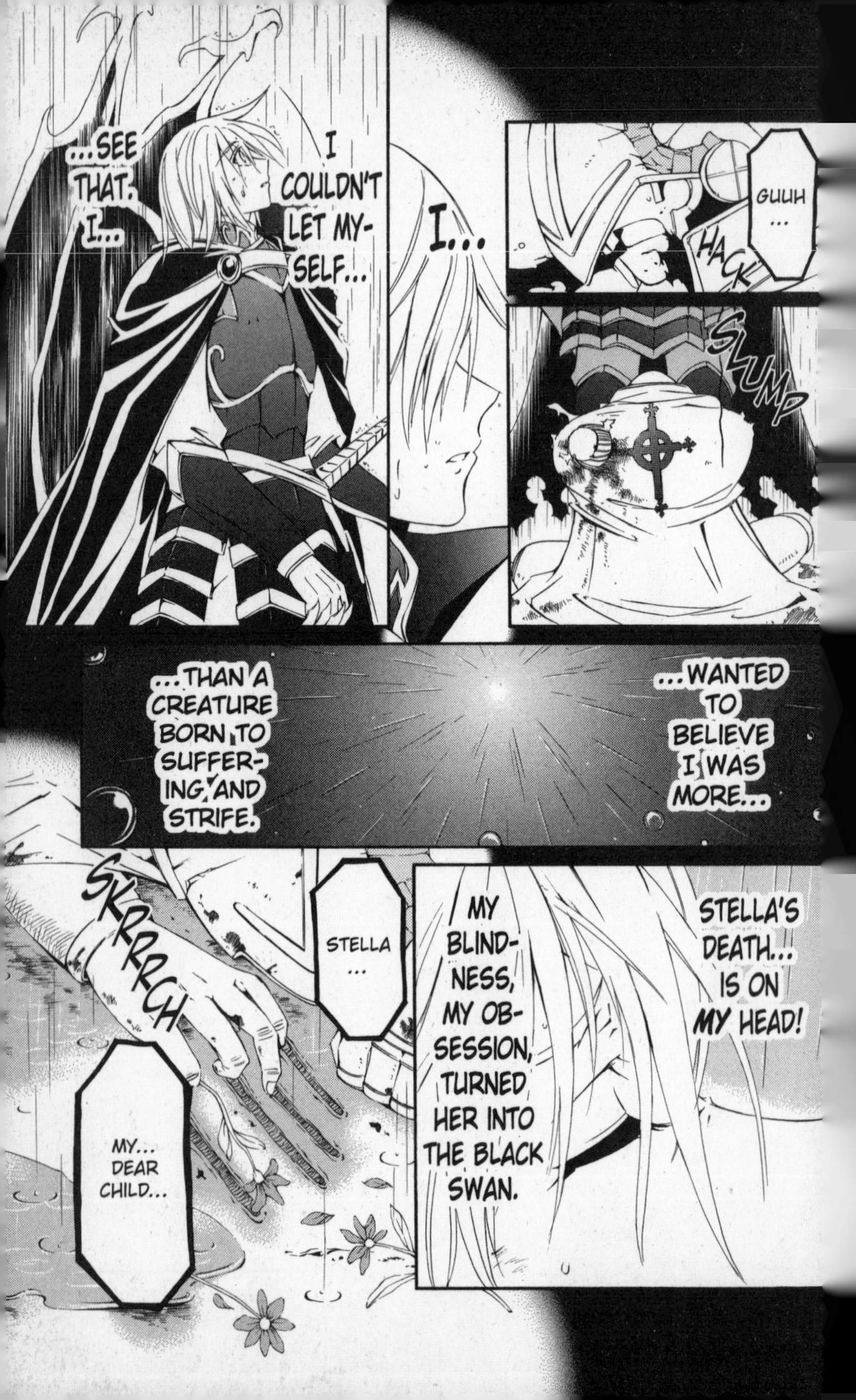
GUUH...
HACK
SLUMP
I...
I COULDN'T LET MY-SELF...
...SEE THAT. I...
...WANTED TO BELIEVE I WAS MORE...
...THAN A CREATURE BORN TO SUFFERING AND STRIFE.
STELLA'S DEATH... IS ON MY HEAD!
MY BLINDNESS, MY OBSESSION, TURNED HER INTO THE BLACK SWAN.
STELLA...
SKRRRCH
MY... DEAR CHILD...

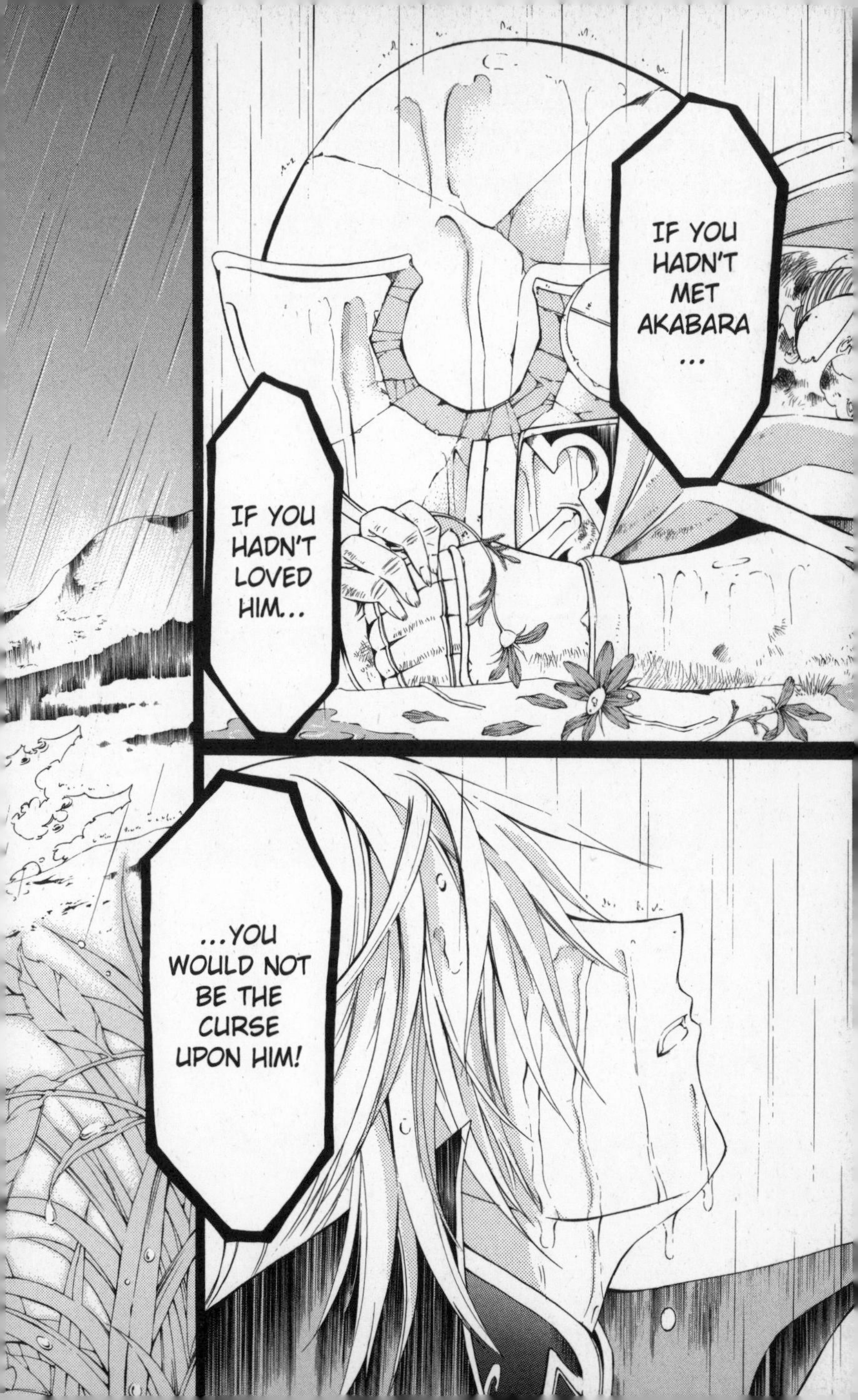
IF YOU HADN'T MET AKABARA ...
IF YOU HADN'T LOVED HIM...
...YOU WOULD NOT BE THE CURSE UPON HIM!

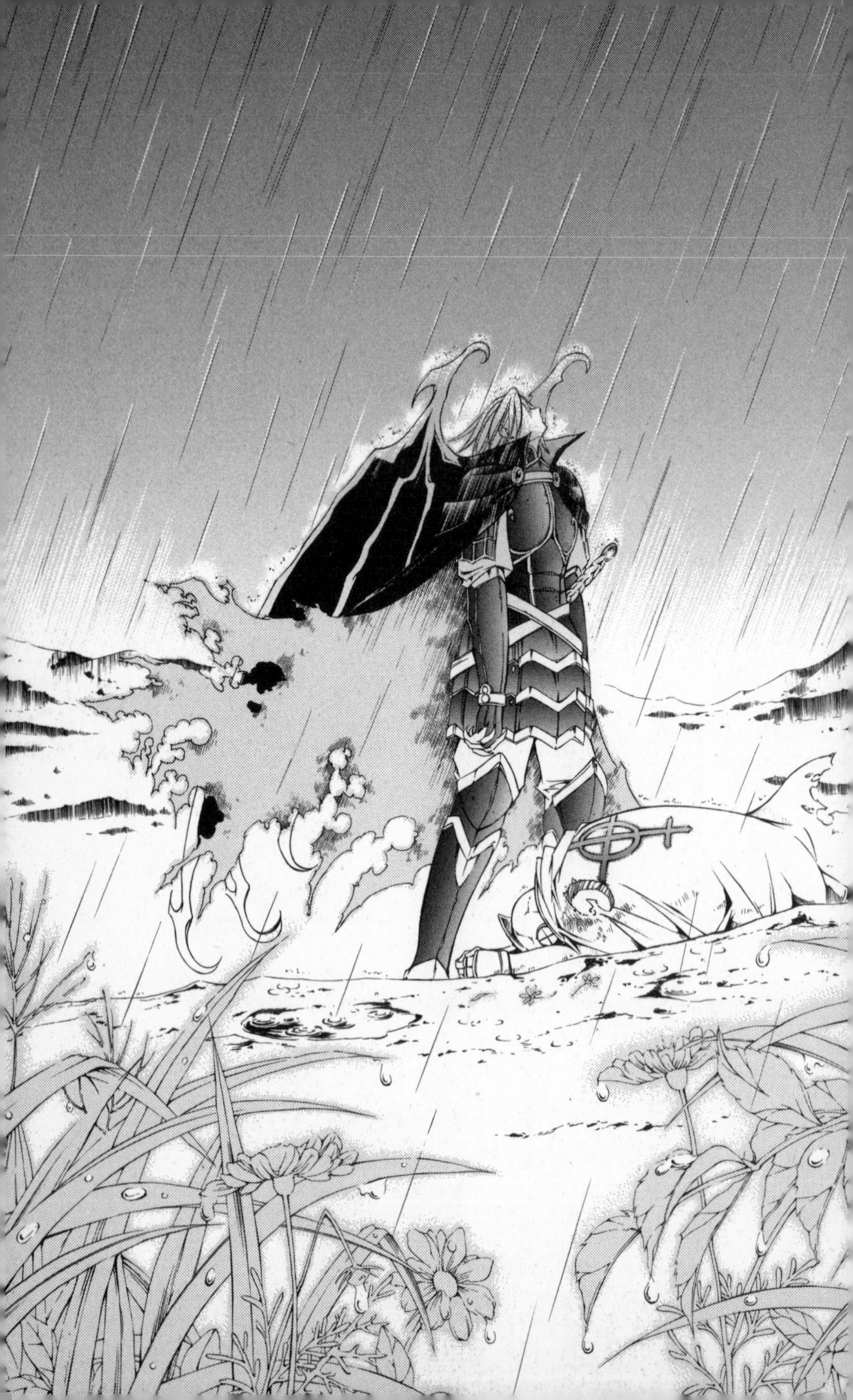

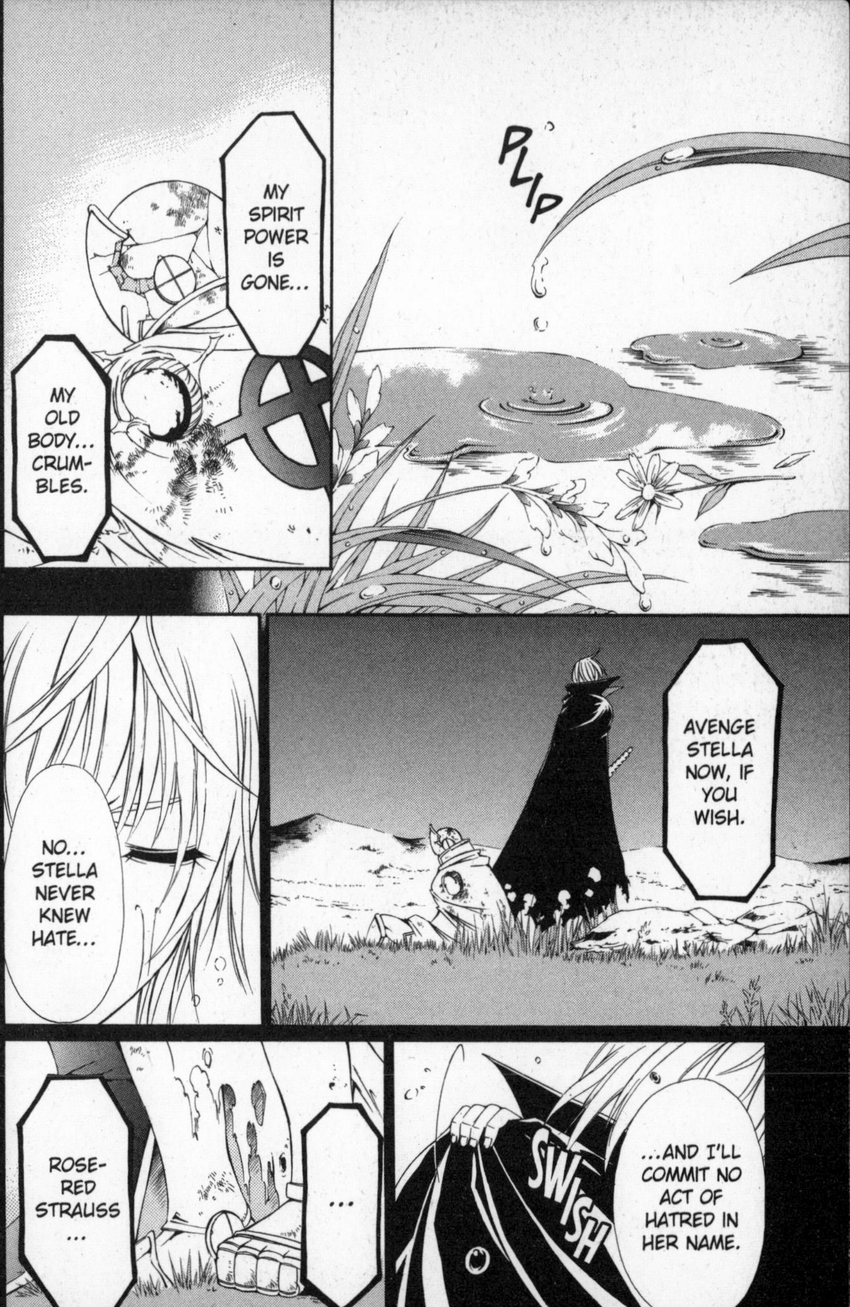
PLIP
MY SPIRIT POWER IS GONE...
MY OLD BODY... CRUMBLES.
AVENGE STELLA NOW, IF YOU WISH.
NO... STELLA NEVER KNEW HATE...
SWISH
...AND I'LL COMMIT NO ACT OF HATRED IN HER NAME.
...
ROSE-RED STRAUSS ...

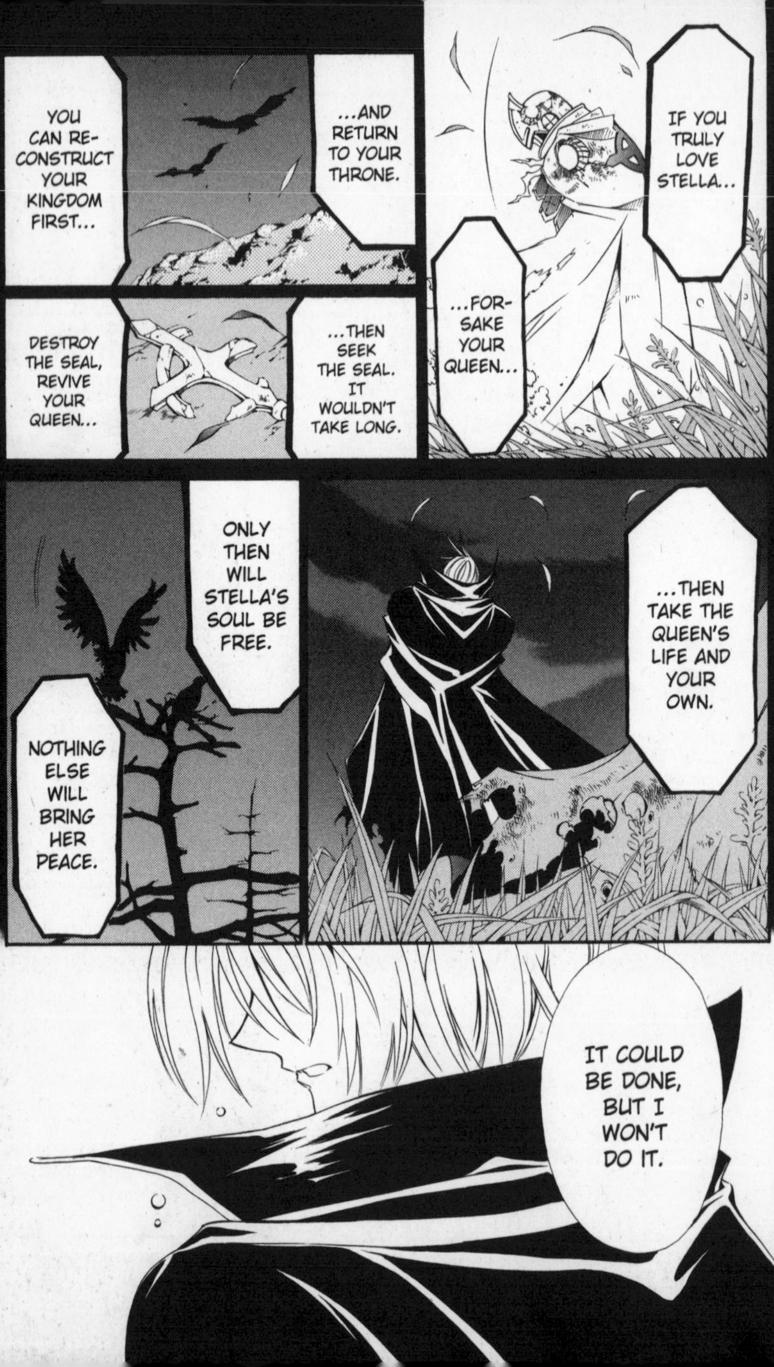
IF YOU TRULY LOVE STELLA...
...FORSAKE YOUR QUEEN...
YOU CAN RECONSTRUCT YOUR KINGDOM FIRST...
...AND RETURN TO YOUR THRONE.
...THEN SEEK THE SEAL. IT WOULDN'T TAKE LONG.
DESTROY THE SEAL, REVIVE YOUR QUEEN...
...THEN TAKE THE QUEEN'S LIFE AND YOUR OWN.
ONLY THEN WILL STELLA'S SOUL BE FREE.
NOTHING ELSE WILL BRING HER PEACE.
IT COULD BE DONE, BUT I WON'T DO IT.

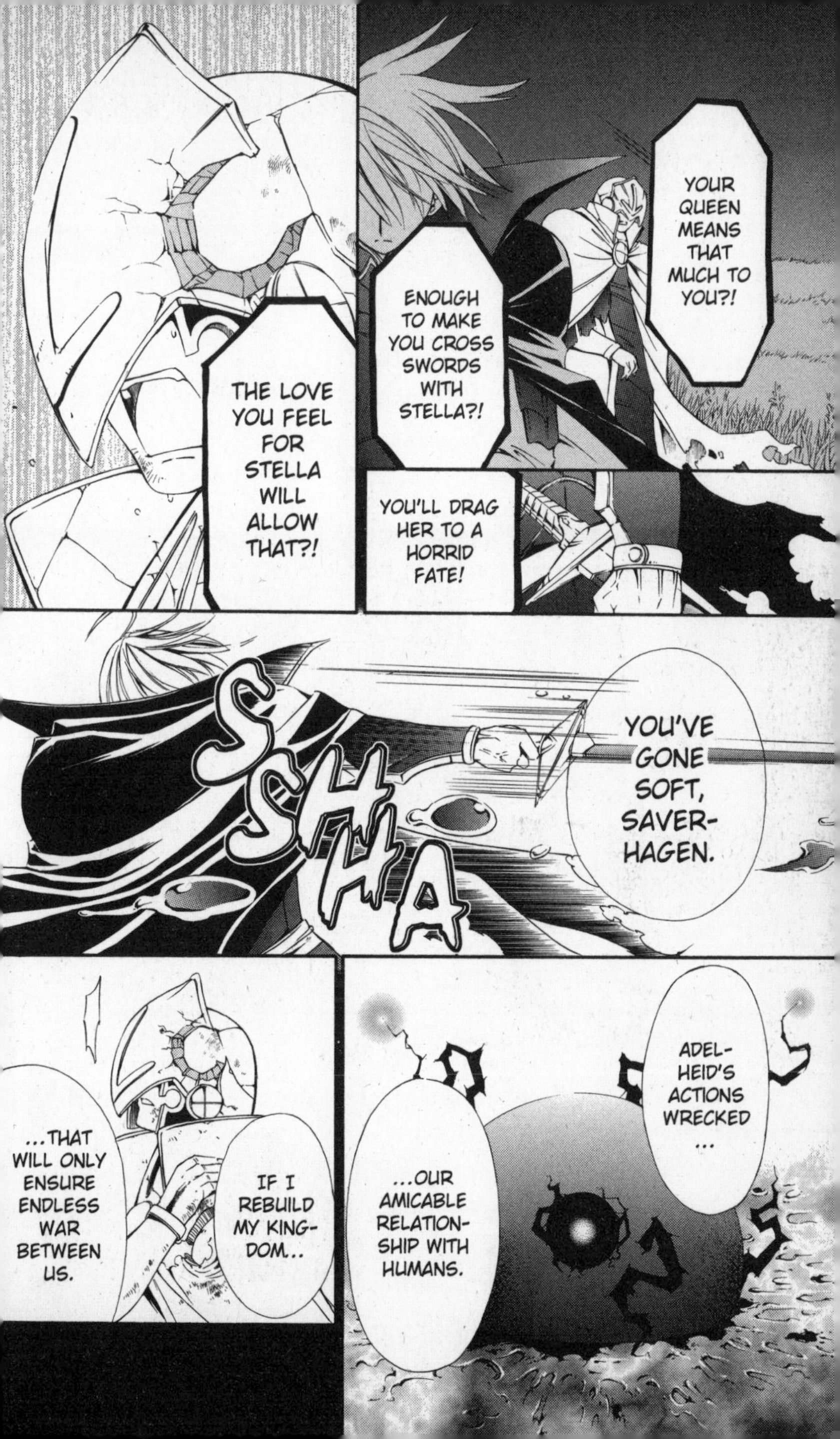
YOUR QUEEN MEANS THAT MUCH TO YOU?!
ENOUGH TO MAKE YOU CROSS SWORDS WITH STELLA?!
YOU'LL DRAG HER TO A HORRID FATE!
THE LOVE YOU FEEL FOR STELLA WILL ALLOW THAT?!
YOU'VE GONE SOFT, SAVER-HAGEN.
SSHA
ADEL-HEID'S ACTIONS WRECKED...
...OUR AMICABLE RELATION-SHIP WITH HUMANS.
IF I REBUILD MY KING-DOM..
...THAT WILL ONLY ENSURE ENDLESS WAR BETWEEN US.

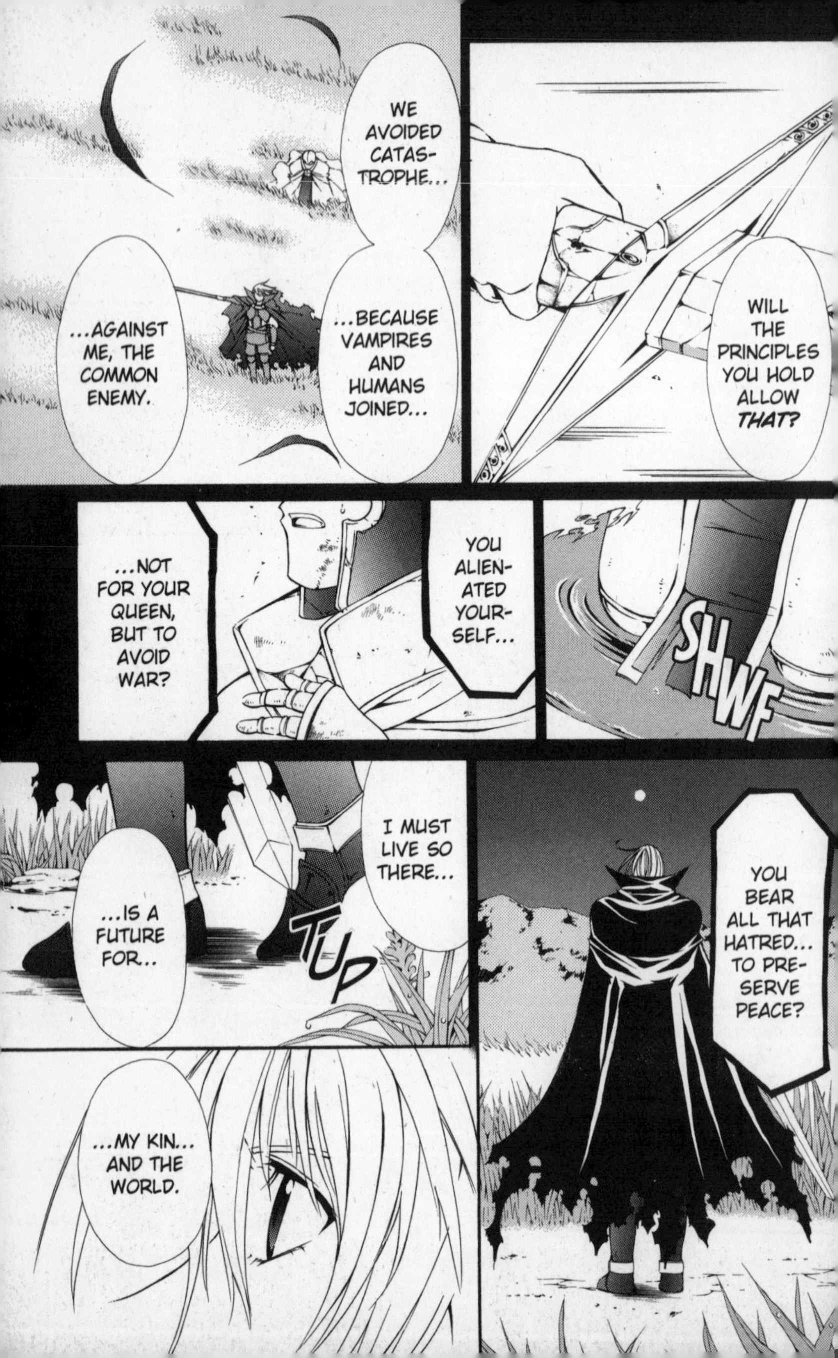
WILL THE PRINCIPLES YOU HOLD ALLOW *THAT?*
WE AVOIDED CATAS-TROPHE...
...BECAUSE VAMPIRES AND HUMANS JOINED...
...AGAINST ME, THE COMMON ENEMY.
SHWF
YOU ALIEN-ATED YOUR-SELF...
...NOT FOR YOUR QUEEN, BUT TO AVOID WAR?
YOU BEAR ALL THAT HATRED... TO PRE-SERVE PEACE?
I MUST LIVE SO THERE...
TUP
...IS A FUTURE FOR...
...MY KIN... AND THE WORLD.

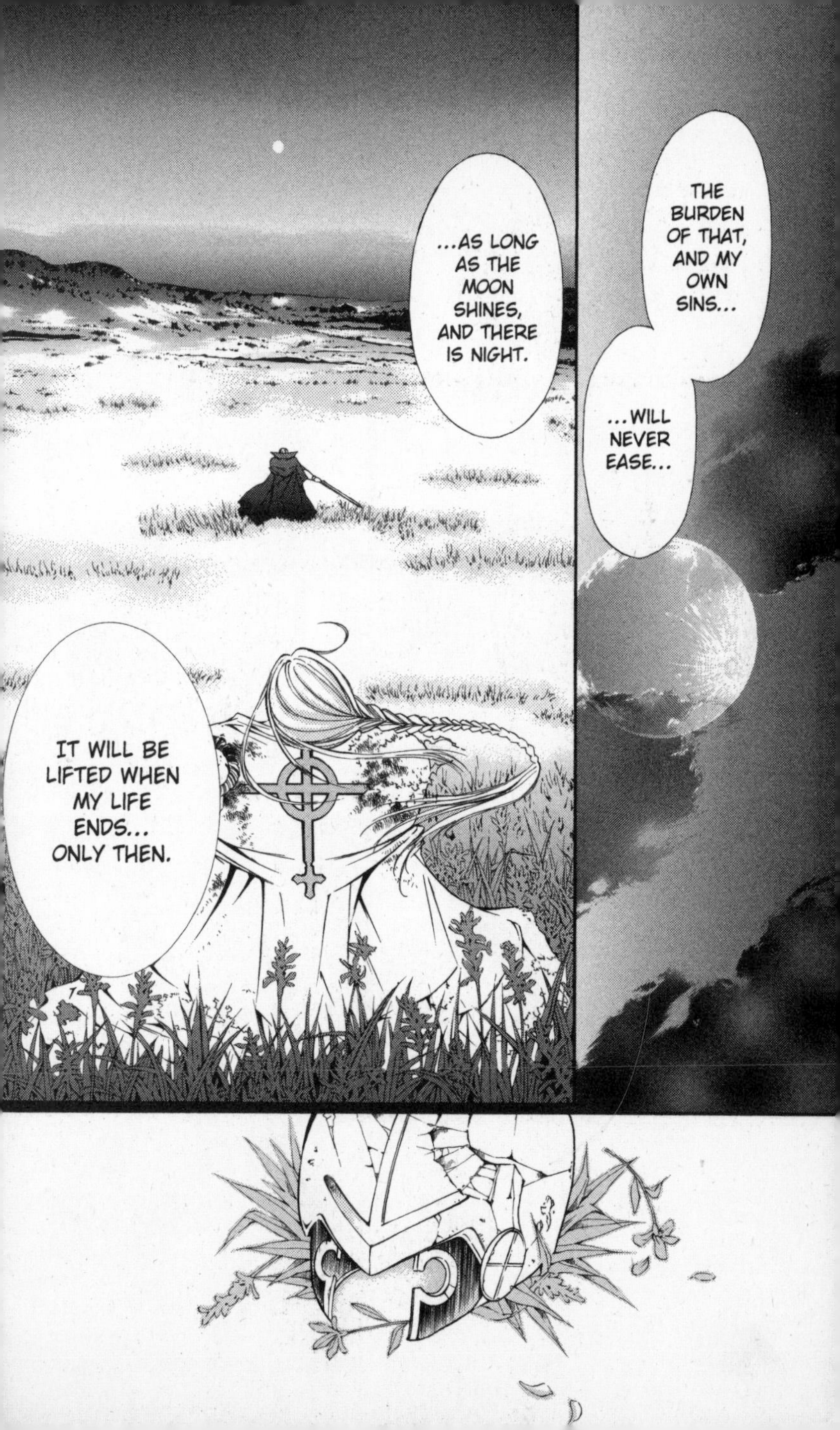
THE BURDEN OF THAT, AND MY OWN SINS...
...WILL NEVER EASE...
...AS LONG AS THE MOON SHINES, AND THERE IS NIGHT.
IT WILL BE LIFTED WHEN MY LIFE ENDS... ONLY THEN.

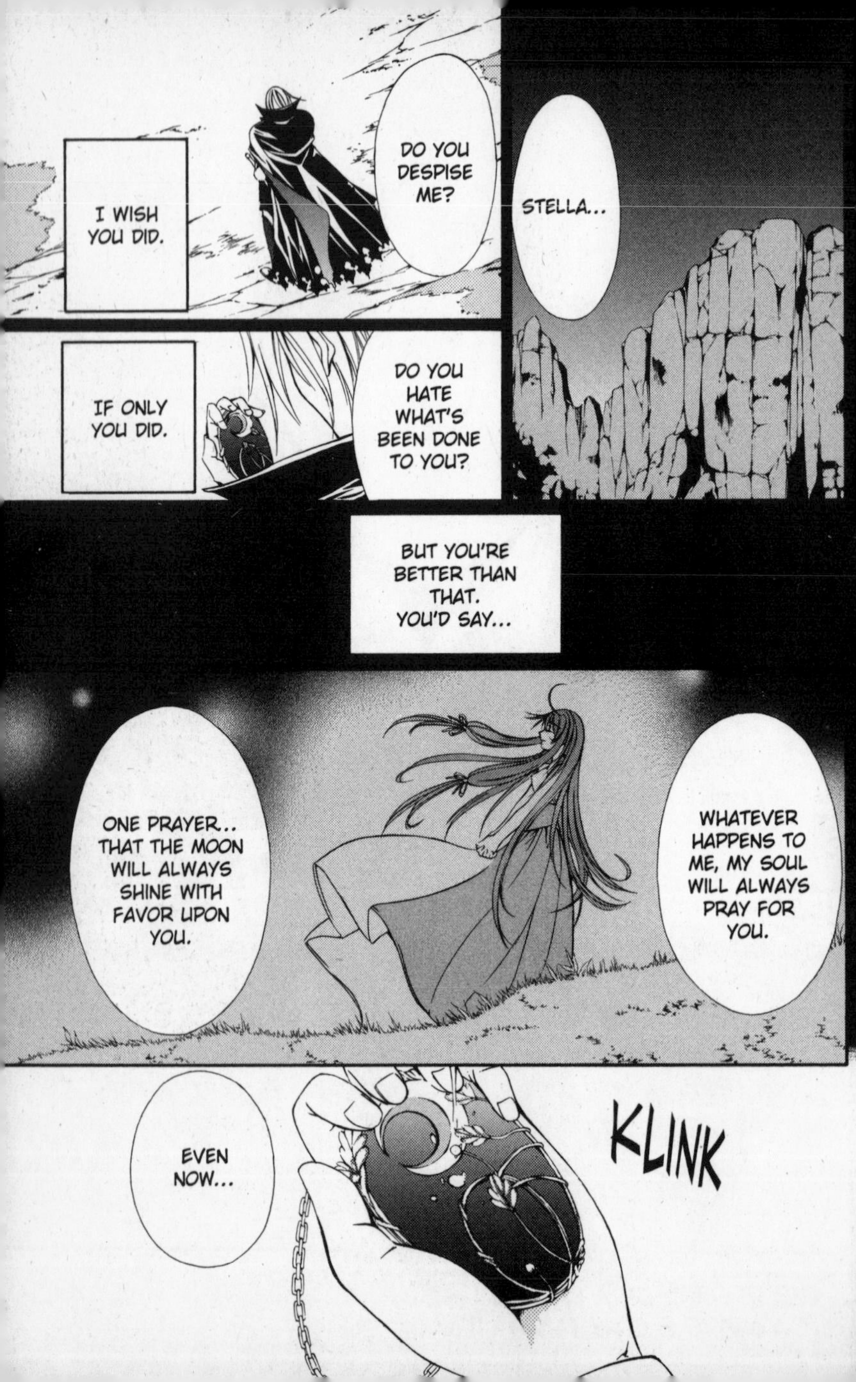
STELLA...
DO YOU DESPISE ME?
I WISH YOU DID.
DO YOU HATE WHAT'S BEEN DONE TO YOU?
IF ONLY YOU DID.
BUT YOU'RE BETTER THAN THAT. YOU'D SAY...
WHATEVER HAPPENS TO ME, MY SOUL WILL ALWAYS PRAY FOR YOU.
ONE PRAYER... THAT THE MOON WILL ALWAYS SHINE WITH FAVOR UPON YOU.
KLINK
EVEN NOW...

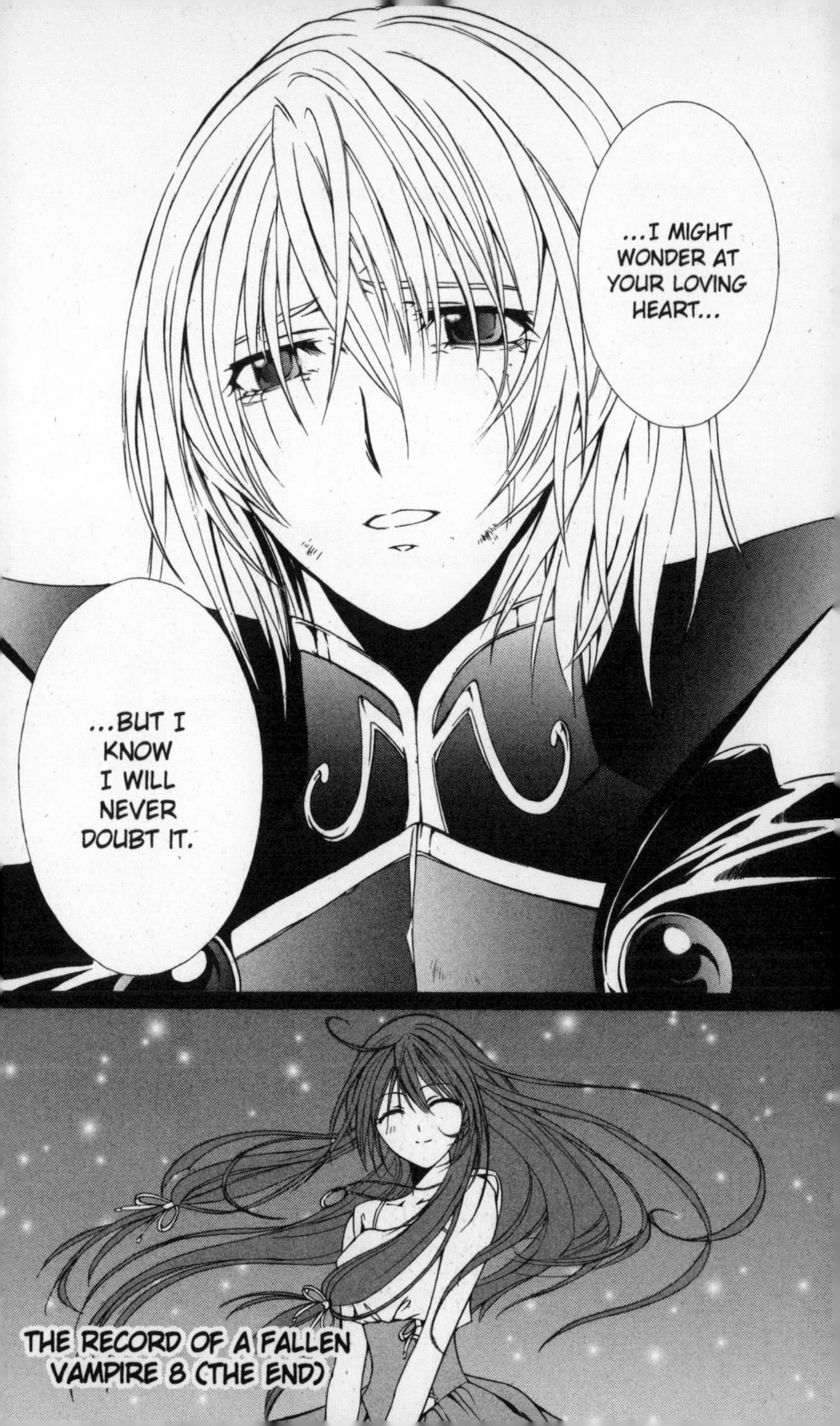
...I MIGHT WONDER AT YOUR LOVING HEART...
...BUT I KNOW I WILL NEVER DOUBT IT.
THE RECORD OF A FALLEN VAMPIRE 8 (THE END)

THE RECORD OF A FALLEN VAMPIRE 8!

MOST OF THE MYSTERIES HAVE UNFOLDED, AND THE STORY IS BARRELING TO ITS GRAND FINALE. THE VAMPIRE KING, HIS BRETHREN AND THE HUMANS WHO HAVE BECOME INVOLVED WITH THEM—WHAT DECISIONS WILL THEY MAKE, AND WHAT FATE AWAITS THEM?

I LOOK FORWARD TO US MEETING AGAIN NEXT VOLUME.

—YURI KIMURA

SPECIAL THANKS

MARUKO ASAGAYA
TEPPEI TAKUMI

AKIRA KIMURA

EDITOR: NOBUAKI YUMURA

REFERENCE:
SEKAI-NO SENSUIKAN
(SUBMARINES OF THE WORLD),
AKIRA SAKAMOTO, BUNRIN-DO

AND TO ALL MY READERS.

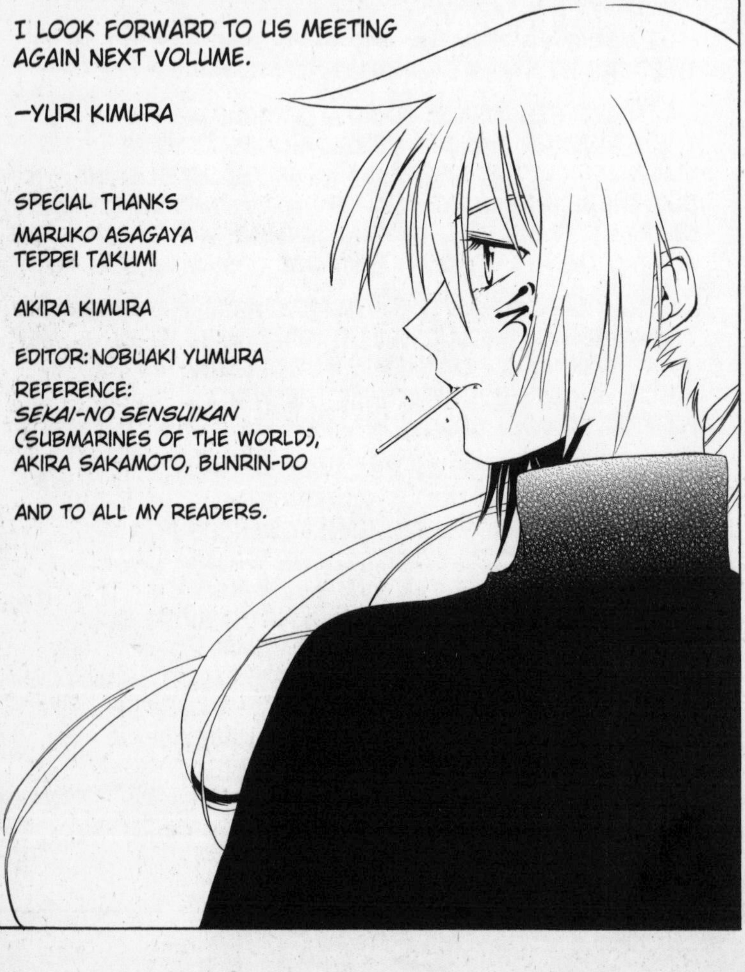

AUTHOR'S AFTERWORD

MY ORIGINAL IDEA WAS TO CREATE A SILLY YET DELIGHTFUL STORY ABOUT VAMPIRES VS. INVADERS FROM OUTER SPACE. YOU COULD SAY THAT IT WAS ALREADY A BIT OFF EVEN IN PART ONE. BUT MORE IMPORTANTLY, THE VAMPIRES, THE MAIN THEME OF THE STORY, DON'T DO ANY BLOODSUCKING.

I'M KYO SHIRODAIRA, AND IN VOLUME 8, YOU CAN SEE THAT THE STORY IS BEGINNING TO DRAW TO A CLOSE.

THE SERIES IS PUBLISHED OVERSEAS AS WELL, AND THE STANDARD CHINESE VERSION USES CHINESE CHARACTERS THAT LITERALLY MEAN "BLOODSUCKING," BUT THERE'S BEEN NO SUCH SCENE. ACTUALLY, BRIDGET CLARIFIED IN CHAPTER 12 THAT ALTHOUGH THEY HAVE THE ABILITY, THEY DON'T DO IT BECAUSE IT'S UNNECESSARY.

THE REASON FOR THIS VAMPIRIC ABILITY IS EXPLAINED IN CHAPTER 36, INCLUDED IN THIS VOLUME, WHICH SOME-WHAT MAINTAINS THE THEME. BUT IT CERTAINLY MAKES READERS QUESTION WHETHER THE WRITER REALLY WANTED TO DO A STORY ON VAMPIRES, DOESN'T IT?

FACT IS, THIS ABILITY BECOMES AN OBSTACLE WHEN CREATING A STORY ABOUT VAMPIRES. BLOODSUCKING CAUSES MANY PROBLEMS: CONSEQUENCES FOR THE VICTIMS HAVE TO BE CAREFULLY WEIGHED; VICTIMIZING PEOPLE MAY INFLATE THE EVIL IMAGE ASSOCIATED WITH VAMPIRES AND CAUSE THE READERS TO AVOID SUCH A THEME; IF THE VICTIMS TURN INTO VAMPIRES AFTER HAVING THEIR BLOOD SUCKED AS THE TRADITIONAL VIEW GOES, THE WORLD WOULD BE FULL OF VAMPIRES AND ALL HELL WOULD BREAK LOOSE. WE HAVE TO BE EXTREMELY CAREFUL WHEN DEALING WITH THIS.

THAT'S WHY THE MODERN-DAY VAMPIRES ARE OFTEN GIVEN MODIFIED CHARACTERISTICS TO RENDER THEM LESS DESPICABLE, SUCH AS FEEDING ON TOMATO JUICE OR ON MEDICAL BLOOD SUPPLIES, OR THAT VICTIMS DON'T BECOME VAMPIRES UNTIL A CERTAIN AMOUNT OF BLOOD IS TAKEN.

WHATEVER THE CASE, VAMPIRES SUCKING BLOOD FROM HUMANS IS PROBABLY NOT A PLEASANT SIGHT, AND SEEING THEM GUZZLING DOWN TOMATO JUICE KIND OF RUINS THE IMAGE. LETTING THEM FEED ON BLOOD JUST ISN'T THAT EASY. THAT'S WHY I AVOIDED INCLUDING THIS PARTICULAR VAMPIRIC ABILITY IN THIS SERIES.

HOWEVER, THERE WILL BE A "GOING ANCESTRAL" SCENE IN THE NEXT VOLUME. THE STORY WILL LIVE UP TO ITS TITLE. THE "WHO WILL SUCK WHOSE BLOOD" QUESTION WILL BE REVEALED IN CHAPTER 41, AS A VERY IMPORTANT CEREMONY OF FAREWELL.

THE STORY WILL END IN THE NEXT VOLUME. WITH EVERYTHING REVEALED, WHAT DECISIONS DO THE CHARACTERS MAKE FOR THE FUTURE? IT WILL BE AN EXTRAVAGANZA OF EVERYTHING, FROM BLOODSUCKING AND INTERGALACTIC WAR WITH BIG MORTAR TO STRAUSS AND KAYUKI'S FINAL BATTLE ON THE SEA. HOW DOES THE TRAGEDY THAT SPANNED A THOUSAND YEARS END?

THERE IS JUST ONE VOLUME LEFT, AND I DO HOPE YOU ENJOY IT.

I PRAY WE MEET AGAIN IN VOLUME 9.

—KYO SHIRODAIRA

THE RECORD OF A FALLEN VAMPIRE

VOL. 8
VIZ MEDIA EDITION

STORY BY: **KYO SHIRODAIRA** ART BY: **YURI KIMURA**

Translation & Adaptation...**A. J. Katsurada**
Touch-up Art & Lettering...**HudsonYards**
Design...**Ronnie Casson**
Editor...**Gary Leach**

VP, Production...**Alvin Lu**
VP, Sales & Product Marketing...**Gonzalo Ferreyra**
VP, Creative...**Linda Espinosa**
Publisher...**Hyoe Narita**

VAMPIRE JYUJIKAI vol.8 © 2007 Kyo Shirodaira, Yuri Kimura/
SQUARE ENIX. All rights reserved. First published in Japan in 2007
by SQUARE ENIX CO., LTD. English translation rights arranged with
SQUARE ENIX CO., LTD. and VIZ Media, LLC.

Printed in the U.S.A.

Published by VIZ Media, LLC
P.O. Box 77010
San Francisco, CA 94107

10 9 8 7 6 5 4 3 2 1
First printing, February 2010

www.viz.com

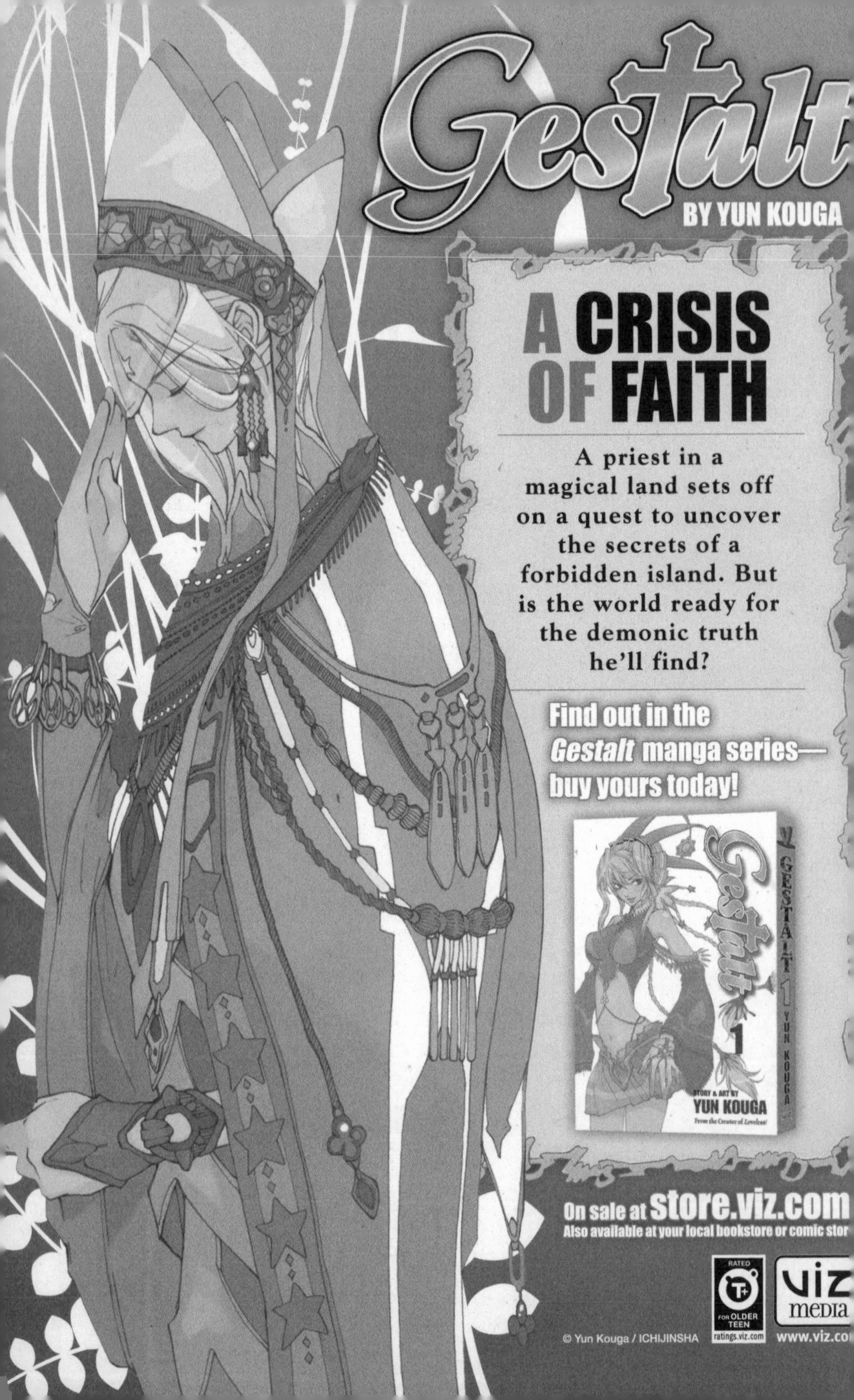
Gestalt
BY YUN KOUGA
A CRISIS OF FAITH
A priest in a magical land sets off on a quest to uncover the secrets of a forbidden island. But is the world ready for the demonic truth he'll find?
Find out in the *Gestalt* manga series—buy yours today!
Gestalt 1
STORY & ART BY YUN KOUGA
GESTALT 1 YUN KOUGA
On sale at store.viz.com
Also available at your local bookstore or comic stor
RATED T+ FOR OLDER TEEN
ratings.viz.com
viz media
www.viz.co
© Yun Kouga / ICHIJINSHA

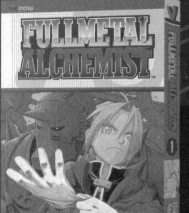
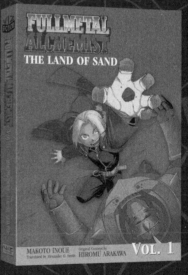
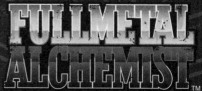

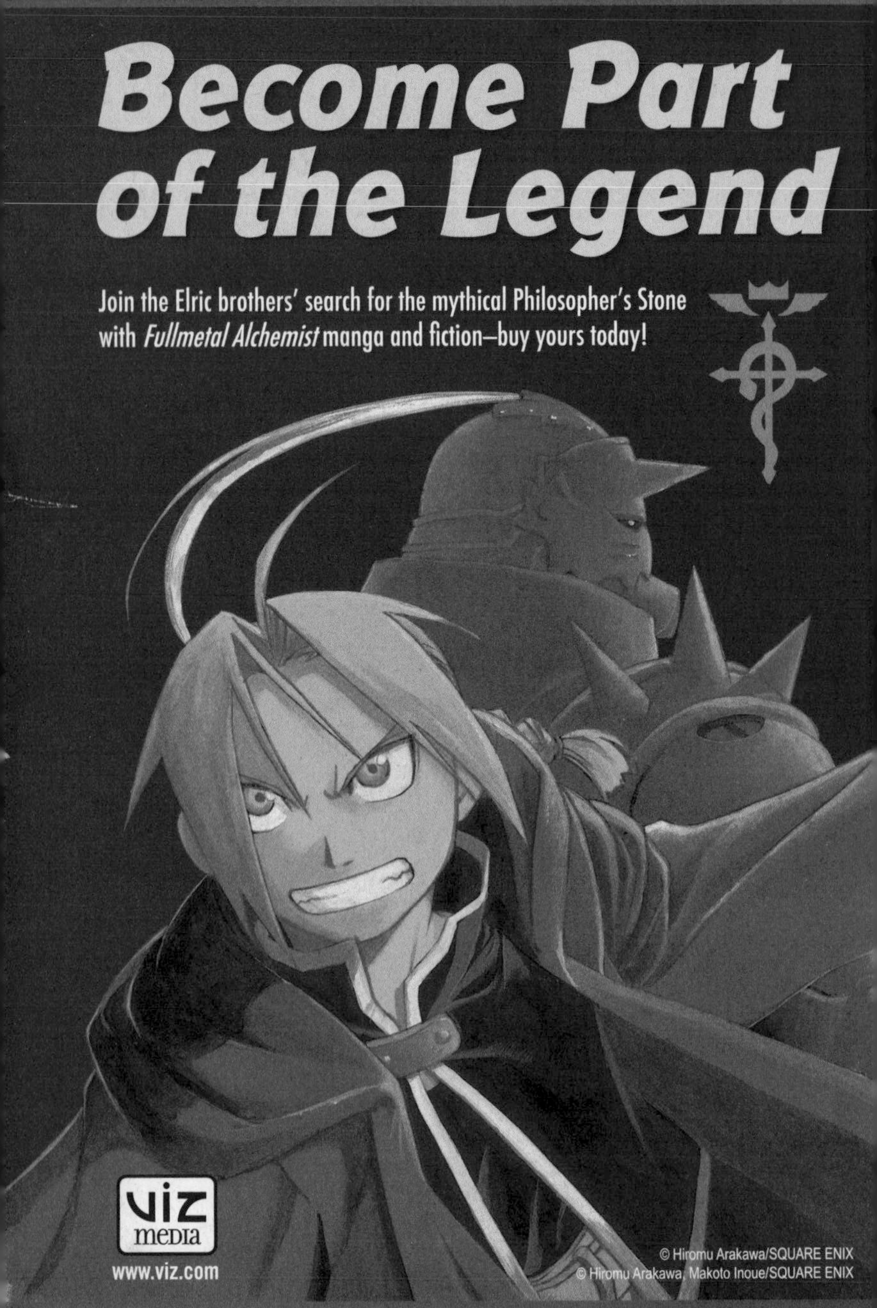
Become Part of the Legend
Join the Elric brothers' search for the mythical Philosopher's Stone with *Fullmetal Alchemist* manga and fiction–buy yours today!
viz media
www.viz.com
© Hiromu Arakawa/SQUARE ENIX
© Hiromu Arakawa, Makoto Inoue/SQUARE ENIX

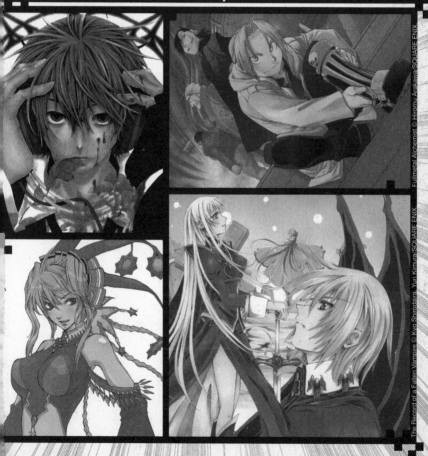